LONG ISLAND

A GUIDE TO NEW YORK'S
SUFFOLK AND NASSAU COUNTIES

Also by Raymond E. and Judith A. Spinzia

Long Island's Prominent North Shore Families:
Their Estates and Their Country Homes,
Volumes I and II

Long Island's Prominent South Shore Families:
Their Estates and Their Country Homes
in the Towns of Babylon and Islip

LONG ISLAND

A GUIDE TO NEW YORK'S
SUFFOLK AND NASSAU COUNTIES

Third Edition

Raymond Edward Spinzia
Judith Ader Spinzia
and
Kathryn Spinzia Rayne

HIPPOCRENE BOOKS, INC.
New York

Third Edition, Revised, 2009

For information, address:
Hippocrene Books, Inc.
171 Madison Avenue
New York, NY 10016
www.hippocrenebooks.com

Library of Congress Cataloging-in-Publication Data

Spinzia, Raymond E.
    Long Island : a guide to New York's Suffolk and Nassau counties / Raymond
Edward Spinzia, Judith Ader Spinzia, and Kathryn Spinzia Rayne.
    —3rd ed., rev.
        p.   cm.
    Includes index.
    Rev. ed. of: Long Island / Raymond E. Spinzia, Judith A. Spinzia, and
Kathryn E. Spinzia. © 1988.
    ISBN-13: 978-0-7818-1213-9
    ISBN-10: 0-7818-1213-5
        1. Long Island (N.Y.)—Guidebooks. 2. Automobile travel—New York
(State)—Long Island—Guidebooks. 3. Parks—New York (State)—Long
Island—Guidebooks. 4. Historic sites—New York (State)—Long Island—
Guidebooks. 5. Museums—New York (State)—Long Island—Guidebooks.
6. Natural areas—New York (State)—Long Island—Guidebooks. 7. Long
Island (N.Y.)—History, Local. 8. Suffolk County (N.Y.)—Guidebooks.
9. Nassau County (N.Y.)—Guidebooks. I. Spinzia, Judith A. II. Rayne,
Kathryn Spinzia. III. Title.

    F127.L8S72 2007
    917.47'210444—dc22   2007050709

Printed in the United States of America.

CONTENTS

MAPS

Maps courtesy of Long Island Regional Planning Board.

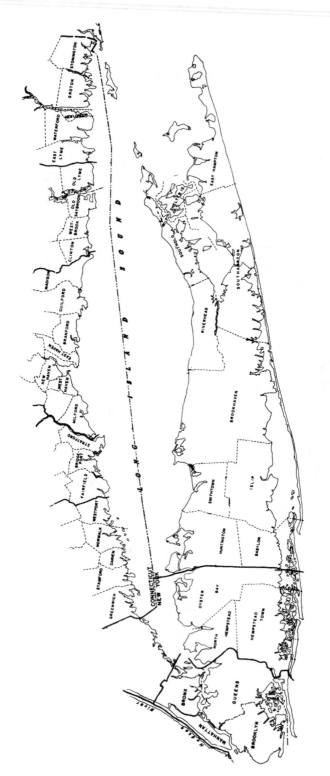

LONG ISLAND

INTRODUCTION

This is a completely revised and updated third edition of the Spinzias' comprehensive guidebook to Long Island's Suffolk and Nassau Counties, first published in 1988. It is organized by town and then subdivided by the various villages and hamlets within the respective towns. Directions are given for each entry from the Long Island Expressway wherever possible; otherwise, directions are given from a central location, usually the village green. All entries are fully discussed with special items of interest mentioned. Facilities at all federal, state, and county parks and preserves as well as forty nature conservancies are delineated, as are archaeological and historical sites and museums. Catalogued and described for the first time are eighty-eight Tiffany stained-glass windows found in Suffolk and Nassau Counties, fifty-four of which, until now, had been lost to art historians. Since most Tiffany windows mentioned are found in churches, which because of thievery and vandalism tend to be closed when there are no services, we have attempted to give readers sufficient information to make their visits to these sites as efficient, informative, and profitable as possible.

Please note that it is always prudent to call historical complexes and museums since the hours posted or published are subject to change.

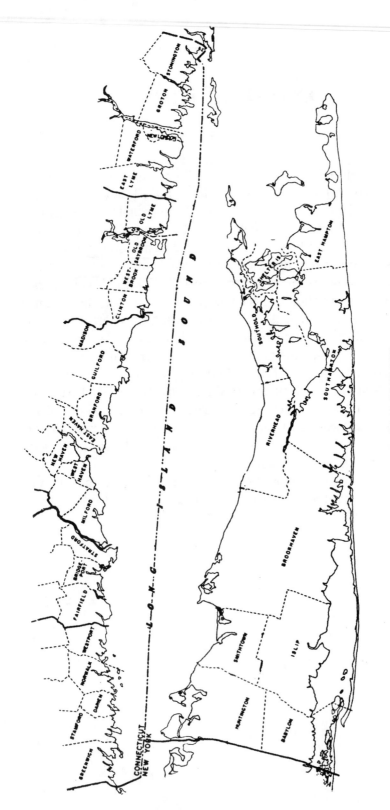

SUFFOLK COUNTY

Suffolk County

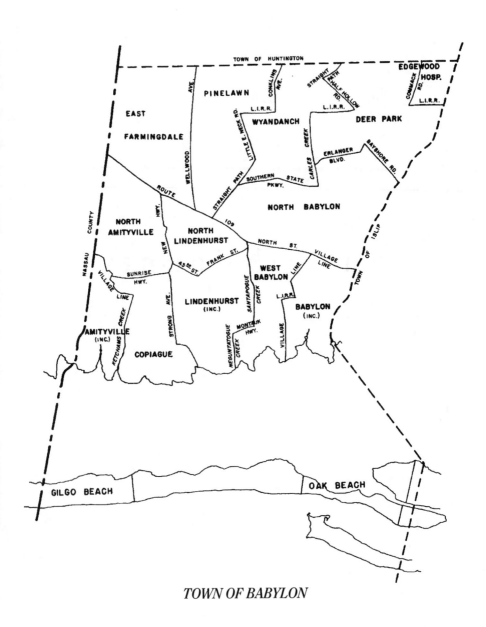

TOWN OF BABYLON

TOWN OF BABYLON

PARKS AND PRESERVES

Federal Parks and Preserves
none

State Parks and Preserves
Belmont Lake State Park (459 acres), North Babylon
Edgewood Oak Brush Plain Preserve (850 acres), Deer Park *(undeveloped)*
Gilgo Beach State Park (1,223 acres), Amityville *(undeveloped)*

County Parks and Preserves
Bergen Point County Golf Course (185 acres), West Babylon
Indian Island County Park (287 acres), Babylon *(undeveloped)*
Van Bourgondien Nurseries County Park (19 acres), West Babylon *(undeveloped)*

Arboretums and Gardens

Amityville

Amityville Historical Society / Lauder Museum

170 Broadway, Amityville
(631) 598-1486

Take the Long Island Expressway to Exit #49 south (Route 110/Amityville). Go south on Route 110/Broadway for 7.5 miles. The museum is on the right (west) side of the road.

The Lauder Museum is located in the old 1909 Bank of Amityville building. The building was acquired by the Amityville Historical Society in 1971 for use as its headquarters and museum. On display are a Victorian parlor with a Beatty Beethoven organ, an 1893 Bellamy Trap carriage, a horse-drawn sleigh, a duck boat with ice runners, and collections of decoys, World War I service medals, 1850–1900 dental instruments, dolls, antique tools, antique metal banks, and a game set of circa 1900 French *Limoges* china.

For those wishing to do historical research, there is a library at the museum with works pertaining to local history.

Edwin Denby's House

99 Bennett Place, Amityville

Not open to the public.

From the Amityville Historical Society/Lauder Museum at the intersection of Route 110/Broadway and Ireland Place in Amityville go south on Route 110/ Broadway for .4 mile. Turn left (east) onto Route 27A/Montauk Highway. Make an immediate right (south) onto Bennett Place; go .3 mile. The house is on the right (west) side of the street.

Edwin Denby (1870–1929) was born in Evansville, IN. He spent his youth in China where his father was a missionary. Edwin was employed for ten years by the Chinese customs service before returning to the United States to enter the University of Michigan, receiving his law degree in 1896. He practiced law in Detroit before being elected to the Michigan state legislature in 1903. In 1905 he was elected to Congress as a representative from the 1st Michigan District and re-elected to Congress for two more terms before being appointed Secretary of the Navy by President Harding.

Denby is said to have been totally ineffective as a Secretary of the Navy and had little influence on naval organization or policy. In spite of this assessment he was reappointed to the position by President Coolidge.

In 1923 Denby became involved in the Teapot Dome scandal. While criminal charges were never brought against him, he resigned rather than continue the embarrassment.

John B. Gambling's House
Bayside Avenue, Amityville

Not open to the public.

From the Amityville Historical Society/Lauder Museum at the intersection of Route 110/Broadway and Ireland Place in Amityville go south on Route 110/ Broadway for .4 mile. Turn left (east) onto Route 27A/Montauk Highway; go .1 mile. Turn right (south) onto Ocean Avenue; go .6 mile. Turn left (east) onto Bayside Avenue. The house is the expanded ranch before you turn into the cul-de-sac.

John Bradley Gambling (1897–1974) was born in Norwich, England. With the outbreak of World War I, he joined the Royal Navy as a radio operator, serving aboard a mine sweeper. After the war he served in the same capacity aboard various merchant ships. He immigrated to the United States and took a job as an engineer at WOR Radio. When Bernarr Macfadden failed to arrive on time for his show, Gambling stepped into the breach and ad-libbed for the entire hour program; six months later, in 1925, he was offered his own show. He progressed through several program formats before establishing the *Rambling With Gambling* show in 1942. In 1958 he retired from radio broadcasting and turned the show over to his son John A., who, in turn, transferred the show to his son John R. Gambling upon his retirement.

The Gamblings spent the winter months in their Manhattan apartment but during the 1940s and 1950s spent weekends and summers in this nine-room house.

Annie Oakley's House
202 Ocean Avenue, Amityville

Not open to the public.

From the Amityville Historical Society/Lauder Museum at the intersection of Route 110/Broadway and Ireland Place in Amityville go south on Route 110/ Broadway for .4 mile. Turn left (east) onto Route 27A/Montauk Highway; go .1 mile. Turn right (south) onto Ocean Avenue; go .5 mile. The house is on the left (east) side of the road.

Phoebe Anne Oakley Mozee (1860–1926) was born in a log cabin in Darke County, OH. At the age of nine her superior talent as a marksman became evident. By the time she was fourteen Annie had earned enough money from hunting to pay off the mortgage on the family's farm. While still in her early teens, she joined Frank Butler's vaudeville act as his assistant, but it was not long before she became the feature performer of the act and Butler became her assistant and later her manager and husband.

In 1885 they joined Buffalo Bill's Wild West Show in which Oakley became an instant national and international success. She performed for Queen Victoria of Great Britain and Wilhelm II, Crown Prince of Germany. The Crown Prince shocked everyone by insisting that Oakley shoot a cigarette from his lips.

In 1901 Oakley became temporarily paralyzed after a railroad accident but recovered and was able to resume her sharpshooting act. She is buried in Brock, OH, near her birthplace.

Walter O'Malley's House
318 Ocean Avenue, Amityville

Not open to the public.

From the Amityville Historical Society/Lauder Museum at the intersection of Route 110/Broadway and Ireland Place in Amityville go south on Route 110/ Broadway for .4 mile. Turn left (east) onto Route 27A/Montauk Highway; go .1 mile. Turn right (south) onto Ocean Avenue; go .8 mile. The house is on the left (east) side of the road.

The son of a New York City Commissioner of Public Markets, Walter O'Malley (1903–1979) was born in The Bronx. He attended Jamaica High School before transferring to Culver Military Academy in Indiana. In 1922 he enter the University of Pennsylvania from which he graduated with honors. He received his law degree from Fordham University and was admitted to the bar in 1930. After establishing his own engineering firm, he became the director of Brooklyn Borough Gas Co. and, in 1932, director of the Brooklyn Dodgers. In 1943 he became the legal representative of the Dodgers and in 1944 organized a syndicate which eventually owned 75% of the team's stock. In 1950 he became president of the corporation, going on to become chairman of the board and its principle owner. In 1957 O'Malley made the unfortunate decision to move the team to Los Angeles, a decision for which many New York fans have never forgiven him.

The O'Malleys lived in this flat-roofed house during the 1950s. The house had been of a more conventional design before it was modified to its present form by O'Malley.

Walt Whitman's House
41 Park Avenue, Amityville

Not open to the public.

From the Amityville Historical Society/Lauder Museum at the intersection of Route 110/Broadway and Ireland Place in Amityville turn left (south) onto Park Avenue; go .3 mile. The house is on the left (east) side of the road.

Walt Whitman (1819–1892), the noted American poet, was born in Huntington Station, Long Island. As a youth he moved to Brooklyn with his parents where he attended school. What little formal education he had ended by 1830. From 1836 to 1841 he taught school in Huntington, Smithtown, and West Babylon.

It is while he was teaching in West Babylon that he lived in this house. The house, which has been enlarged over the years, was moved to this location in

1986 from its original site, where the Great South Bay Shopping Center is today. Whitman lived in the older southern portion of the present structure.

(See also Town of Huntington/Huntington Station/Walt Whitman House and Town of Smithtown/Village of the Branch/Old Schoolhouse.)

BABYLON

Village of Babylon Historical and Preservation Society
117 Main Street, Babylon
(631) 669-1756

Take the Long Island Expressway to Exit #51 south (Route 231/Northport/Huntington). Go south on Route 231/Deer Park Avenue/County Road 35 for 7.3 miles. Turn right (west) onto Main Street/Route 27A/Montauk Highway; go .1 mile. The society's building is located on the right (north) side of the road.

Located in the former Babylon Public Library, the society presents changing exhibits and memorabilia pertaining to the history of Babylon.

EAST FARMINGDALE

Adventureland
2245 Route 110, East Farmingdale
(631) 694-6868

Take the Long Island Expressway to Exit #49 south (Route 110/Amityville). Go south on Route 110 for 2 miles. Adventureland is on the left (east) side of the road.

Opened in 1962, Adventureland, with its thirty rides and attractions, is one of the metropolitan area's largest amusement parks. Among its attractions are a roller coaster, a log flume, a haunted house, a Ferris wheel, bumper cars, rides for children, video games, and pinball machines. A deli-style restaurant is on the premises. Parking is free.

American Airpower Museum
1230 New Highway, East Farmingdale
(at Republic Airport)
(631) 293-6398

Take the Long Island Expressway to Exit #49 south (Route 110/Amityville). Go south on Route 110. Turn left (east) onto Conklin Street. Proceed to New Highway.

Turn right (south) onto New Highway. Pass two hangars and make a right into the museum's parking lot. The museum's entrance is the red hanger door marked American Airpower Museum.

Housed in a 1940s-era hangar, the museum's collection includes a B-17 Flying Fortress, a twin-engine Mitchell bomber, a P-40 Warhawk, a Grumman Avenger, a C-47 Skytrain, a Vought F-4 U Corsair, a Republic P-47 Thunderbolt, a T-6 Texan, a L-39 Albatross, and a 1940s-era control tower. Also located on the premises is a fleet of vintage automobiles and trucks. Due to its strategic location at the airfield, the museum has the only historic aircraft collection in the metropolitan region that can be regularly flown.

(See also Town of Islip/Bayport/Bayport Aerodrome; Town of Hempstead/Garden City/The Cradle of Aviation Museum; and Town of Southampton/Westhampton Beach/ 106th Rescue Group–New York Air National Guard.)

LINDENHURST

Old Village Hall Museum
215 South Wellwood Avenue, Lindenhurst
(631) 957-4385

Take the Long Island Expressway to Exit #49 south (Route 110/Amityville). Go east on the expressway service road (called South Service Road) for .7 mile. Turn right (south) onto Pinelawn Road/Wellwood Avenue. (Further south it is called North Wellwood Avenue/South Wellwood Avenue.) Go 7.2 miles. The museum is on the right (west) side of the road.

The museum is situated in Lindenhurst's first village hall which combined a courthouse, now a main exhibit room; a village clerk's office, now a parlor; and a police station, now a bedroom, toolroom, and kitchen. On display are a Victorian parlor with an Edison phonograph, an 1800s kitchen, a child's bedroom, antique tools, a unicycle, collections of egg cups and *Majolica* china, as well as photographs and memorabilia from Lindenhurst's past.

1901 Depot Restoration
South Broadway, Lindenhurst
(631) 226-1254

Take the Long Island Expressway to Exit #49 south (Route 110/Amityville). Go east on the expressway service road (called South Service Road) for .7 mile. Turn right (south) onto Pinelawn Road/Wellwood Avenue. (Further south it is called North Wellwood Avenue/South Wellwood Avenue.) Go 7.1 miles. Turn right (west) onto West Hoffman Avenue; go .1 mile. Turn left (south) onto South Broadway; go .1 mile. The museum is on the left (east) side of the road.

Located in Irmisch Park, this museum consists of two buildings, a freight house and a depot. The depot, which was built in 1901, was the third train station in the village and was formally presented to the Lindenhurst Historical Society in 1967 for use as a museum. Restored to its original 1901 appearance, it contains railroad memorabilia as well as a teletype machine with the history of Lindenhurst written in Morse Code. The freight house contains old baggage, a scale, trunks, a printing press, and memorabilia of the village's history.

NORTH BABYLON

Belmont Lake State Park – August Belmont Sr. Estate – Nursery Stud Farm
Southern State Parkway, North Babylon
(631) 667-5055

Located off Southern State Parkway at Exit #38.

An avid breeder of thoroughbred horses, Belmont purchased 1,100 acres in North Babylon to be used as a stud farm. Eventually he built a twenty-four-room main residence, thirty outbuildings, and a one-mile racetrack with a grandstand on the property. In 1935 the main residence was demolished by the Long Island State Park Commission, which had acquired a portion of the Belmont estate in the 1920s to establish Belmont Lake State Park. The two canons in front of the commission's headquarters in the park are from a British ship sunk at the Battle of Lake Erie by Commodore Oliver Hazard Perry during the War of 1812. They were recovered by Belmont from a Pittsburgh junkyard.

The 459-acre park offers picnic areas, a picnic pavilion, rowboat rentals, bridle paths, bicycle paths, jogging paths, hiking, lake fishing, ice skating, refreshment stands, athletic fields, and playfields.

(See also Town of Brookhaven/Yaphank/Southaven County Park–Suffolk Club; Town of Hempstead/Elmont/Belmont Park Race Track; Town of Islip/Oakdale/ Connetquot River State Park and Preserve–Southside Sportsmen's Club; and Town of Hempstead/Hempstead/Saint George's Episcopal Church.)

North Babylon Cemetery
Sunrise Highway and Livingston Avenue, North Babylon

Grave of Mario Puzo (1920–1999)

Section 1, Block H, Lot 14

Born in New York City, Puzo was raised above the railroad yards in Manhattan's notorious "Hell's Kitchen." One of six children of Italian immigrants, Puzo served in the United States Army Air Force during World War II. After the war he studied at the New School for Social Research and, later, at Columbia University.

Of the eight books he authored, he is probably remembered most for *The Godfather* (1969). Puzo subsequently sold the rights to *The Godfather* to Paramount Pictures for $85,000. He and Francis Ford Coppola worked on the motion picture's script but, after a fifth rewrite, Puzo withdrew from the project because of differences of opinion with Coppola. Puzo and Coppola later collaborated on the motion picture scripts for *Godfather Part II* and *Godfather Part III*. Puzo was also a collaborator on the scripts for *Earthquake*, *Superman I*, and the sequel, *Superman II*.

PINELAWN

Mount Ararat Cemetery
Pinelawn Road/Wellwood Avenue, Pinelawn
(631) 957-2277

Take the Long Island Expressway to Exit #49 south (Route 110/Amityville). Go east on the expressway service road (called South Service Road) for .7 mile. Turn right (south) onto Pinelawn Road/Wellwood Avenue; go 4.4 miles. The cemetery is on the right (west) side of the road.

Grave of Max Fortunoff (1898–1987)

Section 75, Row A

Fortunoff emigrated from Russia in 1907. By 1922 he and his wife Clara had opened their first store, located under the elevated train on Livonia Avenue in the Brownsville section of Brooklyn. At first they sold only pots and pans but as business improved the store expanded, becoming the largest specialty home furnishing store in the area. In 1964 Fortunoff left Brooklyn for Westbury, Long Island, opening what is still the largest store in the chain. Other stores are located in Manhattan and at two locations in New Jersey.

Known as Mr. F., Fortunoff was a dedicated philanthropist. Among his many philanthropic activities was the restoration of Dowling College, the former Idlehour estate in Oakdale, after its devastating fire in 1974, and the endowment of the college's music program.

(See also Town of Islip/Oakdale/Dowling College–William Kissam Vanderbilt Sr. Estate–Idlehour.)

Grave of William Jaird Levitt Sr. (1907–1986)

Levitt was president of Levitt and Sons, a housing development construction firm that built the 17,500 single-family community of Levittown in Long Island's

Nassau County. Similar communities were built by Levitt and Sons on the Delaware River north of Philadelphia, PA, and in Willingboro Township, NJ.

Levitt's elaborately appointed, thirty-five-room, French Country-style residence, La Colline, is located in Mill Neck. The gatehouse for the estate was a replica of one of his Levittown houses.

(See also Town of Hempstead/Levittown/Levittown Historical Museum and Town of Oyster Bay/Mill Neck/William Jaird Levitt Sr. House–La Colline.)

Grave of Max Weber (1881–1961)

Section 81, Plot G20

Born in western Russia, Weber immigrated to Manhattan with his family at the age of ten. He studied art in Paris between 1905 and 1908 under the influence of the modern school of French artists. After returning to the United States, he was one of the pioneers of modern art in the country. He is known for the abstract works that he painted between 1912 and 1919, as well as the works of his later period which featured figures with expressive gestures giving the illusion of motion.

Pinelawn Memorial Park and Cemetery
Pinelawn Road/Wellwood Avenue, Pinelawn
(631) 249-6100

Take the Long Island Expressway to Exit #49 south (Route 110/Amityville). Go east on the expressway service road (called South Service Road) for .7 mile. Turn right (south) onto Pinelawn Road/Wellwood Avenue; go 2.5 miles. The cemetery is on the left (east) side of the road and the mausoleum area is on the right (west) side of the road.

Garden of *Normandie*

From Pinelawn Road turn left (east) into the cemetery area and take the William H. Locke Memorial Drive for .3 mile. Bear left onto Vista Road; go .4 mile. Turn left and make an immediate right onto Forest Circle Drive; go .1 mile. Turn right onto Normandie Drive South; go .1 mile. The statue is on the left side of the carriage road.

The pride of the French luxury ocean liners and, at the time, the world's fastest, most opulent, and longest ship at more than 1,000 feet, the *Normandie* was built during the depths of the Depression. With her eleven decks, the *Normandie* was able to accommodate 2,170 passengers and a crew of 1,320. She broke the transatlantic speed record on her maiden voyage cruising at an average of almost thirty knots. The record was superseded by the *Queen Mary*, then the *Queen Elizabeth*, and finally by the American liner the *United States*. On February 10, 1942, the *Normandie* exploded, burned, and sank in New York Harbor. To this day it is not certain whether her destruction was the result of enemy sabotage or of careless workers, who at the time were converting her into a troop ship.

The statue of a woman called "Peace" in Pinelawn's Garden of *Normandie* was created by the famous French sculptor Louis DeJean. It was cast by him at a foundry in Neully, France, specifically for the *Normandie*. One of the largest bronze statues to be cast in modern times, the one-and-a-half-ton statue stood in the center of the ship's huge 282-foot-long by 32-foot-high dining salon dwarfing the seven hundred diners. The symbolism of peace is represented by the olive branch held in her right hand. The statue was acquired by the cemetery after it was discovered disassembled in a Brooklyn churchyard.

Grave of "Count" Basie (1904–1984)

From Pinelawn Road turn right (west) into the mausoleum area. Basie is interred in the mausoleum called Forsythia Court South in close proximity to Guy Lombardo. Crypt-Row 57, Tier D, Forsythia Court South

Born William Basie in Red Bank, NJ, he was influenced by the style of Fats Waller and other New York jazz musicians from whom he evolved his famous jazz piano style. He settled in Kansas City, MO, in 1935 after several years of accompanying singers and touring in vaudeville shows. In 1936 he was discovered by a talent scout and brought to New York City. A key figure in the swing era, his piano style was noted for its brightness and simplicity, and his band for its loose, informal arrangements.

Grave of David Merrick (1912–2000)

The grave site is located in Heather Court, southeastern gallery, Tier B, Row 501.

Born in St. Louis, MO, Merrick graduated from Washington University and, later, from St. Louis University School of Law. Infatuated with the theater, he left the legal profession to become a theatrical producer. His forty-year Broadway career, during which he produced over eighty shows, was punctuated by outrageous publicity stunts and ruthless treatment of his actors and staff by the impresario.

Known as the "Indomitable Showman," Merrick won eight Tonys during his career. Among his most memorable shows were: *Fanny* (1954), *The Matchmaker* (1955), *The World of Suzie Wong* (1958), *Destry Rides Again* (1959), *Gypsy* (1959), *Irma La Douce* (1960), *Oliver* (1963), *One Flew Over the Cuckoo's Nest* (1963), *Hello Dolly* (1964), and *42nd Street* (1980).

Grave of Guy Lombardo (1902–1977)

From Pinelawn Road turn right (west) into the mausoleum area. Lombardo is interred in the mausoleum called Forsythia Court South in close proximity to "Count" Basie. Crypt-Row 65, Tier C, Forsythia Court South

Gaetano Albert Lombardo was born in London, Ontario, Canada, to Italian immigrants. By the age of ten he and his younger brother Carmen were performing at garden parties. In the early 1920s he formed a band and was performing at the Winter Garden Hall in London, Ontario. By 1928 he and his Royal Canadians had become famous, noted as they were for "the sweetest music this side of heaven." For almost fifty years his New Year's Eve broadcasts from the Roosevelt and Waldorf-Astoria hotels in New York City were a national event.

Grave of John William Coltrane (1926–1967)

From Pinelawn Road turn left (east) into the cemetery area and take the William H. Locke Memorial Drive for .3 mile. Turn left (north) onto Walt Whitman Drive; go .2 mile. Turn right (east) onto Oak Drive; go .1 mile. Coltrane's grave is in line with the brick wall in front and to the right of a crane sculpture in the Pool of the Heroes. Grave 49, Plot Q, Range 46, Block 1, Section 60

Born in Hamlet, NC, Coltrane was a famous composer and jazz saxophonist noted for his violent style of playing. Because of this and the influence of the music of India in his work, he became a widely imitated and controversial jazz musician of the 1960s. He played with the bands of Dizzy Gillespie and Johnny Hodges as well as with the Miles Davis quintet before forming his own quartet in 1960. He was responsible for popularizing the soprano saxophone.

Grave of Andre Eglevsky (1917–1977)

From Pinelawn Road turn left (east) into the cemetery area and take the William H. Locke Memorial Drive for .3 mile. Bear left onto Vista Road; go .3 mile. Turn right (south) onto the carriage road; go .1 mile. Eglevsky's grave is on the left (east) side of the road. Grave 241, Plot 4, Range 2, Block 9, Section 31

Eglevsky was born in Moscow, Russia, during the Russian Revolution. As the Revolution gained momentum, his mother disguised herself and fled with Andre and her daughter to Constantinople, then to Bulgaria, and ultimately to Nice, France. In France the young Andre began ballet lessons in the hope of improving his frail health. It was quickly evident that he was extremely gifted. By the age of fourteen he had made his debut with the Ballet Russe de Monte Carlo. Within six months he was performing principal roles with the company. Andre rapidly became an established international star, dancing with the American Ballet, the Ballet Russe de Monte Carlo, the Ballet Theatre, the Ballet International, the Grand Ballet de Monte Carlo, and the New York City Ballet under the artistic direction of George Balanchine. (See also Town of Southampton/Sag Harbor/Oakland Cemetery/Grave of George Balanchine.) Critics have described Eglevsky as a "classical dancer of phenomenal ability who danced with clearness, force and ease." In the latter part of the 1950s he formed his own company, the Eglevsky Ballet, which still makes its home in Massapequa, Long Island. He died in Elmira, NY, where his company was scheduled to perform. His grave is marked by a simple, but elegant, bronze plaque embossed with the Russian Orthodox cross.

Grave of Roy Wilkins (1901–1981)

From Pinelawn Road turn left (east) into the cemetery area and take the William H. Locke Memorial Drive for .3 mile. Turn left (north) onto Walt Whitman Drive; go .2 mile. Turn right (east) onto Oak Drive; go .2 mile. Turn left (north) onto Holly Drive; go .1 mile. Turn right (east) onto Constitution Drive North; go .1 mile. Wilkins grave is on the east side of the first brick wall. Grave 19, Plot R, Range 11, Block 3, Section 70

Wilkins was born in Saint Louis, MO. After graduating from the University of Minnesota, he worked for an African-American newspaper, *The Kansas City Call.* In 1931 he joined the National Association for the Advancement of Colored People (NAACP) and edited its magazine, *The Crisis,* from 1934 through 1949. He gradually rose in the administrative structure of the organization and served as executive secretary from 1955 to 1977. Wilkins, the grandson of a slave, became known as "Mr. Civil Rights." He received the Spingarn Metal in 1964 and the Presidential Medal of Freedom from President Johnson in 1969.

Wellwood Cemetery
Pinelawn Road/Wellwood Avenue, Pinelawn
(631) 249-2300

Take the Long Island Expressway to Exit #49 south (Route 110/Amityville). Go east on the expressway service road (called South Service Road) for .7 mile. Turn right (south) onto Pinelawn Road/Wellwood Avenue; go 3.2 miles. Turn left (east) into the cemetery's northernmost gate. Go .2 mile on the carriage road. The graves are on the left (north) side of the carriage road. (A map of the cemetery is available in the cemetery office.)

Graves of Ethel and Julius Rosenberg

Block 5, Plot north half of G12

Both Ethel and Julius were born in New York City. After their marriage in 1939, Julius worked as a civilian employee of the United States Signal Corps, but was fired in 1945 for belonging to the Communist Party. David Greenglass, Julius' brother-in-law, owned a small war surplus business in which Julius worked from 1946 until 1950. In 1949 Klaus Fuchs, a physicist who worked on the atomic bomb project in Los Alamos, confessed to spying for the Soviet Union and incriminated Greenglass, who had also worked at Los Alamos from 1944 to 1945. Greenglass in turn incriminated the Rosenbergs. In 1951 the Rosenbergs were convicted of obtaining and passing information concerning atomic weapons, fuses, and gunfire mechanisms as well as other military secrets on to Soviet agents. Their case was appealed to the United States Supreme Court but the court denied their appeals. Twice President Eisenhower refused appeals for clemency. The Rosenbergs were executed as spies on June 19, 1953, becoming the first Americans given the death penalty for espionage by a United States civil court. Greenglass was sentenced to prison and released in 1960.

WEST BABYLON

Bergen Point County Golf Course
69 Bergen Avenue, West Babylon
(631) 661-8282

Suffolk County Resident Pass is required for admission.

Take the Long Island Expressway to Exit #49 south (Route 110/Amityville). Go east on the expressway service road (called South Service Road) for .7 mile. Turn right (south) onto Pinelawn Road/Wellwood Avenue; go 7.9 miles. Turn left (east) onto Montauk Highway/Route 27A; go 1.2 miles. Turn right (south) onto Bergen Avenue; go .3 mile. The golf course is on the right (west) side of the road.

This 185-acre, eighteen-hole, par-seventy-two golf course offers a putting green, a driving range, a clubhouse, a restaurant, a pro shop, and both electric and pull cart rentals. Cross-country skiing is permitted in the winter.

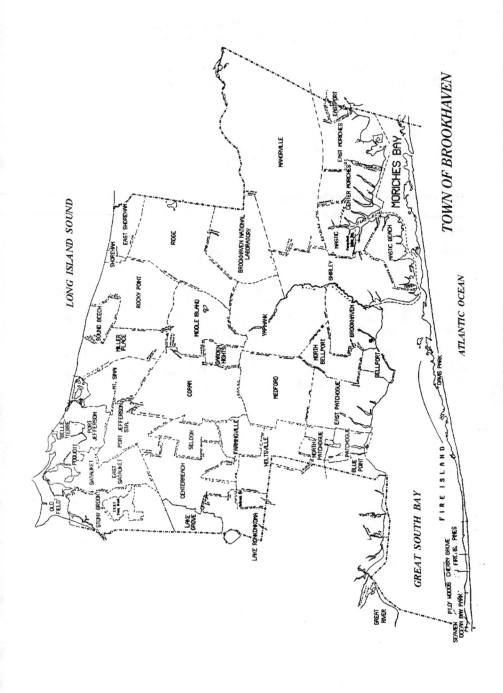

TOWN OF BROOKHAVEN

PARKS AND PRESERVES

Federal Parks and Preserves
Fire Island National Seashore – Sailor's Haven, Fire Island
Fire Island National Seashore – Smith Point, Mastic Beach
Fire Island National Seashore – Sunken Forest, Fire Island
Fire Island National Seashore – Watch Hill, Fire Island
Wertheim National Wildlife Refuge (2,400 acres), Shirley

State Parks and Preserves
Brookhaven Sate Park (2,137 acres), Middle Island *(undeveloped)*
Rocky Point Natural Resources Management Area (5,800), Rocky Point *(undeveloped)*

County Parks and Preserves
Beach County Park (296 acres), Westhampton Beach
Cathedral Pines County Park (321 acres), Middle Island
Cupsogue Smith Point County Park (2,290 acres), Mastic Beach
Lake Ronkonkoma County Park (287 acres), Lake Ronkonkoma *(undeveloped)*
Peconic River County Park (2,010 acres), Manorville *(undeveloped)*
Prosser Pine County Park (56 acres), Yaphank *(undeveloped)*
Robert Cushman County Park (2,200 acres), Manorville *(undeveloped)*
Smith Point County Marina (168 acres), Mastic Beach *(undeveloped)*
Southaven County Park (1,323 acres), Yaphank
Suffolk Hills County Park (985 acres), Brookhaven *(undeveloped)*
Terrell River County Park (260 acres), Center Moriches *(undeveloped)*

Long Island Chapter: The Nature Conservancy
Daniel R. Davis Sanctuary (57 acres), Coram
Finlay – Wolf Pond (9 acres), Ronkonkoma

Arboretums and Gardens

BELLPORT

Bellport–Brookhaven Historical Complex
31 Bellport Lane, Bellport
(631) 286-0888

Take the Long Island Expressway to Exit #65 south (Horse Block Road/Farmingville/ Bellport). Go south on Horse Block Road for 1.3 miles. Turn right (south) onto Bellport Road/Station Road; continue across South Country Road onto Bellport Lane for a total of 4.2 miles. The complex is on the left (east) side of the road.

Post–Crowell House
(part of the Bellport–Brookhaven Historical Complex)
31 Bellport Lane, Bellport

The house was built in 1833 by Hyman Post and was subsequently acquired by Crowell, a local physician. It remained in the Crowell family until 1967 when it was donated to the Bellport–Brookhaven Historical Society by Florence M. Crowell. The house is furnished in period furniture. Of particular interest is the Penbrook table and the circa 1825 linen bedspread which belonged to Elizabeth Post.

Barn
(part of Bellport–Brookhaven Historical Complex)
31 Bellport Lane, Bellport

The barn houses an excellent array of artifacts. There are collections of antiques: bottles, toys, dolls, shoes, weapons, quilts, spinning wheels, and decoys. Also found are Lionel trains from the 1920s and 1930s; a model of the Post–Crowell house; a glass cane; a doctor's carriage; an 1874 scooter boat; an attic loom; and a duck-hunting boat. Of particular interest are the compass carried on the Admiral Perry Polar Expedition; a 1696 record book from the Tangier Smith Estate; textiles, some of which are over two hundred years old; ship's instruments from the SS *Elmer A. Sperry,* a merchant ship built in 1942; and paper money from the Revolutionary and Civil Wars.

Museum Exchange
(part of the Bellport–Brookhaven Historical Complex)
31 Bellport Lane, Bellport

This is a large barn filled with various types of collectibles which are for sale.

Blacksmith Shop
(part of the Bellport–Brookhaven Historical Complex)
31 Bellport Lane, Bellport

Also found on the grounds of this historical complex is a fully equipped, working blacksmith shop.

CENTER MORICHES

Havens House
Main Street, Center Moriches
(631) 878-1776

Take the Long Island Expressway to Exit #69 south (Wading River Road/Wading River/Center Moriches). Go south on Wading River Road for 4.2 miles. Turn right (continuing south) onto Railroad Avenue; go .7 mile. Turn left (east) onto Route 27A/Montauk Highway/Main Street; go .8 mile. The house is on the left (north) side of the road.

The circa 1750 original section of the house has exposed hand-hewn, unplaned support beams with the branch stubs and bark still visible. The larger section of the house was added by the Havens family at the turn of the century. It contains memorabilia as well as collections of pictures, clothes, and antique tools and locks. There is also a small reference library and thrift shop operated by the Center Moriches Historical Society.

CORAM

Daniel R. Davies Sanctuary
(Long Island Chapter: The Nature Conservancy)
Coram–Mount Sinai Road, Coram
(631) 367-3225

Open with prior permission.

Take the Long Island Expressway to Exit #64 north (Route 112/Coram/Medford). Go north on Route 112 for 3.3 miles to Route 25. Turn right (east) onto Route 25; go .2 mile. Turn left (north) onto Coram–Mount Sinai Road; go .3 mile. The sanctuary is on the left (west) side of the road.

This fifty-seven-acre sanctuary is one of Long Island's best examples of a pitch pine/scrub oak ecosystem. Also found here are chestnut oaks, scrub chestnut oaks, chinquapin oaks, trailing arbutus, and lady's slippers. Deer, red fox, small mammals, and bird life abound.

In addition to its ecological importance, the history of the preserve is interesting. Located on its southern border is a field known as the Training Lot. It was here that the militia was trained and decommissioned after the War of 1812.

Please telephone the Conservancy at the above number for permission to visit the sanctuary.

East Patchogue

Swan River Schoolhouse
31 Roe Avenue, East Patchogue
(631) 475-1700

Take the Long Island Expressway to Exit #64 south (Route 112/Coram/Medford). Go south on Route 112 for 4 miles. Turn left (east) onto Route 27A/Main Street/ County Road 80. Go .7 mile bearing right (southeast) onto South County Road/ County Road 36. Go .3 mile. Turn right (south) onto Roe Avenue; go .1 mile. The schoolhouse is on the left (east) side of the road.

This circa 1857 one-room schoolhouse was built on land purchased for $25 in 1857 from Stephen S. Roe. The school remained in use until 1936 when the district was absorbed into the Patchogue Union Free School District #24. In 1962 the building was purchased by the Town of Brookhaven and used until 1970 as a historical museum. In 1970 the town restored it to a one-room schoolhouse. Featured are the original schoolhouse bell, student desks, and some books. Also on display is an 1876 flag, a spinning wheel, an one-hundred-year-old cradle, a pot belly stove, and one of the last gaslights used in Patchogue.

East Setauket

Brewster House
Route 25A/Main Street, East Setauket
(631) 751-2244

Open by appointment only.

Take the Long Island Expressway to Exit #62 north (Nicholls Road/County Road 97/Stony Brook). Go north on Nicholls Road for 9.8 miles to Route 25A. Turn right (east) onto Route 25A; go 1.6 miles. The house is on the left (north) side of the road.

This circa 1665 house is the oldest home in the Three Village area. It was purchased by Joseph Brewster, the son of the first minister of Setauket's Presbyterian church, sometime between 1731 and 1735.

Caleb Brewster, a descendant of Joseph Brewster, was born in Setauket in 1747. (See also Town of Brookhaven/Setauket/Patriot's Rock and Town of Smithtown/Nissequogue/Grave of Richard Smythe [Richard "Bull" Smith].) Not caring for farming, Caleb took to the seas as a whaler and sailed as far as Greenland in search of whale oil. His second voyage took him to England aboard a merchant ship. Upon returning home, he learned that the Revolutionary War had begun. He joined the Continental Army and saw a great deal of action; destroying hay and military supplies at Coram, capturing a British boat on Long Island Sound, leading several whaleboat attacks on segments of the British fleet, and capturing British soldiers at Mastic. Perhaps his most exciting exploits came in 1778 when, as a captain, he joined the Long Island spy ring. It was Brewster who became one of the couriers for Abraham Woodhull and passed messages by whaleboat to patriots in Connecticut.

In 1968 the house was restored to its 1845 appearance based on William Sidney Mount's painting of it, *Long Island Farmhouse*. The painting is on display at the Metropolitan Museum of Art in New York City.

(See also Town of Brookhaven/Mastic Beach/The Manor of Saint George; Town of Brookhaven/Setauket/Presbyterian Church of Setauket; Town of Brookhaven/ Setauket/Richard Woodhull House; Town of Brookhaven/Stony Brook/Hawkins– Mount House; Town of Brookhaven/Stony Brook/The Long Island Museum of American Art, History and Carriages; Town of Oyster Bay/Oyster Bay/Raynham Hall; Town of Oyster Bay/Oyster Bay/Townsend Burying Ground; and Town of Oyster Bay/Oyster Bay/Townsend Museum.)

Sherwood–Jayne House
55 Old Post Road, East Setauket
(631) 692-4664
(The Society for the Preservation of Long Island Antiquities)

Take the Long Island Expressway to Exit #62 north (Nicholls Road/County Road 97/Stony Brook). Go north on Nicholls Road for 9.8 miles to Route 25A. Turn right (east) onto Route 25A; go 1.9 miles. Turn right (south) onto Old Post Road; go .5 mile. The house is on the left (east) side of the road.

This circa 1728 house was built by Matthias Jayne, the son of William Jayne, a chaplain in Oliver Cromwell's army, who came to Setauket around 1670.

In 1908 Howard C. Sherwood bought the house, restored it, and added the wing to the rear of the house. In 1948 he founded the Society for the Preservation of Long Island Antiquities which is dedicated to preserving Long Island's heritage. In his will Sherwood left the bulk of his estate, some $250,000, to the society in order that the organization might continue its work.

Situated behind a huge black oak tree on expansive grounds, the house truly has an idyllic setting. The most notable features of the house are the hand painted wall frescoes in the east parlor and in the east bedroom, which in 1940 were recorded in the Index of American Design, and the Delft fireplace tiles in one of the upstairs bedrooms. The paneling in the west parlor is not original but rather from the Old Parsonage which burned in 1924.

FARMINGVILLE

Bald Hill Cultural Park
South Bicycle Path, Farmingville

Take the Long Island Expressway to Exit #63 north (Farmingville/Selden). Go north on Patchogue–Mount Sinai Road/County Road 83 for 1.5 miles to Bicycle Path Drive. Exit onto Bicycle Path Drive. Turn left (north); go .3 mile. The center is on the left (west) side of the road.

The old Bald Hill Ski Bowl has been converted into a cultural center with an art gallery and outdoor amphitheater. Local artists are given the opportunity to exhibit at the gallery. Musicals, concerts, and dances are held in the amphitheater when weather permits.

Suffolk County Vietnam Veterans' Memorial
Patchogue–Mount Sinai Road, Farmingville

Take the Long Island Expressway to Exit #63 north (Farmingville/Selden). Go north on Patchogue–Mount Sinai Road/County Road 83. The memorial is located in the Suffolk County Vietnam Veterans' Memorial Park at Bald Hill Scenic Overlook in the center median.

Dedicated in 1991, the graceful one-hundred-foot-high red, white and blue tapered spire is truly an inspiring tribute to veterans of the Vietnam War and a positive symbol which was the intent of Robert Fox, a veteran of that war from Massachusetts, from whose concept the memorial was created. It is situated on one of two terminal moraines, left by the retreating glacier, which can be traced in the Island's topography. At an elevation of 321 feet above sea level on one of the highest locations on the Ronkonkoma moraine, the site offers outstanding views of the Island and its surrounding waters.

It should be noted that the memorial is clad in Georgia White Cherokee marble, the same marble used for the Capitol Building and the Lincoln Memorial in Washington, DC.

FIRE ISLAND

Fire Island National Seashore – Sailor's Haven
(631) 589-8980 (ferry); (631) 597-6183 (Visitors' Center)

Take the Long Island Expressway to Exit #53 south (Sagtikos Parkway/Fire Island). Go south on Sagtikos Parkway for 4.1 miles; bear left (east) onto Southern State Parkway. Go east for 6.9 miles on Southern State Parkway to Exit #45 east (Route 27A/Montauk Highway). Go east on Route 27A/Montauk Highway. Stay in the right lane when it joins with Route 27/Sunrise Highway at 1.4 miles. Go .3 mile on Route 27/Sunrise Highway and make a right continuing on Route 27A/ Montauk Highway. Go an additional 4.3 miles to the war memorial at the intersection of Montauk Highway/Route 27A and East Main Street/Middle Road in Sayville. Go east for .2 mile on East Main Street/Middle Road. Turn right (south) onto Foster Avenue; go .6 mile. Turn left (east) onto Terry Street; go .2 mile. Turn right (south) onto River Road to the ferry entrance.

Sailor's Haven has a thirty-six-slip marina with a coin operated pump-out station, guarded swimming, a snack bar, a grocery store, picnic areas, and restrooms. The visitors' center presents changing marine and nautical exhibits and provides information on the park's nature trails. Environmental lectures are given by trained staff. The park is accessible only by ferry or by private boat.

Fire Island National Seashore – Sunken Forest
(631) 289-1810

Take the Long Island Expressway to Exit #53 south (Sagtikos Parkway/Fire Island). Go south on Sagtikos Parkway for 4.1 miles; bear left (east) onto Southern State Parkway. Go east for 6.9 miles on Southern State Parkway to Exit #45 east (Route 27A/Montauk Highway). Go east on Route 27A/Montauk Highway. Stay in the right lane when it joins with Route 27/Sunrise Highway at 1.4 miles. Go .3 mile on Route 27/Sunrise Highway and make a right continuing on Route 27A/ Montauk Highway. Go an additional 4.3 miles to the war memorial at the intersection of Route 27A/Montauk Highway and East Main Street/Middle Road in Sayville. Go east for .2 mile on East Main Street/Middle Road. Turn right (south) onto Foster Avenue; go .6 mile. Turn left (east) onto Terry Street; go .2 mile. Turn right (south) onto River Road to the ferry entrance.

The preserve, which is located below sea level, consists of closely grown trees and vegetation which have created a cool place to take refuge from the blazing sun and heat at the beach. There are guided nature walks through the forest during summer months. Sunken Forest is accessible by private boat or, during the summer months, by ferry from Sayville.

Fire Island National Seashore – Watch Hill

(631) 475-1665 (ferry); (631) 597-6435 (Visitors' Center)

Take the Long Island Expressway to Exit #64 south (Route 112/Coram/Medford). Go south on Route 112 for 3.1 miles. Turn right (west) onto Sunrise Highway/ Route 27; go .4 mile. Turn left (south) onto North Ocean Avenue/County Road 83; go 1.3 miles. Turn right (west) onto Division Street; go .1 mile. Turn left (south) onto Cedar Avenue; go .8 mile. Turn right (west) onto Brightwood Street; go .2 mile to the ferry entrance which is on the left (south) side of the road. This ferry operates only during the summer months.

Watch Hill has a 150-boat marina with coin operated pump-out station, water and electricity, a family campground accommodating twenty-five campers, protected swimming, a snack bar, a grocery store, a first-aid station, a restaurant, and a picnic area. Check at the visitors' center for time and location of guided nature walks. The park is accessible only by ferry or private boat.

HOLTSVILLE

Town of Brookhaven Animal Preserve and Ecology Center

Holtsville Park
249 Buckley Road, Holtsville
(631) 758-9664

Take the Long Island Expressway to Exit #63 (North Ocean Avenue/County Road 83/Mount Sinai/Patchogue). Go south on North Ocean Avenue/County Road 83 for 2 miles. Turn right (west) onto Woodside Avenue; go .9 mile. Turn right (north) onto Buckley Road; go .3 mile. The park is on the right (east) side of the road.

The animal preserve and ecology center is located in the eighty-four-acre Holtsville Park, which is situated on a reclaimed landfill. The animal preserve is an expanding facility with both large and small animals. At last visit there were bison, deer, bald eagles, rabbits, raccoons, pheasants, guinea fowl, chickens, pigs, sheep, peacocks, turkeys, goats, geese, foxes, and a puma. There is a petting zoo and you are encouraged to feed the animals with food available at the preserve.

The ecology center is an integral part of the animal preserve. The center has extensive youth programs for those between the ages of fourteen and twenty who are interested in careers in horticulture, ecology, conservation, and husbandry. Active 4-H clubs, part of the Suffolk County's Cooperative Extension program, are also part of the center's program.

(See also Town of Smithtown/Smithtown/Explorer Scout Nature Museum.)

LAKE GROVE

First Congregational Church of New Village
Route 25, Lake Grove
(631) 585-7330

Take the Long Island Expressway to Exit #60 north (Ronkonkoma Avenue/Lake Ronkonkoma/Sayville). Go north on Hawkins Avenue for 3.3 miles. Turn right (east) onto Route 25/Jericho Turnpike; go .2 mile. The church is on the left (north) side of the road.

The congregation was organized in 1815 and the church was erected in 1818. For the intervening three years services were held in private homes. The church was constructed with the understanding that it was to house, free, all the local Protestant denominations with the Congregationalist congregation occupying it half the time and the Baptist and Presbyterian congregations sharing the remainder of the time. In subsequent years both of the latter denominations built their own churches leaving the Congregationalists alone in the building. In 1963 they also moved to a new, larger building leaving the original church vacant until 1971 when it was acquired by the Town of Brookhaven.

The town restored the building to its original appearance and opened it to the public in 1976. Of particular interest is the bulge in the ceiling over the pulpit, which reflects the shape of the tree used as a beam at that point; the portable pulpit; and the graffiti from another era on the moldings in the main section of the church, as well as on those in the east closet in the rear of the church. The church is on the National Register of Historic Places.

LAKE RONKONKOMA

Cenacle Convent
310 Cenacle Road, Lake Ronkonkoma
(631) 588-8366

Take the Long Island Expressway to Exit #60 (Ronkonkoma Avenue/Lake Ronkonkoma/Sayville). Go north on Hawkins Avenue for 1 mile. Turn right (east) onto Portion Road; go 1.2 miles. Turn left (north) onto Cenacle Road; go .2 mile. Turn left (west) into the retreat house grounds. Follow road to retreat house. The former home of Maude Adams is on the left just before you reach the retreat house. Her grave is on the grounds.

Grave of Maude Adams (1872–1953)

Please call the retreat house to obtain directions to the grave site and permission to visit the grounds.

Maude Ewing Adams Kiskadden was born in Salt Lake City, UT. The daughter of an actress, Maude made her debut at nine months of age. As a youngster, she was able to grasp the motivation of a part long before she could read. By 1897 she had become a star, her greatest role being the role of Peter Pan in 1906. Although this role was created by Nina Boucicault in London in 1904, it was Adams' interpretation of the role together with the costume she designed that made the play a resounding success. The costume, with its feathered hat and round collar, became a national fashion style and Adams, a national idol.

Never married, her private life was beyond reproach. While nominally a Protestant, she was deeply religious and spent some months in a convent in Tours, France. She is buried on her 400-acre former estate which she deeded to the Sisters of Saint Regis for the care and understanding that they extended to her during the long recuperation period after her nervous breakdown. No other religious order would help her because she was an actress.

It was said of her, "Charm is a sort of bloom upon a woman. If you have it, you don't need to have anything else."

Finlay–Wolf Pond
(Long Island Chapter: The Nature Conservancy)
Ronkonkoma Avenue, Lake Ronkonkoma
(631) 367-3225

Open with prior permission.

Take the Long Island Expressway to Exit #60 north (Ronkonkoma Avenue/Lake Ronkonkoma). Go north on Ronkonkoma Avenue for 1.2 miles. The preserve is on the right (east) side of the road just .1 mile beyond the intersection with Portion Road.

This nine-acre preserve is a combination kettlehole pond, freshwater wetlands, field, and upland wood. There is a variety of vegetation including red maple and beech trees, bladderwort, bullhead lilies, fragrant water lilies, calamus, swamp honeysuckles, sweet pepperbushes, and button-bushes. The preserve also has five species of fern that are protected by New York State.

Please call the Conservancy at the above telephone number to obtain permission to visit the preserve.

Lake Ronkonkoma Historical Museum
328 Hawkins Avenue, Lake Ronkonkoma
(631) 467-3152

Take the Long Island Expressway to Exit #60 (Ronkonkoma Avenue/Lake Ronkonkoma/Sayville). Go north on Hawkin's Avenue to the museum.

The collections contain Long Island Indian artifacts, period postcards, and maps. Local family memorabilia have been collected illustrating the Bavarian roots of many of the early families of the area. Also, an effort has been made to collect and exhibit material relevant to the career of stage actress Maude Adams, who lived nearby.

(See also Town of Brookhaven/Lake Ronkonkoma/Cenacle Convent.)

MANORVILLE

The Animal Farm and Petting Zoo

184A Wading River Road, Manorville
(631) 878-1785

Take the Long Island Expressway to Exit #69 south (Wading River Road/Wading River/Center Moriches). Go south on Wading River Road for 2.5 miles. The petting zoo is on the right (west) side of the road.

The Animal Farm is designed for children and the young-at-heart as a petting and feeding zoo. Found at the site are American buffalo, llama, Grand Canyon burros, monkeys, peacocks, parrots, and a wide assortment of barn animals. There are rides for children, a puppet theater, a picnic area, and an antique automobile museum.

Long Island Game Farm and Zoological Park

Chapman Boulevard, Manorville
(631) 878-6644

Take the Long Island Expressway to Exit #70 south (Eastport Manor Road/Manorville/Eastport). Go south on Port Jefferson–Westhampton Road/County Road 111/ Captain Daniel Roe Blvd. for .4 mile. Turn right (west) onto Chapman Boulevard; go 1.3 miles. The game farm is on the left (east) side of the road.

The park has many diverse and exotic animals, both wild and tamed. Children will delight in the petting zoo and in a chance to feed baby animals. There is an oceanarium with a sea lion show as well as a chimpanzee show. Picnic facilities are available.

Manorville Historical Society Museum

50 North Street, Manorville
(631) 369-2250

Take the Long Island Expressway to Exit #70 south (Eastport Manor Road/Manorville/Eastport). Go north on Port Jefferson–Westhampton Road/County Road 111 to North Street. Turn left (west) onto North Street. Proceed to museum.

The museum is located in a 1929 two-room schoolhouse. One room is a period display of a classroom. The other museum room houses artifacts pertinent to Long Island schools.

MASTIC BEACH

Fire Island National Seashore – Smith Point
Fire Island, Mastic Beach
(631) 281-3010

Take the Long Island Expressway to Exit #68 south (William Floyd Parkway/ County Road 46). Go south on William Floyd Parkway for 7.8 miles to the park.

This section of Fire Island National Seashore offers nature walks and swimming. There is a boardwalk for people with disabilities as well as an information pavilion with restrooms.

(See also Town of Brookhaven/Fire Island/Fire Island National Seashore–Sailor's Haven; Town of Brookhaven/Fire Island/Fire Island National Seashore–Sunken Forest; and Town of Brookhaven/Fire Island/Fire Island National Seashore–Watch Hill.)

The Manor of Saint George
Neighborhood Road, Mastic Beach
(631) 281-5034

Take the Long Island Expressway to Exit #68 south (William Floyd Parkway/ County Road 46). Go south on William Floyd Parkway for 6.2 miles. Turn right (west) onto Neighborhood Road and go .1 mile to the manor gate.

In the 1670s, at the age of twenty-two, Colonel William "Tangier" Smith, a former page at the court of Charles II of England, began public office in the royal city of Tangier in Morocco. (See also Town of Brookhaven/Ridge/Longwood Estate.) Strategically located opposite Gibraltar, Tangier had been given by the king of Portugal as part of a dowry occasioned by the marriage of his daughter to Charles II. In 1682 Colonel Smith was appointed mayor of Tangier but hopes of establishing a major trading seaport were already beginning to fade and in 1683 the port was abandoned, but not before being totally destroyed by the British. To compensate Colonel Smith for his sizable personal financial losses, he was allowed to purchase 10,000 acres of land in the present Town of Brookhaven. With the granting of a royal patent establishing the Manor of Saint George in 1693 by the English sovereigns William and Mary, Colonel Smith's lands extended from Long Island Sound to the Atlantic Ocean and from present-day Islip to Riverhead.

During the Revolutionary War the manor house was occupied by the British who built a stockade fort at the site and named it Fort George. In 1780 the fort was destroyed by Continental soldiers under the command of Major Benjamin Tallmadge. Tallmadge also led the raid on Fort Franklin in 1781 and was the senior intelligence officer for George Washington. (See also Town of Huntington/Lloyd Harbor/Henry Lloyd Manor.) Indeed, it was to Tallmadge that Major John Andre was brought after the latter's capture and it was Tallmadge who escorted Andre to the gallows. (See also Town of Brookhaven/East Setauket/Brewster House; Town of Brookhaven/Mastic Beach/Woodhull Cemetery/Grave of Nathaniel Woodhull; Town of Brookhaven/Setauket/Presbyterian Church of Setauket; Town of Brookhaven/Setauket/Richard Woodhull House; Town of Oyster Bay/Oyster Bay/Raynham Hall; Town of Oyster Bay/Oyster Bay/Townsend Burying Ground; and Town of Oyster Bay/Oyster Bay/Townsend Museum.)

The Smiths were also ardent patriots. Indeed, Judge William Smith had served as President pro tempore of the Provincial Congress and his son, General John Smith, had been imprisoned by the British and was later to become a United States Senator from New York State. It was General John Smith who built the present manor house after the Revolutionary War.

Over the years the manor has played an active role in United States military endeavors. During the War of 1812 cannons were placed there to protect the inlet from British ships and during World War I an army airfield was located just south of the manor house while its grounds were used for recreational purposes by military personnel stationed at Camp Upton. (See also Town of Brookhaven/Upton/Brookhaven National Laboratories.)

The manor house, which is situated on the remaining 127 acres of the manorial lands, is impeccably decorated with eighteenth- and nineteenth-century furnishings. Of particular interest are the parquet floors with differing designs in each room, marble fireplaces, original beams in the kitchen, and Persian and Indian rugs.

Also located on the grounds is the Smith family cemetery.

Smith Point County Park

Fire Island, Mastic Beach
(631) 852-1313 (for park and camping information)

Suffolk County Resident Pass is required for admission.

Take the Long Island Expressway to Exit #68 south (William Floyd Parkway/County Road 46). Go south on William Floyd Parkway for 7.8 miles to the park.

This 2,290-acre park, which overlooks both the Atlantic Ocean and the Great South Bay, is the largest oceanfront park on Fire Island. It offers supervised ocean swimming, surfing, ocean fishing, bike hostels, nature trails, shuffleboard courts, picnic areas, and controlled hunting of waterfowl. There is a pavilion for renting beach umbrellas and cabanas. The pavilion also houses a snack bar. There are facilities for people with disabilities.

Available on a first-come, first-served basis is a camping area with restrooms and showers. Beach buggies are allowed to drive on the western section of the beach only by permit.

William Floyd Estate

245 Park Drive, Mastic Beach
(631) 399-2030

Take the Long Island Expressway to Exit #68 south (William Floyd Parkway/ County Road 46). Go south on William Floyd Parkway for 6.2 miles. Turn left (east) onto Neighborhood Road; go 1.9 miles. Turn left (north) onto Whittier Drive (which becomes Mastic Beach Road). Go .6 mile on Whittier Drive/Mastic Beach Road. Turn left onto Aspen Road and then right onto Park Drive.

Born in Mastic on December 17, 1734, William Floyd was a signer of the Declaration of Independence, New York State Senator, and soldier. The eldest son of Nicoll and Tabitha Smith Floyd, he inherited the family estate in Mastic Beach at the age of eighteen when both his parents died of typhus. He quickly became known for his hospitality. William Floyd joined the militia and rose to the rank of major-general. While serving in this capacity, he was able to repulse the first British attack on Long Island, but in 1776 he was forced to seek refuge in Connecticut. His estate was virtually ruined by the occupying British soldiers. After the war, Floyd returned to Mastic Beach and rebuilt his estate. In 1795 he was an unsuccessful candidate for lieutenant governor of New York State when he was defeated by Stephen Van Rensselaer. In 1801 and again in 1808 he was elected New York State Senator. He died at the age of eighty-seven on August 4, 1821.

His descendants lived at the Mastic Beach estate for 250 years before donating it to the National Park Service. The house has been on the National Register of Historic Places since 1971. The 613-acre estate contains the main house, twelve buildings, and a family graveyard. The vast majority of its furnishings belonged to the Floyd family and cover a period from the 1700s to the 1940s. Of particular interest is the portrait of William Floyd, one of the few in existence.

(See also Town of Smithtown/Nissequogue/Grave of Richard Smythe [Richard "Bull" Smith] and Town of Brookhaven/Mastic Beach/Woodhull Cemetery/Grave of Nathaniel Woodhull.)

Woodhull Cemetery

Neighborhood Road, Mastic Beach

Take the Long Island Expressway to Exit #68 south (William Floyd Parkway/ County Road 46). Go south on William Floyd Parkway for 6.2 miles. Turn left (east) onto Neighborhood Road; go 2 miles. The cemetery is on the right (south) side of the road.

Grave of Nathaniel Woodhull (1722–1776)

The grave site is centrally located in this small cemetery and can easily be viewed from outside the locked fence.

Woodhull was born at The Manor of Saint George, his mother being the granddaughter of Richard "Bull" Smith. (See also Town of Brookhaven/Mastic Beach/

The Manor of Saint George and Town of Smithtown/Nissequogue/Grave of Richard Smythe [Richard "Bull" Smith].) Woodhull entered the military at an early age rising to the rank of major by the outset of the French and Indian War (1755–1763). During the war he served with General Abercromby at the Battles of Crown Point and Fort Ticonderoga, with General Amherst as a colonel in the Third Regiment of New York Provincials during the invasion of Canada, and with General Bradstreet at the 1758 Battle of Fort Frontenac, Kingston, Ontario. In 1761 Woodhull married Ruth F. Floyd, the sister of William Floyd, and, after the war, settled down to farm and pursue a career in politics. (See also Town of Brookhaven/Mastic Beach/William Floyd Estate.) He served as Suffolk County's representative to the convention that chose delegates to the First Continental Congress and became president of the New York Provincial Congress, which in 1775 assumed control of the colony placing Suffolk and Queens counties under Woodhull's jurisdiction. A brigadier-general, Woodhull was responsible for the defense of Long Island. In 1776, when the British were threatening Manhattan from Brooklyn, Woodhull was ordered to Jamaica to remove stock and supplies thus impeding the British advance. With the Patriot's defeat at the Battle of Long Island, Woodhull's retreat was cut off. Captured near Jamaica, he was ordered by a British soldier to say, "God save the King." When he responded, "God save us all," the unarmed Woodhull was attacked with a broadsword and severely wounded in the head and arm, the latter being badly mangled from the shoulder to the wrist. The next day he was placed on a prisoner-of-war ship in New York Harbor, a ship which had previously been used to transport livestock. Due to the severity of his wounds, he was moved to a nearby house where his arm was amputated. He died on September 20, 1776, as a result of his wounds.

MIDDLE ISLAND

Cathedral Pines County Park
Yaphank–Middle Island Road, Middle Island
(631) 852-5500

Suffolk County Resident Pass is required for admission.

Take the Long Island Expressway to Exit #68 north (William Floyd Parkway/County Road 46). Go north on William Floyd Parkway for 1.7 miles to Longwood Road (opposite the entrance to Brookhaven National Laboratories). Turn left (west) onto Longwood Road; go 1.9 miles. The entrance to the park is across Yaphank–Middle Island Road.

This 321-acre park was formerly the Prosses Pines and Camp Wilderness. It is currently divided into two sections. The eastern section is manned during the summer months by an environmental staff which offers films, lectures, and slide shows on conservation. Guided nature walks are also offered on an appointment basis. The western section of the park offers hiking, nature walks along marked trails, primitive camping facilities for organized youth groups, and bike hostels. Plans are being formulated for the restoration of the circa 1790 Dayton House and barn complex which are located within the park.

MILLER PLACE

Miller House
North Country Road, Miller Place
(631) 928-0821

Take the Long Island Expressway to Exit #63 north (County Road 83/North Ocean Avenue/Mount Sinai/Patchogue). Go north on North Ocean Avenue/Patchogue–Mount Sinai Road for 8.5 miles. Turn right (east) onto Route 25A; go .4 mile. Bear left (continuing east) onto Echo Avenue; go .2 mile. Turn left (north) onto Pipe Stove Hollow Road; go .1 mile. Turn right (east) onto North Country Road/County Road 20; go .7 mile. The house is on the left (north) side of the road.

In the early 1700s Andrew Miller became the first permanent settler in the area which now bears his name. This 1720 house was built by his grandson William Miller and was occupied by their descendants until 1978 when it was sold to the Miller Place Historical Society. Despite two additions, one in 1740 and one in 1816, the house with its exposed beams with wooden peg construction and Dutch door still retains much of its charm. An area of the interior construction has deliberately been left exposed so that the original beams, which are still covered with bark, may be viewed. Also of interest are the eighteenth-century pantry shelves which, according to the Society for the Preservation of Long Island Antiquities, are the only original eighteenth-century pantry shelves remaining on Long Island. The house is on the National Register of Historic Places.

OLD FIELD

Flax Pond
Crane Neck Road, Old Field

From the village green in Setauket go north on Main Street for 1.7 miles to Mount Grey Road. Turn left (west) onto Mount Grey Road; go .6 mile. Turn right (north) onto Crane Neck Road; go .6 mile. The pond is on the right (east) side of the road. (Look for the wooden bridge.)

A special permit from the Department of Environmental Conservation, Albany, NY, is required in order to visit this protected area.

Originally a freshwater pond that was left by the retreating Wisconsin glacier, it was used by early settlers for retting flax so that the fiber could be extracted for spinning. In 1803 an inlet to Long Island Sound was dug converting it to a saltwater pond. Fishing, clamming, and oystering were popular sports on the pond until 1942 when sand mining in the pond threatened its very existence. Fortunately, the mining operation lasted only three years and no irreparable harm was done.

The pond is currently owned and protected by the State University of New York and the New York State Department of Environmental Conservation.

Old Field Lighthouse
Old Field Road, Old Field

Not open to the public.

From the village green in Setauket go north on Main Street. Continue straight onto Old Field Road for a total of 3.1 miles to the Long Island Sound and the lighthouse.

In 1823 the federal government appropriated $2,500 for the construction of the lighthouse. In 1824 an additional $1,500 was authorized in order that the lighthouse might be completed. It remained in operation until 1868 when the present structure was built. The light consisted of nine whale oil lamps which were seated in a large lantern with parabolic reflectors.

The lighthouse was purchased by the village in 1935 and is presently the home of the Old Field constable. The old keeper's house is now the Old Field Village Hall.

(See also Town of East Hampton/Cedar Point/Cedar Point Lighthouse; Town of East Hampton/Montauk/Montauk Lighthouse; Town of Huntington/Eaton's Neck/ Eaton's Neck Lighthouse; Town of Islip/Fire Island/Fire Island Lighthouse; and Town of Southold/Southold/Horton Lighthouse.)

PATCHOGUE

The Bay Mist
Watch Hill Boat Terminal, Patchogue
(631) 475-1606

Take the Long Island Expressway to Exit #64 south (Route 112/Coram/Medford). Go south on Route 112 for 3.1 miles. Turn right (west) onto Sunrise Highway/ Route 27; go .4 mile. Turn left (south) onto North Ocean Avenue/County Road 83; go 1.3 miles. Turn right (west) onto Division Street; go .1 mile. Turn left (south) onto Cedar Avenue; go .8 mile. Turn right (west) onto Brightwood Street; go .2 mile to the dock.

The Bay Mist has two completely enclosed and heated decks which can accommodate two hundred people. From early spring through January 1st, theme cruises such as Big Band, Italian Feast, Fourth of July, 50s Theme Night, and New Year's Eve parties are given on the Great South Bay. The boat may also be rented for special occasions.

Lakeview Cemetery
Main Street, Patchogue

Take the Long Island Expressway to Exit #61 (County Road 19/Holbrook/Patchogue). Go south on Patchogue–Holbrook Road/County Road 19 (which later joins Waverly Avenue) for 4.9 miles. Turn left (east) onto Main Street/County Road 85; go .1 mile. The main entrance to the cemetery is on the left (north) side of the road.

Grave of Elizabeth Oakes Smith (1806–1893)

The grave site is on the far east side of the cemetery. It is the second gravestone from the open area; about eight feet from the fence.

Born in Yarmouth, ME, Elizabeth had a longing for education but was convinced by her parents to put aside her hopes of higher education and a career as headmistress of a girls' school. In 1823 she married Seba Smith, a man nearly twice her age. With the loss of the family fortune in The Panic of 1837, Elizabeth began writing under the *nom de plume* Ernest Helfenstein to supplement her husband's meager income. Through her books, magazine articles, and lectures, espousing such causes as woman's suffrage and the improvement of living conditions in Manhattan's slums, she became a prominent reformer.

Patchogue Village Center for the Performing Arts
71 East Main Street, Patchogue
(631) 207-1313

The theater is located in the center of Patchogue's business district.

Opened in 1923, the 1,166-seat theater was arguably one of the largest and most ornate theaters on Long Island. For the first six years of its existence, it hosted first-run feature films, Broadway plays, vaudeville, and burlesque. It was purchased in 1929 by the Prudential Theater Circuit and functioned as a motion picture theater for the next forty years. Since then it has had several owners. In 1980 United Artists purchased the building and destroyed much of its ornate features during a conversion to a three-theater-multiplex motion picture house.

In 1997 the Village of Patchogue purchased the theater and began the laborious task of restoring it to its former glory. The restorations completed, the theater now hosts Broadway plays, ice shows, local drama productions, dance performances, and live concerts ranging from rock to classical music.

PORT JEFFERSON

Children's Maritime Museum

101 East Broadway, Port Jefferson
(631) 331-3277

Take the Long Island Expressway to Exit #64 north (Route 112/Port Jefferson). Go north on Route 112 for 10 miles. Turn right onto East Broadway.

Appropriately located in the more-than-a-century-old Bayles Chandlery building, the museum occupies over 1,200-square-feet of the building's first floor. Exhibits are based on historical, scientific, and artistic dimensions of Long Island's maritime heritage. They utilize the constructivism approach to learning thereby provoking thought in problem solving.

(See also Town of East Hampton/Amagansett/The Town of East Hampton Marine Museum; Town of Islip/West Sayville/Long Island Maritime Museum; Town of Riverhead/Riverhead/Atlantis Marine World; and Town of Southampton/Sag Harbor/ Sag Harbor Whaling and Historical Museum.)

John R. Mather House Museum

115 Prospect Street, Port Jefferson
(631) 473-2665

Take the Long Island Expressway to Exit #64 north (Route 112/Port Jefferson). Go north on Route 112 for 3.2 miles. Bear left and continue on Route 112 across Route 25. At 8.7 miles go straight as the road becomes Route 25A west. When you have traveled a total of 10 miles, turn right (east) onto Main Street. Go .1 mile bearing right up the hill and onto Prospect Street. Continue another .1 mile on Prospect Street. The house is on the left (north) side of the road.

In 1880 John Willse moved from Setauket to Drown Meadow, which became Port Jefferson in 1836, and immediately established a shipbuilding business. John's daughter Irena married his apprentice Richard Mather and their son John Richard was born in 1814. With the death of Willse in 1814, Richard assumed ownership of the shipyard. Two years later Richard died in an accident while constructing the schooner *Catherine Rodgers* for his father who was a sea captain. Drown Meadow's shipbuilding industry came to a halt until Richard's brother Titus Mather took over management of the family business in 1819.

In 1821 Richard's widow Irena married William L. Jones, who was in the process of establishing his own shipyard in Drown Meadow. John Richard became a partner in the Jones shipyard and continued the business when Jones retired in 1844.

John Richard Mather died in 1899 leaving Mather House to his daughter Irena and his son. The circa 1840 Mather House is now the home of the Historical Society of Greater Port Jefferson. Decorated in period furniture, it has small collections of lusterware and postcards. There is also a small reference library. The

37

tool shed has a large collection of antique tools. Also located on the grounds is a circa 1875 two-bedroom house which was moved from the center of town to make room for a parking lot. Of interest here are a small loom, a folding crib, and some original window panes.

In 1928 John Richard's grandson bequeathed $500,000 for the construction of Port Jefferson's Mather Hospital and endowed it with an additional $400,000.

The Martha Jefferson
Port Jefferson Harbor, Port Jefferson
(631) 331-3333

Take the Long Island Expressway to Exit #64 north (Route 112/Port Jefferson). Go north on Route 112 for 10 miles. Make a right (east) onto Arden Place. Go .1 mile. Make a left (north) into the entrance to parking lot #1.

A 140-person-capacity replica of a paddle-wheel boat, the *Martha Jefferson* offers scenic tours of Long Island Sound and private charters. Brunch and dinner cruises are also offered. It features a climate-controlled area, open-air deck, dance floor, and a bar on each of its two decks.

(See also Town of Oyster Bay/Glen Cove/*Paddle Steamer Thomas Jefferson*; Town of Brookhaven/Patchogue/*The Bay Mist*; Town of Islip/Fire Island/*Moonchaser*; and Town of Hempstead/Freeport/Nautical Cruise Lines.)

RIDGE

Brookhaven Volunteer Firefighter's Museum
Fireman's Memorial Park
Route 25, Ridge
(631) 924-8114

Located in a restored 1889 firehouse, the museum has two floors of firefighting mementos, nine trucks, and six additional pieces of equipment. The memorial park, in which the museum is located, is dedicated to New York City fire and police personnel from the town that perished in the September 11, 2001, terrorist attack on New York's World Trade Center.

Longwood Estate

Smith Road, Ridge
(631) 732-3751 Extension 227

Take the Long Island Expressway to Exit #68 north (William Floyd Parkway/ County Road 46/Brookhaven Lab./Wading River). Go north on William Floyd Parkway for 1.7 miles to Longwood Road (opposite the entrance to Brookhaven National Laboratories). Turn left (west) onto Longwood Road; go .4 mile. Turn right (north) onto Smith Road; go .2 mile. The entrance is on the right (east) side of the road.

This circa 1790 thirty-five-acre farm is presently being restored by the Town of Brookhaven with help from the Society for the Preservation of Long Island Antiquities. The twenty-two-room house was the home of Mr. and Mrs. Elbert Smith, a direct descendant of William "Tangier" Smith who settled in Setauket in 1656. (See also Town of Brookhaven/Mastic Beach/The Manor of Saint George.) The farm consists of a main house, several service buildings, and a pond. Among the service buildings is the circa 1872 Ridge Schoolhouse which was moved to the estate and which also is being restored.

The estate is the site of the annual Brookhaven Country Fair which features Revolutionary War encampments, re-enactments of Revolutionary battles, craft demonstrations, period music, Indian exhibits, and colonial games.

SETAUKET

The Village Green

Main Street, Setauket

Take the Long Island Expressway to Exit #62 north (Nicholls Road/County Road 97/Stony Brook). Go north on Nicholls Road for 9.8 miles to Route 25A. Turn right (east) onto Route 25A; go 1.3 miles. Turn left (north) onto Main Street; go .4 mile to the village green.

The village green, which is owned by both the Caroline and Presbyterian churches, is somewhat smaller than the original village green which was laid out by settlers more than 325 years ago. This triangular plot was the sight of a fort built in 1675 by the early settlers as protection against an Indian uprising which never materialized.

Caroline Church of Brookhaven

Strong's Neck Road, Setauket
(631) 941-4245

Located on the north end of the village green in Setauket.

Built in 1729, the church was originally called Christ Church. When Queen Caroline, the consort of George II, donated a silver communion service to the church in 1730, its name was changed to Caroline Church as a gesture of gratitude and respect. Because it was an Anglican church, the British soldiers tended to respect the church and even attended its services during the Revolutionary War. After the war the church, with its loyalist congregation, fell on hard times. Most of the loyalist congregation moved to Canada, thus there was no money for much-needed repairs. With the aid of Trinity Church in New York City the Caroline Church was able to survive but it was not until about 1814 that the church was again financially sound.

Of particular interest is the twist in the church's tower which is a result of the warping of the hand-hewn oak corner post; the bullet marks sustained during the Battle of Setauket in 1777; the Union Jack and Crown cut into the weather vane; the painted stained-glass windows; the exposed original beams; and a carillon which plays "God Save the Queen," or, if you prefer, "My Country Tis of Thee." It now has the distinction of being the oldest Episcopal church in New York State and the second oldest Episcopal church in the United States.

Caroline Church of Brookhaven Cemetery

Strong's Neck Road, Setauket
(631) 941-4245

Located on the north end of the village green in Setauket.

Grave of John Ward Melville (1887–1977)

The grave site is in the far northwestern section of the cemetery.

Melville was born in Brooklyn, NY. After graduating from Columbia University in 1909, he worked as a shoe salesman. He served in the quartermaster general's office in its shoe leather division during World War I. After the war, he was employed by John Ward Shoes as a manager, buyer, vice-president, and, ultimately, as chairman of the board of what was to become Melville Shoe Company, which in turn became famous through its Thom McAn trademark.

A dynamic force, Melville's philanthropy was responsible for the preservation of the colonial atmosphere of the hamlets of Three Village and Stony Brook as he single-handedly tried to stem the tide of modernism that was encroaching into North Shore communities. (See also Town of Brookhaven/Stony Brook/Stony Brook Post Office.)

His collections of over three hundred horse-drawn vehicles and nineteenth-century paintings provided the nucleus for The Long Island Museum of American

Art, History and Carriages. (See also Town of Brookhaven/Stony Brook/The Long Island Museum of American Art, History and Carriages.)

In the mid-1950s he donated 450 acres to New York State for the creation of the State University at Stony Brook. Envisioning a small college, the architecture of which would blend harmoniously with the colonial atmosphere of the surrounding communities, he was extremely disappointed when the state went ahead with plans for a modernistic campus which would service a population of some twelve thousand students.

Emma S. Clark Memorial Library
120 Main Street, Setauket
(631) 941-4080

Located on the west side of the village green in Setauket.

The building, with its brick exterior and oak interior set off beautifully by exposed beams, is built in the Queen Anne-style of architecture. The 1892 stained-glass window in the reading room, by the New York studio Heinigke and Bowen, pictures the Archangel Gabriel. The library houses approximately 80,000 volumes and has a fine collection of Long Island and local history.

Old Field Farm
West Meadow Road, Setauket
(631) 246-8983

Take the Long Island Expressway to Exit #62 north (Nicholls Road/County Road 97/Stony Brook). Go north on Nicholls Road for 9.8 miles to Route 25A. Turn left (west) onto Route 25A. At the first traffic light, turn right onto Quaker Path. Bear left at the fork onto Grey Road. Turn left onto West Meadow Road (aka Trustees Road).

Built by Ward Melville at the headwaters of West Meadow Creek, the equestrian center was originally known as North Shore Show Grounds. Now owned by Suffolk County, it features a Colonial Revival-style stable, a grandstand, and competition rings. Call the above telephone number for the schedule of events.

Patriot's Rock
Main Street, Setauket

From the village green in Setauket go north on Main Street for .1 mile. The rock is on the left (west) side of the road.

The rock has significance for two reasons. The Reverend Nathaniel Brewster, a member of the first graduating class of Harvard College (1642) and Setauket's first ordained minister, is said to have preached his first sermon atop the huge boulder. (See also Town of Smithtown/Nissequogue/Grave of Richard Smythe/Richard "Bull"

41

Smith and Town of Brookhaven/East Setauket/Brewster House.) And, during the Battle of Setauket in 1777 General Parson positioned his artillery on this site while attacking the British who held a fortified position in the Presbyterian church.

Presbyterian Church of Setauket
Main Street, Setauket
(631) 941-4271

The church is located on the east side of the village green in Setauket.

This, the third church to be erected on this site, was founded by the Puritans about 1660. Known originally as the First Presbyterian Church of Brookhaven, it is the oldest organized church in the Town of Brookhaven. The first building was erected in 1669, the second in 1714, and the present one in 1812. During the Revolutionary War British soldiers caused considerable damage to the building by stabling their horses in the church.

The adjacent cemetery is particularly interesting as it is the final resting place for several famous Long Islanders. The grave of John Thompson, one of the town's founders, is located directly behind the church and in front of the wrought iron fence. The grave of Abraham Woodhull, the chief of the Long Island spy ring, is located to the rear of the church just behind and to the north of the wrought iron fence; and the grave of the famous painter William Sidney Mount is located to the rear and south of the church about eight rows from the road. Mount's distinctive grave stone, on top of which is a carved cross, bears the inscription "As a painter, eminent and original; as a man, exemplary and beloved."

(See also Town of Brookhaven/East Setauket/Brewster House; Town of Brookhaven/Setauket/Richard Woodhull House; Town of Brookhaven/Setauket/Thompson House; Town of Brookhaven/Stony Brook/Hawkins–Mount House; Town of Brookhaven/Stony Brook/The Long Island Museum of American Art, History and Carriages; Town of Hempstead/Hempstead/Denton Village Green; and Town of Oyster Bay/Oyster Bay/Raynham Hall.)

Richard Woodhull House
Dyke Road, Setauket

From the north end of the village green in Setauket turn east onto Dyke Road towards Strong's Neck. Go .5 mile on Dyke Road. The marker for the site is on the left (west) side of the road.

The original structure on the site was built in 1690 by Richard Woodhull, one of the founders of Setauket and the great-grandfather of Abraham Woodhull. Abraham, who lived here, became the chief of the Long Island spy ring during the Revolutionary War and was known by the code name "Samuel Culper Sr." An ardent patriot, Woodhull recruited Robert Townsend (who was known by the code name "Samuel Culper Jr."), Caleb Brewster, and Austin Roe, among others, into the spy ring. Townsend's mission was to report British troop and ship movements in the Manhattan area to Woodhull. His reports were written in disappearing ink which had recently been invented by James Jay, whose brother John Jay was to become the first Chief Justice of the Supreme Court. The message was carried on horseback to Woodhull in Setauket by Austin Roe. Woodhull in turn gave the message to Caleb Brewster, who sailed across Long Island Sound and delivered it to Major Tallmadge, the chief of Washington's spy network. Perhaps the most important intelligence gathered by the Long Island spy ring was the plot of Major Andre and Benedict Arnold for the surrender of West Point to the British. So successful were Townsend and Woodhull in keeping their identities secret, it was not until the 1930s that historians were able to verify their true identities and the roles that they played in the Revolution.

Unfortunately, the Woodhull house was destroyed by fire in 1931.

(See also Town of Brookhaven/East Setauket/Brewster House; Town of Brookhaven/Mastic Beach/The Manor of Saint George; Town of Brookhaven/Setauket/Presbyterian Church of Setauket; Town of Huntington/Lloyd Harbor/Henry Lloyd Manor; Town of Oyster Bay/Oyster Bay/Raynham Hall; Town of Oyster Bay/Oyster Bay/Townsend Burying Ground; and Town of Oyster Bay/Oyster Bay/Townsend Museum.)

Saint German of Alaska Eastern Orthodox Church
140 Main Street, Setauket
(631) 751-6009

From the village green in Setauket go south on Main Street for .2 mile. The church is on the right (west) side of the road.

In 1976 the circa 1890 building, which had been the Roman Catholic Church of Saint James, was remodeled into the Eastern Orthodox Church of Saint German of Alaska. The interior was renovated, icons were placed on the walls, and a large crystal chandelier hung overhead. The pointed steeple was replaced by a single onion dome with an Eastern Orthodox cross.

Setauket Neighborhood House
95 Main Street, Setauket
(631) 751-6208

From the village green in Setauket go north on Main Street for .2 mile. Turn left (west) continuing on Main Street; go .1 mile. The house is on the left (south) side of the road.

In 1820 the house was moved from its original site on Setauket Bay to its present location by Dr. John Elderkin. Here, during the 1860s, John Elderkin Jr. converted the house into a combination stagecoach stop, post office, and inn called the Elderkin Hotel.

In 1918 it was purchased by Eversley Childs, an Old Field industrialist, and presented to the community. Since then it has served as a meetinghouse and polling place administrated by the Setauket Neighborhood Association. The house, which is available for public use, has been restored to its Victorian appearance. Two rooms are decorated and furnished in the Victorian Empire-style.

Thompson House

North Country Road (not Route 25A), Setauket
(631) 692-4664

From the village green in Setauket go north on Main Street for .2 mile. Turn left (west) continuing on Main Street; go .8 mile. When you cross Ridgeway Avenue, Main Street becomes North Country Road (not Route 25A). The house is on the left (east) side of the road.

The Reverend William Thompson arrived in New England in 1634. By 1672 his descendants had settled in Setauket and built this circa 1700 salt box-style house.

Benjamin Thompson, a member of the sixth generation of Thompsons to live in the house, was the noted Long Island historian who in 1839 published his book *History of Long Island,* which is still considered the cornerstone of Long Island history.

The house, which is maintained by the Society for the Preservation of Long Island Antiquities and is on the National Register of Historic Places, is characterized by a steep roof and forty-one-inch-long shingles made of bog cedar. The collection of furniture displayed in the house is one of the finest on Long Island and contains representative pieces of three distinctive Long Island styles of furniture: the double-paneled blanket chest; the *kas,* a large cupboard found in areas settled by the Dutch; and the splatback chair, a country version of the Queen Anne-style. The splatback chair was made in 1790 by Nathanial Dominy IV. Another Dominy piece on display is a clock made in 1797.

Located to the rear of the house are an herb garden and a family graveyard.

(See also Town of Brookhaven/Setauket/Presbyterian Church of Setauket and Town of Islip/West Bay Shore/Sagtikos Manor.)

Tucker–Jones House

Main Street at Ridgeway Avenue, Setauket
(631) 751-8960

From the village green in Setauket go north on Main Street for .2 mile. Turn left (west) continuing on Main Street; go .7 mile. The house is on the left (east) side of the road.

This circa 1850 two-and-a-half-story house was the home of a sea captain. It was rebuilt in 1908 when the original structure was destroyed by fire. On the grounds are a barn which was restored in 1975 and a fully equipped blacksmith shop.

SHIRLEY

Wertheim National Wildlife Refuge
Smith Road, Shirley
(631) 286-0485

Open with prior permission.

Take the Long Island Expressway to Exit #68 south (William Floyd Parkway/ County Road 46). Go south on William Floyd Parkway for 3 miles. Turn right (west) onto Route 27A/Montauk Highway. Go .7 mile on Route 27A/Montauk Highway. Turn left (south) onto Old River Road (which becomes Smith Road); go .3 mile. The park is on the right (west) side of the road.

This 2,400-acre federal preserve is operated by the Fish and Wildlife Services of the Department of Interior. A total of 1,800 acres of the preserve's wetlands were donated to the federal government in 1947 by Maurice Wertheim. The government took title to the land in 1975 at the death of Wertheim's widow Cecile. Since 1950 the government has acquired six hundred contiguous acres adjoining the original Wertheim donation and has plans for acquiring additional property when money becomes available.

At present, use of the preserve is limited to boaters who travel the reed-rimmed waterways and to educational groups.

STONY BROOK

The Hercules Pavilion
Main Street at the village green, Stony Brook

Take the Long Island Expressway to Exit #62 north (Nicholls Road/County Road 97/Stony Brook). Go north on Nicholls Road for 9.8 miles to Route 25A. Turn left (west) onto Route 25A; go 1.6 miles. Turn right (north) onto Main Street; go .5 mile to the village green, which is on the left (west) side of the road.

Hercules is the figurehead from the *USS Ohio,* a seventy-four-gun ship built in 1820 at the Brooklyn Navy Yard. In 1884 the ship was decommissioned and dynamited near Greenport and sold for scrap. (See also Town of Southold/Greenport/ Margaret Ireland House.) The one-and-a-half-ton figurehead was preserved and mounted on a pedestal at the Canoe Place Inn in Hampton Bays. It remained at that location some sixty years. In 1954 it was purchased by the Village of Stony Brook, restored, and repainted in its original colors. Legend has it that any woman who kisses Hercules will be married within the year.

Next to the covered pavilion in which Hercules stands is a fully equipped whale boat.

The Country House Restaurant
Main Street and Route 25A, Stony Brook
(631) 751-3332

From the Hercules Pavilion at the village green in Stony Brook go south on Main Street for .5 mile. The Country House is on the left (east) side of the road at the intersection of Main Street and Route 25A.

This circa 1710 farmhouse was built by Obadiah Davis after moving to Stony Brook from Mount Sinai. In 1838 the English actor Thomas Hadaway purchased the house and held séances that were attended by painter-inventor William Sidney Mount. Subsequent owners continued to farm the land and indeed it was successful until the early 1900s. In 1967 it became the 1710 House Restaurant and then later became known as the Hadaway House Restaurant. It is presently the Country House Restaurant.

On the hill slightly north of the house is a cemetery in which four Revolutionary War patriots—Caleb Davis, Joseph Wells, Obadiah Davis, and John Williamson—are buried.

Hawkins–Mount House
Main Street/Route 25A and Stony Brook Road, Stony Brook
(631) 751-0066

From the Hercules Pavilion at the village green in Stony Brook go south on Main Street for .9 mile, continuing south when it becomes Route 25A. The house is on the left (east) side of the road at the intersection of Route 25A and Stony Brook Road.

Built in 1757 by Major Eleazer Hawkins, the house has been used as a post office, a store, and a tavern. If you look closely at the west facade you will see the inscription "Jonas Hawkins Store and Ordinary." Not content with the quiet life of an innkeeper, Jonas occasionally acted as a courier for the Long Island spy ring.

The famous American painter William Sidney Mount, who was born in Setauket on November 26, 1807, and whose grandmother was a Hawkins, lived in this house from 1836 until his death in 1868. Written comments about the weather and paint dabs are still visible on one wall of Mount's attic studio. (See also Town of Brookhaven/East Setauket/Brewster House; Town of Brookhaven/Setauket Presbyterian Church of Setauket; and Town of Brookhaven/Stony Brook/The Long Island Museum of American Art, History and Carriages.)

The house, which is owned by The Long Island Museum of American Art, History and Carriages, is on the National Register of Historic Places. It is only open for a few days each year in December.

The Long Island Museum of American Art, History and Carriages
1200 Main Street/Route 25A, Stony Brook
(631) 751-0066

From the Hercules Pavilion at the village green in Stony Brook go south on Main Street for .5 mile to the intersection of Route 25A. The museums are located on both sides of the road.

This multi-building complex houses the Melville collection of more than three hundred horse-drawn vehicles, a harness maker's shop, a blacksmith shop, an 1818 schoolhouse, a nineteenth-century printing shop, and an eighteenth-century barn. Changing displays of costumes, textiles, ceramics, housewares, dolls, and toys can be viewed in the various galleries. The museum also has a permanent collection of decoys and a miniature rooms gallery. Its collection of nineteenth-century American paintings is renowned, especially the collection of paintings by William Sidney Mount.

(See also Town of Brookhaven/East Setauket/Brewster House; Town of Brookhaven/Setauket/Caroline Church of Brookhaven Cemetery/Grave of John Ward Melville; Town of Brookhaven/Setauket/Presbyterian Church of Setauket; and Town of Brookhaven/Stony Brook/Hawkins–Mount House.)

Museum of Anthropology
Social and Behavioral Science Building, State University at Stony Brook
Nicholls Road, Stony Brook
(631) 689-6000

Take the Long Island Expressway to Exit #62 north (Nicholls Road/County Road 97/Stony Brook). Go north on Nicholls Road for 8.9 miles. Turn left into the main entrance of SUNY Stony Brook (opposite Daniel Webster Drive); go .1 mile. Turn left and go .1 mile to parking garage on left.

The museum has changing displays, dioramas, maps, and prehistoric artifacts relevant to Long Island. It is operated by students.

Museum of Long Island Natural Sciences

Earth and Space Sciences Building, State University at Stony Brook
Nicholls Road, Stony Brook
(631) 632-8230

Take the Long Island Expressway to Exit #62 north (Nicholls Road/County Road 97/Stony Brook). Go north on Nicholls Road for 8.9 miles. Turn left into the main entrance of SUNY Stony Brook (opposite Daniel Webster Drive); go .1 mile. Turn left and go .1 mile to parking garage on left.

Featured are changing exhibits about Long Island's natural history. There is a permanent exhibit of the geological history of Long Island. Special programs are available to schools and groups.

Staller Art Gallery

State University at Stony Brook
Nicholls Road, Stony Brook
(631) 632-7240

Take the Long Island Expressway to Exit #62 north (Nicholls Road/County Road 97/Stony Brook). Go north on Nicholls Road for 8.9 miles. Turn left into the main entrance of SUNY Stony Brook (opposite Daniel Webster Drive); go .1 mile. Turn left and go .1 mile to parking garage on left.

Located in the Staller Center for the Arts, the 4,700-square-foot gallery offers five exhibitions of contemporary art each year.

Staller Performing Arts Center

State University at Stony Brook
Nicholls Road, Stony Brook
(631) 632-2787

Take the Long Island Expressway to Exit #62 north (Nicholls Road/County Road 97/Stony Brook). Go north on Nicholls Road for 8.9 miles. Turn left into the main entrance of SUNY Stony Brook (opposite Daniel Webster Drive); go .1 mile. Turn left and go .1 mile to parking garage on left.

The Staller Performing Arts Center offers classical and contemporary music programs, ballet, plays, films, and lecture series. It hosts the Stony Brook Film Festival during the summer months.

Stony Brook Post Office
Main Street, Stony Brook

Located on the east side of Main Street opposite the village green in Stony Brook.

The post office is part of a nineteenth-century Federal-style shopping center built by Ward Melville. It is most unusual in that the eagle that adorns its facade flaps it wings on the hour.

(See also Town of Brookhaven/Setauket/Caroline Church of Brookhaven Cemetery/Grave of John Ward Melville.)

Three Village Inn
Dock Road, Stony Brook
(631) 751-0555

Located on the north side of Dock Road opposite the village green in Stony Brook.

The original part of the restaurant was built in 1751 by a farmer named Richard Hallock. His son George was not particularly interested in farming and is responsible for building the town's first wharf and becoming the town's first major shipbuilder. The Hallock homestead was purchased by Jonas Smith around 1850. A ship owner with a fleet of thirty-two ships, Smith was one of the country's most influential ship owners with offices at 66 South Street, New York City, near the present site of the South Street Seaport Museum.

The house was eventually bought by Mrs. Frank Melville in 1929 and renovated for the Woman's Exchange Organization to be used as a tea room. Over the years the tea room grew into a fine restaurant with rooms for overnight guests.

The original colonial fireplace is still visible near the bar; original beams with pegged joints can be seen in the Exchange Room.

UPTON

Brookhaven National Laboratories – Camp Upton
William Floyd Parkway, Upton
(631) 344-8000

The Exhibit Center is open to schools and special interest groups with tours available by special arrangement during the winter and to individuals during the summer. Call for dates when tours are available.

Take the Long Island Expressway to Exit #68 north (William Floyd Parkway/ County Road 46/Brookhaven National Lab./Wading River). Go north on William Floyd Parkway for 1.7 miles. The complex is on the right (east) side of the road.

Camp Upton, which was named after the Civil War General Emory Upton, was built by the United States Army during World War I on 10,000 acres of swampy, mosquito-infested land. Used to train troops, its most famous soldier was probably Irving Berlin. Berlin wrote the popular song "Oh, How I Hate to Get Up in the Morning" based on his experiences at the camp.

At the completion of World War I the camp was used as a demobilization center for returning soldiers. During World War II the camp was reactivated, but this time by the United States Army Air Corps, which used the facilities to train pilots.

In 1947 the site became Brookhaven National Laboratories which is operated by a consortium of universities. Fundamental research in diverse fields is carried out at the complex.

(See also Town of North Hempstead/Roslyn/Trinity Episcopal Church.)

WESTHAMPTON BEACH

Cupsogue Beach County Park
Dune Road, Westhampton Beach
(631) 852-8111

Take the Long Island Expressway to Exit #70 south (Eastport Manor Road/Manorville/Eastport). Go south on Port Jefferson–Westhampton Road/County Road 111/ Captain Daniel Roe Blvd. for 4.7 miles. Go east on Sunrise Highway/Route 27 for 4.1 miles to Exit #63 south (County Road 31/Westhampton Beach). Go south for a total of 5.6 miles on Old Riverhead Road which becomes Oak Street which then becomes Potunk Lane which at 4.4 miles curves left becoming Jessup Lane. Turn right (west) onto Dune Road/County Road 89. Go 4.7 miles to the park which is located at the end of the road.

This 296-acre park is located on Fire Island extending from the western terminus of Dune Road west to the Moriches Inlet. During the summer there is supervised swimming, a wooden pavilion where beach chairs and umbrellas may be rented, as well as a refreshment stand. Other activities offered are surfing, fishing, and duck hunting (in season). There are restrooms as well as facilities for people with disabilities.

YAPHANK

Hawkins–Jacobsen House
Yaphank Avenue, Yaphank
(631) 924-3879

Take the Long Island Expressway to Exit #68 south (William Floyd Parkway/ County Road 46). Go south on William Floyd Parkway for .6 mile. Turn right (west) onto Moriches Road/Middle Island Road which becomes Broadway/ Moriches Road and then becomes East Main Street; go 1.7 miles. Turn left (south) onto Yaphank Road; go 50 feet. The house is on the right (west) side of the road.

This circa 1850 house, which is located on one-and-one-third acres adjacent to the northern section of Southaven County Park, is the best example of Victorian-style architecture in the Yaphank area. Although owned by the Suffolk County Historic Trust, the restoration was completed by the Yaphank Historical Society. The house, which was featured in the January 1986 issue of *House Beautiful* decorating magazine, is truly a gem of Victorian design. The historical society plans to use the house as a resource center with lectures, garden parties, quilting bees, and concerts. It has been on the National Register of Historic Places since 1986.

Southaven County Park – Suffolk Club
Victory Boulevard, Yaphank
(631) 854-1414

Suffolk County Resident Pass required for admission.

Take the Long Island Expressway to Exit #68 south (William Floyd Parkway/ County Road 46). Go south on William Floyd Parkway for 2.8 miles to the Sunrise Highway service road (which becomes Victory Boulevard). Turn right (west) onto the Sunrise Highway service road/Victory Boulevard. Go 1 mile to park's main entrance which is on the right (north) side of the road.

This 1,323-acre park was the first park opened by the Suffolk County Parks Department. It was originally known as the Suffolk Club, a private organization established in 1858 by August Belmont Sr. as a hunting club. (See also Town of Babylon/North Babylon/Belmont Lake State Park–August Belmont Sr. Estate–Nursery Stud Farm; Town of Hempstead/Elmont/Belmont Park Race Track; Town of Hempstead/Garden City/Vanderbilt Motor Parkway Toll House; and Town of Islip/Oakdale/Connetquot River State Park and Preserve–Southside Sportsmen's Club.)

The park offers a myriad of activities such as guided nature walks, nature trails, hiking, picnicking, bridle paths, dog and horse shows, canoeing, rowboating and boat rentals, trap and skeet shooting, freshwater fishing, and hunting. Ice skating is available when weather permits. There is also a camping facility which accommodates three hundred tenters, trailers, and members of organized youth groups. The park is also a bicycle hostel stop. The camping ground has sanitary and water facilities as well as accommodations for people with disabilities.

There are plans to restore the circa 1810 Hard–Homan House, which is located on Yaphank Road in the northern portion of the park, and the circa 1920 Anson Wales Hard Jr. house, located in the southern portion of the park. At the present time neither house is open to the public.

(See also Town of Islip/West Sayville/West Sayville County Park–Anson Wales Hard Jr. Estate–Meadow Edge.)

Suffolk County Farm and Educational Center

4600 Yaphank Avenue, Yaphank
(631) 852-4600

Take the Long Island Expressway to Exit #67 south (Yaphank Road/Brookhaven). Go south on Yaphank Avenue/County Road 21 for .4 mile. The farm is on the right (west) side of the road.

The educational center is located on a nineteenth-century farm which is operated by Suffolk County and the Cornell Cooperative Extension. Featured demonstrations have been created to emphasize horticultural, agricultural, and nutritional aspects important to good health. Feeding and petting of farm animals is permitted in selected areas of the farm.

Suffolk County Police Museum
30 Yaphank Avenue, Yaphank
(631) 852-6011

Take the Long Island Expressway to Exit #67 south (Yaphank Road/Brookhaven). Go south on Yaphank Avenue/County Road 21 to the museum.

The museum displays articles pertaining to police enforcement from 1600 sheriffs to present law enforcement. Also found in the museum are a re-created 1927 police station house and a 1960 police car.

(See also Town of Hempstead/Garden City/Nassau County Police Museum.)

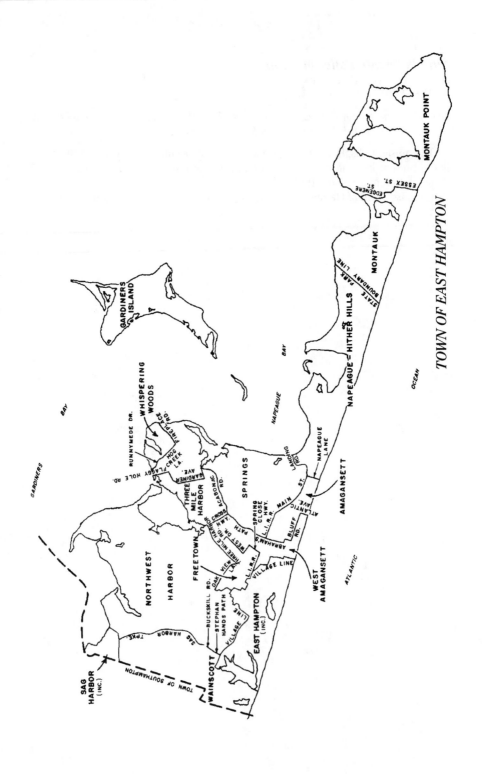

TOWN OF EAST HAMPTON

TOWN OF EAST HAMPTON

Parks and Preserves

Federal Parks and Preserves
Amagansett National Wildlife Refuge (36 acres), Amagansett

State Parks and Preserves
Amsterdam Beach State Park (122 acres), Montauk *(undeveloped)*
Camp Hero State Park (119 acres), Montauk *(undeveloped)*
Hither Hills State Park (1,755 acres), Montauk
Montauk Downs State Park (160 acres), Montauk
Montauk Point State Park (724 acres), Montauk
Napeague State Park (1,300 acres), East Hampton Beach *(undeveloped)*
Shadmoor State Park (99 acres), Montauk *(undeveloped)*

County Parks and Preserves
Cedar Point County Park (608 acres), Cedar Point
Montauk County Park (1,126 acres), Montauk
Northwest Harbor County Park (337 acres), Sag Harbor *(undeveloped)*
Theodore Roosevelt County Park (1,126 acres), Montauk *(undeveloped)*

South Fork – Shelter Island Chapter: The Nature Conservancy
Accabonac Harbor Preserve (130 acres), Springs
Atlantic Double Dunes Preserve, Amagansett

Arboretums and Gardens
none

Amagansett

Atlantic Double Dunes Preserve
(South Fork – Shelter Island Chapter: The Nature Conservancy)
Atlantic Avenue, Amagansett
(631) 329-7689

Open with prior permission.

From the war memorial at the intersection of Route 27/Main Street/Montauk Highway and Atlantic Avenue in Amagansett go south on Atlantic Avenue for .9 mile.

The preserve is an oceanfront sanctuary extending from Amagansett to East Hampton. This truly unique area is abundantly populated with tree swallows, flickers, and hawks. It includes over 100 plant species and hosts more than 130 species of birds. Caution is advised since the area is posted as tick-infested.

Please call the Conservancy at the above telephone number to obtain permission to visit the preserve.

Commercial Fisherman's Museum
Route 27/Main Street, Amagansett
(631) 324-4083

From the war memorial at the intersection of Route 27/Main Street/Montauk Highway and Atlantic Avenue in Amagansett go west on Route 27/Main Street/Montauk Highway for .6 mile. The museum is on the right (north) side of the road.

The museum is located in the circa 1760 Schellinger House. (See also Town of East Hampton/Amagansett/Miss Amelia's Cottage; Town of East Hampton/East Hampton/Pantigo Mill; and Town of Southampton/Bridgehampton/Beebe Windmill.) Research has found that the house originally had a central chimney with three fireplaces on the main floor and one on the second floor. In 1830 the house was modified with several structural changes made. The original chimney was replaced by a central staircase, windows were enlarged, the front door was paneled, and a triangular fireplace was installed. Restoration is currently planned so that the exterior of the house will be restored to its eighteenth-century appearance. The house presently is being used as a museum with photo exhibits depicting the lifestyles of commercial fishermen of Long Island.

The East Hampton Town Marine Museum
Bluff Road, Amagansett
(631) 324-6850

From the war memorial at the intersection of Route 27/Main Street/Montauk Highway in Amagansett go south on Atlantic Avenue. Continue on Atlantic Avenue for .6 mile to Bluff Road. Turn right (west) onto Bluff Road; go .2 mile. The museum is on the left (south) side of the road.

The purpose of the museum is to depict the economic, social, and political impact that fishing and whaling have had on the local community. It is operated by the East Hampton Historical Society and is located in a former World War II naval barracks. Found in the museum are whaling boats, a wagon, clamming and whaling equipment, and a diorama of Fort Pond Bay.

(See also Town of Brookhaven/Port Jefferson/Children's Maritime Museum; Town of Islip/West Sayville/Long Island Maritime Museum; Town of Riverhead/Riverhead/Atlantis World; and Town of Southampton/Sag Harbor/Sag Harbor Whaling and Historical Museum.)

Miss Amelia's Cottage
Route 27/Main Street and Windmill Lane, Amagansett
(631) 267-3020

From the war memorial at the intersection of Route 27/Main Street/Montauk Highway and Atlantic Avenue in Amagansett go west on Route 27/Main Street/ Montauk Highway for .7 mile. The cottage is on the right (north) side of the road.

This circa 1725 cottage was named after Mary Amelia Schellinger who lived in it from 1841 until her death in 1930. (See also Town of East Hampton/Amagansett/ Commercial Fisherman's Museum; Town of East Hampton/East Hampton/Pantigo Mill; and Town of Southampton/Bridgehampton/Beebe Windmill.) Restored by the Amagansett Historical Society, the house has a large central chimney with three fireplaces and a divided "good morning" staircase that leads to the second floor. Among the furnishings in the house are excellent examples of Dominy furniture such as a candle table and two clocks, one of which Dominy made with only an hour hand. Other items found in the house are collections of flowing blue china, dolls, toys, and an exquisite clock from Glasgow, Scotland.

Roy K. Lester Carriage Museum
Route 27/Main Street, Amagansett
(631) 267-3020

From the war memorial at the intersection of Route 27/Main Street/Montauk Highway and Atlantic Avenue in Amagansett go west on Route 27/Main Street/ Montauk Highway for .7 mile. The museum is located on the right (north) side of the road.

The museum, which is owned and operated by the Amagansett Historical Society, contains wagons, carriages, omnibuses, and station wagons. The pride of the collection is the restored brougham manufactured by Brewster and Company, which certainly could be considered the Rolls Royce of its day. Plans are now being made for the restoration of the other vehicles as well as the opening of a second carriage house and the establishment of a carriage workshop staffed partly by volunteers.

Saint Thomas Episcopal Church
Route 27/Main Street, Amagansett
(631) 267-3080

From the war memorial at the intersection of Route 27/Main Street/Montauk Highway and Atlantic Avenue in Amagansett go west on Route 27/Main Street/ Montauk Highway for .7 mile. The church is on the left (south) side of the road.

This quaint country-style church was built in 1907. It is unique in that its windows are unstained leaded glass and its interior is made entirely of chestnut.

APAQUOGUE

Grantland Rice's House
West End Road, Apaquogue

Not open to the public.

From the village green in East Hampton go west on Route 27/Main Street/Montauk Highway. At .2 mile continue straight (south) onto Ocean Avenue; go .5 mile. Turn right (west) onto Lily Pond Road; go 1.3 miles. Turn left (southwest) onto West End Road; go 1.6 miles. The house is on the left (south) side of the road.

A sportswriter and poet, Rice (1880–1945) was born in Tennessee. He received his undergraduate degree from Vanderbilt University in 1901. Upon graduation, he obtained employment as a journalist working for a number of newspapers including *The Nashville Daily News* (1901), *Atlanta Journal* (1902–1904), *Nashville Tennessean* (1906–1910), *New York Evening Mail* (1911–1914), and the *New York Tribune* (1914–1930), before having his own syndicated column. It was Rice who first used the term "the four horsemen of the Apocalypse" when referring to the backfield of the Notre Dame football team. In 1943 he was given an Academy Award Oscar for the best one-reel picture produced that year.

Rice built this large two-story house on four acres next to that of his friend Ring Lardner. (See also Town of East Hampton/Apaquogue/Ring Lardner's House– Still Pond and Town of North Hempstead/Kings Point/Ring Lardner's House–The Mange.) Like Lardner, Rice was forced to move his house back some 200 feet behind the dunes due to the severe erosion caused by the 1931 hurricane. Rice lived in this house from 1928 until his death in 1945. He is buried in Woodlawn Cemetery, The Bronx, NY.

Ring Lardner's House – Still Pond
West End Road, Apaquogue

Not open to the public.

From the village green in East Hampton go west on Route 27/Main Street/Montauk Highway. At .2 mile continue straight (south) onto Ocean Avenue; go .5 mile. Turn right (west) onto Lily Pond Road; go 1.3 miles. Turn left (southwest) onto West End Road; go 1.5 miles. The house is on the left (south) side of the road.

Ringgold Wilmer Lardner (1885–1933) gained prominence as a journalist, short-story writer, and playwright whose dialectic style of writing was compared to that of Mark Twain in *Huckleberry Finn.* Lardner died of a heart attack at the age of forty-eight. He is interred at the Fresh Ponds Crematorium in Middle Village, Queens – *Gothic Section, 3807.*

This thirteen-room, shingled house was his home from 1928 to 1933. It was originally built further up on the dunes but was moved to its present site because of the severe erosion caused by the 1931 hurricane.

(See also Town of North Hempstead/Kings Point/Ring Lardner's House–The Mange.)

CEDAR POINT

Cedar Point County Park
Alewive Brook Road, Cedar Point
(631) 852-7620

Suffolk County Resident Pass is required for admission.

From Route 27/Main Street/Montauk Highway turn north opposite the village green in East Hampton onto Buell Lane/Route 114. (Buell Lane becomes Sag Harbor Turnpike.) Go 2 miles and turn right (east) onto Stephan Hands Path. Go .7 mile on Stephan Hands Path to North West Road, bearing left onto Old North West Road. Continue for 3.8 miles (turning right at the 2 mile mark). Turn left onto Alewive Brook Road; go .1 mile. The park entrance is on the right side of the road.

Located on Gardiner's Bay, this 608-acre park is designed for trailer and tent camping. It has 190 general campsites, 60 sites for club camping, and a 200-person organized youth group camping area. There are water and sanitary facilities but no hook ups. A general store is located within the park and there are facilities for people with disabilities. The park offers swimming, picnicking with grills, bridle paths, nature trails, hunting, fishing, and rowboating. And for the adventuresome, a two-mile, round-trip hike out to the Cedar Point Lighthouse is possible.

Cedar Point Lighthouse
Alewive Brook Road, Cedar Point

From Route 27/Main Street/Montauk Highway turn north opposite the village green in East Hampton onto Buell Lane/Route 114. (Buell Lane becomes Sag Harbor Turnpike.) Go 2 miles and turn right (east) onto Stephan Hands Path. Go .7 mile on Stephan Hands Path to Old North West Road, bearing left onto Old North West Road. Continue for 3.8 miles (turning right at the 2 mile mark). Turn left onto Alewive Brook Road; go .1 mile. The park entrance is on the right side of the road.

Built in 1838 by the federal government, the lighthouse was purchased by Phelan Beale at public auction in 1936 for $2,002. It remained a private residence until its acquisition by Suffolk County. The county is seeking funds to restore the lighthouse which suffered severe damage in 1974 when the entire interior of the building was gutted by a fire, deliberately set by vandals. There is a nature trail leading to the lighthouse.

EAST HAMPTON

Clinton Academy
151 Main Street, East Hampton
(631) 324-6850

From the village green in East Hampton go east on Route 27/Main Street/Montauk Highway for .2 mile. The academy is on the left (north) side of the road.

Named after New York State Governor George Clinton and established in 1784, the academy was the first private co-educational institution in the state. The curriculum encompassed the philosophies of the Latin grammar school and that of the English academic school. Thus, students learned practical subjects such as geometry, surveying, accounting, navigation, mathematics, and science, as well as Latin and Greek. With the development of statewide education in the nineteenth century the academy began a twenty-year decline and closed in 1881.

Anna Symmes Harrison (1775–1864), the first First Lady to have a formal education, began her schooling at Clinton Academy during the Revolutionary War. Her mother, Anna Tuttle, was born in Southold, Long Island, and died shortly after young Anna's birth. Her father, John Cleves Symmes, also born in Southold, disguised himself in a British uniform and brought Anna from New Jersey to the Southold home of her maternal grandparents. The Tuttles, a prominent East End family, saw to her education which also included years at what was then considered to be the finest girls' school in New York City. She rejoined her father and his new wife and traveled to Ohio, where her father was responsible for the settlement and growth of Cincinnati. There she met William Henry Harrison, the son of Benjamin Harrison, a signer of the Declaration of Independence, who was then a young military officer and who would become our ninth president. In her home in North Bend, OH, Anna educated not only her own children but neighbor children as well. Her grandson, son of one of her ten children, also became president; Benjamin Harrison was our twenty-third president.

An ironic aside, with William Henry Harrison's death in February 1841, just one month after his inauguration, his vice-president John Tyler became president. Only a few years later Tyler would marry young Julia Gardiner of East Hampton, the daughter of David Gardiner. (See also East Hampton/East Hampton/Old Cemetery/Grave of David Gardiner and Grave of John Alexander Tyler.)

The building, which housed the academy, was remodeled in 1886 and used for a myriad of community functions. In 1921 it was acquired by the East Hampton Historical Society and restored to its original eighteenth-century appearance. Today the academy is on the National Register of Historic Places and is a museum housing an antique Edison projector, an 1861 piano, an 1825 school desk, an 1800 microscope, as well as other memorabilia relevant to the school and its role in the community.

Gardiner's Windmill

James Lane, East Hampton

Not open to the public.

Located on private property directly opposite (south) the East Hampton village green, cemetery, and memorial to Lion Gardiner.

Built in 1804 by Nathaniel Dominy V, this smock-type mill with intermediate gears driving two pairs of millstones replaced a 1769 post-type mill. It cost $1,320 to build and was owned by Miller Dayton, Jeremiah Osborne, and John Gardiner. (See also Town of East Hampton/East Hampton/Old Cemetery and Town of Islip/West Bay Shore/Sagtikos Manor.) By 1884 the thirteenth Lord of the Manor, Jonathan Thompson Gardiner, acquired sole ownership. The Gardiner family continued to operate the mill until the early 1920s. The mill, which is on the National Register of Historic Places, is presently in desperate need of repair. Its shaft is rotten and its sails are missing.

Cedar Lawn Cemetery

Cooper Lane, East Hampton

From the village green in East Hampton go east on Route 27/Main Street/Montauk Highway for .7 mile. Bear left before the Old Hook Mill onto North Main Street/West Main Street and continue under the railroad bridge. Go .1 mile from the Old Hook Mill to Cedar Street. Turn left (north) onto Cedar Street; go .6 mile. Turn left (west) onto Cooper Lane; go .6 mile. The cemetery is on the right (north) side of the road.

Grave of Childe Hassam (1859–1935)

Turn right (north) into the cemetery at the third carriage road. Turn left (west); go .1 mile. Turn right (north); go .1 mile. The grave site is on the right (east) side of the carriage road within a hedged plot. Lot 32, Section C

American-born Frederick Childe Hassam, together with Theodore Robinson, John H. Twachtman, and J. Alden Weir, is considered one of the four pioneers in American Impressionism. The movement, influenced by the works of French painters such as Monet, Renoir, and Degas developed in America largely due to these four artists. Hassam painted in the French tradition, choosing New England subjects and flooding these subjects with natural sunlight. His use of color is greatly praised. Together with J. Alden Weir he founded The Ten in 1898. This group did much to advance the acceptance of Impressionism in America. Hassam was not only known as a painter, but also as an illustrator.

(See also Town of Southold/East Marion/East Marion Cemetery/Grave of Mark Rothko.)

Guild Hall Museum
158 Main Street, East Hampton
(631) 324-0806

From the village green in East Hampton go east on Route 27/Main Street/Montauk Highway for .1 mile. The museum is on the right (south) side of the road opposite the Clinton Academy.

Opened in 1931, the Guild Hall consists of the 393-seat John Drew Theater, which is used for musical and dramatic productions as well as films and concerts; three art galleries; and a sculpture garden. While the museum concentrates on regional artists, displaying a collection of over one thousand works, it also features special exhibits of internationally known artists.

Hayground Windmill
Windmill Lane, East Hampton

Not open to the public.

From the village green in East Hampton go east on Route 27/Main Street/Montauk Highway for .9 mile to Egypt Lane (bearing right at the Old Hook Mill). Turn right (south) onto Egypt Lane; continue for .8 mile. Turn left (east) onto Further Lane; go .4 mile. Turn right (south) onto Windmill Lane and go to the end of the road. The mill is on private property.

This smock-type windmill was built on the village green of Hayground in 1809 by an unknown millwright. It remained in use until 1919 giving it the distinction of being the last windmill to operate on Long Island. Prior to its purchase by Robert Dowling and its relocation to his estate in East Hampton, the mill was used commercially as a tearoom and as an artist's studio. (See also Town of Islip/Oakdale/Dowling College–William Kissam Vanderbilt Sr. Estate–Idlehour.) The cap, frame, and fantail were restored in 1981–1982. The mill is on the National Register of Historic Places.

(See also Town of East Hampton/East Hampton/Gardiner's Windmill; Town of East Hampton/East Hampton/Old Hook Mill; Town of East Hampton/East Hampton/Pantigo Mill; Town of East Hampton/Wainscott/Wainscott Windmill; Town of Shelter Island/Shelter Island/Shelter Island Windmill; Town of Southampton/Southampton/The Good Ground Windmill; Town of Southampton/Water Mill/Water Mill Windmill; and Town of Southampton/Bridgehampton/Beebe Windmill.)

Home Sweet Home
14 James Lane, East Hampton
(631) 324-0713

Located opposite the village green in East Hampton on James Lane which is one street south of and parallel to Route 27/Main Street/Montauk Highway.

This 1660 salt box-style house was the childhood home of John Howard Payne. At the age of fourteen he began publishing the *Thespian Mirror* which became a popular weekly dramatic paper. At fifteen he wrote *Julia,* his first full length play. During his life he wrote some sixty-five plays, but he is remembered most for the song "Home Sweet Home" from his 1823 opera *Clari* which premiered at Covent Garden in England.

The contents of the house span the seventeenth, eighteenth, and nineteenth centuries. Among its more prized displays is a chest made in 1640 in New Haven, CT, which has been documented as the oldest piece of furniture made in the colonies. Also to be found is an extensive collection of lusterware china, a Cromwellian helmet, and complete collections of Staffordshire and Wedgwood china. Both the house and the windmill behind it are on the National Register of Historic Places.

Long Island Collection
East Hampton Public Library
159 Main Street, East Hampton
(631) 324-0222

From the village green in East Hampton go east on Route 27/Main Street/Montauk Highway for .1 mile. The library is on the left (north) side of the road opposite the Guild Hall.

The collection was established in 1930 when the Long Island historian Morton Pennypacker donated his extensive collection of Long Island materials to the East Hampton Library.

Paintings, lithographs, and etchings of Thomas Moran and his family are displayed in the rooms that house the Long Island Collection. (See also Town of East Hampton/East Hampton/Old Cemetery/Graves of Mary and Thomas Moran.) The library is beautifully appointed with antique furniture including an eight-foot-tall, one-stroke Dominy clock (c. 1820–1825).

Lyman Beecher Homestead
Huntting Lane, East Hampton

Not open to the public.

From the village green in East Hampton go east on Route 27/Main Street/Montauk Highway for .5 mile. The house is on the right (south) side of the road facing Huntting Lane.

The Reverend Lyman Beecher, the fiery Presbyterian minister, social reformer, president of Lane Theological Seminary, and founder of the American Bible Society, lived in East Hampton for a period of time. This circa 1740 house was purchased by him in 1799, for the sum of $800 to accommodate his very large family of thirteen children. These incredibly intelligent children were interested and active in social reform, and were recognized for teaching, writing, and preaching. The best known of these are: Harriet Beecher Stowe, the author of *Uncle Tom's Cabin* and *Life Among the Lowly;* Henry Ward Beecher, the eminent preacher who was famous for his fiery oratory for suffrage and against slavery; Edward Beecher, president of Illinois College in Jacksonville, IL; Thomas Kennicut Beecher, progressive and beloved Congregational teacher and minister at Park Church in Elmira, NY; and Catharine Esther Beecher, teacher and activist who worked for the liberalization of education for women.

Most Holy Trinity Roman Catholic Church
Buell Lane/Route 114, East Hampton
(631) 324-0134

From Route 27/Main Street/Montauk Highway turn north opposite the village green in East Hampton onto Buell Lane/Route 114; go north for .4 mile. The church is on the left (west) side of the road.

This unique church has unusually shaped clear leaded-glass windows including those in the dormers on both the north and south sides of the building. The roof slopes abruptly to about eight feet above the ground on the north side and slopes to a covered portico on the south side. The entire interior, including the ceiling, is wainscotted with stained and highly polished narrow pieces of wood. The tapestries behind the altars, the font, and the hexagonal carved wood lanterns hanging from the ceiling on both sides of the church are both unusual and beautiful.

Mulford Farm

10 James Lane, East Hampton
(631) 324-6850

Located opposite the village green in East Hampton on James Lane which is one street south of and parallel to Route 27/Main Street/Montauk Highway.

Upon arrival in East Hampton John Mulford purchased this circa 1680 house and became very active in civic affairs. His son Samuel was appointed captain of the militia and in 1705 was elected to the Provincial Congress. A noted firebrand, Samuel became enraged at the tax imposed on whale oil and traveled to England to lobby for its abolition. To thwart London's pickpockets he placed fishhooks in his pockets. Within days he became the talk of London. Indeed the tactic made him so well known that he was granted an audience with the king and managed to have the unpopular tax repealed. He is buried across the street in the Old Cemetery on the village green. The Mulford Farm was worked from 1712–1944 by eight generations of the family before it was acquired by the East Hampton Historical Society. It is the best example of seventeenth-century salt box-style architecture remaining in the village. In spite of ongoing restoration, there are several rooms open for viewing. Of particular interest is the exposed seaweed insulation. The decorated beams and door frames are very unusual in a house of this era. The house is on the National Register of Historic Places.

The Nature Trail

David's Lane, East Hampton

From the village green in East Hampton go east on Route 27/Main Street/Montauk Highway for .9 mile (bearing right at the Old Hook Mill). Turn right (south) onto Egypt Lane; go .6 mile. Turn right (west) onto David's Lane; go .1 mile. The park is on the right (north) side of the road.

A truly delightful wildlife sanctuary with typical Long Island flora and fauna, this seventeen-acre preserve contains a stream with bridges and paths along its wooded banks, a site that will calm the most jangled nerves. Migratory waterfowl are easily seen and enjoyed even if you choose not to leave your car. A small parking area, accommodating about six cars, is right at the edge of the stream on David's Lane. Split-log benches are also provided. Please note that picnics, fires, dogs, bicycles, and guns are prohibited.

Old Cemetery

Main Street, East Hampton

Located on Route 27/Main Street/Montauk Highway between the lake and the village green and opposite the Home Sweet Home and Mulford Farm Complex.

Grave of David Gardiner (1784–1844)

The grave site is located just east of that of Lion Gardiner (see below). It is marked by a tall obelisk.

David Gardiner, a New York State Senator, died in a tragic accident aboard the *USS Princeton*. A steam frigate of revolutionary design invented by John Ericson, it was the first ship to have propelling machinery below the water line. During a ceremonial trip on the Potomac River, the fire power of its twelve-inch cannons was demonstrated for the distinguished passengers. They included President Tyler, several cabinet members, and federal and state legislators including Senator Gardiner, as well as members of their respective families. One of the cannons exploded, killing, among others, Secretary of State Upshur, Secretary of the Navy Gilmer, and New York State Senator Gardiner. President Tyler and Senator Gardiner's daughter Julia, unhurt, were literally blown into each other's arms by the percussion. This chance encounter between the fifty-four-year-old widower President Tyler and the twenty-four-year-old Julia Gardiner culminated four months later in marriage. (See also Town of East Hampton/East Hampton/Old Cemetery/Grave of John Alexander Tyler.)

Grave of Lion Gardiner (1599–1663)

The grave site is marked by an ornate monument with a reclining knight in armor.

In 1635 Gardiner was in the Low Countries serving as an engineer in the army of the Prince of Orange. He was persuaded to join a group of English colonists interested in settling in New England. A man of decision, he landed at Boston in 1635 and was immediately employed by the Massachusetts Bay Colony to design and build fortifications in Boston Harbor. The following spring he moved to Saybrook, CT, where he remained for four years. Not only did he design and erect defenses for the settlement, but he also appears to have been responsible for their military protection, a duty which he performed with some distinction during the Pequot Indian War of 1637. (See also Town of Oyster Bay/Mill Neck/Underhill Burying Ground/Grave of Captain John Underhill.) While living in Saybrook, his wife bore their son David, the first white child born in the settlement. A few years later, Gardiner purchased and moved to the Isle of Wight off eastern Long Island, renaming it Gardiner's Island. In 1686 the Gardiners were given full manorial rights to the island which has remained in the family to this date.

The elaborate monument marking the grave of Lion Gardiner in the cemetery was designed by James Renwick (1818–1895), who also designed Saint Patrick's Cathedral in Manhattan and the castle-style building of the Smithsonian Museum in Washington, DC.

Upon exhumation in the 1800s, Gardiner's armor-clad skeleton showed him to be six-feet-tall with red hair. Legend has it that his hair was clipped at that time and put into Tiffany rings and given to descendants.

(See also Town of East Hampton/East Hampton/Gardiner's Windmill and Town of Islip/West Bay Shore/Sagtikos Manor.)

Grave of Mary Nimmo Moran (1842–1899)

The grave site is located 150 feet south of that of Lion Gardiner. It is marked by an imposing eight-column monument.

Born in Strathaven, Scotland, Mary Moran immigrated to the United States as a youth with her family. Always interested in art, she took painting lessons and eventually became a student of the noted artist Thomas Moran, whom she married in 1862. They lived in Philadelphia, PA, for ten years before moving to Newark, NJ, Manhattan, and ultimately to East Hampton. Mary, known for her landscape etching, was the first woman member of the British Society of Painter-Etchers.

(See also Town of East Hampton/East Hampton/Long Island Collection–East Hampton Public Library.)

Grave of Thomas Moran (1837–1926)

The grave site is located 150 feet south of that of Lion Gardiner. It is marked by an imposing eight-column monument.

A noted landscape painter and etcher, Moran was born in Bolton, England. At the age of seventeen he immigrated to the United States with his parents and brothers. He worked in Philadelphia for two years as a wood-engraver before taking up oil painting. Under the tutelage of his brothers, who were also painters, he became an accomplished artist. In the 1860s, he returned to Europe several times, visiting France, Italy, and England, where he was profoundly influenced by Turner. In 1871 he returned to the United States to accompany F. V. Hayden on an expedition to the West. Moran made several western trips during which he painted his famous *The Grand Canyon,* which measures eight feet by twelve feet, and the *Chasm of the Colorado.* Both were purchased by Congress for $10,000 and are displayed in the United States Capitol Building. His name is still linked to the West today, not only through his painting but by other lasting memorials: Mount Moran in Wyoming and Moran Point in Arizona are named in his honor.

In 1884 he built a summer home at 229 Main Street in East Hampton, which still stands directly across the street from the cemetery, where he continued painting landscapes. Moran was internationally acclaimed, becoming a fellow of the British Society of Painter-Etchers. John Ruskin, the famous nineteenth-century English essayist and critic, claimed that Moran was one of the best etchers in America.

Grave of John Alexander Tyler (1848–1883)

The grave site is located just east of that of Lion Gardiner. It is marked by a tall broken column.

The son of President John Tyler and Julia Gardiner Tyler, John Alexander Tyler was born at the Tyler estate Sherwood Forest on the James River in Virginia.

With the advent of the Civil War he, like his father who became a member of the Confederate Congress, remained loyal to the Southern cause. At the age of sixteen, he joined the First Virginia Artillery Battalion under the command of Robert E. Lee. As the war progressed, his mother Julia, dressed as a farmer's wife, fled their Sherwood Forest estate by driving a hay wagon with her younger children secreted in the hay. After returning to New York, she raised money for the Confederate cause. Along with the other surviving members of the Confederate Army, John Alexander was paroled in 1865 by the peace agreement signed at Appomattox Court House.

He spent the next eight years studying in Europe, first at Carlsruhe Baden and then at Freiberg Saxony from which he graduated as a mining and civil engineer. He joined the German army and served in the First Umlan Regiment under the command of Prince John of Saxony. Actively engaged in the Franco–Prussian War (1870–1871), he was personally decorated for distinguished service by Emperor Wilhelm I.

In 1873 Tyler returned to the United States to an appointment of U. S. Surveyor of Indian Lands. In 1883 he died in New Mexico after attaining the position of Inspector of Surveys for the New Mexico Territory. His body was returned to Long Island for interment with his grandfather, David Gardiner, in East Hampton. The graves of his father and mother are in Hollywood Cemetery in Richmond, VA.

(See also Town of East Hampton/East Hampton/Old Cemetery/Grave of David Gardiner.)

Old Hook Mill

36 North Main Street, East Hampton
(631) 324-0713

From the village green in East Hampton go east on Route 27/Main Street/Montauk Highway for .8 mile. The mill is located at the fork in the road.

This smock-type mill, which has been on the National Register of Historic Places since 1978, was built in 1806 by Nathaniel Dominy V and replaced an older 1736 post-type mill which had been constructed on the same site. The massive main post of the previous mill was retained for the new mill and still is seen today. Over the years ownership of the mill was expanded from four to eight in order to increase cash flow necessary for repairs. By 1850 ownership was consolidated in the hands of Nathaniel Dominy VII and Charles Hedges. In 1859 Dominy bought out Hedges, thus becoming the mill's sole owner. In 1922 the Village of East Hampton bought and restored the mill. In 1986 it was again completely restored. The Old Hook Mill is unique in that it has more original machinery than any other mill on Long Island.

(See Index for complete list of windmills in area.)

Osborn–Jackson House

101 Main Street, East Hampton
(631) 324-6850

From the village green in East Hampton go east on Route 27/Main Street/Montauk Highway for .3 mile. The house is on the left (north) side of the road.

This circa 1740 house is the administrative office of the East Hampton Historical Society. It is also a museum with several rooms devoted to colonial quilting and weaving. Of special interest is the large barn frame loom which is still used by members of the society.

Pantigo Mill

14 James Lane, East Hampton

Located opposite the village green in East Hampton on James Lane which is one street south of and parallel to Route 27/Main Street/Montauk Highway.

Located behind the Mulford Farm and the Home Sweet Home Museum, this smock-type mill is the third mill to occupy this man-made hill. It was built in 1804 by Samuel Schellinger for Huntting Miller to replace an earlier 1771 post-type mill. (See also Town of East Hampton/Amagansett/Commercial Fisherman's Museum and Town of East Hampton/Amagansett/Miss Amelia's Cottage.) In 1832 Miller bequeathed the mill to his grandson Captain William Hedges, who in 1845 sold it to David A. Hedges who then moved it to his property on Pantigo Road. Gustav Buek, who lived in the Payne house (Home Sweet Home Museum), bought the mill in 1917 from Hiram Sanford who had moved it to the corner of Egypt Lane and Pantigo Road. Buek moved the mill to the rear of his house where it can be seen today. The mill has been placed on the National Register of Historic Places.
(See Index for complete list of windmills in area.)

Paul Tillich's House

84 Woods Lane, East Hampton

Not open to the public.

From the village green in East Hampton go west on Route 27/Main Street/Montauk Highway. At .2 mile continue right (west) on Route 27/Montauk Highway as it becomes Woods Lane; go an additional .4 mile. The house is on the right (north) side of the road.

Paul Johannes Tillich (1896–1965), one of the foremost contemporary Protestant theologians and philosophers of the twentieth century, was born in Starzeddel, Prussia. He received his doctorate degree from the university at Breslau in 1912 and was ordained a Lutheran minister in the same year. Tillich served in the German army as a chaplain during World War I. After the war, he became a professor of theology and philosophy at several prestigious German universities. It was during this time that Tillich wrote many of his major works. An ardent anti-Nazi, he was the first non-Jewish professor to be dismissed from a German university. He immigrated to the United States in 1933 to join the faculty of Union Theological Seminary. In 1954 he joined the faculty of Harvard University Divinity School and later that of the University of Chicago. Through his lectures and twenty-five books, Tillich helped to define the role of the Christian faith in the twentieth century.

Paul and Hannah Tillich bought this house in 1943 and used it as a summer home until 1965. He wrote most of his major work *Systematic Theology* (1951–1963) while summering in East Hampton. Paul Tillich died in 1965 and is buried in Paul Tillich Park, New Harmony, IN.

Town House
Main Street, East Hampton

From the village green in East Hampton go east on Route 27/Main Street/Montauk Highway for .2 mile. The Town House is on the left (north) side of the road.

Built in 1731, this small building is adjacent to the Clinton Academy. It was originally used as a town hall for public meetings. Later, during the 1800s, it served as a schoolhouse. At present it is closed but plans are under consideration to convert the building into a visitors' center.

MONTAUK

Hither Hills State Park
Route 27/Montauk Highway, Montauk
(631) 668-2554

Located on Route 27/Montauk Highway just west of the Village of Montauk. The park entrance is on the right (south) side of the road.

This 1,755-acre park features tent and trailer campsites, a pump-out station, showers, restrooms, a picnic area, an athletic field, a food stand, and a general store. Fishing is also permitted.

Montauk County Park – Deep Hollow Dude Ranch
Route 27/Montauk Highway, Montauk
(631) 668-2744

Suffolk County Resident Pass required for admission.

From the east end of the Village of Montauk go 3 miles east on Route 27/Montauk Highway. The main park entrance is on the left (north) side of the road.

The 1,126-acre Montauk County Park (formerly the Deep Hollow Dude Ranch) offers activities ranging in interest from the historical such as the Third House, the Pharaoh Museum, an Indian burial ground, and an archaeological dig; to recreational activities as diverse as a three-mile nature trail, a bridle path, horse rental, a picnic area, a bike hostel, ice skating, swimming, fishing, and a camping site.

The entrance for the nature trail, the Indian burial ground, and the archaeological dig is reached by going north on East Lake Drive from its intersection with Route 27/Montauk Highway for 2.8 miles. The park entrance is on the right (east) side of the road. Be prepared to walk a considerable distance.

(See also Town of East Hampton/Montauk/The Pharaoh Museum and Town of East Hampton/Montauk/The Third House.)

Montauk Downs State Park
South Fairview Avenue, Montauk
(631) 668-5000

From the east end of the Village of Montauk go east on Route 27/Montauk Highway for 1 mile. Turn left (north) onto West Lake Drive/County Road 77; go .6 mile. Make a left (west) onto Fairview Avenue; go .3 mile. The park is on the right (north) side of the road.

This 160-acre park has an eighteen-hole golf course, a clubhouse, a golf/tennis pro shop, locker rooms, tennis courts, driving range, a swimming pool, and a restaurant.

Montauk Lighthouse
Montauk Point, Montauk
(631) 668-2544

Take Route 27/Montauk Highway east to the end of the road on the South Fork. The lighthouse is located in Montauk State Park.

The lighthouse, the oldest on Long Island and on the National Register of Historic Places since 1969, was commissioned in 1790 by George Washington. Its land was surveyed in 1792 by Ezra L'Hommedieu and purchased the same year by the federal government from the Town of East Hampton. (See also Town of Southold/Southold/First Presbyterian Church of Southold.) The hundred-foot-high tower was built by John McComb Jr. in 1795 using red limestone imported from Connecticut. McComb also built the Eaton's Neck Lighthouse (1798), New York City Hall (1812), and Castle Clinton National Monument in New York City's Battery Park (1808–1811). (See also Town of Huntington/Eaton's Neck/Eaton's Neck Lighthouse.) The Montauk Lighthouse stands on Turtle Hill which is sixty-nine feet above sea level and which was 297 feet from the shoreline at the time of the lighthouse's construction. Unfortunately, due to erosion, the lighthouse is now only fifty feet from the cliff's edge. In 1858 the original light, which was stationary and

71

fueled by whale oil, was replaced by a flashing signal which, in turn, was replaced by a revolving light powered by electricity.

Located at the base of the lighthouse in the keeper's house is the Lighthouse Museum. On display are oil, kerosene, coal, and electric lights used in various lighthouses. There are also reproductions of Coast Guard vessels, a display of the erosion problems the lighthouse is confronting, and a continuous slide show on the history of the lighthouse. Visitors are permitted to climb the 137 spiraled steps to the top of the lighthouse.

(See also Town of East Hampton/Montauk/Montauk State Park.)

The Pharaoh Museum
Montauk County Park
Route 27/Montauk Highway, Montauk
(631) 668-5022

From the east end of the Village of Montauk go east on Route 27/Montauk Highway for 3 miles. The museum is located on the left (north) side of the road in Montauk County Park.

The museum is named after Jeremiah Pharaoh, a local Indian who served as a seaman and for nine years sailed throughout the world. On display are aboriginal tools, pottery, a wigwam, photographs of the Pharaoh family, documents in reference to the demise of the Montauk Indians, exhibits of archaeological dating techniques, and the re-creation of an excavation area.

(See also Town of Southampton/Shinnecock Hills/Shinnecock Nation Cultural Center and Museum.)

The Second House
Route 27/Montauk Highway, Montauk
(631) 668-5340

Going east on Route 27/Montauk Highway, it is located on the left (north) side of the road just before entering the Village of Montauk.

Montauk was originally owned and used by the Town of East Hampton as a cattle and sheep range. In 1666 the first herds were driven to Montauk in May and remained there until November, making Montauk the nation's first cattle and sheep ranch. The First House was built to house men responsible for keeping the animals on their respective ranges. The Second House was built in 1797 also as a line shack. It was added onto over the years and eventually became a school. In 1910 it became the summer house of David Kennedy. After the death of the Kennedys the house remained empty for many years until its purchase in the late 1960s by the Town of East Hampton. The house has been completely restored and is maintained and operated by the Montauk Historical Society. On display are a spinning wheel, antique tools, an organ, dolls, period clothing, antique sewing machines, and Victorian furniture.

Montauk State Park
Montauk Point, Montauk
(631) 668-5000

Take Route 27/Montauk Highway east to the end of the road on the South Fork.

This 724-acre park has a picnic area, a refreshment stand, a surf fishing station, and a hiking trail. By far the park's major attraction is the Montauk Lighthouse and Museum.
(See also Town of East Hampton/Montauk/Montauk Lighthouse.)

The Third House
Montauk County Park
Route 27/Montauk Highway, Montauk
(631) 852-7878

From the east end of the Village of Montauk go east on Route 27/Montauk Highway for 3 miles. The house is located on the left (north) side of the road in the Montauk County Park.

In 1898 the house became the headquarters of Teddy Roosevelt's Rough Riders. They were quarantined at Montauk while they recuperated from typhoid, dysentery, and yellow fever prior to their demobilization after the Spanish–American War. The house is also historically significant because it was here that President McKinley persuaded Teddy to run for governor of New York. Located in the house are pictures of Roosevelt and his Rough Riders taken during their stay at Montauk.
(See also Town of Islip/Sayville/Roosevelt County Park–John Ellis Roosevelt Estate–Meadow Croft; Town of Oyster Bay/Oyster Bay/Christ Episcopal Church; Town of Oyster Bay/Oyster Bay/First Presbyterian Church; Town of Oyster Bay/Oyster Bay/Young's Memorial Cemetery/Grave of Theodore Roosevelt; and Town of Oyster Bay/Cove Neck/Sagamore Hill National Historic Site–Theodore Roosevelt Estate–Sagamore Hill.)

Windjammer Cruise
Viking Landing Dock
West Lake Drive, Montauk
(631) 283-6041

Go east on Route 27/Montauk Highway through the Village of Montauk for 1 mile past the traffic circle flagpole. Turn left (north) onto West Lake Drive/County Road 77; go 2 miles. Turn right (east) onto Flamingo Avenue and continue for .2 mile to the Viking Landing Dock.

The *Appledore* was built in 1978 in the style of a nineteenth-century New England coastal schooner. It is eighty-six-feet-long and carries thirty-seven passengers. If you are looking for a nineteenth-century nautical experience, this is it!

(See Town of Brookhaven/Patchogue/*The Bay Mist*; Town of Brookhaven/Port Jefferson/*Martha Jefferson*; Town of Riverhead/Riverhead/Whale Watching; and Town of Oyster Bay/Glen Cove/*Paddle Steamer Thomas Jefferson*.)

SPRINGS

Accabonac Harbor Preserve
(South Fork – Shelter Island Chapter: The Nature Conservancy)
Springs–Fireplace Road, Springs
(631) 267-3748

Open with prior permission.

From the village green in East Hampton go east on Route 27/Main Street/Montauk Highway for .8 mile. Just before the Old Hook Mill bear left at fork in the road onto North Main Street. Go .5 mile to Springs–Fireplace Road. Bear right onto Springs–Fireplace Road; go 4.2 miles. The preserve is on the right (east) side of the road.

This 130-acre preserve is actually a complex consisting of two separate preserves: the Merrill Lake Sanctuary and the Kaplan Meadows Sanctuary. Both preserves are located on a 1,000-acre tidal estuary which has provided an abundance of marine resources to the local population since the Indians first settled in the area. Among the diverse wildlife found are several rare and endangered species, such as diamondback terrapin, mink, American oyster, and the chuck-will's-widow. One of the goals of the Conservancy is to acquire the land between these two preserves so that a contiguous harbor-wide preserve at Accabonac Harbor may be created.

Please telephone the Conservancy at the above number to obtain permission to visit the preserve.

Green River Cemetery
Accabonac Road, Springs

From the village green in East Hampton go east on Route 27/Main Street/Montauk Highway for .7 mile. Bear left just before the Old Hook Mill and turn right (south) after the cemetery by the mill and before the railroad trestle onto Gay Lane. Make an immediate left (east) onto Accabonac Road; go 3.6 miles. The cemetery is on the left (north) side of the road opposite Lilia Lane.

Grave of James Brooks (1906–1992)

Born in St. Louis, MO, Brooks attended Southern Methodist University in Dallas, TX, and was a student of Martha Simkins at the Dallas Art Institute prior to relocating to Manhattan, where he continued his studies at the Arts Student League. After three years at the League, he worked as a commercial artist and during the Depression traveled in the West and Midwest painting scenes in the Social Realist-style popular in that era. During that time he also was a muralist for the WPA's Federal Arts Project. His best remembered WPA painting is the 12-foot by 235-foot mural entitled *Flight* in the rotunda of New York's LaGuardia Airport. He was drafted into the army in 1942. After the war, Brooks resumed painting but by that time his style had changed to Cubism.

In 1957 he moved to East Hampton where he was deeply influenced by Jackson Pollack's Abstract Expressionism.

Grave of Stuart Davis (1894–1964)

The grave site is on the west side of the cemetery. It is marked by a highly polished black granite stone with his unique signature chiseled across it.

Born in Philadelphia, PA, of parents who were themselves both artists, Stuart Davis burst upon the art scene at the age of nineteen with his first show. Shortly thereafter he experimented with an Illusionistic style inspired by the Cubistic school, an American urban style he retained throughout his career, revealing his view of the tempo and noise of the city, of traffic, and of jazz; of flashing lights and garish city scenes including billboards. His obsession with interconnected planes in the 1920s included his now famous still life of an eggbeater, electric fan, and a rubber glove titled *Eggbeater No. 2* (1927) and *Lucky Strike* (1921). In the 1930s he created several murals, some under the auspices of the WPA. Examples of this period can be seen in Radio City Music Hall and in Rockefeller Center. In the 1940s and 1950s Davis introduced vivid use of colors to his flat patterns and planes, strong lighting and shadowing effects, both boldly simple and complex.

Grave of Elaine de Kooning (1918–1989)

The grave site is on the right (west) side of the westernmost carriage road about fifteen feet to the right (north) of Abraham Rattner's grave and twenty-five feet to the left (south) of Stuart Davis' grave.

Born in New York City, Elaine Fried de Kooning was raised in the Sheepshead Bay section of Brooklyn. In 1936, upon graduation from Erasmus High School, she entered Hunter College, but her love for art and desire to paint convinced her to transfer to Leonardo de Vinci Art School, which was also located in Manhattan. In 1938 Elaine again transferred, this time to the American Artists' School where she studied sculpture, watercolors, and oils. She met Willem de Kooning and became his art pupil for some five years before their marriage in 1943.

Through the years Elaine became recognized in her own right as an artist of diverse techniques which ranged from Realism to the Gestural Abstract Expressionism of the New York School. She once referred to herself as an escape artist who always tried to avoid style but rather was more interested in character because character comes out of a work, while style is imposed on it.

In addition to being an artist, Elaine was a writer for *Art News*, a set designer, and a member of the faculties of numerous universities and art schools including: Yale University, Rice University, New York Studio School in Paris, Brandeis University, Carnegie–Mellon University, University of Pennsylvania, and Parsons School of Fine Art in Manhattan. She held the Lamar Dodd Chair at the University of Georgia and the Milton and Sally Avery Chair at Bard College.

Grave of Jimmy Ernst (1920–1984)

The grave site is about forty yards from the road and about twenty yards to the left (east) side of the westernmost carriage road.

Born in Bruehl, Germany, Jimmy was the son of the Surrealist painter Max Ernst. He attended school in Germany before immigrating to New York City in 1938, where he embarked on an art career without any formal art training. His early period was influenced more by the Surrealism of Matta than that of his father. Later phases included his jazz period, a white and black period, and his Gothic period.

His grave is marked by a small pink rock with the inscription, "Artists and Poets are the raw nerve ends of humanity by themselves they can do little to save humanity without them there would be little worth caring."

Grave of Frederick Kiesler (1892–1965)

The grave site is on the right (west) side of the westernmost carriage road about fifteen feet to the left (south) of the grave of Stuart Davis. It is marked by a black marble stone which is positioned flush to the ground.

Kiesler was educated in his native Vienna, Austria, at the Tchnische Hochschule and the Academy of Fine Arts. Before immigrating to the United States in 1926 he began his architectural career working on Vienna's first slum clearance and rehousing project.

A faculty member of the Julliard School of Music and Columbia University School of Architecture, he taught that ". . . architects make first rate stage directors, but stage design makes much better architects." In addition to designing opera sets for the Julliard School of Music and the Metropolitan Opera, Kiesler designed the exhibition hall for Columbia University's School of Architecture and was a Correalism-styled sculptor. Both his architecture and sculpture stressed infinity.

Grave of Lee Krasner (1908–1984)

The grave site is on the north side of the cemetery just in front of that of Jackson Pollock.

Lee Krasner belongs to the first generation of the New York School-of-Action painters whose popularity spanned the 1940s and 1950s. The proponents of the movement included her husband Jackson Pollock, Willem de Kooning, and Arshile Gorky. Krasner's painting style, which is characterized by color of movements and moods in nature, was influenced by Matisse, Picasso, Mondrian, and Pollock.

(See also Town of East Hampton/Springs/Pollock–Krasner Museum and Study Center.)

Grave of Abbott Joseph Liebling (1904–1963)

The grave site is on the left (south) side of the carriage road directly opposite the graves of Jackson Pollock and Lee Krasner.

A noted journalist and author, Liebling was educated at Dartmouth College, Columbia University, and the Sorbonne in France. He served with distinction on the staff of the *New Yorker* magazine from 1935 until his death in 1963. During World War II he was the magazine's war correspondent in France, Great Britain, and North Africa for which he was a recipient of the Knight of the Legion of Honor by France.

Grave of Jean Stafford Liebling (1915–1979)

The grave site is on the left (south) side of the carriage road directly opposite the graves of Jackson Pollock and Lee Krasner.

Stafford had a propensity for surrounding herself with literary figures; all three of her husbands were writers, the most famous being the poet Robert Lowell. A novelist and author of short stories, Stafford was awarded the Pulitzer Prize for fiction in 1970 for her book *Collected Stories*. The main theme of her stories tended to be of the conflicts that arose between women and children as they battled feelings of alienation and isolation.

Grave of Constantino Nivola (1912–1988)

The grave site is to the north of the easternmost carriage road along the northern fence of the cemetery.

Nivola was a native of Sardinia where, as a youth, he learned sculpturing as an apprentice stonemason. He came to the United States in 1939 when it became evident that Fascist Italy was being drawn into the Nazi sphere of influence. He settled in Manhattan and learned English in part by reading dictionaries. By 1948 Nivola and his family were summering in Springs, but it was not until 1970, by which time his children were out of school, that he became a permanent resident of Springs.

Considered by many to be America's greatest architectural sculptor of the last century, Nivola's sculptures ranged in size from the 35,000-square-foot mural at the Hartford Insurance Company's headquarters in Hartford, CT, to abstract figurines, small enough to be held in your hand.

Grave of Frank O'Hara (1926–1966)

The grave site is directly opposite the grave of Stuart Davis on the left (east) side of the westernmost carriage road.

O'Hara, a noted poet, art critic, and associate curator of the Museum of Modern Art, was born in Baltimore, MD. He received his undergraduate degree from Harvard University and his graduate degree from the University of Michigan. A member of the New York School of Poets, he collaborated with the New York School of Second Generation Painters in what became known as "poem painting." He said of his own work, ". . . I don't think my experiences are clarified or made beautiful for myself or anyone else, they are just there in whatever form I can find them. What is clear to me in my work is probably obscure to others and vice versa. . . ." O'Hara's life was cut short in a freak accident on Fire Island when he was hit by a dune buggy whose driver was blinded by approaching headlights.

Grave of Jackson Pollock (1912–1956)

The grave site is in the back (northern section) of the cemetery. A huge boulder, in which a bronze plaque with his signature is embedded, marks his grave. His grave is behind that of his wife Lee Krasner.

Jackson Pollock, born on January 28, 1912, in Cody, WY, and raised in the Southwest, arrived in New York City in 1929 where he studied, along with his brother Charles, with Thomas Hart Benton, one of the most conventional American artists. Interestingly, he referred to his experience with Benton as "something against which to react very strongly" and strongly he did react, pioneering a controversial Abstract Impressionistic style which incorporated globs and random drips and emotional effects created by "attacking the canvas." Overpainting, glazing, swirling, and textural variation with both brush and palette knife characterize his later works.

Pollock lived in a nineteenth-century farmhouse on Springs–Fireplace Road in Springs from 1945 until his tragic death at age forty-four in an automobile accident in East Hampton on August 12, 1956. (See also Town of East Hampton/Springs/Pollock–Krasner Museum and Study Center.)

People continue to visit his grave on or near the anniversary of his death, leaving mementos as tributes, including real and artificial flowers, gallon paint cans, paintings, and poems. The boulder, marking his grave site, hosts oddly shaped lichen communities in random abstraction—perhaps a natural tribute.

Grave of Abraham Rattner (1895–1978)

The grave site is on the west side of the cemetery approximately one hundred feet to the left (south) of the grave of Stuart Davis.

Born in Poughkeepsie, NY, Rattner was originally interested in architecture and city planning and studied at George Washington University's School of Architecture before winning an art scholarship to the Pennsylvania Academy of Fine Arts in 1916. He spent the period between the world wars studying at the Beaux-Arts, Sorbonne, Ranson, and Calorossi academies in France while perfecting his painting technique, which has been described as Senso-Realism showing echoes of Cubism and Futurism characterized by bright colors. With the advent of World War II he returned to the United States where he taught art and perfected his unique painting style.

Rattner lived at 30A Egypt Lane in East Hampton. His grave is marked by a circular black marble headstone embossed with his distinctive signature on the front. The back of the stone is inscribed:

"Abraham Rattner, 1895–1978 '. . . but now my eye hath seen thee.' Job 42:5."

Grave of Ad Reinhardt (1913–1967)

The grave site is on the west side of the cemetery directly in front of that of Stuart Davis. It is marked by a small white rectangular stone which is flush to the ground.

Adolph Frederick Reinhardt was born in Buffalo, NY. He received his undergraduate degree from Columbia University in 1935 and continued his art studies at the National Academy of Design and later at the American Artists' School. His paintings were essentially abstract in style although his earlier works show the influence of Cubism. In later years, Reinhardt developed a rather individualistic style, the subtlety of which challenges the viewer.

Pollock–Krasner Museum and Study Center
830 Springs–Fireplace Road, Springs
(631) 324-4929

From the village green in East Hampton go east on Route 27/Main Street/Montauk Highway for .8 mile. Bear left just before the Old Hook Mill onto North Main Street; go .5 mile. Bear right onto Springs–Fireplace Road; go 4 miles. The museum is on the right (east) side of the road.

In 1945 Jackson Pollock and Lee Krasner bought this house, five acres, and a barn with money borrowed from a local bank and from art patron Peggy Guggenheim. For the next eleven years Pollock lived and painted here. Now owned by Stony Brook University, it is a museum dedicated to the works of Pollock and Krasner. Intended primarily to be a research facility, the museum has a library, a

79

small collection of prints, Pollock's books and records, and videotapes of East End artists.

(See also Town of East Hampton/Springs/Green River Cemetery/Grave of Jackson Pollock/Grave of Lee Krasner.)

Willem de Kooning's House
182 Woodbine Drive, Springs

Not open to the public.

From the village green in East Hampton go east on Route 27/Main Street/Montauk Highway for .8 mile. Just before the Old Hook Mill bear left at the fork in the road onto North Main Street; go .5 mile. Bear right onto Springs–Fireplace Road; go 3 miles. Turn left (north) onto Woodbine Drive; go .2 mile. The house is on the left (west) side of the road.

Willem de Kooning (1904–1997) was born in Rotterdam, The Netherlands. He studied art at the Rotterdam Academy of Fine Arts and Techniques for eight years prior to arriving in the United States in 1926 as a stowaway aboard the British freighter *SS Shelly*.

In 1927 he relocated from Hoboken, NJ, to Manhattan where his style of painting was influenced by Arshile Gorky. By 1938 de Kooning gradually became identified with New York's Abstract-Expressionist movement and by the mid 1950s he was considered one of its leading proponents.

In the early 1960s he relocated permanently to Springs where he owned this house and another on Accabonac Road across from the Green River Cemetery. (See also Town of East Hampton/Springs/Green River Cemetery.)

In 1964 de Kooning was awarded the Presidential Medal of Freedom by President Lyndon Johnson.

THREE–MILE HARBOR

Boat Shop
Gann Road, Three–Mile Harbor
(631) 267-6544

From the village green in East Hampton go east on Route 27/Main Street/Montauk Highway for .8 mile. Bear left just before the Old Hook Mill onto North Main Street. Go .5 mile to the fork in the road. Take Three–Mile Harbor Road/County Road 40; go 4 miles from the fork in the road. Turn left (west) onto Gann Road; go .3 mile onto the dock. The Boat Shop is on the left side of the dock.

The shop has educational dioramas as well as a collection of fishing, whaling, and other nautical artifacts. Its program is designed as a training program for boat building. The Boat Shop is sponsored by the East Hampton Marine Museum and the Town of East Hampton.

WAINSCOTT

Wainscott Windmill
Main Street, Wainscott

Not open to the public.

From the intersection of Route 27/Montauk Highway and Route 24 in Wainscott go east on Route 27/Montauk Highway for 16.3 miles. Turn right (south) onto Town Line Road; go 1.1 miles. Turn left (east) onto Main Street; go 1.3 miles through the Georgica Association property. Bear right at the fork. The mill is located next to the tennis courts.

This smock-type mill was built on Mill Hill in the Village of Southampton by Jeremiah Jagger and Joshua Sayers and replaced a mill that had been destroyed by fire in 1812. Sometime during the 1840s it was purchased by Captain Barney Green and moved to another location on Mill Hill. In 1858 the mill was moved again but this time to Wainscott, where it remained in operation until 1910 when it was forced to close due to the lack of grain that resulted when Long Island farmers switched from growing wheat to raising potatoes. In 1912 the mill became the Wainscott Public Library for a period of time. In 1922 it was purchased by Lathrop Brown, moved just west of the Montauk Lighthouse, and incorporated into his new summer home. When the federal government acquired his property in 1942, Brown donated the mill to the Georgica Association, which moved the mill back to Wainscott. It has been on the National Register of Historic Places since 1978.

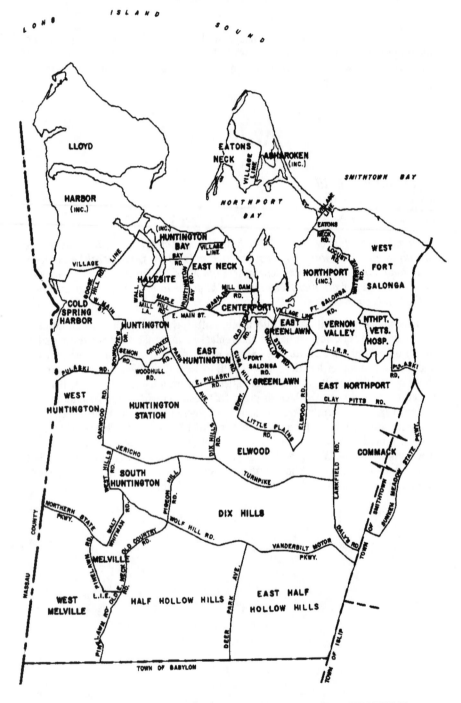

TOWN OF HUNTINGTON

TOWN OF HUNTINGTON

PARKS AND PRESERVES

Federal Parks and Preserves
Target Rock National Wildlife Refuge (80 acres), Lloyd Harbor

State Parks and Preserves
Caumsett State Park (1,500 acres), Lloyd Harbor
Cold Spring Harbor State Park (40 acres), Cold Spring Harbor *(undeveloped)*
Trail View State Park (40 acres), Woodbury *(undeveloped)*
Walt Whitman House (1 acre), Huntington Station

County Parks and Preserves
Berkeley Jackson County Parkland (102 acres), Elwood
Makamah County Nature Preserve (160 acres), West Fort Salonga
West Hills County Park (854 acres), West Huntington

Long Island Chapter: The Nature Conservancy
Matheson Meadows Sanctuary (40 acres), Lloyd Harbor
Uplands Farm Sanctuary (93 acres), Cold Spring Harbor
Van Wyck – Lefferts Mill, Lloyd Harbor

Arboretums and Gardens

CENTERPORT

Betty Allen Twin Ponds Nature Park
Route 25A, Centerport

Take the Long Island Expressway to Exit #51 north (Route 231/Northport/Hun-tington). Go north on Route 231/Deer Park Avenue for 2 miles. Bear right (northeast) onto East Deer Park Road; go .8 mile. Turn right (east) onto Route 25/Jericho Turnpike; go .2 mile. Turn left (north) onto Elwood Road; go 4 miles. Turn left (west) onto Route 25A; go 1.2 miles. The park is on the left (south) side of the road.

This is the only town-owned nature preserve included in this guide. The woman to whom it is dedicated was an outstanding naturalist and dear friend of the authors. This thirty-acre preserve with its lakes and nature walks is open to all people at all times for a quiet walk or a quiet commune with nature, just as Betty wished it to be.

Suffolk County Vanderbilt Museum and Planetarium – William Kissam Vanderbilt Jr. Estate – Eagle's Nest
180 Little Neck Road, Centerport
(631) 854-5555

Take the Long Island Expressway to Exit #51 north (Route 231/Northport/Hun-tington). Go north on Route 231/Deer Park Avenue for 2 miles. Bear right (northeast) onto East Deer Park Road; go .8 mile. Turn right (east) onto Route 25/ Jericho Turnpike; go .2 mile. Turn left (north) onto Elwood Road; go 4 miles. Turn left (west) onto Route 25A; go 1.5 miles. Turn right (north) onto Little Neck Road; go 1.3 miles. The museum is on the right (east) side of the road.

Known as Eagle's Nest, the forty-three-acre estate of William Kissam Vander-bilt Jr. offers a commanding view of Northport Harbor and Eaton's Neck. Origi-nally a six-room, Japanese-style, country house, Vanderbilt transformed it into a twenty-four-room mansion with a Spanish-Moroccan design. Italian Renaissance furniture, paneling from English manor houses, Persian Kurd rugs, thirteenth-century Portuguese fireplaces, a 2,000-pipe organ, and numerous fifteenth-century oil paintings are just a few of the fine treasures that were acquired to furnish the mansion. Located on the grounds are six marble columns from ancient Carthage and two iron eagles from New York City's old Grand Central Station. Integral parts of the mansion are the Habitat and Memorial wings which contain wildlife exhibits. Eagle's Nest has been on the National Register of Historic places since 1985.

A separate building, the Hall of Fishes, was built by Vanderbilt to house his vast marine science collection and his natural history collection, the largest on Long Island. To insure that his guests would tour his museum, Vanderbilt placed the first hole of his eight-hole golf course on the roof of the Hall of Fishes, the only access to the first hole being a route through his museum.

The Planetarium with its sixty-foot dome and sixteen-inch Cassegrain reflecting telescope is one of the largest in the country. Special shows are held throughout the year. Call the Planetarium at the above number for changing schedule of events.

(See also Town of Islip/Islip/Saint Mark's Episcopal Church; Town of Islip/Oakdale/ Connetquot River State Park and Preserve–Southside Sportsmen's Club; and Town of Islip/Oakdale/Dowling College–William Kissam Vanderbilt Sr. Estate–Idlehour.)

Suydam Homestead and Barn Museum
1 Fort Salonga Road/Route 25A, Centerport
(631) 754-1180

Take the Long Island Expressway to Exit #51 north (Route 231/Northport/Hun-tington). Go north on Route 231/Deer Park Avenue for 2 miles. Bear right (northeast) onto East Deer Park Road; go .8 mile. Turn right (east) onto Route 25/Jericho Turnpike; go .2 mile. Turn left (north) onto Elwood Road; go 4 miles. Turn left (west) onto Route 25A; go 1.5 miles. The homestead museum is on the left (south) side of the road.

Originally just a one-room dwelling, the circa 1730 house was occupied by members of the Suydam family for nearly 150 years. During that time the Suy-dams expanded the house several times to its present size.

Sometime in the 1950s its ownership passed out of the family. In 1989 the house was purchased by the Greenlawn–Centerport Historical Association, which has meticulously restored it to an eighteenth-century structure. The association also did an extensive archeological excavation on the grounds which unearthed numerous artifacts, now displayed in one of the house's rooms. Two other rooms in the house have been furnished in period furniture. The house is on the National Register of Historic Places.

In 1997 the association constructed a barn behind the homestead to house its extensive collection of period furniture, farm tools, wagons, clothing, and house-hold objects.

(See also Town of Huntington/Greenlawn/Greenlawn–Centerport Historical Asso-ciation Library.)

COLD SPRING HARBOR

Cold Spring Harbor Whaling Museum
301 Main Street, Cold Spring Harbor
(631) 367-3418

Take the Long Island Expressway to Exit #45 north (Manetto Hill Road/Plainview/ Woodbury). Go north on Woodbury Road for 3.4 miles. Turn left (north) onto Route 108/Harbor Road; go 1.6 miles. Turn right (east) onto Route 25A; go 1.2 miles. The museum is on the left (north) side of the road.

From 1838 to 1858 Cold Spring Harbor was a major whaling port on Long Island's North Shore. On display in the museum are hundreds of items of the Yankee whaling era including a fully equipped whaling boat. Also featured are prints, harpoons, model ships, whale bones, a diorama of the town circa 1850, and scrimshaw. A most unusual example of scrimshaw is done on a lobster claw. There is a small but interesting gift shop.

Dolan DNA Learning Center
334 Main Street, Cold Spring Harbor
(516) 367-5179

Take the Long Island Expressway to Exit #45 north (Manetto Hill Road/Plainview/ Woodbury). Go north on Woodbury Road for 3.4 miles. Turn left (north) onto Route 108/Harbor Road; go 1.6 miles. Turn right (east) onto Route 25A; go 1.4 miles. The learning center is on the right (south) side of the road.

Affiliated with the Cold Spring Harbor Laboratory, the learning center focuses on improving the understanding of DNA science by middle and high school students. Its presentations include unique biotechnological interactive exhibits and computer multimedia that stress a hands-on approach. There is also a multi-image, surround-sound film entitled *Long Island From Ice Age To the End of the Twentieth Century*. During the summer months the center hosts a DNA Boot Camp.

The Gallery
Main Street and Shore Road, Cold Spring Harbor
(631) 692-4664

Take the Long Island Expressway to Exit #45 north (Manetto Hill Road/Plainview/ Woodbury). Go north on Woodbury Road for 3.4 miles. Turn left (north) onto Route 108/Harbor Road; go 1.6 miles. Turn right (east) onto Route 25A; go 1.2 miles. The Gallery is on the left (north) side of the road.

Located in the former Cold Spring Harbor Public Library, The Gallery is operated by the Society for the Preservation of Long Island Antiquities. It hosts lectures and presents exhibits on all aspects of local history and cultural heritage.

The Gallery's shop features a collection of Long Island-related books and gift items.

(See also Town of Brookhaven/East Setauket/Sherwood–Jayne House; Town of Brookhaven/Setauket/Thompson House; Town of Huntington/Lloyd Harbor/Joseph Lloyd Manor; and Town of Huntington/Lloyd Harbor/Van Wyck–Lefferts Tide Mill.)

Norman Mattoon Thomas' House

106 Goose Hill Road, Cold Spring Harbor

Not open to the public.

From the village green at the intersection of Route 25A/Main Street and Park Avenue/County Road 35 in Huntington go west on Route 25A/Main Street for 1 mile. Turn right (north) onto West Neck Road; go 1.1 miles. Turn left (west) onto Huntington Road; go .5 mile. Turn left (south) onto Goose Hill Road; go 100 feet. The house is on the left (east) side of the road.

Norman Mattoon Thomas (1884–1968) was the Socialist Party's presidential candidate six times from 1928 to 1948. Born in Marion, OH, he attended Bucknell College (now Bucknell University), Lewisburg, PA, for one year before transferring to Princeton Theological Seminary from which he graduated in 1905. After graduation he worked as a volunteer for the East Side Settlement in the slums of Manhattan before being ordained a Presbyterian minister in 1911. He joined the Socialist Party in 1918, helped found the Civil Liberties Union (1920), was the Socialist Party's candidate for governor of New York (1924) and for mayor of New York City (1925 and 1929), and became the leader of the Socialist Party after the death of Eugene Debs (1926). Many of his programs, such as the five-day work week, old age pensions, unemployment, accident, and health insurance programs, low cost public housing, slum clearance, minimum wage laws, nuclear disarmament, and opposition to United States involvement in Vietnam, were later to be adopted by the major political parties. Thomas espoused his views not only through lectures but also through the twenty books which he authored.

The U-shaped house was designed by Mrs. Thomas, the former Frances Violet Stewart (1881–1947). The Thomases moved into this house in 1929; Mr. Thomas continued to live at this address in Cold Spring Harbor until his death in 1968. Thomas' remains were cremated and his ashes were scattered in Long Island Sound.

Uplands Farm Sanctuary
(Long Island Chapter: The Nature Conservancy)
Lawrence Hill Road, Cold Spring Harbor
(631) 367-3225

Open with prior permission.

Take the Long Island Expressway to Exit #45 north (Manetto Hill Road/Plainview/ Woodbury). Go north on Woodbury Road for 3.4 miles. Turn left (north) onto Route 108/Harbor Road; go 1.5 miles. Turn right (east) onto Lawrence Hill Road; go .4 mile. The sanctuary is on the right (south) side of the road.

This ninety-three-acre sanctuary is a part of the George Nichol Sr. estate, Uplands, that was worked as a dairy farm from the 1920s. It presently houses the headquarters of the Long Island Chapter: The Nature Conservancy. In addition to its offices, there is the Uplands Farm Environmental Center with an auditorium, a library, and classrooms. The sanctuary itself consists of fields and upland hardwood stands of dogwood, apple, maple, and hickory trees.

Please call the Conservancy at the above telephone number to obtain permission to use the sanctuary.

COMMACK

Jewish Sports Hall of Fame
and The Long Island Jewish Discovery Museum
74 Hauppauge Road, Commack
(631) 462-9800

Take the Long Island Expressway to Exit #52 north. Go north on Commack Road to Hauppauge Road. Turn left (west) onto Hauppauge Road. The Hall of Fame is on the right (north) side of the road.

Located in the Suffolk Jewish Community Center, the museum features plaques and memorabilia of over fifty Jewish athletes, broadcasters, sports writers, and team owners. Among those included in the collection are: Red Auerback, Marty Glickman, Hank Greenberg, Sandy Koufax, Dolph Schayes, and Warner Wolf.

In the same building is The Long Island Jewish Discovery Museum, which is designed as an interactive family museum focusing on Jewish history, heritage, and the Hebrew language.

Telephone Pioneers Museum
445 Commack Road, Commack
(631) 543-1371

Take the Long Island Expressway to Exit #52 north. Go north on Commack Road. The museum is on the left (west) side of the road.

Staffed by Telephone Pioneers of America volunteers, the museum depicts the evolution of the telephone through dioramas and automated talking displays. The museum contains over one hundred telephones from all eras, a letter from Alexander Graham Bell's protégée Thomas Watson, and historic telephone directories.

The museum is accessible to people with disabilities. Special care has been taken in order that visitors using wheelchairs may operate the displays.

(See also Town of Huntington/Huntington Station/New York Telephone Museum.)

DIX HILLS

Saint Andrew's Orthodox Church
1095 Carlls Straight Path, Dix Hills
(631) 586-1611

Take the Long Island Expressway to Exit #51 south (Route 231/Northport/Babylon). Go south on Route 231/Deer Park Avenue for 1.8 miles. Turn left (east) onto Old Country Road; go .8 mile. Turn left (north) onto Carlls Straight Path; go .5 mile. The church is on the left (west) side of the road.

This wooden church is a contemporary reproduction of Russian churches which were built entirely of wood and without the use of iron nails. Its exterior is similar to churches found at the eighteenth-century restoration village in Suzdal, Russia. The church's interior, however, interprets the traditional Russian Orthodox architecture in a more modern manner with cool white plaster walls contrasting with the rustic warmth of wood. Lecterns, sconces, and a chandelier are of brass. The altar is adorned with icons although there was no iconostasis when last visited. A skylight illuminates the icon of The Holy Family. One striking difference between this church and those we have seen in Russia is that pews have been installed as an accommodation for the parishioners.

(See also Town of Oyster Bay/Sea Cliff/Church of Our Lady of Kazan.)

EATON'S NECK

Eaton's Neck Lighthouse
Lighthouse Road, Eaton's Neck
(631) 261-6959

Open only by appointment. Arrangements must be made in writing.

Take the Long Island Expressway to Exit #51 north (Route 231/Northport/Huntington). Go north on Route 231/Deer Park Avenue for 2 miles. Bear right (northeast) onto East Deer Park Road; go .8 mile. Turn right (east) onto Route 25/Jericho Turnpike; go .2 mile. Turn left (north) onto Elwood Road; go 4 miles. Cross Route 25A; continue north on Reservoir Avenue for .4 mile. Bear left (north) onto Church Street; go .3 mile. Cross Main Street and continue north on Ocean Avenue; go 4.9 miles, bearing left onto Eaton's Neck Road. Turn right (north) onto Lighthouse Road and go 1.1 miles to its end. The lighthouse is on the United States Coast Guard Station.

The waters off Eaton's Neck are known for their treachery and have caused numerous shipwrecks. In order to safeguard coastal shipping, the federal government decided to build a lighthouse at Eaton's Neck. In 1798 it purchased ten acres on the northern tip of Eaton's Neck from John Gardiner. John McComb Jr., the designer of the Montauk Lighthouse (1795) and New York City Hall (1812), was commissioned to design this lighthouse. The second oldest lighthouse on Long Island, it is 73-feet-tall and, because of its bluff elevation, rises 144 feet above the water. Its beacon was visible for eighteen miles. The lighthouse's beacon no longer shines but the building is used as a command center controlling five other lighthouses from Throgs Neck to Stratford Shoals in Connecticut. The lighthouse has been on the National Register of Historic Places since 1973.

(See also Town of Brookhaven/Old Field/Old Field Lighthouse; Town of East Hampton/Cedar Point/Cedar Point Lighthouse; Town of East Hampton/Montauk/Montauk Lighthouse; Town of Islip/Fire Island/Fire Island Lighthouse; and Town of Southold/Southold/Horton Lighthouse.)

ELWOOD

Berkeley Jackson County Parkland
Manor Road, Elwood
(631) 854-4949

Suffolk County Resident Pass is required for admission.

Take the Long Island Expressway to Exit #51 north (Route 231/Northport/Huntington). Go north on Route 231/Deer Park Avenue for 3.1 miles. Turn right (east) onto Route 25/Jericho Turnpike; go .2 mile. Turn left (north) onto Manor Road; go .2 mile. The park entrance is a dirt road on the right (east) side of the road.

This undeveloped 102-acre park is a limited use nature park. It is predominately a woodland preserve. Guided nature walks are given by environmental specialists for interested organizations. Telephone the above number to arrange group visits.

FORT SALONGA

Booker T. Washington's House
Cousins Street, Fort Salonga

Not open to the public.

Take the Long Island Expressway to Exit #53 north (Sagtikos Parkway/Sunken Meadow Parkway). Go north on the Sagtikos Parkway/Sunken Meadow Parkway for 7.3 miles to Exit #SM5 west (Route 25A/Huntington). Go west on Route 25A for 2.3 miles. Turn right (north) onto Fresh Pond Road; go .8 mile. Turn left (west) onto Cousins Street; go 1 mile. The house is at the top of the hill on the right (north) side of the road overlooking Long Island Sound.

Booker Taliaferro Washington (1858–1915) was born in Hale's Ford, VA. Upon graduation from Hampton Institute in 1875, he was employed as a teacher at Wayland Seminary in Washington, DC, for four years before returning to the Hampton Institute as a teacher. In 1881 he was appointed principal of the Tuskegee Institute. Through his books and lectures, which stressed economic independence for African-Americans through education, he became the foremost advocate of African-American education.

After 1905 Washington spent his summers in this nineteenth-century house which overlooks Long Island Sound. He died in 1915 and is buried on the grounds of Tuskegee Institute in Tuskegee, AL.

GREENLAWN

Greenlawn–Centerport Historical Association Library
30 Broadway, Greenlawn
(631) 754-1180

Take the Long Island Expressway to Exit #51 north (Route 231/Northport/Huntington). Go north on Route 231/Deer Park Avenue for 2 miles. Bear right (northeast) onto East Deer Park Road; go .8 mile. Turn right (east) onto Route 25/Jericho Turnpike; go .2 mile. Turn left (north) onto Elwood Road; go 2.7 miles. Turn left (west) onto Pulaski Road; go 1.6 miles. Turn right (north) onto Broadway; go .4 mile. The Harborfields Public Library is on the left (west) side of the road.

Located in the Harborfields Public Library, the association has a separate room for their extensive collection of local history material. The historical association holds an annual pickle festival and an annual antique show as fundraisers for its Suydam Homestead and the newly acquired John Gardiner Farm. The latter, which is presently being restored and not open to the public at this time, is on the corner of Deer Park Avenue and Little Plains Road.

(See also Town of Huntington/Centerport/Suydam Homestead and Barn Museum.)

Saint Paraskevi Greek Orthodox Church
Shrine Place and Pulaski Road, Greenlawn
(631) 261-7272

Take the Long Island Expressway to Exit #51 north (Route 231/Northport/Huntington). Go north on Route 231/Deer Park Avenue for 2 miles. Bear right (northeast) onto East Deer Park Road; go .8 mile. Turn right (east) onto Route 25/Jericho Turnpike; go .2 mile. Turn left (north) onto Elwood Road; go 2.7 miles. Turn left (west) onto Pulaski Road; go .8 mile. The church is on the right (north) side of the road.

This most unusual church, built in 1965, has a domed ceiling decorated with stained-glass hemisphere windows depicting the life of Christ. The ornate altar is faced with life-sized gold icons so typical of Greek, Russian, and Byzantine decor. Contemporary icons decorate the walls. A lovely grotto, entered from the passageway between the church and the parish house, also contains small icons.

A festival, featuring ethnic foods, is held each year.

HALESITE

Nathan Hale Rock
Mill Dam Road and New York Avenue, Halesite

From the village green at the intersection of Route 25A/Main Street and Park Avenue/County Road 35 in Huntington go west on Route 25A/Main Street for .7 mile. Turn right (north) onto Route 110/New York Avenue; go .9 mile. The rock is on the left (west) side of the road.

The rock commemorates the bravery of Nathan Hale, who was born in Coventry, CT, on June 6, 1755. He graduated from Yale College on September 8, 1773, and enlisted as a lieutenant in the Seventh Connecticut Regiment on July 6, 1775. He was appointed a captain in the Continental Army on September 1, 1775, and volunteered as a spy in September of 1776. He was captured by the British less than one month later while on a spy mission in the Huntington area. Before being executed in New York City on September 22, 1776, he uttered the now famous phrase, "I regret that I have but one life to lose for my country."

HUNTINGTON

The Arsenal
525 Park Avenue, Huntington
(631) 351-3244

Take the Long Island Expressway to Exit #51 north (Route 231/Northport/Huntington). Go north on Route 231/Deer Park Avenue which becomes Park Avenue/ County Road 35 for 7 miles. The Arsenal is on the left (west) side of the road .2 mile south of the village green in Huntington.

This circa 1740 building was used by the colonial militia to conveniently store their weapons rather than transporting them from their homes to the village commons for the monthly militia drills. During the Revolutionary War the Provincial Congress sent two shipments of gun powder totaling 1,100 pounds to be stored in the arsenal. The building, which is the only known colonial arsenal on Long Island, was purchased by the Town of Huntington in 1974 and has been restored to its 1776 appearance. It is presently the home of the Huntington Militia which conducts tours of the building providing a view of the life of a Revolutionary soldier.

Conklin House
2 High Street, Huntington
(631) 427-7045 (Huntington Historical Society)

From the village green in Huntington at the intersection of Route 25A/Main Street and Park Avenue/County Road 35 go west on Route 25A/Main Street for .7 mile. Turn left (south) onto Route 110/New York Avenue; go .2 mile. The house is on the right (west) side of the road at the intersection of Route 110/New York Avenue and High Street.

Built in the mid-1700s by David Conklin on an old Indian trail, the house, which is on the National Register of Historic Places, was originally a small salt box-style home. It was added onto in the 1800s and possibly in the early 1900s, gradually expanding it to the present fifteen-room house. It is furnished in eighteenth- and nineteenth-century furnishings. Of special interest are a chair from the Widow Platt's tavern in Huntington and a table from the Ketcham home in Amityville. Both pieces of furniture were used by George Washington during his 1790 tour of Long Island. Also of interest are examples of pottery made in Huntington, the doll collections, and the cast-iron table forged in Sheffield, England, which has an unusual painted top depicting a North African scene.

Heckscher Park and Art Museum
2 Prime Avenue, Huntington
(631) 351-3250

From the village green at the intersection of Route 25A/Main Street and Park Avenue/County Road 35 in Huntington go west .4 mile on Route 25A/Main Street. The park and museum are on the right (north) side of the road.

The park's lake was used at various times by the colonists as a sheep bath and water supply for a whiskey still. In 1860 it was converted into a trout farm by Stephen W. Gaines. The lake and its adjacent land were subsequently purchased by Ebenezer Prime II who built a watermill which derived its power from the lake. In winter ice blocks were cut from the lake and stored in an icehouse for sale during the summer. August Heckscher Sr., a German immigrant who made a fortune in Manhattan real estate and in coal and zinc mines, acquired the land from the Primes in 1917 and transformed it into a park. In 1920 he deeded the park and its museum to the Town of Huntington.

The museum's collection consists of works of art ranging from the sixteenth century to the twentieth century and encompasses examples of traditional as well as contemporary American and European paintings, drawings, prints, and sculpture. Concerts are held in the park's Chapin Bandstand during the summer.

Huntington Historical Society
209 Main Street, Huntington
(631) 427-7045

From the village green at the intersection of Route 25A/Main Street and Park Avenue/County Road 35 in Huntington go west .5 mile on Route 25A/Main Street. The historical society is on the right (north) side of the road.

The society's office, research library, and exhibition gallery are located in the old Huntington Trade School, which was built in 1905 as the first school of manual learning in Huntington. The building was designed by Josiah Cleaveland Cady, the renowned architect who also designed the American Museum of Natural History and the old Metropolitan Opera House, both in Manhattan, the First Presbyterian Church in Oyster Bay, and the Soldiers' and Sailors' Memorial Building in Huntington. (See also Town of Huntington/Huntington/Huntington Town Historian's Office and Town of Oyster Bay/Oyster Bay/First Presbyterian Church.) This building is on the National Register of Historic Places.

Huntington Rural Cemetery Association

555 New York Avenue, Huntington

From the village green in Huntington at the intersection of Route 25A/Main Street and Park Avenue/County Road 35 go west on Route 25A/Main Street for .7 mile. Turn left (south) onto Route 110/New York Avenue; go .6 mile. The cemetery is on the right (west) side of the road.

Grave of Harry Chapin (1942–1981)

The grave site is about 100 yards southwest of the Smith family circle in the center of the cemetery and on top of the hill. It is marked by a large rock.

Chapin was born and raised in Greenwich Village. Music came naturally to him, an ability, no doubt, influenced by the career of his father who was a drummer in the Woody Herman and Tommy Dorsey bands. As a child, Harry played the trumpet and guitar but gave up thoughts of a career in music to enter the Air Force Academy and later Cornell University. After working for a short period in the film industry, he formed a group in 1964 which played folk music in Greenwich Village and recorded. His biggest hit "Taxi" was recorded in 1972. He once described his style as "story song," a narrative form which stemmed from "talking blues." After moving to Huntington Bay, he continued performing folk music in an era devoted to electrified rock.

He was killed in an automobile accident on the Long Island Expressway when his Volkswagen "bug" was struck by a tractor-trailer truck.

In 1986 Congress authorized the United States Mint to issue a bronze medal in recognition of Chapin's tireless efforts in raising money for humanitarian causes and especially for his efforts on behalf of the "War on World Hunger" campaign. His humanitarian projects have been continued, in his name, by his wife Sandy.

Huntington Town Historian's Office

228 Main Street, Huntington
(631) 351-3244

From the village green at the intersection of Route 25A/Main Street and Park Avenue/County Road 35 in Huntington go west on Route 25A/Main Street for .5 mile. The office is on the left (south) side of the road.

The historian's office is located in the Soldiers' and Sailors' Memorial Building which was erected in 1892. The building was designed by Josiah Cleaveland Cady who also designed the old Metropolitan Opera House and the American Museum of Natural History, both in Manhattan, as well as the Huntington Trade School located across the street from the historian's office and the First Presbyterian Church in Oyster Bay. (See also Town of Huntington/Huntington/Huntington Historical Society and Town of Oyster Bay/Oyster Bay/First Presbyterian Church.) The building housed the collection of the Huntington Public Library until 1957.

95

At present, it is being used as the office of the town historian. Located here are the town's early documents, maps, and records.

Kissam House

434 Park Avenue, Huntington
(631) 427-7045 (Huntington Historical Society)

From the village green at the intersection of Route 25A/Main Street and Park Avenue/County Road 35 in Huntington go south on Park Avenue/County Road 35 for .3 mile. The house is on the left (east) side of the road.

The present Federal-style house was probably built just after the Revolutionary War for Dr. Daniel Whitehead Kissam, a relative through his paternal grandmother of a patentee of the villages of Huntington, Oyster Bay, and Newtown. Daniel began practicing medicine in 1787 in Glen Cove. The same year he married Elizabeth Tredwell, a cousin of The Reverend Samuel Seabury, the first Bishop of the Episcopal Church in America. (See also Town of Hempstead/Hempstead/Saint George's Episcopal Church and Town of Huntington/Huntington/Saint John's Episcopal Church.)

In 1795 Kissam moved to Huntington and either built or bought the present house now known as the Kissam House, which is currently owned and operated by the Huntington Historical Society. Seventeenth- and eighteenth-century furnishings are displayed in this two-and-one-half-story structure. Of particular interest is the Eli Terry clock, one of very few surviving. The house, which was acquired by the Huntington Historical Society in 1967, is on the National Register of Historic Places.

There is a museum shop located at the rear of the property where an ever-changing inventory of antiques is offered for sale.

The Old Burying Ground

Main Street, Huntington

From the village green at the intersection of Route 25A/Main Street and Park Avenue/County Road 35 in Huntington go west on Route 25A/Main Street for .5 mile. The cemetery is on the left (south) side of the road.

In an effort to inflict as much humiliation as possible on the Patriots during the occupation of Huntington, British soldiers tore down the Old First Church and used its wood to build their encampment, Fort Golgotha, in the midst of the Old Burying Ground. (See also Town of Huntington/Huntington/Old First Church of Huntington and Town of Huntington/Lloyd Harbor/Henry Lloyd Manor.) Tombstones were used as crude ovens and, according to legend, the bread that was baked in these ovens had the reverse inscriptions of the early headstones. So intent were the British in vilifying the Patriots, when the patriot, The Reverend Prim, rector of the Old First Church, died in 1779, Colonel Thompson, also known as Count Rumford, pitched the entrance to his tent in such a manner that he would be trodding over the grave of that "damned rebel."

Incidentally, Count Rumford was not a British count but rather a count in the Holy Roman Empire. Rumford was born in Massachusetts and was a patriot until the petty jealousies of others prevented him from obtaining a position of leadership in the Continental Army. Frustrated, he joined the Loyalists and was given command of the King's Dragoons, the loyalist regiment that constructed Fort Franklin and Fort Golgotha. After the war he went to France and amassed a fortune, a portion of which he gave as an endowment to Harvard College (Harvard University).

The Old Burying Ground was placed on the National Register of Historic Places in 1981.

Old First Presbyterian Church of Huntington
125 Main Street, Huntington
(631) 427-2101

From the village green at the intersection of Route 25A/Main Street and Park Avenue/County Road 35 in Huntington go west on Route 25A/Main Street for .3 mile. The church is on the right (north) side of the road.

For some twelve years the early Congregationalist settlers held their religious services either in each other's homes or in the Town Hall. In 1665 they built their first church. It was a primitive wooden building with oil paper for windows and roughly hewn pews and pulpit. In 1715 it was dismantled and a new larger, more ornate, church was built on the same site. During the Revolutionary War the British used the church as a stable and store house. They finally dismantled it and used the wood to build Fort Golgotha in the middle of the Old Burying Ground which was located a few hundred yards from the church. (See also Town of Huntington/Huntington/The Old Burying Ground and Town of Huntington/Lloyd Harbor/Henry Lloyd Manor.) The church's bell was taken and used on a British frigate. In 1784 a new church (Presbyterian) was built on the site of the Old First Church. That same year the British returned the church bell but, due to a large crack, it was unusable and had to be recast. The new bell was mounted in the church's tower in 1789.

The church is now on the National Register of Historic Places.

Saint John's Episcopal Church
12 Prospect Street, Huntington
(631) 427-1752

From the village green at the intersection of Route 25A/Main Street and Park Avenue/County Road 35 in Huntington go west on Route 25A/Main Street for .9 mile. The church is on the left (south) side of the road on the corner of Prospect Street.

The Anglican congregation was organized in 1745. Four years later they established their first church on Park Avenue behind the present site of the Bethel A.M.E. Church. Samuel Seabury was their first lay reader; he was later to become the first Episcopal bishop in America and is buried in Saint James Episcopal Church in New London, CT. (See also Town of Hempstead/Hempstead/Saint George's Episcopal Church and Town of Huntington/Huntington/Kissam House.) During the Revolution the British used the church as a barracks and a storehouse fortifying it with an embankment and cannons. In 1862 the church was demolished and a new Gothic-style church built. It burned down in 1905. The present church was erected in 1908 on a new site. Unfortunately, the only remains of the two previous churches are portions of the churchyards.

HUNTINGTON STATION

New York Telephone Museum
50 West 4th Street, Huntington Station
(631) 587-9949

Take the Long Island Expressway to Exit #49 north (Route 110/Huntington). Go north on Route 110/New York Avenue for 5 miles. Turn left (west) onto West 4th Street; go .1 mile. The museum is on the left (south) side of the road.

The museum, which is located on the second floor of the New York Telephone Company Building, traces the history of telephone communication. On display is a replica of the first telephone made by Alexander Graham Bell as well as an impressive collection of obsolete, but still functional, telephones.
(See also Town of Huntington/Commack/Telephone Pioneers Museum.)

Walt Whitman House
246 Old Walt Whitman Road, Huntington Station
(631) 427-5240

Take the Long Island Expressway to Exit #49 north (Route 110/Huntington). Go north on Route 110/New York Avenue for 2.4 miles. Turn left (west) onto Old Walt Whitman Road; go .3 mile. The house is on the right (east) side of the road.

This circa 1816 house was built by Walt's father just nine years prior to Walt's birth. While he was still a child, the family moved to Brooklyn but Walt continued to spend summers on Long Island at the Cold Spring Harbor home of his maternal grandparents, the Van Velsors. Throughout his life Whitman spent as much time on Long Island as possible, as a teacher in Smithtown, Huntington, and Babylon; and as publisher of *The Long Islander*, a newspaper he founded in 1858 in Huntington which is still published today. (See also Town of Smithtown/Village of The Branch/Old Schoolhouse.)

The house, which was acquired and restored by the New York State Division for Historical Preservation in 1957 and has been on the National Register of Historic Places since 1985, contains period furniture including a few original Whitman pieces, Whitman memorabilia, a small reference library, and a gift shop. Special events, including concerts and poetry readings, are held throughout the year. Available at the small gift shop is a map designed for a self-driven tour of the houses associated with Whitman in the nearby community of West Hills.

LLOYD HARBOR

Billy Joel's House
Lloyd Harbor Road, Lloyd Harbor

Not open to the public.

From the village green at the intersection of Route 25A/Main Street and Park Avenue/County Road 35 in Huntington go west on Route 25A/Main Street for 1 mile. Turn right (north) onto West Neck Road (which becomes Lloyd Harbor Road); go 4.5 miles. The house is located at the end of the causeway, on the left (north) side of the road surrounded by a high wall.

The noted singer, songwriter, and performer Billy Joel was born in The Bronx in 1949 and raised in Hicksville and Levittown. His music is influenced by American soul singers and The Beatles; indeed, Joel himself claims to have modeled his musical style after that of Paul McCartney. Joel attained immediate success with his second album *With Piano Man* (1973) for which he was awarded a gold album. His fifth and sixth albums, *The Stranger* and *52nd Street*, both achieved platinum record status. Joel composed music in the more classical style for his 2001 album *Fantasies & Delusions*.

Joel lived in this house during the late 1980s, moved then to the Hamptons, and, subsequently, into an estate house on Centre Island, directly across the harbor from this house.

Caumsett State Park – Marshall Field III Estate – Caumsett

25 Lloyd Harbor Road, Lloyd Harbor
(631) 423-1770

From the village green at the intersection of Route 25A/Main Street and Park Avenue/County Road 35 in Huntington go west on Route 25A/Main Street for 1 mile. Turn right (north) onto West Neck Road (which becomes Lloyd Harbor Road); go 5.1 miles. The park entrance is on the left (east) side of the road.

In 1921 Marshall Field III purchased 1,750 acres in Lloyd Neck for his estate. He named it *Caumsett*, the original Matinecock Indian name for the area, meaning "place by a sharp rock." Marshall Field III was the grandson of the famous department store pioneer and philanthropist. In 1922 he engaged the Manhattan architect John Russell Pope to create a Beaux-Arts English-styled estate that would be self-sufficient and a combination of country-club, hunting preserve, and home. The estate, as designed by Pope, had facilities for virtually every sport except golf. It also had a cattle and dairy farm, and supplied its own vegetables, water, and electricity.

In 1961 fifteen hundred acres of the estate were acquired by New York State and transformed into a park offering nature walks, horseback riding, hiking, bicycling, cross-country skiing, and surf fishing. There are no restrooms, water, or picnicking facilities. It should be noted that no provisions have been made to make this park accessible for people with disabilities.

The estate was placed on the National Register of Historic Places in 1979.

Henry Lloyd Manor

41 Lloyd Harbor Road, Lloyd Harbor
(631) 549-6987

From the village green at the intersection of Route 25A/Main Street and Park Avenue/County Road 35 in Huntington go west on Route 25A/Main Street for 1 mile. Turn right (north) onto West Neck Road (which becomes Lloyd Harbor Road); go 5.4 miles. The house is on the left (east) side of the road.

James Lloyd, a successful businessman, purchased a tract of land on Horse's Neck from Thomas Hart. James subsequently married Griseld Sylvester of Shelter Island who owned the rest of Horse's Neck. (See also Town of Shelter Island/Shelter Island/Cemetery and Monument to Quaker Martyrs; Town of Shelter Island/Shelter Island/Shelter Island Windmill; and Town of Southampton/Sag Harbor/Custom House.) The marriage not only united the couple but also brought them ownership of all of Horse's Neck which later became known as Lloyd's Neck. In 1685 Lieutenant Governor Thomas Dongan made James Lloyd the First Lord of the Manor. Holdings also included large tracts of land in what is now Queens Village. After James' death, his son Henry became the Second Lord of the Manor and built the manor house in 1711. Unlike his father, Henry, who inherited the title and property at age twenty-one, enjoyed the role of Lord of the Manor. He executed his manorial rights, to a fault, prohibiting poaching and insisting on payment for timber and thatch that the townspeople of Huntington cut on his land. When Henry died, his eldest son, also named Henry, inherited the title and one-third of the land. Henry, a businessman who lived in Boston, hoped to sell his business and move to the manor. With the advent of the Revolution, Henry, with his Tory sympathies moved instead to London, England, where he died in 1795.

Because of the manor's strategic location overlooking Lloyd Harbor, the British occupied it and built Fort Franklin nearby. The fort, whose construction was supervised by Count Rumford, was the site of a battle on July 12, 1781, when patriots under the command of Major Tallmadge crossed the Sound but failed in their attempt to destroy the fort. (See also Town of Brookhaven/Mastic Beach/The Manor of Saint George; Town of Brookhaven/Setauket/Richard Woodhull House; Town of Huntington/Huntington/The Old Burying Ground; and Town of Huntington/Huntington/Old First Presbyterian Church.) At the end of the war New York State confiscated the estate but it was purchased a few years later by Henry's nephew John and has remained in the family until recently. (See also Town of Huntington/Lloyd Harbor/Joseph Lloyd Manor.)

While the name of Lloyd has slipped into obscurity, that of one of their slaves, Jupiter Hammon, the first African-American poet in the United States, is becoming increasingly recognized.

The house was restored by the Lloyd Harbor Historical Society and is open to the public.

Joseph Lloyd Manor
Harbor Road and Lloyd Lane, Lloyd Harbor
(631) 692-4664

From the village green at the intersection of Route 25A/Main Street and Park Avenue/County Road 35 in Huntington go west on Route 25A/Main Street for 1 mile. Turn right (north) onto West Neck Road (which becomes Lloyd Harbor Road); go 5.1 miles. The house is located on the left (east) side of the road.

With the death of Henry Lloyd I on March 18, 1763, his son Joseph inherited one-quarter of the manor's property, the rest being divided among his brothers. Joseph built his manor house on Lloyd's Neck in 1766. During the Revolution none of the Lloyds remained at the manor. Joseph's brother Henry, a loyalist, moved to London, England, where he died in 1795. Joseph, a patriot, fled to Connecticut where he became increasingly despondent. Believing the patriot cause was lost after their defeat at Charlestown, he committed suicide. The property of all the Lloyds, which was desirable for its abundant timber and strategic location, was confiscated by the British. Indeed, much of the manor's timber was used to build local fortifications. So severe was the deforestation by the British that it took fifty years for refoliation to occur.

After the war, John Lloyd, Joseph's nephew, returned and purchased the lands of Henry which had been confiscated by New York State. The advent of the depression of 1873 caused the demise of the family holdings and the passage of the house to a series of successive owners until it was acquired by the Society for the Preservation of Long Island Antiquities in 1968. The manor house which is on the National Register of Historic Places has been fully restored. Of particular interest are the museum-quality examples of Chippendale, Queen Anne, Federal, and Empire furnishings. A lovely eighteenth-century garden is located on the manor grounds.

(See also Town of Brookhaven/Mastic Beach/The Manor of Saint George; Town of Brookhaven/Mastic Beach/William Floyd Estate; Town of Hempstead/Lawrence/Rock Hall Museum; Town of Huntington/Lloyd Harbor/Henry Lloyd Manor; and Town of Oyster Bay/Oyster Bay/Raynham Hall.)

Matheson Meadows Sanctuary
(Long Island Chapter: The Nature Conservancy)
Fort Hill Drive, Lloyd Harbor
(631) 367-3225

Open with prior permission.

From the village green at the intersection of Route 25A/Main Street and Park Avenue/County Road 35 in Huntington go west on Route 25A/Main Street for 1 mile. Turn right (north) onto West Neck Road (which becomes Lloyd Harbor Road); go 5.1 miles. Turn left (west) onto Fort Hill Lane; go .2 mile to Fort Hill Drive. The sanctuary is the meadow on both sides of Fort Hill Drive.

This forty-acre sanctuary is a large meadow separated by a road. The area was used as a pasture for cows and sheep until the late 1930s. It was subsequently farmed until the 1950s and then used as a pasture for horses until the 1970s. The sanctuary is overgrown with bittersweet, burdock, poison ivy, honeysuckle, milkweed, and other flowering plants, primarily daisies. The sanctuary supports a wide variety of wildlife such as woodcocks, bobolinks, meadow voles, Norway rats, great horned owls, and red-tailed hawks.

Please telephone the Conservancy at the above number to obtain permission to visit the sanctuary.

Museum of Long Island's Gold Coast
101 Brown's Road, Lloyd Harbor
(631) 571-7600 or 424-8230

Take the Long Island Expressway to Exit #49 north (Route 110/Huntington). Go north on Route 110/New York Avenue for 8 miles. Turn left (west) onto Route 25A/ Main Street. Travel through the Village of Huntington to West Neck Road. Turn right (north) onto West Neck Road; go 2 miles. Turn right onto John Davies Lane. Make a quick left onto Southdown Road and another quick right onto Brown's Road. The entrance is on the left side of the road.

In 1973 George McKesson Brown's 80,000-square-foot French Chateau-style mansion West Neck Farm, the estate's boat house, and thirty-three of the surrounding acres were acquired by Suffolk County. The museum, which is located in Brown's mansion, features exhibits and artifacts of the Gold Coast era.

The mansion, which is on the National Register of Historic Places, is available for catered affairs.

Saint Patrick's Cemetery
Huntington Road, Lloyd Harbor

Take the Long Island Expressway to Exit #49 north (Route 110/Huntington). Go north on Route 110/New York Avenue for 8 miles. Turn left (west) onto Route 25A/ Main Street. Travel through the Village of Huntington to West Neck Road. Turn right (north) onto West Neck Road; go 1.1 miles. Turn left (west) onto Huntington Road; go .2 mile. The cemetery is on the right (north) side of the road.

Grave of Charles Ludlam (1943–1987)

Follow the carriage road bearing left up the hill. Go half way up the hill. The grave site is on the left about 75 feet from the carriage road.

Ludlam, a native Long Islander, was born in Floral Park and raised in New Hyde Park and Greenlawn. As a youth he was fascinated by theater and at the age of seventeen founded his own theater group in Northport. In 1961 he entered Hofstra University with a performing arts scholarship but was persuaded by his professors to major in both writing and acting. Upon graduation in 1965 he moved to Manhattan and by 1967 had established his own theater group known as the Ridiculous Theatrical Company. During his short career, Ludlam wrote thirty-two plays and acted in virtually all of them, winning six "Obies." He once said, "Life provides an inexhaustible source of the ridiculous, so I never have to worry about running out of material." One could only wonder how much more he could have shown us about ourselves had he lived longer.

Seminary of the Immaculate Conception – Roland Ray Conklin Estate – Rosemary Farm

West Neck Road, Lloyd Harbor
(631) 423-0483

From the village green at the intersection of Route 25A/Main Street and Park Avenue/County Road 35 in Huntington go west on Route 25A/Main Street for 1 mile. Turn right (north) onto West Neck Road; go 3.2 miles. The seminary is on the right (east) side of the road.

The seminary is located on the former Roland Ray Conklin estate, Rosemary Farm. The circa 1908 English-style manor house, designed by the noted painter, musician, and architect Wilson Eyre, was destroyed by arson in 1990. Located on the property are the remnants of an open-air amphitheater in which Sarah Bernhardt, John Philip Sousa, and both John and Ethel Barrymore performed. The towered carriage house is the only structure that remains of the Conklin estate.

In 1924 the property was purchased by the Brooklyn Diocese. The seminary was built in 1930 at a cost of over $2.5 million. No mortgage was necessary as the entire cost was paid without any indebtedness being incurred. The Romanesque-style building literally surrounds the chapel. The chapel with its white stucco walls, stenciled beamed ceiling, wrought iron grill and gate creates a distinctly Byzantine atmosphere. The Skinner organ which comprises four separate organs, has 1,800 pipes and is played from the three manual keyboards and a pedal keyboard. The small bell that hangs outside the lower crypt area came from the Convent de la Candalaria in Cadiz, Spain. It was cast in 1656 with gold and silver as part of the manufacturing process to assure a magnificent tone.

Target Rock National Wildlife Refuge – Ferdinand Eberstadt Estate – Target Rock

Lloyd Harbor Road, Lloyd Harbor
(631) 271-2409

From the village green located at the intersection of Route 25A/Main Street and Park Avenue/County Road 35 in Huntington go west on Route 25A/Main Street for 1 mile. Turn right (north) onto West Neck Road (which becomes Lloyd Harbor Road); go 7.4 miles. The refuge is on the right side of the road.

In 1967 Ferdinand Eberstadt, a Manhattan investment banker, donated his eighty-acre estate, Target Rock, to the United States Department of Interior with the understanding that it be preserved as a wildlife refuge and center for environmental education. The refuge consists of a salt marsh, a pond, tidal waters, a thicket, and, interestingly, formal gardens. Because of the diversity of the habitat, 191 species of birds have been identified at the refuge. A guide pamphlet of the one-mile nature walk is available at the refuge.

In 1995 the estate's main residence was demolished by the federal government.

Van Wyck–Lefferts Tide Mill
(Long Island Chapter: The Nature Conservancy)
(631) 367-3225

Open with prior permission.

Since the only land access to the mill is through private property, it is imperative that you call the Conservancy at the above telephone number to obtain permission to visit the mill.

This tidal mill was built on the Huntington Harbor shoreline in 1793 by Abraham Van Wyck. With its intricate wooden gears, it is one of the few watermills on the East Coast that has not totally succumbed to the ravages of time and the elements. The mill which operated until the 1880s, has been on the National Register of Historic Places since 1978.

In 1969 Arthur Gwynne's family donated a portion of their estate Mill Cove and the Van Wyck–Lefferts Tide Mill to the Conservancy. The mill is being partially restored with the help of the Society for the Preservation of Long Island Antiquities.

NORTHPORT

Jack Kerouac's House
7 Judy Ann Court, Northport

Not open to the public.

Take the Long Island Expressway to Exit #51 north (Route 231/Northport/Huntington). Go north on Route 231/Deer Park Avenue for 2 miles. Bear right (northeast) onto East Deer Park Road; go .8 mile. Turn right (east) onto Route 25/Jericho Turnpike; go .2 mile. Turn left (north) onto Elwood Road; go 4 miles. Cross Route 25A; continue north on Reservoir Avenue for .4 mile. Bear left (north) onto Church Street; go .3 mile. Turn right (east) onto Dogwood Road; go .3 mile. Turn right (south) onto Judy Ann Court. The house is on the right (west) side of the road.

Kerouac (1922–1969) was born in Lowell, MA. He attended local parochial schools and the Horace Mann School in Manhattan before receiving an academic and athletic scholarship to Columbia University in 1940. After one year at Columbia, he enlisted in the United States Navy but was given a psychiatric discharge after two months. Before returning to Columbia in 1942, he worked at odd jobs in service stations and served for awhile in the Merchant Marine during the Battle of the Atlantic. His second attempt at college lasted only one semester. After leaving Columbia for a second time, his apartment near the university became the gathering place for the university's young intellectuals which included Allen Gingsberg, who later achieved notoriety as a proponent of the mind-altering drug

LSD and poet of the "beat generation." From 1943 to 1950 Kerouac roamed the United States and Mexico before returning to his mother's house in Lowell to write *The Town and the Country* (1950), which dealt with his adolescence. At twenty-eight Kerouac was hailed by critics as the best and most promising of the young novelists. After his initial success with *The Town and The Country*, he abandoned the traditional writing process of write-rewrite for a new genre which is described as spontaneous composition, that is, writing without ever refining or correcting the text. Others have referred to it as unintelligible. Kerouac's second book *On The Road* was written in three weeks utilizing this new technique. The term "beat generation" first made its appearance in this book. Published seven years after its completion, it embodies the complete rejection of conventional middle-class values in favor of a totally uninhibited lifestyle. *On The Road*, highly controversial at the time of its publication, has subsequently sold over 500,000 copies. His later books were also of the same genre but none has received the same attention as did *On The Road*.

Kerouac lived in this modest development ranch with his mother from 1963 to 1964. During this time he tried several times to end his life on the road by lying on the streetcar tracks on Main Street in Northport. He died in Saint Petersburg, FL, of massive internal bleeding caused by a neglected hernia condition. He is buried in Edison Cemetery in Lowell, MA.

Northport Historical Society Museum
215 Main Street, Northport
(631) 757-9859

Take the Long Island Expressway to Exit #51 north (Route 231/Northport/Huntington). Go north on Route 231/Deer Park Avenue for 2 miles. Bear right (northeast) onto East Deer Park Road; go .8 mile. Turn right (east) onto Route 25/Jericho Turnpike; go .2 mile. Turn left (north) onto Elwood Road; go 4 miles. Cross Route 25A; continue north on Reservoir Avenue for .4 mile. Bear left (north) onto Church Street; go .3 mile. Turn left (west) onto Main Street; go .3 mile. The museum is on the right (north) side of the road.

Established in 1974, the museum is located in the former Carnegie Library Building. Featured are changing exhibits of local history, and collections of photographs and tools. The museum shop has antiques, collectibles, and an excellent self-guided walking tour brochure of the Northport area.

Trinity Episcopal Church
130 Main Street, Northport
(631) 261-7670

Take the Long Island Expressway to Exit #51 north (Route 231/Northport/Huntington). Go north on Route 231/Deer Park Avenue for 2 miles. Bear right (northeast) onto East Deer Park Road; go .8 mile. Turn right (east) onto Route 25/Jericho Turnpike; go .2 mile. Turn left (north) onto Elwood Road; go 4 miles. Cross Route 25A; continue north on Reservoir Avenue for .4 mile. Bear left (north) onto Church Street; go .3 mile. Turn left (west) onto Main Street; go .4 mile. The church is on the left (south) side of the road.

This unimposing gray frame church was built in 1889 by the same craftsmen who built the Edward Thompson Publishing Company on Woodbine Avenue in Northport. Over the years it has been remodeled several times. The south and east wings were built in 1899 and the north section was added in the 1950s. Remnants of the four equally sided triangular roofline of the original structure are still visible. The interior is in the Gothic Revival-style with Gothic paneling on the pews, communion railing, choir stalls, and altar.

Three beautiful Tiffany windows can be seen here. The Knight (1899) – Beebe (1906) Memorial window on the east wall is signed "TIFFANY STVDIOS" and is documented in Tiffany Studios' records. Based on the painting, *Christ in Gethsemane*, by Johann Heinrich Hofman, the window depicts Jesus praying in the Garden of Gethsemane and is surrounded by decorative panels with distinctive jewel glass grape clusters and shields decorated with glass jewels. The spotlighting or cellar lighting effect on the centrally placed praying figure and the sky at sunset over the Palestinian village are especially effective. Drapery glass, especially the dark purple in Jesus' robes, and mottled glass of fine quality have been incorporated. The extensive plating used in this window gives a dramatic three-dimensional effect.

On the west wall is found the Parrott Memorial (1887) window, *Saint John.* The centrally placed figure of the studious Saint John in intensely deep blue robes is contained in a hemisphere surrounded by a pink brick effect. Although Tiffany did execute several hemisphere windows, this was not a common memorial type. It is striking. The pink and blue pastel mottled glass sky is typically Tiffany. Both drapery glass and mottled glass have been used. Although it is unsigned, it is documented in the surviving records of Tiffany Studios.

Spectacular beyond words is the Brown Memorial window, *Our Saviour,* directly over the altar and the centerpiece of a Greek cross. A serene Saviour is shown against an unusual background of pink, rose, lavender, and gold. A central lighting effect is incorporated by the artist that is brilliantly enhanced by morning sunlight. Because of its position over the altar, it has not been possible to determine if it is indeed signed, but it is documented in the records of Tiffany Studios.

West Fort Salonga

Makamah County Nature Preserve

Makamah Road, West Fort Salonga
(631) 854-4949

Suffolk County Resident Pass is required for admission.

Take the Long Island Expressway to Exit #53 north (Sagtikos Parkway/Sunken Meadow). Take the Sagtikos Parkway/Sunken Meadow Parkway north for 7.2 miles. Go west on Route 25A for 3.2 miles. Turn right (north) onto Makamah Road; go .5 mile. There is a footpath on the left (west) side of the road leading into the park.

This 160-acre park is a limited use nature park consisting of a woodland, a thicket, a marsh, and several small streams. The diverse nature of the habitats found in this park, make this preserve an excellent place for nature walks, hiking, and birdwatching.

West Huntington

West Hills County Park – Henry Lewis Stimson Estate – Highold

Reservoir Road, West Huntington
(631) 854-4423

Suffolk County Resident Pass is required for admission.

Take the Long Island Expressway to Exit #49 north (Route 110/Huntington). Go north on Route 110/New York Avenue for 2.4 miles. Turn left (west) onto Walt Whitman Road; go .3 mile. Turn left onto West Hills Road; go 1 mile. Turn left (south) onto Reservoir Road; go .6 mile. The park is at the end of the road.

For horseback riding, picnic facilities, and Sweet Hollow Hall; take the Long Island Expressway to Exit #49 north (Route 110/Huntington). Go north on Route 110/New York Avenue for 1.5 miles and make a U-turn. Go south on Route 110/New York Avenue for .2 mile to just before the westbound entrance to Northern State Parkway. Turn right (west) onto Gwynne Road and go .5 mile to the park entrance.

For Jayne's Hill and picnicking areas; take the Long Island Expressway to Exit #49 north (Route 110/Huntington). Go north on Route 110/New York Avenue for 2.4 miles. Turn left onto Walt Whitman Road; go .3 mile. Turn left onto West Hills Road; go 1 mile. Turn left (south) onto Reservoir Road; go .6 mile. The Jayne's Hill entrance is at the end of the road.

This 854-acre park is the former Henry Lewis Stimson estate, Highold. Stimson served as Secretary of State in the Hoover administration and Secretary of War in the Taft, Franklin Delano Roosevelt, and Truman administrations. (See also Town of Oyster Bay/East Norwich/Muttontown Preserve–Egerton L. Winthrop Estate and Benjamin Moore Estate–Chelsea; and Town of Oyster Bay/Laurel Hollow/Memorial Cemetery of Saint John's Church.)

The park offers nature trails, horseback riding, stables, horse shows, bike hostels, picnicking, and campgrounds accommodating 180 campers. Located in the park is Sweet Hollow Hall, which was once a Presbyterian church. The hall has forty-eight rooms and serves as a conference center, meeting hall, and theater for non-profit organizations. There are restrooms and facilities in the park for people with disabilities.

Jayne's Hill, a favorite spot of poet Walt Whitman, is in West Hills County Park. The hill is the highest peak on Long Island, rising 401.5 feet above sea level. Because of its serenity, this park is referred to as "a park lover's park."

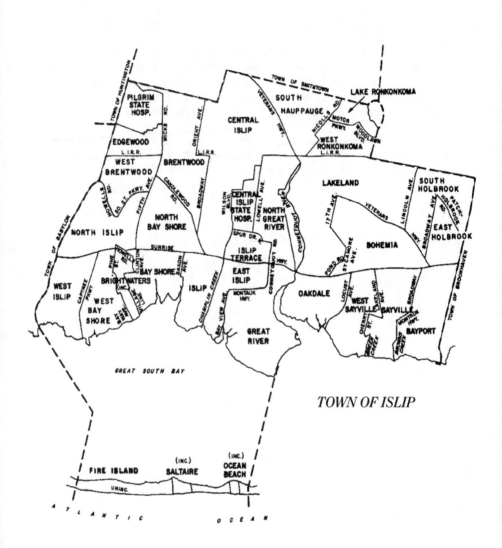

TOWN OF ISLIP

TOWN OF ISLIP

PARKS AND PRESERVES

Federal Parks and Preserves
Sayville National Wildlife Refuge (985 acres), Sayville
Seatuck National Wildlife Refuge (196 acres), Islip

State Parks and Preserves
Bayard Cutting Arboretum (690 acres), Great River
Brentwood State Park (52 acres), Brentwood *(undeveloped)*
Captree State Park (298 acres), Fire Island
Connetquot River State Park and Preserve (3,473 acres), Oakdale
Heckscher State Park (1,657 acres), East Islip
Robert Moses State Park (875 acres), Fire Island

County Parks and Preserves
Bohemia Equestrian Center (174 acres), Bohemia
Brookside County Park (5.4 acres), Sayville
Gardiner's County Park (231 acres), West Bay Shore
Islip Greenbelt County Park (153 acres), Islip *(undeveloped)*
Lakeland County Park (40 acres), Lakeland
Roosevelt Estate County Park (65 acres), Sayville *(undeveloped)*
San Soucci Lakes County Nature Preserve (302 acres), Bayport
Timber Point County Country Club (239 acres), Great River
Timber Point County Marina (part of Timber Point County Country Club),
    Great River
West Sayville Golf Course (250 acres), West Sayville

Long Island Chapter: The Nature Conservancy
Hollins Preserve (30 acres), East Islip
Orr Preserve (14 acres), East Islip
Thorne Preserve (87 acres), West Bay Shore

Arboretums and Gardens
Bayard Cutting Arboretum (690 acres), Great River

Bayport

Bayport Aerodrome
Third Avenue, Bayport
(631) 732-6509

Take the Long Island Expressway to Exit #62 south (Nicolls Road/Stony Brook/ Blue Point). Go south on Nicolls Road/County Road 97 for 4.9 miles. Turn right (west) onto Route 27A/Montauk Highway; go .8 mile. Turn right (north) onto Third Avenue and go 1.1 miles to the aerodrome.

Owned by the Town of Islip, this grass-covered, unpaved airstrip is reminiscent of the aerodromes of the turn of the century. It is home base to a few dozen vintage aircraft, all of which are privately owned and operational. Found here are several World War II trainers, E R Coupes, J 3 Cubs, and a replica 1925 Pientenpol, among others, that may be seen during the free tour which can be arranged at the gate. On designated weekends there are fly-ins of vintage aircraft. Call for further information about these weekends. (See also Town of Babylon/East Farmingdale/American Airpower Museum; Town of Hempstead/Garden City/The Cradle of Aviation Museum; and Town of Southampton/Westhampton Beach/106th Rescue Group – New York Air National Guard.)

Bay Shore

Bay Shore Historical Society
22 Maple Avenue, Bay Shore
(631) 665-4637

From Route 27A/Montauk Highway/Main Street turn south onto Maple Avenue. Go .4 mile. The society's headquarters is one the right (west) side of the street.

Featured in the Victorian-style, c. 1820 house are a parlor and a kitchen furnished in the period, permanent exhibition rooms, and a reference library. A separate building in the rear of the property houses period tools.

BOHEMIA

Bohemia Equestrian Center

Sycamore Avenue, Bohemia
(631) 854-4949

Suffolk County Resident Pass is required for admission.

Take the Long Island Expressway to Exit #57 south (Veterans' Memorial Highway/ Route 454/Hauppauge/Patchogue). Go south on Veterans' Memorial Highway/ Route 454 for 3.7 miles. Turn right onto Sycamore Avenue; go .7 mile. The park is on the right side of the road.

This 174-acre park is designed for equestrians. At present the park has bridle paths and a ring for horse shows. Plans are still being formulated for the further development of this park.

Bohemia Union Cemetery Association

Church Street, Bohemia

Take the Long Island Expressway to Exit #59 (Ocean Avenue/Ronkonkoma/Oak-dale). Go south on Ocean Avenue/County Road 93 for .9 mile. Stay on County Road 93 when it forks left at .9 mile to become Lakeland Avenue. Continue south on Lakeland Avenue for an additional 2.2 miles. Turn right (west) onto Church Street; go .2 mile. The cemetery is on the left (south) side of the road.

Monument to Jan Hus (c. 1369–1415)

The monument is located in the center of the cemetery and is easily visible from the road.

Jan Hus (John Huss) was born in Husinetz near Budweis, Czechoslovakia. Educated in Prague, he was ordained a priest in 1401. Hus was influenced by the English religious reformer John Wycliffe who advocated a church without property, challenged the doctrine of papal infallibility, condemned the sale of indulgences, and encouraged the elimination or weakening of many of the functions performed by priests. In addition, he believed in direct access to God by individuals including the receiving of both bread and wine by communicants at the Eucharist and celebration of the Mass in Czechoslovakian instead of Latin. As a result, Hus was excommunicated in 1410 for teaching Wycliffe's doctrines and his own beliefs as put forth in his thesis, *De Ecclesia (On The Church)*. In 1414 he was invited by Emperor Sigismund to defend his views at the Council of Constance. In spite of a guarantee of safety by King Wenceslaus and Emperor Sigismund, Hus was betrayed by the king and the emperor, condemned by the Council as a heretic, and burned at the stake. This act of treachery aroused his followers and led to the Hussite War

(1419–1434), which had both religious and political overtones. Martin Luther was greatly influenced by the works of Jan Hus.

This area of Long Island was settled in 1855 by Czechoslovakian settlers and was named by them Bohemia in honor of a province in their native land. A quick look at the names of families interred in this small cemetery will confirm the Czechoslovakian influence. Indeed, so closely did the early settlers identify with their homeland that they erected this monument to Jan Hus in 1893. It is reputed to have been the first monument in America dedicated to his memory.

Gold Star Parents' Monument
4250 Veterans' Memorial Highway, Bohemia

Take the Long Island Expressway to Exit #57 south (Veterans' Memorial Highway/ Route 454/Hauppauge/Patchogue). Go south on Veterans' Memorial Highway/ Route 454 for 5.3 miles. The monument is in front of the office building called MacArthur Plaza on the right (south) side of the road.

The Gold Star Parents' Monument is unique in that it is believed to be the first and, at present, the only monument in the country dedicated to the parents who have lost their children in the service of our country.

A national competition for the monument's design was held. The commission was awarded to Eileen Barry, an Islip resident. The bronze statue depicts resigned parents, arms linked in strength; the mother holding a folded burial flag with gold stars while the father is releasing the spirit of a child represented by a dove. They stand in a black marble fountain which symbolized the turbulence of their sorrow and sacrifice. On the front of the fountain is inscribed, "Our mission is to assist those who bear the sacred name of 'Gold Star Parents' and to help each other to bear the cross of sorrow which has come to us through the sacrifices our sons and daughters made for freedom and democracy."

The Gold Star Organization was founded in 1928. Their mission is embodied in the above inscription.

EAST ISLIP

Broadhollow Theatre Company
Bay Way Arts Center
265 East Main Street, East Islip
(631) 581-2700

The theater is located on the north side of Route 27A/East Main Street/Montauk Highway in East Islip.

In existence since 1972, the theater company stages plays and musicals. It also has an educational program, a children's theater, and additional theater sites in Lindenhurst and Elmont.

Heckscher State Park – George C. Taylor Estate
Heckscher Parkway, East Islip
(631) 581-2100

Take the Long Island Expressway to Exit #53 south (Sagtikos Parkway/Fire Island). Go south on Sagtikos Parkway for 4.1 miles; bear left (east) onto Southern State Parkway. Go east for 8.4 miles on Southern State Parkway/Heckscher Parkway to park entrance.

This 1,657-acre park is on part of the 6,893-acre estate of George C. Taylor, Deer Range Farm. The estate's mansion, built in 1886, was demolished in 1933. The park has three beaches on the Great South Bay, a pool, a bathhouse, a boat ramp, camping and fishing facilities, athletic fields, bridle paths, bike and hiking paths, nature trails, a picnic pavilion, and a refreshment stand. During the summer concert programs are presented while cross-country skiing is permitted in the winter.

Hollins Preserve
(Long Island Chapter: The Nature Conservancy)
Bayview Avenue, East Islip
(631) 367-3225 (Conservancy)
(631) 224-5436 (South Shore Nature Center)

Open with prior permission.

Take the Long Island Expressway to Exit #53 south (Sagtikos Parkway/Fire Island). Go south on Sagtikos Parkway for 4.1 miles; bear left (east) onto Southern State Parkway. Go east on Southern State Parkway for 6.9 miles to Exit #45 west (Route 27A/Montauk Highway). Go west on Route 27A/Montauk Highway for 1 mile. Turn left (south) onto Bayview Avenue; go 1.2 miles. The preserve is on the left (east) side of the road.

This thirty-acre preserve is managed for the Conservancy by the South Shore Nature Center. It consists of a gently sloping glacial till, a freshwater marsh, a saltwater marsh, and a stream. Because the preserve contains an abundance of plant species that are protected by New York State, it is being considered for natural landmark status. Wildlife abounds here with deer, foxes, rabbits, raccoons, opossums, egrets, herons, and ducks. Located across the street is the Conservancy's Orr Preserve.

Please call either the Nature Center or the Conservancy at the telephone numbers above to obtain permission to visit either preserve.

The Islip Art Museum
50 Irish Lane, East Islip
(631) 224-5420

Take the Long Island Expressway to Exit #56 south (Route 111/Smithtown/Islip). Go south on Route 111 for 5.6 miles. Turn left (east) onto Route 27A/Montauk

Highway; go .5 mile. Turn left (north) onto Irish Lane; go .2 mile. The entrance is on the left (west) side of the road.

The museum is located in the main residence of the former estate of Harry Kearsarge Knapp Sr., Brookwood. Over the years the estate has had several owners including The Orphan Asylum Society of Brooklyn which renamed the site Brookwood Hall.

In 1967 the mansion, its carriage house, gatehouse and its surrounding thirty-eight acres were purchased by the Town of Islip.

The museum's collection focuses on contemporary art by Long Island artists. The estate's carriage house is, at present, a center for experimental art.

Orr Preserve
(Long Island Chapter: The Nature Conservancy)
Bayview Avenue, East Islip
(631) 367-3225 (Conservancy)
(631) 224-5436 (South Shore Nature Center)

Open with prior permission.

Take the Long Island Expressway to Exit #53 south (Sagtikos Parkway/Fire Island). Go south on Sagtikos Parkway for 4.1 miles; bear left (east) onto Southern State Parkway. Go east on Southern State Parkway for 6.9 miles to Exit #45 west (Route 27A/Montauk Highway). Go west on Route 27A/Montauk Highway for 1 mile. Turn left (south) onto Bayview Avenue; go .8 mile. The entrance to the preserve is at the South Shore Nature Center on the right (west) side of the road.

This fourteen-acre preserve, which is managed by the South Shore Nature Center, is traversed by a boardwalk and consists of a freshwater pond, a stream, and a wooded area. Red maple, black cherry, white oak, black tupelo, sassafras, and black oak trees are found in the drier northeastern section of the preserve. Sweet pepperbushes, swamp azaleas, and skunk cabbages are found near the freshwater pond. A large variety of wildlife including small mammals, reptiles, amphibians, and birds are found in the preserve.

Located across the street is the Conservancy's Hollins Preserve. Please call either the Nature Center or the Conservancy at the telephone numbers above to obtain permission to visit either preserve.

South Shore Nature Center
Bayview Avenue, East Islip
(631) 224-5436

Take the Long Island Expressway to Exit #53 south (Sagtikos Parkway/Fire Island). Go south on Sagtikos Parkway for 4.1 miles; bear left (east) onto Southern State Parkway. Go east on Southern State Parkway for 6.9 miles to Exit #45 west

(Route 27A/Montauk Highway) for 1 mile. Turn left (south) onto Bayview Avenue; go .8 mile. The entrance is on the right (west) side of the road.

This two-hundred-acre facility is operated by the Town of Islip. It is a composite of several preserves: the Gregory Bird Sanctuary, the Hollins Wetlands, the Orr Preserve, and the Hollins Preserve. The combined lands include eight distinct habitats. Found here are a field, an upland forest, a succession forest, a freshwater marsh, a saltwater marsh, bottom lands, and transition areas, making the environmental center the only one on Long Island to have such a wide range of habitats in one area. There is a small museum in the information center containing exhibits of turtles, bees, birds, and Indian artifacts, as well as a saltwater aquarium and a research library. The center offers an extensive and varied schedule of environmental programs throughout the year.

(See also Town of Islip/East Islip/Hollins Preserve and Town of Islip/East Islip/ Orr Preserve.)

Town of Islip Clam Hatchery
Bayview Avenue, East Islip
(631) 224-5654

Take the Long Island Expressway to Exit #53 south (Sagtikos Parkway/Fire Island). Go south on Sagtikos Parkway for 4.1 miles; bear left (east) onto Southern State Parkway. Go east on Southern State Parkway for 6.9 miles to Exit #45 west (Route 27A/Montauk Highway). Go west on Route 27A/Montauk Highway for 1 mile. Turn left (south) onto Bayview Avenue; go 1.7 miles. Enter the East Islip Marina. Turn right; go .4 mile to the hatchery.

Islip proudly claims title to the first large scale shellfish hatchery in New York State to be municipally operated. Started in 1986, a crop of twenty-one million seed clams was realized in 1987. An annual crop of thirty-six million seed clams is planned. At the present time commercially-available small seed clams are raised in tanks on the premises and then transferred to protected field units in the Great South Bay for further growth before their final transfer to the unprotected areas of the Great South Bay where they complete their growth cycle and are then harvested by commercial shell-fishermen. There are plans to eventually produce the small seed clams through mariculture right here in the hatchery. This will not only reduce costs but also increase the quality of seed clams available to the Shellfish Management Program and, thus, stem the decline of the shellfishing industry in the Great South Bay of Long Island.

Guided tours may be arranged for individuals or groups by calling the above telephone number.

(See also Town of Oyster Bay/Cold Spring Harbor/Cold Spring Harbor Fish Hatchery.)

FIRE ISLAND

Captree State Park
Fire Island
(631) 669-0449

Take the Long Island Expressway to Exit #53 south (Sagtikos Parkway/Fire Island). Go south for 4 miles on Sagtikos Parkway to Southern State Parkway. Go west on Southern State Parkway for 1 mile to Exit #40 south (Robert Moses Causeway). Take Robert Moses Causeway south for 7.5 miles to the exit for Captree State Park. Go .5 mile to the park entrance.

This 298-acre park is located on the western end of Fire Island. It has a refreshment stand, restrooms, a surf fishing pier, a boat basin, charter and open fishing boats, and a bait and marine fuel station. Since a section of the park is a bird sanctuary and protected nesting area, this is an excellent place for bird watching or just watching a sunset.

Fire Island Lighthouse
Fire Island National Seashore, Fire Island
(631) 321-7028

Take the Long Island Expressway to Exit #53 south (Sagtikos Parkway/Fire Island). Go south for 4 miles on Sagtikos Parkway to Southern State Parkway. Go west on Southern State Parkway for 1 mile to Exit #40 south (Robert Moses Causeway). Take Robert Moses Causeway south for 8.7 miles to traffic circle. Go around the circle and go east for 2 miles past parking lots numbered four and five to the edge of Fire Island National Seashore. The lighthouse is clearly visible from the road.

The original circa 1826 Fire Island Lighthouse did not have sufficient height for its signal to project far enough out to sea, nor was its construction of the sturdiness necessary to withstand the often fierce South Shore weather. Consequently, on March 3, 1857, Congress appropriated $40,000 to construct a much stronger 168-foot lighthouse on the same site. The new lighthouse went into operation on November 1, 1858, with a signal capable of being seen for twenty-one miles at sea. It remained in operation for 116 years before it was decommissioned in 1974. In 1976 management of the lighthouse was transferred to the National Parks Service. The lighthouse was listed on the National Register of Historic Places in 1981.

Unfortunately, the intervening years have not been kind to this historic treasure which was the first glimpse of America for many immigrants entering New York Harbor. To renovate the ravages of time and neglect the Fire Island Lighthouse Society has been formed. The goal of the society has been to refurbish the lighthouse, relight its lamp, and develop a surrounding ninety-acre tract of land for educational and recreational programs. The first phase of the restoration was completed in the spring of 1986 with the relighting of the beacon and the opening of an information and exhibition center in the former lightkeeper's cottage. It should be noted that the lighthouse is presently surrounded by a "clothes-optional" beach which some visitors might find objectionable.

Moonchaser
Captree Boat Basin
Captree State Park
Fire Island
(631) 661-5061

Take the Long Island Expressway to Exit #53 south (Sagtikos Parkway/Fire Island). Go south for 4 miles on Sagtikos Parkway to Southern State Parkway. Go west on Southern State Parkway for 1 mile to Exit #40 south (Robert Moses Causeway). Take Robert Moses Causeway south for 7.5 miles to the exit for Captree State Park.

The 250-person-capacity boat *Moonchaser* offers scenic tours of the Great South Bay. Its enclosed main deck and canopied upper sun deck are ideal for public excursions or private chartered affairs.

Robert Moses State Park
Fire Island
(631) 669-0470

Take the Long Island Expressway to Exit #53 south (Sagtikos Parkway/Fire Island). Go south 4 miles on Sagtikos Parkway to Southern State Parkway. Go west on Southern State Parkway for 1 mile to Exit #40 south (Robert Moses Causeway). Take Robert Moses Causeway south for 8.5 miles to the park entrance.

Located on the western end of Fire Island, this 875-acre park offers swimming, surf fishing, pitch-putt golf, playfields, and both anchorage and transient dockage. A refreshment stand, restrooms, a picnic area with charcoal grills, and a bathhouse are available.

GREAT RIVER

Bayard Cutting Arboretum – William Bayard Cutting Estate – Westbrook
Montauk Highway, Great River
(631) 581-1002

Take the Long Island Expressway to Exit #53 south (Sagtikos Parkway/Fire Island). Go south on Sagtikos Parkway for 4.1 miles; bear left (east) onto Southern

119

State Parkway. Go east for 6.9 miles on Southern State Parkway to Exit #45 east (Route 27A/Montauk Highway). Go east on Route 27A/Montauk Highway for .6 mile. The arboretum is on the right (south) side of the road.

This 690-acre arboretum was once part of Westbrook, the 931-acre estate of William Bayard Cutting. Cutting made his fortune in banking, railroads, and ferry boat service from Brooklyn to Manhattan. In 1884 he bought the property from George Lorlliard. Construction of the Tudor-style manor house, designed by Charles C. Haight, began in 1886. It incorporates walls, ceilings, and staircases of ornately carved wood paneling, most of which was purchased in England; many beautiful fireplaces including one in the dining room decorated with mosaic work reportedly done by Louis Comfort Tiffany; many stained-glass windows, also attributed to Tiffany; and a magnificent tapestry-covered dining room wall. In 1887 Frederick Law Olmsted, the designer of New York City's Central Park, was commissioned to create a private arboretum for the estate. The estate, which was given as a gift to the New York State by Olivia B. James and her mother Mrs. William Bayard Cutting, is on the National Register of Historic Places. (See also Town of Islip/Great River/Emmanuel Episcopal Church and Town of Islip/Islip/Saint Mark's Episcopal Church.)

The house, which is partially furnished with original Cutting furnishings, contains a refreshment stand and meeting rooms. It is open to the public.

The arboretum has nature walks with labeled plants. During the spring, summer, and fall there are guided nature walks and during the winter there are indoor concerts.

Emmanuel Episcopal Church
Great River Road, Great River
(631) 581-3964

Take the Long Island Expressway to Exit #53 south (Sagtikos Parkway/Fire Island). Go south on Sagtikos Parkway for 4.1 miles; bear left (east) onto Southern State Parkway. Go east for 6.9 miles on Southern State Parkway to Exit #45 east (Route 27A/Montauk Highway). Go east on Route 27A/Montauk Highway for .2 mile. Turn right (south) onto Great River Road; go 1 mile. The church is on the right (west) side of the road.

On November 16, 1862, William Nicoll, descendant of the patentee and vestryman at Saint Mark's, Islip, officially gave the initial parcel of property on which Saint Mark's Youngsport Chapel was erected. The first service was celebrated on that date by The Reverend Reuben Riley of Saint Mark's Episcopal Church, Islip. The Youngsport Chapel remained a mission of Saint Mark's until it was transferred to Saint John's, Oakdale, in 1873. In October 1877 it was incorporated as Emmanuel Church. Enlarged and altered many times over the years, it has admirably preserved the look of the small country church, which was the parish of William Bayard Cutting, William Laurence Breese, Frederick Gilbert Bourne, and William Nicoll, the founder who served as warden here for twenty-two years.

The lancet-arched main entrance is on the southeast corner with an unusual oak door which is also lancet-shaped and faced with beautiful brass filigree work, hand-wrought brass hinges, and ornate brass doorknobs. On the east wall, just as you enter, is the Plumb Memorial window (1879) which pictures Evangelists Matthew, Mark, Luke, and John. It is painted and etched French stained-glass externally plated with American opalescent glass and is strikingly beautiful. Mr. James Neale Plumb, whose estate Deer Range Farm is now part of nearby Hecksher State Park, also contributed the bell tower in 1877.

The Hobbs Memorial window on the chancel wall behind the altar, *Christ and Child with Adoring Angels*, pictures a centrally positioned figure of Christ with a child, a common theme of Tiffany Studios. The child's robe is composed of pearl white opalescent drapery glass and the robes of Christ are of lavender drapery glass. The attractive Gothic frame of this memorial is reminiscent of the 1908 Sage Memorial window in The First Presbyterian Church in Far Rockaway. The two side lancet panels depict angels. Beautiful opalescent lilies, symbolizing the Resurrection, and iris, symbolizing remembrance, both flowers consistently identified with Tiffany designs, are depicted across the landscape, integrating the small Gothic panels into a single scene. The signature "TIFFANY STVDIOS NEW YORK" places this window between 1900 and 1915; the church dates it from 1902. Repainting of faces has greatly altered this window. The trees shown are excellent examples of the Tiffany mottled glass technique.

A small floral window on the north wall of the chancel with poppies, symbolizing sleep, and lilies is also signed "TIFFANY STVDIOS NEW YORK" suggesting that this ornamental and perhaps the similar, but unsigned, window, also with poppies, opposite on the south wall of the chancel may have been made about the same time as the Hobbs Memorial.

The Sarah Nicoll Memorial window (1913) in the choir alcove on the south side of the church and the William Nicoll Memorial window (1900) in the baptismal alcove on the north side are attributed to Tiffany by the parish but are unsigned and undocumented except for a note in the Tiffany Studios' records in reference to ornamental window(s) done in this church. The former includes the Crown of Heaven motif with floral work, strikingly similar to a pair of documented Tiffany windows in the McCormick mausoleum in Wildwood Cemetery in Williamsport, PA, while the latter features a glass jewel cross with mottled decoratives and floral work. Both are of very fine quality. Note that the glass forms a trefoil within the lancet.

A large number of ornamental windows are also attributed to Tiffany by the parish and date from 1903. These are all quite similar and unsigned except for the Dover Memorial window on the north wall. The signature in the lower right hand corner, "TIFFANY STVDIOS NEW YORK," is discernable only with difficulty.

Although still beautiful, the true beauty of these windows was greatly distorted, at our last visit, by a mottled blue protective covering on the outside.

The rectory, constructed in 1889 and located to the north of the church building, was a gift of William Bayard Cutting. Before you leave, note the lych gate at the entrance to the cemetery behind the church; there are few to be seen in the United States today and this is a particularly lovely one.

(See also Town of Islip/Great River/Timber Point County Country Club–William Laurence Breese Estate; Town of Islip/Oakdale/Connetquot River State Park and Preserve–Southside Sportsmen's Club; Town of Islip/Oakdale/Frederick Gilbert Bourne Estate–Indian Neck Hall; and Town of Islip/Oakdale/Saint John's Episcopal Church.)

(There are more Tiffany windows in this area of Islip. See also Town of Islip/ Great River/Bayard Cutting Arboretum–William Bayard Cutting Estate–Westbrook; Town of Islip/Sayville/Saint Ann's Episcopal Church; and Town of Islip/Islip/Saint Mark's Episcopal Church.)

Timber Point County Country Club – William Laurence Breese Estate

Great River Road, Great River

(631) 854-4949

Suffolk County Resident Pass is required for admission.

Take the Long Island Expressway to Exit #53 south (Sagtikos Parkway/Fire Island). Go south on Sagtikos Parkway for 4.1 miles; bear left (east) onto Southern State Parkway. Go east for 6.9 miles on Southern State Parkway to Exit #45 east (Route 27A/Montauk Highway). Go east on Route 27A/Montauk Highway for .2 mile. Turn right (south) onto Great River Road; go 1.4 miles to the club's entrance.

Located on the former William Laurence Breese estate, Timber Point, this 239-acre, 27-hole golf club is adjacent to the Timber Point County Marina. The club's greens and fairways are attractively set beside the marina and bay. It offers a P.G.A.-staffed pro shop, locker rooms, a bar, a lounge, a clubhouse with dining room, a practice putting green, a driving range, and both electric and pull cart rentals. Also found at the club are asphalt tennis courts, bridle paths, a livery stable which rents horses and ponies, and a riding ring. Cross-country skiing is permitted in the winter.

Timber Point County Marina

Great River Road, Great River

(631) 854-4949

Suffolk County Resident Pass is required for admission.

Take the Long Island Expressway to Exit #53 south (Sagtikos Parkway/Fire Island). Go south on Sagtikos Parkway for 4.1 miles; bear left (east) onto Southern State Parkway. Go east for 6.9 miles on Southern State Parkway to Exit #45 east (Route 27A/Montauk Highway). Go east on Route 27A/Montauk Highway for .2 mile. Turn right (south) onto Great River Road; go 1.4 miles to the entrance of Timber Point County Country Club. Follow signs to the marina.

Located within the Timber Point County Country Club, this marina offers the opportunity for both water and land activities. The marina has 159 seasonal berths,

71 of which are designed for larger, deeper draft vessels and 78 for vessels up to 29 feet in length. There are eight transient slips for stays of up to 72 hours. Fuel, oil, and sewage pump-out facilities are also available. The adjacent golf course offers full golf facilities. Tennis courts and horseback riding facilities are also available.

ISLIP

Saint Mark's Episcopal Church
754 Montauk Highway, Islip
(631) 581-4950

Take the Long Island Expressway to Exit #56 south (Route 111/Smithtown/Islip). Go south on Route 111 for 5.6 miles to Route 27A/Montauk Highway. The church is at the intersection of Montauk Highway and Route 111 on the south side of Montauk Highway.

If you never entered this incredibly beautiful parish church, a desire for the fascinatingly different could be satisfied by a study of the roof angles and pitches and of the symbolic roof decorations of Nordic design. Some of these gargoyles are of the so-called "dragon style" descending from designs used on Viking (Norse) ships. The cross atop the east entrance is typical of thirteenth-century Norwegian stave churches. The original shake wooden roof shingles have been replaced by the practicality of a contemporary roof. If you arrive just before a service, you will see and hear the external rolling pull-bell over the east entrance rung. This same bell called parishioners to worship in 1847, when the parish was organized.

Saint Mark's was inspired by several Norwegian churches including *Fantoft,* which is located in Bergen, Norway (to which it was moved in 1884 from Fortun). Only about thirty of these stave churches *(stavkirker)* survive today demonstrating a construction where vertical planks or staves are either anchored directly into the ground or are connected to a horizontal base. Large tree trunks, located in St. Mark's basement under the main beam, still helped to support the church building until they were removed in 1990. William Kissam Vanderbilt Sr. financed the church at a cost of $15,000, importing the materials necessary and the Scandinavian craftsmen to reproduce what he had seen on a visit to Norway in the mid-1800s. It was designed by Richard Morris Hunt who also designed other Vanderbilt projects including Biltmore in Asheville, NC; the original Idlehour in Oakdale, Long Island; Marble House and The Breakers, both in Newport, RI; and early work on the Metropolitan Museum of Art, a project subsequently finished by his son, Richard Howland Hunt, designer of the present Idlehour mansion. The present rectory was also designed by Richard Morris Hunt and completed in the same year as the church. The Vanderbilt gift for the church construction was conditional on the building of the rectory. The architecturally different, but complimentary, parish house was designed by Isaac Henry Green II, the noted Long Island Beaux-Arts architect, in 1890.

The present 1880 church replaced an earlier white frame church building dating from the late 1840s which was sold to the Roman Catholic diocese and became part of the parish hall of Saint Mary's Church in East Islip. In 1893, the church was expanded, doubling the seating capacity. These additions were made possible by the gifts of many but principally by those of Robert Fulton Cutting, William Bayard Cutting, William Kissam Vanderbilt Sr., Harry Bowly Hollins Sr., and Henry Duncan Wood Sr. A very large contribution was also made by the employees of William Kissam Vanderbilt Sr. William Bayard Cutting was also on the vestry here in 1885–1886 but left Saint Mark's allegedly due to a dispute with the Vanderbilts over treatment of help and workmen. Cutting helped finance the building of Emmanuel Episcopal Church in Great River and Helen Suydam Cutting (Mrs. Robert Fulton Cutting) and her brother, Walter L. Suydam, financed Saint Ann's Episcopal Church in Sayville. (See also Town of Islip/Great River/Bayard Cutting Arboretum–William Bayard Cutting Estate; Town of Islip/Great River/Emmanuel Episcopal Church; and Town of Islip/Sayville/Saint Ann's Episcopal Church.)

The less than gentile behavior attributed to the Vanderbilts is alluded to in descriptions of their arrival at church on Sunday mornings—perhaps apocryphal. As their carriages approached the church trumpeters were said to blow a fanfare announcing the family. The whole "kit and caboodle" then disembarked and processed to their front pew. On the north wall, is the Vanderbilt Memorial window made by Heaton, Butler, and Bayne of London in 1921 and entitled *Christ on the Road to Emmaus* (Luke 24:29). This was the gift of William Kissam Vanderbilt Jr., Harold Stirling Vanderbilt, and their sister, Consuelo, who was confirmed here in Saint Mark's in 1893 and later married the Duke of Marlborough at Saint Thomas' on Fifth Avenue in Manhattan. Evidence uncovered during the post-fire recovery period in late-1989 confirms that the Vanderbilt family pew was the large open pew to the east of the south transept entrance.

Documentation, found by these authors, confirms that the original 1878 Tiffany window, Louis Comfort Tiffany's first ecclesiastical figure window, was still in the church on the day of its consecration on June 21, 1880. The three apse windows, replacing the earlier stained-glass rendering of Saint Mark, were documented by the authors in April 1989. The vestry records confirm that these windows were not only by Tiffany but a gift of Louis Comfort Tiffany to the parish in 1895. He did not sign any of the three triptych windows. Saint Mark, who is regarded as an interpreter of Saint Peter, is often shown writing as he is in this window. The centrally positioned Saint Mark with a winged lion, traditional symbol of Saint Mark, is surrounded by panels of decorative patterns emphasizing blues and greens and including pressed glass and much jewel glass. The almost abstract ship at full sail in the left window and the landscape with fig tree in the right window are almost overwhelmed by the decorative techniques. Careful examination of the center panel of the left triptych will reveal a stunning example of flashed or etched glass—glass which appears to be blue-gray forming the sea on which the ship is sailing. Biblical references to Mark 4:39-40 and Mark 11:24; Revelation 21:3 and Luke 6:31; and Mark 11:13 and Galatians 5:22-23 at the bottom of the windows are preceded by illuminated initials as seen in medieval iconography. This, unusual in

Tiffany work, is an intriguing contrast to the very contemporary, abstract design of these windows.

In the chancel is the ornately carved reredos with icon work of exceptional quality given in 1919. The silver altar cross, set with extraordinary crystal representations of Christ and His disciples, was a gift to the church in 1891 but dates to the Italian Renaissance. The church was also the fortunate recipient of a rare Germanic Crusader's Cross which dates from the late fourteenth century and which has been completely restored by artisans of the Metropolitan Museum of Art.

The Redmond Memorial window, *Saint John,* on the south wall is a very early Tiffany window in the European style with decorative panels balancing the theme and proclaiming Christ's words from John 14:27. Saint John is traditionally shown with a book as he is here. However, he is also represented by an eagle, which symbolizes power and the ability to soar to heaven, suggesting divine inspiration. Although Tiffany made many windows showing Saint John, this is the only one which the authors have seen in which he included the eagle. Fine drapery glass has been used to form the Evangelist's robes. There is much greater use of primary colors here than in later Tiffany works. Although unsigned, this is documented in the Tiffany Studios' records and is dated 1895 in the church's records.

Next to the Redmond Memorial on the south wall is the Peters Memorial. This truly magnificent, albeit typical Tiffany, is really a set of three windows or a triptych window recorded in the Tiffany records as *Floral Design*—a considerable understatement. The center panel features a yellow glass jeweled cross circled with concentric circles of blue shaded to lavender glass jewels; they are rough hewn stones such as seen in beach glass mosaics. The beautiful Tiffany opalescent lilies, symbolizing the Resurrection, are seen on all three panels as well as pansies, which are the floral emblem of Trinity Sunday and symbolize thoughtful recollection. This Memorial is signed, "TIFFANY GLASS & DECORATING COMPANY, NEW YORK." The signature was used from approximately 1890–1899; this window dates from 1899.

Over the north transept is the Henry Baldwin Hyde Sr. Memorial window, *Recording Angel.* According to church records it was given in 1899, consistent with the use of heavy drapery glass in the robes of the angel and in those of the kneeling winged hero. The passage "The Spirit shall return onto God who gave it." (Ecclesiastes 12:7) is represented by the presentation of a dove, symbolizing the spirit, to the recording angel. The sword, representing the occupations of the mortal life, has been put behind the petitioner. A pearl white opalescent glass scroll lies across the angel's knees and she holds a laurel wreath, symbolic of victory. Unfortunately, the addition of a belfry in 1919 obscures the window as no natural light now passes through its many plating layers. Tiffany incorporated the effects of the natural lighting into his art. Sadly, this window can never be seen, enhanced by the unique light from the North, as Tiffany wished, since it is now artificially backlighted. It is unsigned, but listed in Tiffany Studios' records.

Over the south transept is the Johnson Memorial window, *Choir of Angels.* The Tiffany Studios' records refer to this window as the Carroll Memorial. It bears the passage "Blessed are the Dead which die in the Lord—That they may rest from their labors" (Revelation 14:13). The centrally positioned angel appears to be singing while the angel on the left is playing a stringed lute. Notice that the strings appear to be embedded iron bars, a technique used infrequently by Tiffany, but only by Tiffany. The angel on the right is playing a violin without a fingerboard. Again, heavy drapery glass and the use of small glass composites, for example in the wings, characterize this early period piece. This window is not only signed, it is copyrighted as well. The inscription reads "COPYRIGHT 1898 TIFFANY GLASS & DECORATING COMPANY NEW YORK." This, and, for that matter, all the Tiffany windows in St. Mark's date from the period prior to the 1900 formation of Tiffany Studios.

On the north wall is the unusual Knapp Memorial window—deceptively plain. (See also Town of Islip/East Islip/Islip Art Museum–Harry Kearsarge Knapp Sr. Estate–Brookwood.) The small painted and stained-glass pieces integrated into this window are medieval German work; several are especially early, perhaps as early as the twelfth century. More of these medieval medallions can be seen in the windows of the Islip Art Museum, which occupies the Brookwood estate of the Knapps. One of the figures depicted is that of a pope, totally unexpected in an Anglican Church but certainly an artistic treasure. This memorial dates from 1913.

Other fine windows are examples of the work of Mayer of Munich, Connick Studio of Boston, Willet Stained Glass Studios of Philadelphia, and Hardman Studio of England.

Ornamental Tiffany windows with a brick pattern at the bottom and pressed glass rondelles on top, which were in the early church and which have since been removed to allow for the installation of memorials, are in storage.

As you turn to leave this beautifully wainscotted church look up over the east entrance. There is an unusual trefoil pebble cluster window in a circular frame of the type done by Tiffany. It appears to incorporate both the pebble cluster effect and that of the better known glass jewels. This type of Tiffany window is less well known and rarely signed; there are few surviving today. Another may be seen as Saint Ann's Episcopal Church in Sayville, although that one is a rose, or petal window, rather than a trefoil. Neither is mentioned in surviving Tiffany Studios' records although a newspaper article from 1880 indicates that this window is by Tiffany and that it was in the church on the occasion of its consecration. It was evidently moved with the back wall when Saint Mark's was doubled in size in 1893.

On December 5, 1989, Saint Mark's Church suffered a devastating fire. Many of the glorious windows were damaged or destroyed. An amazing restoration of the stained-glass windows was done by Jack Cushen of East Marion.

This church is a treasure and surely should be on your itinerary. The very fact that it contains museum quality Tiffany pieces from his early period makes it a must to see.

(See also Town of Hempstead/Garden City/Vanderbilt Motor Parkway Toll House; Town of Huntington/Centerport/Suffolk County Vanderbilt Museum–William Kissam Vanderbilt Jr. Estate–Eagle's Nest; Town of Islip/Oakdale/Connetquot River State Park and Preserve–Southside Sportsmen's Club; and Town of Islip/Oakdale/Dowling College–William Kissam Vanderbilt Sr. Estate–Idlehour.)

LAKELAND

Lakeland County Park

Johnson Avenue, Lakeland
(631) 853-2727

Suffolk County Resident Pass is required for admission.

Take the Long Island Expressway to Exit #57 south (Veterans' Memorial Highway/ Route 454/Hauppauge/Patchogue). Go south on Veterans' Memorial Highway/ Route 454 for .9 mile. Turn left (east) onto Nichols Road; go .5 mile. Turn right (south) onto Johnson Avenue; go .6 mile. The park is on the right side of the road.

This forty-acre park was established with help from federal and New York State matching funds. It has been designed especially for people with disabilities. The nature trails, playgrounds, court games, picnic areas, and both parking facilities and restrooms are designed to make them readily accessible to people with disabilities. There are guardrails for people with visual needs, boardwalks for people using wheelchairs with carefully positioned safety railings, and descriptive pamphlets for people with hearing impairment. Cassette programs have been developed as guides to hikers with disabilities for exploring a one-tenth mile trail. Unique texturing of walking surfaces and braille guideposts enable people with visual impairment to walk this trail alone in perfect safety.

OAKDALE

Connetquot River State Park and Preserve – Southside Sportsmen's Club

Montauk Highway, Oakdale
(631) 581-1005

Take the Long Island Expressway to Exit #53 south (Sagtikos Parkway/Fire Island). Go south on Sagtikos Parkway for 4.1 miles; bear left (east) onto Southern State Parkway. Go east on Southern State Parkway for 6 miles to Exit #44 east (Route 27/Sunrise Highway). Go east on Route 27/Sunrise Highway for 2.2 miles and make the first allowable U-turn (opposite the Suffolk County Water Authority Building). Go west on Route 27/Sunrise Highway for .9 mile. The park is on the right (north) side of the road.

This 3,473-acre park was once the Southside Sportsmen's Club, a private organization which was founded in 1866 and used as a game preserve devoted to fishing and hunting. Its list of members included Charles Tiffany, Ogden Goelet, Oliver Hazard Perry Belmont, Frederick Gilbert Bourne, James Gordon Bennett, and the Whitneys, Cuttings, Lorillards, and Vanderbilts. Among the distinguished visitors were President Grant, General Sherman, Daniel Webster, and Henry Clay. Local

Beaux-Arts architect Isaac Henry Green II designed the circa 1885 main clubhouse and annex by incorporating into the clubhouse the earlier circa 1820 Snedecor Inn. The resulting structure, which is on the National Register of Historic Places, is an unusual example and combination of nineteenth-century Colonial Revival- and Shingle-style architecture. An interesting feature is the fan light window over the door. It has leaded tracery with bottle glass rondures.

On display are decoys made by George Combs, Verity shore birds, antique guns, rare books, antique fishing equipment, Francis Law's bird collection, and the original clubhouse kitchen.

Also found in the park is a circa 1760 grist mill built by the Nicols family, founders of the Town of Islip. The mill, which is on the National Register of Historic Places, remained in operation for one hundred years.

This park offers guided nature walks, trout fishing, hiking trails, bridle paths, and cross-country skiing.

(See also Town of Babylon/North Babylon/Belmont Lake State Park–August Belmont Sr. Estate–Nursery Stud Farm; Town of Brookhaven/Yaphank/Southaven County Park–Suffolk Club; Town of Hempstead/Elmont/Belmont Race Track; Town of Hempstead/Garden City/Vanderbilt Motor Parkway Toll House; Town of Huntington/Centerport/Suffolk County Vanderbilt Museum–William Kissam Vanderbilt Jr. Estate–Eagle's Nest; Town of Islip/Great River/Emmanuel Episcopal Church; Town of Islip/Islip/Saint Mark's Episcopal Church; Town of Islip/Oakdale/Dowling College–William Kissam Vanderbilt Sr. Estate–Idlehour; Town of Islip/Oakdale/ Frederick Gilbert Bourne Estate–Indian Neck Hall; and Town of Oyster Bay/Old Westbury/New York Institute–Whitney Estate.)

Dowling College—William Kissam Vanderbilt Sr. Estate – Idlehour
Idle Hour Boulevard, Oakdale
(631) 589-6100

Take the Long Island Expressway to Exit #53 south (Sagtikos Parkway/Fire Island). Go south on Sagtikos Parkway for 4.1 miles; bear left (east) onto Southern State Parkway. Go east for 6.9 miles on Southern State Parkway to Exit #45 east (Route 27A/Montauk Highway). Go east on Route 27A/Montauk Highway. Stay in the right lane when it joins with Route 27/Sunrise Highway at 1.4 miles. Go .3 mile on Route 27/Sunrise Highway and make a right continuing on Route 27A/ Montauk Highway. Go .4 mile. Turn right (south) onto Idle Hour Boulevard; go .3 mile. The college is on the right (west) side of the road.

In 1876 William Kissam Vanderbilt Sr., the grandson of Commodore Cornelius Vanderbilt, commissioned Richard Morris Hunt to design the mansion on his eight-hundred-acre country estate Idlehour. Unfortunately, it was destroyed by fire in 1899. The present 115-room structure was designed by Hunt's son, Richard Howland Hunt, a noted Beaux-Arts architect who completed the design of the Metropolitan Museum of Art, a commission which his father had originally begun. Hunt used Medieval and Renaissance styles of architecture from various European countries in his design of the new main house.

With Vanderbilt's death in 1920 the estate passed through several owners, one of whom, reportedly, was "Dutch" Schultz, the notorious rum runner and gambler. In 1938 the mansion was used by the Royal Fraternity of Master Metaphysicians which called it Peace Haven; their leader James Schafer was later sent to jail for embezzlement. The National Dairy Association occupied the mansion from 1948 to 1960, using it as their headquarters. In 1962 the mansion and some of the other estate buildings became Adelphi Suffolk College, Suffolk County's first liberal arts college. In 1968 the college separated from Adelphi University and was renamed in honor of Robert W. Dowling, a member of the college's board of trustees and chief benefactor. (See also Town of East Hampton/East Hampton/Hayground Windmill.) The estate's coach house is now the gymnasium; the former powerhouse is the arts center; and the main house is used for classrooms and administrative offices. The stables, barns, and service buildings have been converted into apartments and are collectively known as the Artists' Colony.

In 1974 a fire severely damaged the main house destroying the living room, men's smoking room, and the magnificent main hall staircase. Repairs to the main residence were financed by the Fortunoff family. Unfortunately, historic elements were not restored. The Hunt Room, with its sculpture of Diana, survived the fire and is an excellent example of the former grandeur of the estate.

The former Vanderbilt mansion is available for catered affairs.

(See also Town of Babylon/Pinelawn/Mount Ararat Cemetery/Grave of Max Fortunoff; Town of Hempstead/Garden City/Vanderbilt Motor Parkway Toll House; Town of Huntington/Centerport/Suffolk County Vanderbilt Museum–William Kissam Vanderbilt Jr. Estate–Eagle's Nest; and Town of Islip/Islip/Saint Mark's Episcopal Church.)

Frederick Gilbert Bourne Estate – Indian Neck Hall
Montauk Highway, Oakdale

Take the Long Island Expressway to Exit #53 south (Sagtikos Parkway/Fire Island). Go south on Sagtikos Parkway for 4.1 miles; bear left (east) onto Southern State Parkway. Go east for 6.9 miles on Southern State Parkway to Exit #45 east (Route 27A/Montauk Highway). Go east on Route 27A/Montauk Highway. Stay in the right lane when it joins with Route 27/Sunrise Highway at 1.4 miles. Go .3 mile on Route 27/Sunrise Highway and make a right continuing on Route 27A/ Montauk Highway. Go an additional 1.8 miles. It is on the right (south) side of the road.

Frederick Gilbert Bourne (1851–1919) was the director of the Singer Sewing Machine Company and responsible for transforming it into the huge international organization it is today, although it no longer manufactures sewing machines. The Beaux-Arts Georgian-style mansion of his 2,000-acre estate, known as Indian Neck Hall, was designed by Ernest Flagg. The one-hundred-room, year-round family home, initially measuring 300-feet-long by 125-feet-wide, contained a skating rink, a bowling alley, a Turkish bath, and a swimming pool in its basement. At the time of its construction in 1900 it was said to be the largest mansion on Long

Island. The estate was landscaped with over 10,000 trees. The drive to the mansion requires passing over an artificial lake on a marble-faced bridge; when built, the bridge alone cost $30,000.

Over the years Bourne made three major alterations to the mansion. One was the demolition of the music room in 1908 and the construction of a much larger one to accommodate a pipe organ with over 7,000 pipes. In 1912 the ceiling of the main stairway was raised to accommodate the pipework of the hall organ. At the time of its installation, these two units combined are said to have been the largest privately owned house organ in the world. When removed in 1948, it still ranked as the third largest. The final major alteration was the addition of the clock tower in 1912.

In 1926 the Christian Brothers purchased the mansion, its auxiliary buildings, and 156 acres of the Bourne estate as the new home for LaSalle Military Academy, formerly the Clason Point Military Academy. The academy, which was recognized as one of the most prestigious military high schools in the nation, celebrated its centennial in 1983.

In 2001 the academy, then renamed LaSalle Center, sold the school to St. John's University. In 2006 the estate was purchased by the Joint Industry Board of the Electrical Industry, which in turn rented the facility to St. John's University.

To rent the mansion for a catered event, please call (631) 277-7800.

(See also Town of Islip/Oakdale/Connetquot River State Park and Preserve–Southside Sportsmen's Club; Town of Islip/Oakdale/Saint John's Episcopal Church; and Town of Islip/West Sayville/West Sayville County Golf Course–Anson Wales Hard Jr. Estate–Meadow Edge.)

Saint John's Episcopal Church
Montauk Highway, Oakdale
(631) 581-4950 (St. Mark's Episcopal Church, Islip)

Take the Long Island Expressway to Exit #53 south (Sagtikos Parkway/Fire Island). Go south on Sagtikos Parkway for 4.1 miles; bear left (east) onto Southern State Parkway. Go east for 6.9 miles on Southern State Parkway to Exit #45 east (Route 27A/Montauk Highway). Go east on Montauk Highway/Route 27A. Stay in the right lane when it joins with Sunrise Highway/Route 27 at 1.4 miles. Go .3 mile on Sunrise Highway/Route 27 and make a right continuing on Montauk Highway/Route 27A. Go an additional 1.8 miles. The church is on the left (north) side of the road.

William Nicoll III built this church on his estate in 1765. It was originally called Charlotte Church to honor the wife of King George III and was the only place of worship in the area for over eighty years. During the Revolution British troops occupied the church causing severe damage to the building. The local community was so outraged by these acts of deliberate destruction and wanton sacrilege that the church's name was changed to Saint John's Church in 1784. In 1916 the church and its grounds were renovated by Frederick Gilbert Bourne whose estate, Indian Neck Hall, was located directly across the street. (See also Town of Islip/Oakdale/Frederick Gilbert Bourne Estate – Indian Neck Hall.)

This small frame church has closed pews, sixteen-over-sixteen double-hung windows with long shutters, a slave gallery, split shake roof, and lovely stained-glass windows over the altar. Surrounded as it is by an old graveyard, which dates to Revolutionary times, it bears a remarkable resemblance to the Caroline Church in Setauket, which is the only church on Long Island older than Saint John's. (See also Town of Brookhaven/Setauket/Caroline Church of Brookhaven.)

In 2003, overseen by the Department of Mission and the rector of St. Mark's Church, Islip, grant applications for historic preservation of St. John's Church were approved by the Diocese of Long Island.

SAYVILLE

Islip Grange Restoration Complex
Montauk Highway and Broadway Avenue, Sayville
(631) 224-5430

Take the Long Island Expressway to Exit #53 south (Sagtikos Parkway/Fire Island). Go south on Sagtikos Parkway for 4.1 miles; bear left (east) onto Southern State Parkway. Go east for 6.9 miles on Southern State Parkway to Exit #45 east (Route 27A/Montauk Highway). Go east on Route 27A/Montauk Highway. Stay in the right lane when it joins with Route 27/Sunrise Highway at 1.4 miles. Go .3 mile on Route 27/Sunrise Highway and make a right continuing on Route 27A/ Montauk Highway. Go an additional 4.3 miles to the war memorial on Route 27A/ Montauk Highway and Collins Avenue in Sayville. Go east on Route 27A/Montauk Highway for 1.1 miles. Turn left (north) onto Broadway Avenue; go .1 mile. The entrance to the complex is on the left (west) side of the road.

Owned by the Town of Islip and reflecting pre-Civil War rural village life, this twelve-acre complex consists of pre-1900 buildings moved to this site from various areas within the town. Located here are a country cottage with a shake roof, barns, a church, two houses, and a farm windmill.

The Robinson House
(part of the Islip Grange Restoration Complex)
Montauk Highway and Broadway Avenue, Sayville

Benjamin Tuthill built this circa 1840 house at a site west of Greene Avenue on Montauk Highway in Sayville. Its Classical-style architecture is unique in that it was built using balloon framing construction which was invented in 1833 by August Deodat Taylor, a Connecticut architect. This light construction was vastly different from the heavily timbered New England braced frame construction and thus was a innovation in home design.

The Reformed Protestant Dutch Church of West Sayville
(part of the Islip Grange Restoration Complex)
Montauk Highway and Broadway Avenue, Sayville

This structure is a three-quarter-scale reproduction of the original church which still stands on the north side of Main Street in West Sayville, but in a drastically altered state. In the mid 1800s Dutch immigrants came to the Oakdale and West Sayville area because of employment opportunities in the oyster industry. By 1866 Tuckertown (now, West Sayville) had attracted so many Dutch immigrants that a Reformed Protestant Dutch church was built in 1867 in the Classical-style. The church remained in use until 1907 when a new larger one was built. The original structure became the home of Mr. and Mrs. Charles Emerson Peppard. It was eventually sold and now houses a storage company.

Ockers Barns
(part of the Islip Grange Restoration Complex)
Montauk Highway and Broadway Avenue, Sayville

These circa 1800 barns were moved from the Ockers homestead on Montauk Highway in Oakdale. Of interest is the mortise and tenon joint method of construction in which wooden dowels were used instead of costly nails. Indeed, nails were so expensive at this time that it was not uncommon for people to burn down their barns and sift through the ashes to recover the precious nails.

American Farm Windmill
(part of the Islip Grange Restoration Complex)
Montauk Highway and Broadway Avenue, Sayville

This circa 1895 farm windmill was used by the Powell family on their estate located on Handsome Street and Greene Avenue near the Great South Bay in Sayville. Before being donated to the Grange Restoration, it was used on the Udell farm located on the west side of Johnson Avenue near Veterans' Memorial Highway in Bohemia. Of particular interest are the two metal sails displayed with the windmill which contrast with the wooden sails found on windmills further east on the Island.

Roosevelt County Park – John Ellis Roosevelt Estate – Meadow Croft
Middle Road, Sayville
(631) 472-4625

From the war memorial located at the intersection of Route 27A/Montauk Highway and Collins Avenue in Sayville bear right onto South Main Street; go .4 mile. The entrance is on the left (north) side of the road.

132

The sixty-five-acre John Ellis Roosevelt estate Meadow Croft is located in the Roosevelt County Park section of Sans Souci Lakes County Nature Preserve. John Ellis Roosevelt (1853–1939), a successful Manhattan investment banker, was a cousin and legal advisor to President Theodore Roosevelt. In 1891 he commissioned Isaac Henry Green II to design the main building for the estate. Green, a noted Beaux-Arts architect from Sayville, also designed many other buildings on Long Island's South Shore including the Hard estate in West Sayville, Saint Ann's Episcopal Church in Sayville, the parish house of Saint Mark's Episcopal Church in Islip, the Maidstone Club in East Hampton, and some of the outbuildings on the Bourne estate in Oakdale.

Meadow Croft is a fine example of Colonial Revival-style architecture. The Gold Coast estate and summerhouse has been restored through the cooperative efforts of Suffolk County, the Sayville Historical Society, and the Bayport Heritage Association. It was placed on the National Register of Historic Places in 1987.

(See also Town of East Hampton/Montauk/The Third House; Town of Oyster Bay/Oyster Bay/Christ Episcopal Church; Town of Oyster Bay/Oyster Bay/First Presbyterian Church; Town of Oyster Bay/Oyster Bay/Young's Memorial Cemetery/ Grave of Theodore Roosevelt; and Town of Oyster Bay/Cove Neck/Sagamore Hill National Historic Site–Theodore Roosevelt Estate–Sagamore Hill.)

Saint Ann's Episcopal Church
257 South Main Street, Sayville
(631) 589-6522

From the war memorial located at the intersection of Route 27A/Montauk Highway and Collins Avenue in Sayville bear right onto South Main Street; go .3 mile. The church is on the left (north) side of the road.

To reach the graves of Teddy Roosevelt's cousins, go fifty feet beyond the church's parking lot to the third dirt carriage road. The Roosevelts' graves are in front marked by a large stone cross. To reach the grave of General Philippe Regis Denis de Keredern de Trobriand, turn left (west) onto the third dirt carriage road; go .1 mile. The grave is on the right side of the carriage road marked by a dark gray marble gravestone which is positioned horizontally.

Saint Barnabas Chapel was the original name of this parish and it was a mission of Saint John's Episcopal Church in Oakdale until 1874 when it became Saint Ann's Episcopal Church. Supposedly the name choice was a personal request of John R. Suydam Sr. in honor of his wife Ann Middleton Lawrence Suydam. (See also Town of Islip/Oakdale/Saint John's Episcopal Church.) This lovely stone church, built in 1887, was donated by Helen Suydam Cutting (Mrs. Robert Fulton Cutting) and her brother Walter L. Suydam, replacing the 1866 mission on land initially presented by their father. The original building was pivoted around to the east and attached at the back of the present building.

Designed by the architect Isaac Henry Green II, who is buried in the cemetery behind, the church incorporates the apse aspect of early Roman basilicas. It is in the apse of this church that one finds a series of seven windows executed by Louis Comfort Tiffany between 1888 and 1892 before the actual formation of Tiffany Studios but documented in the surviving records of Tiffany Studios. Since these were made during his early period it is not unusual that there is no drapery glass or fractured glass. Some plating effects and fine mottled glass, especially in the velvet-like texture of the gold robes of the three figures, are apparent. The center window features a haloed Christ in red robes with hands outstretched at waist level. The glass used to make these red robes is very unusual. In most figure windows Tiffany used drapery glass but here the glass has been extensively scored. Characteristic lilies are at his right. This panel is flanked by two windows picturing adoring angels; the one on the left holds a lily while the angel on the right holds an incense burner. The latter is particularly notable for the quality of the stained-glass imagery wherein the smoke from the burning incense seems to rise and drift into the heavens, symbolizing prayers ascending to God. These center windows have an unusual purity with considerable painting of very fine quality.

To the right and left of these three central windows are four lily windows, two on each side, picturing the flowers entwined around a cross. These are elegantly beautiful windows albeit identical. They are further trimmed with bright blue, red, and gold glass jewels in heavy lead settings, so typical of the early period of Tiffany designs.

Over the south entrance is a pebble cluster round window, historically referred to as a rose or petal window, whether it has petals or not. Composed primarily of red, gold, and brown glass jewels, it is strikingly bordered with blue and gold glass jewels. Pure gold between the plating layers gives this a glorious quality. Although unsigned, it is most probably of Tiffany design. Few of this style remain, yet this lovely one and a trefoil pebble cluster window of similar style in Saint Mark's Episcopal Church in Islip are within a few minutes drive of each other. (See also Town of Islip/Islip/Saint Mark's Episcopal Church.)

In the narthex are two small hemisphere windows with rondures of bull's eye or crown glass. Although not documented by the parish or in Tiffany Studios' records, we strongly suspect that these too are decoratives from Tiffany Studios. There is evidence that the windows now in place in the nave of the church, made by Lamb Studios, replaced windows of this poorer quality which were often installed just "to fill the opening" until better quality windows could be financed.

The bronze Prescott Memorial plaque on the east wall also was executed by Tiffany and is signed "TIFFANY GLASS AND DECORATING COMPANY." It features a dove with decorations. Next to it is a lovely memorial to Edith Corse Evans who was "Lost at Sea in SS *Titanic* April 15, 1912." It is a haunting reminder of the ripple effect of life and death all the more ironic when you consider that Louis Comfort Tiffany was supposed to have sailed on the ill-fated maiden voyage of the *Titanic*.

The church itself is quite beautiful with a beamed and wainscotted ceiling and lower wall wainscotting divided from the cool white wall by a chair rail. Fine brass appointments including the altar rail, the lectern decorated with an eagle, candlesticks, vases, and the cross set this church apart.

Behind the church is the parish cemetery where the names of many Sayville and other South Shore families are quickly recognized. Members of the Suydam family are buried here. Of special interest are the graves of three of Teddy Roosevelt's cousins and that of General Philippe Regis Denis de Keredern de Trobriand (1816–1897), who was born in Tours, France, and died in Bayport, Long Island. Trobriand and Lafayette are said to be the only two Frenchmen to attain such high rank in the United States Army. (See also Town of Islip/Sayville/Sayville Historical Society Complex.)

For information on other sites in the area with Tiffany stained-glass windows see Town of Islip/Great River/Bayard Cutting Arboretum–William Bayard Cutting Estate–Westbrook; Town of Islip/Great River/Emmanuel Episcopal Church; and Town of Islip/Islip/St. Mark's Episcopal Church. All are open to the public.

Sayville Historical Society Complex
43 Edwards Street, Sayville
(631) 563-0186

From the war memorial located at the intersection of Route 27A/Montauk Highway and Collins Avenue in Sayville turn right (south) onto Collins Avenue; go .3 mile. The historic complex is on the left (east) side of the road facing Edwards Street.

In 1761, while returning home from the French and Indian War, John Edwards passed through what is now known today as Sayville. He was so enchanted with the area that he immediately moved his family there from East Hampton. In the same year he built the first house in Sayville which remained standing until 1913 when it was destroyed by a fire. In 1785 his son Matthew built a house on the corner of Gillette Avenue and Edwards Street. In 1838 it was moved by Matthew's son James to its present site on Edwards Street. It was occupied by seven generations of the Edwards family before Clarissa Edwards donated it to the Sayville Historical Society. Completely restored, it is furnished in period furniture and has large collections of antique lamps, ice skates, toys, and dolls. There is also a reference library available for research on local history.

The complex includes the Edwards' Homestead, a museum, and a gift shop. In a barn that was originally on the former Budenos dairy farm, which was located on Broadway Avenue in Sayville, the society has established a museum next to the Homestead. It contains collections of shells, ink wells, miniature shoes, bottles, jars, memorabilia, and military uniforms. Of special interest is the Civil War uniform of General Philippe Regis Denis de Keredern de Trobriand, the only Frenchman other than Lafayette to attain this high rank in the American Army. (See also Town of Islip/Sayville/Saint Ann's Episcopal Church.)

WEST BAY SHORE

Gardiner's County Park

Route 27A/Montauk Highway, West Bay Shore
(631) 854-4949

Suffolk County Resident Pass is required for admission.

Take the Long Island Expressway to Exit #53 south (Sagtikos Parkway/Fire Island). Go south for 4 miles on Sagtikos Parkway to Southern State Parkway. Go west on Southern State Parkway for 1 mile to Exit #40 south (Robert Moses Causeway). Take Robert Moses Causeway south for 3.2 miles to Exit #RM2 east (Route 27A/Montauk Highway/Bay Shore). Go east on Route 27A/Montauk Highway for .8 mile. The park is on the right (south) side of the road opposite Sagtikos Manor.

The land that this 231-acre park encompasses was originally owned by the Gardiner family and later became part of their estate, Sagtikos Manor. The park consists of grass fields, inland woods, and a marsh. It offers nature trails, an environmental center, and guided nature walks. Restrooms are available.

Sagtikos Manor

Montauk Highway, West Bay Shore
(631) 854-0939

Take the Long Island Expressway to Exit #53 south (Sagtikos Parkway/Fire Island). Go south for 4 miles on Sagtikos Parkway to Southern State Parkway. Go west on Southern State Parkway for 1 mile to Exit #40 south (Robert Moses Causeway). Take Robert Moses Causeway south for 3.2 miles to Exit #RM2 east (Route 27A/ Montauk Highway/Bay Shore). Go east on Route 27A/Montauk Highway for .8 mile. The Manor is on the left (north) side of the road opposite Gardiner's County Park.

In 1692 Stephanus Van Cortlandt purchased from the Secatogue Indians 1,200 acres of land which extended from the Great South Bay northward to the middle of the Island. He received a manorial grant for the land in 1697 and built his manor house the same year naming it *Sagtikos* which is an Indian word meaning "snake that hisses." In 1707 Van Cortlandt's heirs sold the manor along with its extensive lands to Timothy Carle (Carll), a wealthy Huntington farmer. In 1758 the manor was purchased for £1,200 by Jonathan Thompson of Setauket, a wealthy farmer and judge. (See also Town of Brookhaven/Setauket/Thompson House.) In 1772 Thompson gave the manor house along with 1,207 acres as a wedding gift to his son Isaac and his new bride Mary Gardiner of East Hampton. The manor house remained in the Thompson/Gardiner family from 1758 until 2002, when it was purchased by Suffolk County from Robert David Lion Gardiner, the sixteenth and last Lord of the Manor. The manor has been on the National Register of Historic Places since 1976. (See also Town of East Hampton/East Hampton/Old Cemetery/

Grave of Lion Gardner.) During the Revolutionary War British soldiers were frequently quartered on the manor grounds and many British officers stayed at the
house. The most distinguished of these was General Henry Clinton, who in 1778
ultimately became commander-in-chief of British forces in North America. After
the war the manor house was host to President George Washington during his
1790 tour of Long Island. Both the Clinton and the Washington rooms are furnished as they were when their respective guests visited.

The original manor house was added onto in the late nineteenth century. Both
the old section and the newer section are furnished with period furniture and
paintings. Of particular interest are the Washington and Clinton related furnishings and the Spanish upright "giraffe" piano. (See also Town of Southampton/Sag
Harbor/Sag Harbor Whaling and Historical Museum.)

On the ten remaining acres of the manor grounds are a family graveyard and a
formal garden.

Thorne Preserve
(Long Island Chapter: The Nature Conservancy)
Mariner's Lane, West Bay Shore
(631) 367-3225

Open with prior permission.

Take the Long Island Expressway to Exit #53 south (Sagtikos Parkway/Fire Island).
Go south 4 miles on Sagtikos Parkway to Southern State Parkway. Go west on
Southern State Parkway for 1 mile to Exit #40 south (Robert Moses Causeway).
Take Robert Moses Causeway south for 3.2 miles to Exit #RM2 east (Route 27A/
Montauk Highway). Go east on Route 27A/Montauk Highway for 1.5 miles to
the Admiralty Town House development. From the security gate turn left (east)
onto Admiral's Drive East; go .2 mile. Turn left onto Mariner's Lane, make a quick
right, and continue on Mariner's Lane to the end at the designated parking space.

This eighty-seven-acre preserve is located on the former Landon Ketchum
Thorne Sr. estate, Thorneham. It consists of sandy shore, salt marshes, meadows,
freshwater swamps, woodlands, streams, and thickets. The predominant vegetation
is cord grass. There is a profusion of both water and shorebirds.

Please call the Conservancy at the above telephone number to obtain prior permission to use the preserve. This is important since arrangements to go through
the security gate at the Admiralty Town House must be made in advance.

WEST SAYVILLE

Long Island Maritime Museum
Montauk Highway, West Sayville
(631) 854-4974

Take the Long Island Expressway to Exit #53 south (Sagtikos Parkway/Fire Island). Go south on Sagtikos Parkway for 4.1 miles; bear left (east) onto Southern State Parkway. Go east for 6.9 miles on Southern State Parkway to Exit #45 east (Route 27A/Montauk Highway). Go east on Route 27A/Montauk Highway. Stay in the right lane when it joins with Route 27/Sunrise Highway at 1.4 miles. Go .3 mile on Route 27/Sunrise Highway and make a right continuing on Route 27A/Montauk Highway. Go an additional 3.1 miles. The museum entrance is on the right (south) side of the road.

Located on the grounds of the West Sayville County Golf Course, the museum is dedicated to preserving the marine heritage of Suffolk County. In addition to changing displays of nautical artifacts there are permanent exhibits depicting relics from wrecked sailing ships, pirate gear found in the sand dunes of Southampton, an exhibit of the Bellport Life Saving Station, and photographs and models of ships built on Long Island. The outdoor pavilion has a collection of small boats typical of nineteenth-century Long Island. Moored at the dock is the oyster sloop *Priscilla,* which was built in 1888 in Patchogue and which still sails the Great South Bay as a mobile exhibit. Of particular interest are the restoration workshops and the annual vintage boat show.

Located on the grounds of the Long Island Maritime Museum, is the William Rudolph Oyster House. It has displays of oystering equipment, shells, and a photographic exhibit of Dutch immigrants.

West Sayville County Golf Course – Anson Wales Hard Jr. Estate – Meadow Edge
Montauk Highway, West Sayville
(631) 854-4949

Suffolk County Resident Pass is required for admission.

Take the Long Island Expressway to Exit #53 south (Sagtikos Parkway/Fire Island). Go south on Sagtikos Parkway for 4.1 miles; bear left (east) onto Southern State Parkway. Go east for 6.9 miles on Southern State Parkway to Exit #45 east (Route 27A/Montauk Highway). Go east on Route 27A/Montauk Highway. Stay in the right lane when it joins with Route 27/Sunrise Highway at 1.4 miles. Go .3 mile on Route 27/Sunrise Highway and make a right continuing on Route 27A/Montauk Highway. Go an additional 3.1 miles. The entrance is on the right (south) side of the road.

This 250-acre, eighteen-hole, par-seventy-two golf course was formerly the estate of Anson Wales Hard Jr., the son-in-law of Frederick Gilbert Bourne. (See also Town of Islip/Oakdale/Frederick Gilbert Bourne Estate–Indian Neck Hall). With fairways extending from both sides of the entrance to protected wetlands, this is truly an idyllic setting. The club offers tennis courts, a game room, locker rooms, P.G.A.-staffed pro shop, a putting green, a driving range, and both hand and electric golf cart rentals. There is a lounge, bar, and restaurant in the former Hard mansion. These facilities are also available for catered affairs.

Also located on the grounds is the Long Island Maritime Museum, dedicated to preserving the county's marine heritage. (See also Town of Islip/West Sayville/Long Island Maritime Museum.)

TOWN OF RIVERHEAD

TOWN OF RIVERHEAD

PARKS AND PRESERVES

Federal Parks and Preserves
none

State Parks and Preserves
Jamesport State Park (530 acres), Jamesport *(undeveloped)*
Otis Pike Preserve and Peconic Headwaters Natural Resources Management Area
    (4,500 acres), Calverton *(undeveloped)*
Wildwood State Park (769 acres), Wading River

County Parks and Preserves
David Sarnoff Pine Barrens Preserve (2,700 acres), Riverhead *(undeveloped)*
Indian Island County Golf Course (157 acres), Aquebogue
Indian Island County Park (287 acres), Aquebogue

Long Island Chapter: The Nature Conservancy
Reppa Pond Preserve (6 acres), Wading River
Wading River Marsh Preserve (96 acres), Wading River

Arboretums and Gardens

Aquebogue

Indian Island County Golf Course
Cross River Drive, Aquebogue
(631) 852-3233

Take the Long Island Expressway to Exit #73. Go east on Route 25/Main Road for 4.4 miles to County Road 105/Cross River Drive. Turn right (south) onto County Road 105; go 1.5 miles to Indian Island Golf Course exit. Turn left (east) into the park entrance.

Opened in 1972, this 157-acre, eighteen-hole, par-seventy-two golf course features a driving range, a practice putting green, locker rooms, a pro shop, and electric and pull cart rentals. There is a dining room, a lounge, and a bar in the clubhouse.

Indian Island County Park
Hubbard Avenue, Aquebogue
(631) 852-3233

Suffolk County Resident Pass is required for admission.

Take the Long Island Expressway to Exit #73. Go east on Route 25/Main Road for 4.4 miles to County Road 105/Cross River Drive. Turn right (south) onto County Road 105; go .8 mile to Indian Island County Park exit. Go 50 yards; turn left (east). The entrance to the park will be in front of you.

There are one hundred year-round general campsites, fifty group sites, bike hostel facilities, and an organized youth group camping site for one hundred people at this 287-acre park. Water and sanitary facilities are conveniently located nearby. Additionally, the park offers picnicking, nature trails, bird watching, and horseback riding (although, no horse rentals). There is also a zoo containing some seventy-five small animals. Facilities have been provided for people with disabilities.

Calverton

Skydive Long Island
4062 Grumman Boulevard, Calverton
(631) 208-3900

Take the Long Island Expressway to Exit #69 north (Wading River Road/Wading River). Go north on Wading River Road for 2.8 miles to Grumman Blvd. Turn right (east) onto Grumman Blvd.; go 1.5 miles. There is a blue and white Skydrive sign with an arrow. On the left side there is a guard booth. Once inside the property follow the blue and white signs to the Skydive facility.

Open to both the novice and experienced, Skydive Long Island was established in 1986. A full service skydiving drop zone, it is the only student training facility of its kind on Long Island.

(See also Town of Southampton/Westhampton Beach/Sky Sailors Glider Flights.)

Splish Splash
2549 Splish Splash Drive, Calverton
(631) 727-3600

Take the Long Island Expressway to Exit #72 west (Riverhead/Calverton). From the west ramp, turn left at the first traffic light onto Splish Splash Drive.

Located on ninety-six acres, Splish Splash was voted one of the top five water parks in the country by the Travel Channel and number one in the Tri-State area. Included are over twenty water features for children and adults.

NORTHVILLE

Hallockville Museum Farm Restoration
6038 Sound Avenue, Northville
(631) 298-5292

Proceeding east on Route 25/Main Road into Mattituck make an extremely sharp left onto Sound Avenue/Truck Route 25; go 1 mile. Turn left (west) continuing on Truck Route 25. When Truck Route 25 turns, you continue straight on Sound Avenue for 2.1 miles. The restoration is on the right (north) side of road.

This group of historic buildings, which is owned by Suffolk County, consists of eight farmhouses, five barns, and related structures. All of the eighteenth- and nineteenth-century homes, with the exception of the circa 1765 Zachariah Hallock home, were built by the sons and grandsons of Captain Zachariah Hallock. The unique feature of this restoration is that each building is on its original site. The museum presents a profile of Long Island agrarian lifestyles from the eighteenth to the twentieth century. The Hallock Homestead has been on the National Register of Historic Places since 1984.

RIVERHEAD

Atlantis Marine World Aquarium
431 East Main Street, Riverhead
(631) 208-9200

Take the Long Island Expressway to Exit #72 (Riverhead/Calverton). Go east on Route 25 into Riverhead. The aquarium is located in the center of Riverhead's business district.

The aquarium features over one hundred exhibits. Included are thirteen fresh and saltwater tanks with sharks, sting rays, and tropical fish. It is one of the few facilities of its kind where guests may swim in a shark tank or snorkel with sting rays.

Dinosaur Walk Museum
221 East Main Street, Riverhead
(631) 369-6556

Take the Long Island Expressway to Exit #72 (Riverhead/Calverton). Go east on Route 25 into Riverhead. The museum is located in the center of Riverhead's business district.

Designed to dispel the ferocious image of dinosaurs portrayed in motion pictures, the Dinosaur Walk Museum has over fifty life-sized exhibits of prehistoric animals. Also featured are a puzzle station, a coloring station, and a fossil dig for children, a video center, and a gift shop.

The Fauna Society Serpentarium at Riverhead
213 East Main Street, Riverhead
(631) 722-5488

Take the Long Island Expressway to Exit #72 (Riverhead/Calverton). Go east on Route 25 into Riverhead. The Serpentarium is located in the center of Riverhead's business district.

Featured are over two hundred reptiles in seventy live exhibits. Included are snakes, alligators, frogs, turtles, and lizards.

Fresh Pond Schoolhouse
133 East Main Street, Riverhead
(631) 727-0407

Take the Long Island Expressway east to Exit #72 (Riverhead/Calverton). Go east on Route 25 for 3.4 miles to Peconic Avenue. Turn right onto Peconic Avenue; go .1 mile. Turn left into the municipal parking lot. Go through parking lot for .2 mile. The schoolhouse is on the left.

This circa 1822 one-room schoolhouse was moved to its present location from Baiting Hollow. Furnished in period furniture, it demonstrates the educational atmosphere of an earlier time.

Long Island Science Center
11 East Main Street, Riverhead
(631) 208-8000

Take the Long Island Expressway to Exit #72 (Riverhead/Calverton). Go east on Route 25 into Riverhead. The museum is located in the center of Riverhead's business district at the intersection of West Main Street and Peconic Avenue.

The center is a children's hands-on, interactive science and technology museum. Featured are diverse exhibits on such subjects as magnets, electricity, structural engineering, archaeology, rain forests, butterflies, and wireless communication.

An intern program provides experience with the design and creation of interactive exhibits and working with the public.

Polish Festival
Polish Town, Riverhead

Take the Long Island Expressway to Exit #72 (Riverhead/Calverton). Go east on Route 25 for 2.9 miles. Turn left onto Marcy Avenue. Go .1 mile to Pulaski Street and the center of Polish Town.

Once a year during the summer months Polish Town, a small neighborhood community located in Riverhead, has a Polish festival. The festival starts with a mass in Polish at St. Isidore's Church named for the patron saint of farmers. After mass the congregation goes outside to witness the *Hejnal,* a re-enactment of the thirteenth-century invasion of Poland by the Tartars. Later, there is a fully costumed eighteenth-century peasant wedding, as well as polka contests. Throughout the two-day festival, visitors are able to purchase handicrafts, foods, and imported Polish goods from the 150 booths located at the festival site. Check a local newspaper for the dates and times of the festival as this is an ideal time to visit Polish Town with its brightly adorned buildings and unique street signs decorated with the Polish eagle.

(See also Town of North Hempstead/Port Washington/The Polish Museum.)

Railroad Museum of Long Island
416 Griffin Avenue, Riverhead
(631) 727-7920

Take the Long Island Expressway to Exit #72 (Riverhead/Calverton). Go east on Route 25 into Riverhead. The museum is located in the center of Riverhead's business district.

Established in 1990, the museum site is a former lumberyard opposite the village's Long Island Rail Road station. Featured are three steam locomotives, a diesel locomotive, the first Long Island Rail Road all-aluminum, double-decker passenger car, baggage cars, and a post office car. A ride on a mini-train from the 1964–1965 New York World's Fair is also available. Unfortunately accessibility for people with disabilities into the exhibits is limited.

The indoor museum has photographs and memorabilia related to railroading, and a gift shop.

This site functions as the restoration facility for the museum's rolling stock. Its Greenport facility, located in a former Long Island Rail Road freight house, has changing exhibits of railroad artifacts.

(See also Town of Southold/Greenport/Railroad Museum of Long Island.)

Riverhead Raceway
Old Country Road, Riverhead
(631) 727-0010

Take the Long Island Expressway to Exit #73 (Old Country Road). Go east on Old Country Road/County Road #58 for .6 mile. The track is on the right (south) side of the road.

This quarter-mile track offers NASCAR, modified, street stocks, Charger division, Blunderbust division, and drag races as well as demolition derbies.

(See also Town of Southampton/Westhampton/Westhampton Raceway.)

Suffolk County Historical Society Museum
300 West Main Street, Riverhead
(631) 727-2881

Take the Long Island Expressway to Exit #72 (Riverhead/Calverton). Go east on Route 25 for 3.1 miles. The museum is on the left side of the road.

The museum portrays the entire three hundred years of Suffolk County history. To be found are furniture, gun, model, decoy, scrimshaw, and china collections as well as a fully equipped blacksmith's shop. One of the museum's more unusual items is the dog or sheep treadmill used to generate power. Of special interest is the early Stars and Stripes Continental flag of John Hulbert, which he carried as part of the Bridgehampton contingent at the Battle of Ticonderoga.

The Weathervane gift shop, located on the lower level, offers a large selection of genealogical and Long Island-related books as well as gifts. An extensive genealogical library, concentrating on the ancestry of early Long Island families, can be found on the main floor of the museum.

Whale Watching
428 East Main Street, Riverhead
(631) 369-9840

Take the Long Island Expressway to Exit #72 (Riverhead/Calverton). Go east on Route 25 into Riverhead. The foundation is located in the center of Riverhead's business district.

The Okeanos Foundation has created a marine mammal program to aid stranded, sick, or injured animals. It has also established study programs which are available to schools, environmental organizations, and interested groups. The study programs consist of a combination of lectures, field trips, slide presentations, and a cruise on its seventy-two-foot boat the *Finback II*. The purpose of these cruises, which incidentally are open to the general public, is to chart the behavior, population, and distribution of marine mammals and to aid in their conservation.

If you want a truly enjoyable experience watching whales frolic in the ocean, make a reservation, pack a lunch, bring your camera, and join the crew of the *Finback II*.

Wading River

Reppa Pond Preserve
(Long Island Chapter: The Nature Conservancy)
Sound Avenue, Wading River
(631) 367-3225

Open with prior permission.

Take the Long Island Expressway to Exit #69 north (Wading River Road/Wading River). Go north on Wading River Road/Wading River Manor Road for a total of 7 miles. About .4 mile after the road crosses Route 25A it feeds onto North Country Road which leads into the center of the village. Turn right (north) onto Sound Avenue (the one in town); continue for .4 mile. The pond is on the right side of the road.

This six-acre pond and woodland preserve was donated by Gertrude K. Reppa. The freshwater pond is surrounded by red maples, willows, sweet pepperbushes, water hemlocks, and rare bee balms. The swampy areas sustain a variety of reptiles, amphibians, and birdlife.

Please call the Conservancy at the above telephone number for permission prior to visit.

Wading River Historical Society
North Country Road, Wading River
(631) 929-4082

The society's headquarters are located near the center of the village of Wading River on North Country Road .1 mile north of Sound Avenue.

The house was built by Able Raynor in 1826 and is believed to have once stood on the hill behind its present location. It is furnished in period furniture and contains the society's collections of antique clothing, paintings, and craft items.

Wading River Marsh Preserve
(Long Island Chapter: The Nature Conservancy)
Sound Avenue, Wading River
(631) 367-3225

Open with prior permission.

Take the Long Island Expressway to Exit #69 north (Wading River Road/Wading River). Go north on Wading River Road/Wading River Manor Road for a total of 7 miles. About .4 mile after the road crosses Route 25A it feeds onto North Country Road which leads into the center of the village. Turn right (north) onto Sound Avenue (the one in town); continue for .8 mile. The entrance to the preserve is a trail on the right side of a driveway on the left side of the road. For parking instructions please call the Conservancy at the above telephone number.

This ninety-six-acre tidal marsh preserve tends to flood during abnormally high tides and storms. Archeological excavations have determined that in 3,000 B.C. Indians hunted, gathered shellfish, and harvested nuts in this area. Colonists were attracted to the area by good farm land, an abundant supply of salt hay, and a stream capable of powering a grist mill.

Today the preserve hosts over one hundred different species of birds and an untold number of marine species.

Please call the Conservancy at the telephone number above for permission prior to visit.

Wildwood State Park – Robin/Wagg/Meyer Estate
Hulse Landing Road, Wading River
(631) 929-4314

Take the Long Island Expressway to Exit #69 north (Wading River Road/Wading River). Go north on Wading River Road/Wading River Manor Road for 6 miles to Route 25A (Be careful not to turn at Route 25). Turn right (east) onto Route 25A; go 1.1 miles to Sound Avenue. Angle left onto Sound Avenue; go 1.1 miles to Hulse Landing Road. Go .9 mile on Hulse Landing Road, bearing right at fork to park entrance.

Located on the former Robin/Wagg/Meyer estate this 769-acre park offers tent and trailer campsites, picnic areas, swimming, hiking, fishing, and athletic fields. Showers, restrooms, and food stands have been provided. Cross-country skiing is permitted in the winter.

TOWN OF SHELTER ISLAND

TOWN OF SHELTER ISLAND

PARKS AND PRESERVES

Federal Parks and Preserves
none

State Parks and Preserves
none

County Parks and Preserves
none

South Fork – Shelter Island Chapter: The Nature Conservancy
Mashomack Preserve (2,039 acres), Shelter Island

Arboretums and Gardens

Shelter Island

Cemetery and Monument to Quaker Martyrs
Route 114, Shelter Island

From the south ferry go north for 2.8 miles on Route 114 to the intersection of Manwaring Road and Route 114 (opposite the white entrance gates to Sylvester Manor). Turn left, continuing on Route 114. Go .3 mile on Route 114 to a dirt road on the right side of the road. (Entrance columns read "Sylvester Manor.") Proceed on the dirt road, bearing left, for .2 mile to the cemetery and monument.

The monument is located on what was once part of Sylvester Manor. Nathaniel Sylvester and his wife Grissel, who were fleeing Cromwellian England, arrived at Shelter Island in 1652 and were among the first Friends to arrive in America. Sylvester, the first resident owner on Shelter Island, prospered as a sugar merchant in the Barbados trade. He built his manor house and became noted for sheltering Friends seeking refuge from the Puritan Court of Massachusetts. Among the visitors at the manor was George Fox, the founder of the Quakers. The monument was dedicated by John Greenleaf Whittier, a Friend, in 1884 to the memory of Nathaniel Sylvester and the last four Friends to be executed on the Boston Common: Mary Dyer, William Robinson, Marmaduke Stevenson, and William Leddra. Located to the right of the monument is a small clearing in the woods used for quiet meditation and meetings.

(See also Town of Huntington/Lloyd Harbor/Henry Lloyd Manor; Town of North Hempstead/Manhasset/Manhasset Friends Meeting House; Town of Oyster Bay/Jericho/Jericho Friends Meeting House; Town of Oyster Bay/Matinecock/Matinecock Friends Meeting House; Town of Oyster Bay/Mill Neck/Underhill Burying Ground/ Grave of Captain John Underhill; Town of Oyster Bay/Oyster Bay/Council Rock; Town of Shelter Island/Shelter Island/Shelter Island Windmill; Town of Southampton/Sag Harbor/Custom House; and Town of Southold/Southold/Whitaker Historical Collection–Southold Free Library.)

Chapel in the Grove (Union Chapel)
Wesley Street, Shelter Island

From the south ferry go north on Route 114 for 4.2 miles to Grand Avenue. Turn left onto Grand Avenue; go .2 mile. Turn right onto Wesley Street; go .1 mile. The church is on the left side of the road.

In 1871 a group of Methodists from Brooklyn purchased three hundred acres on Shelter Island for the establishment of a Christian summer camp. The camp drew thousands of people who arrived by day steamer from New England and by special trains from Brooklyn and New York City. The chapel, Shelter Island's oldest public building, was built in 1875 and has been on the National Register of Historic Places since 1984. Of particular interest are two marine mosaic windows made of translucent stones, beach glass, and seashells by a local artist, Walter Cole Brigham.

(See also Town of Shelter Island/Shelter Island/Saint Mary's Episcopal Church and Town of Southampton/Southampton/Saint Andrew's Dune Church.)

Havens House
16 South Ferry Road/Route 114, Shelter Island
(631) 749-0025

From the south ferry go north on Route 114 for 1.7 miles. The house is on the left (west) side of the road.

This circa 1700 house was the home of James Havens, a member of the Provincial Congress. In subsequent years it has been used as a post office and general store by the Havens family who maintained ownership until 1925. Now the home of the Shelter Island Historical Society and the local chapter of the DAR, it is furnished with nineteenth-century furnishings. On display are collections of dolls, quilts, fans, clothes, and local memorabilia. Parts of the original construction have been left exposed for inspection.

Mashomack Preserve
(South Fork Shelter Island Chapter: The Nature Conservancy)
Route 114, Shelter Island
(631) 749-1001

From the south ferry go north for .9 mile on Route 114. The preserve is on the right (east) side of the road.

The preserve consists of 2,039 acres of salt marshes, freshwater ponds, oak woodlands, pine swamps, and interlacing tidal creeks. This variety of habitats hosts numerous wildlife such as ruby-throated hummingbirds, muskrats, foxes, deer mice, harbor seals, terrapins, cedar waxwings, woodpeckers, towhees, catbirds, warblers, owls, hawks, red-wing blackbirds, ospreys, great blue herons, glossy ibis, black skimmers, and herons. The trails are marked by gold arrows and maps are available in the trail house just beyond the parking area.

Tour reservations, group visits, and motorized tours for people with disabilities may be arranged by telephoning the preserve office at the above number. No special arrangements must be made by individuals wishing to visit this preserve.

Saint Mary's Episcopal Church
Saint Mary's Road, Shelter Island
(631) 749-0770

From the south ferry go north on Route 114 for 2.8 miles to Manwaring Road. Turn right onto Manwaring Road; go .4 mile. Turn right onto Saint Mary's Road; go .2 mile. The church is on the left side of the road.

The original church was erected in 1873 on land donated by Dr. Samuel M. Nicoll. For twenty-five years the church was served by visiting Episcopalian ministers. In 1883 the congregation was formally incorporated and in 1887 the rectory was built. During a violent storm in 1892 the church's steeple was struck by lightning causing the entire structure to burn to the ground. The rectory, only forty feet away, was saved by covering the roof with wet carpeting. Shortly after the fire the present building was erected and additional land was donated by the Nicoll family for a cemetery. Records indicate that the unsigned geometric patterned Nicoll Memorial windows were made by Tiffany. Also of interest is the Samuel Nicoll Memorial marine mosaic window made of translucent stones, beach glass, and seashells by the local artist Walter Cole Brigham.

(See also Town of Shelter Island/Shelter Island/Chapel in the Grove (Union Chapel) and Town of Southampton/Southampton/Saint Andrew's Dune Church.)

Shelter Island Windmill
Manwaring Road, Shelter Island

From the south ferry go north on Route 114 for 2.8 miles to Manwaring Road. Turn right onto Manwaring Road; go .2 mile. The windmill is on the left side of the road in the middle of a field.

This smock-type windmill was built in 1810 by Nathaniel Dominy V and was located at the western end of the village of Southold. In 1839 it was moved to Shelter Island and remained in operation until about 1879 when it was purchased by Lillian Horsford and retained as a landmark. The mill was used briefly from 1917–1918 to provide food for Shelter Island residents due to shortages caused by World War I. In 1926 the mill was moved to its present site on the grounds of historic Sylvester Manor. It has been on the National Register of Historic Places since 1978.

(See also Town of Huntington/Lloyd Harbor/Henry Lloyd Manor; Town of Shelter Island/Shelter Island/Cemetery and Monument to Quaker Martyrs; and Town of Southampton/Sag Harbor/Custom House.)

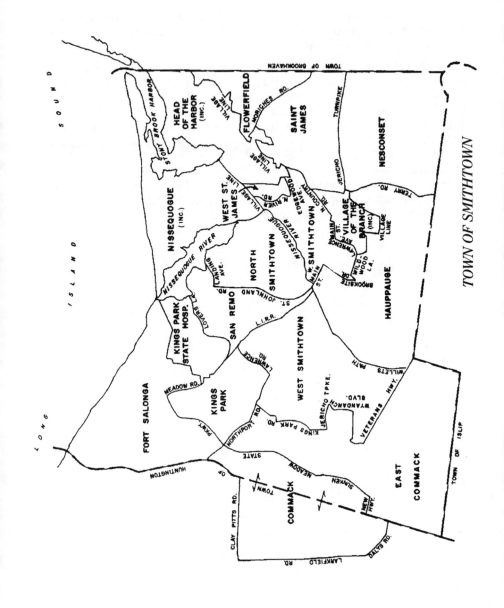

TOWN OF SMITHTOWN

TOWN OF SMITHTOWN

PARKS AND PRESERVES

Federal Parks and Preserves
none

State Parks and Preserves
Caleb Smith State Park (543 acres), Smithtown
Governor Alfred E. Smith/Sunken Meadow State Park (1,266 acres), Kings Park
Nissequogue River State Park (527 acres), Kings Park

County Parks and Preserves
Arthur Kunz County Park (97 acres), Smithtown *(undeveloped)*
Blydenburgh County Park (588 acres), Hauppauge/Smithtown
Lake Ronkonkoma County Park (98 acres), Lake Ronkonkoma *(undeveloped)*
Landing Avenue-Nissequogue River Park (97 acres), Nissequogue *(undeveloped)*
Nissequogue River County Wetlands Park (35 acres), Smithtown
Riverside Conservation Area and County Park (35 acres), Smithtown
Smithtown Greenbelt County Park (118 acres), Hauppauge/Smithtown
   (undeveloped)

Long Island Chapter: The Nature Conservancy
Butler–Huntington Woods (66 acres), Saint James
David Weld Sanctuary (114 acres), Nissequogue
East Farm Preserve (55 acres), Head of the Harbor
Vail Blydenburgh Sanctuary (27 acres), Nissequogue

Arboretums and Gardens

Commack

Hoyt Farm
New Highway, Commack
(631) 360-7644

Take the Long Island Expressway to Exit #56 north (Route 111/Smithtown/Islip). Go north on Route 111 for 1.3 miles. Turn left (west) onto Veterans' Memorial Highway/Route 454 (which merges with Route 347). Go 1.6 miles on Route 454/ Route 347 to New Highway. Turn left (south) onto New Highway; go 1.7 miles. The park is on the left (south) side of the road.

This 133-acre tract of land was donated by the Hoyt family to the Town of Smithtown. Approximately eighty-five percent of the land is dedicated to wildlife preservation and nature trails. The balance of the land has been developed as a sports and recreational area with ball fields and a covered picnic area. Restrooms are provided.

The farmhouse, a portion of which dates back to 1770, was built by John Wicks. The dining room and living room have been furnished in Federal period furniture and may be visited. The remaining rooms in the house are provided for the park ranger and his family and are closed to the public.

Hauppauge

Armed Forces Plaza
Veterans' Memorial Highway, Hauppauge

Take the Long Island Expressway to Exit #56 north (Route 111/Smithtown/Islip). Go north on Route 111 for 1.3 miles. Turn left (west) onto Veterans' Memorial Highway/Route 454 (which merges with Route 347). Go .6 mile. The memorial is on the left (south) side of the road.

The memorial is dedicated to those who served in World War II and the Korean Conflict.

The World War II monument is a granite map of the world with thirty-two bronze plaques listing the major conflicts in which American forces were involved.

The Korean Conflict is remembered with three bronze statues—a soldier, a map of Korea, and an armed forces nurse.

Blydenburgh County Park

Veterans' Memorial Highway, Hauppauge
(631) 854-3713

Suffolk County Resident Pass is required for admission.

Take the Long Island Expressway to Exit #56 north (Route 111/Smithtown/Islip). Go north on Route 111 for 1.3 miles. Turn left (west) onto Veterans' Memorial Highway/Route 454 (which merges with Route 347). Go a total of .9 mile. The park is on the right (north) side of the road.

This 588-acre park has forty general camping sites, ten organized youth group sites, and 250 trailer and tent sites. It has sanitary facilities but no hook ups. The park also has nature trails, bridle paths (but no horse rentals), dog and horse shows, bike hostels; and offers facilities for picnicking, hiking, rowboating with rowboat rentals, ice-skating (weather permitting), and freshwater fishing. In the Smithtown section of the park are the Mill House and New Mill which are presently being restored by Suffolk County. (See also Town of Smithtown/Smithtown/ The Mill House, Stump Pond, and New Mill.) The Explorer Scout Nature Museum is also found in this section of the park.

(See also Town of Smithtown/Smithtown/Explorer Scout Nature Museum.)

HEAD OF THE HARBOR

East Farm Preserve

(Long Island Chapter: The Nature Conservancy)
Shep Jones Lane, Head of the Harbor
(631) 367-3225

Open with prior permission.

From the village green located at the intersection of Route 25/Jericho Turnpike/Main Street and Route 111 in Smithtown (Village of the Branch) go north on Route 25A/North Country Road for 4.1 miles. Turn left (west) onto Shep Jones Lane; go .5 mile. The preserve is on the left (south) side of the road.

A large portion of this fifty-five-acre preserve was farmed as early as 1693 by the early settler Timothy Mills and later by tenant farmers. The preserve comprises one-quarter of the Mills Pond Historic District, which is listed on the National Register of Historic Places. Consisting of hedgerows, wet and dry woodlands, and fields, the preserve supports a wide variety of bird, small mammal, and amphibian life.

Please telephone the Conservancy at the above number to obtain permission to visit the preserve.

Mills Pond House
Route 25A, Head of the Harbor
(631) 862-6575

From the village green located at the intersection of Route 25/Jericho Turnpike/ Main Street and Route 111 in Smithtown (Village of the Branch) go north on Route 25A/North Country Road for 3.8 miles. Turn right (east) onto Mills Pond Road; go .1 mile. The entrance is on the right (south) side of the road.

In 1693 Timothy Mills of Jamaica purchased land from Adam Smith, the son of the patentee of Smithtown. Mills' original pre-1700 house was partially destroyed by fire. In 1838 William Wickham Mills rebuilt the house adding a three-story addition thus transforming it into the present Greek Revival-style house which has been on the National Register of Historic Places since 1973. The balustraded roof trim is more typical of the earlier Georgian-style architecture or of the later Renaissance Revival period than that of Greek Revival. The interior contains gold-veined black marble mantle pieces, ornamental plaster ceiling centers, and wooden Doric columns. Located on the grounds to the west of the house is the circa 1764 family cemetery.

The house is presently the home of the Smithtown Arts Council and is used as an art gallery with changing exhibits.

Stanford White Estate – Box Hill
580 Moriches Road, Head of the Harbor

Not open to the public.

From the village green located at the intersection of Route 25/Jericho Turnpike/ Main Street and Route 111 in Smithtown (Village of the Branch) go north on Route 25A/North Country Road for 2.7 miles. Turn left (west) onto Moriches Road; go 1.1 miles. The estate is located on the northeast corner of Moriches Road and Cordwood Path.

The noted architect Stanford White was born November 9, 1853, in Manhattan. He was educated as an architect at the University of New York and became the chief assistant to H. H. Richardson for the design and construction of Trinity Church in Boston. After further study in Europe, he became a partner in the firm of McKim, Mead, and White which specialized in Beaux-Arts style architecture and was one of the most prominent Beaux-Arts firms in America. Among its many designs were those of the original Madison Square Garden, the old Pennsylvania Station, the Washington Square Arch, the Herald Building, the Brooklyn Museum, the Pierpont Morgan Library, and many of Long Island's estates and churches. In addition, they designed the Vanderbilt mansion in Hyde Park, the Boston Public Library on Copley Square, the Rhode Island State Capitol Building in Providence, and the U.S. Army War College in Washington, DC; and remodeled the White House during the administration of Theodore Roosevelt, eliminating most of decorating elements previously installed by Louis C. Tiffany.

At the age of twenty-three White married the fifteen-year-old daughter of Judge John Lawrence Smith, a descendant of Richard "Bull" Smith, the patentee of Smithtown. One hundred acres of land in Head of the Harbor became the site of Box Hill, a two-and-a-half story summer retreat with pebble and stucco exterior built in 1872, which has been on the National Register of Historic Places since 1973. While dining at the elaborate roof garden in Madison Square Garden in 1906, White was shot by Harry K. Thaw, the cocaine-crazed, outraged husband of White's liaison Evelyn Nesbitt. White is buried in the small cemetery behind Saint James Episcopal Church. Box Hill is privately owned by one of White's thirty-four grandchildren.

(See also Town of Smithtown/Head of the Harbor/Stanford White House; Town of Smithtown/Saint James/Saint James Episcopal Church; and Town of Smithtown/ Village of the Branch/Judge J. Lawrence Smith House–The Homestead.)

Stanford White House
Harbor Road, Head of the Harbor

Not open to the public.

From the village green located at the intersection of Route 25/Jericho Turnpike/ Main Street and Route 111 in Smithtown (Village of the Branch) go north on Route 25A/North Country Road for 2.7 miles. Turn left (west) onto Moriches Road; go 1.1 miles. Turn right (north) onto Cordwood Path; go .7 mile, turning right (east) at a small park on the Nissequogue River onto Harbor Road. The house is on the right (south) side of the road.

Stanford White, the noted and flamboyant architect, designed and built this very interesting three-story frame house for his sister-in-law here at the northern end of his estate Box Hill. The house, which gives the appearance of being octagonal or crown-shaped, has an eastward extension and beautifully placed porches overlooking the Nissequogue River. It also has a rather fanciful widow's walk around the "crown." Unfortunately, the house can not be visited since it is privately owned.

(See also Town of Smithtown/Head of the Harbor/Stanford White Estate–Box Hill; Town of Smithtown/Saint James/Saint James Episcopal Church; and Town of Smithtown/Village of the Branch/Judge J. Lawrence Smith House–The Homestead.)

Stony Brook Grist Mill
Harbor Road and Main Street, Head of the Harbor
(631) 751-2244

From the village green located at the intersection of Route 25/Jericho Turnpike/ Main Street and Route 111 in Smithtown (Village of the Branch) go north on Route 25A/North Country Road for 5.1 miles to Main Street in Stony Brook. Continue north on Main Street for .3 mile. Turn left (west) onto Harbor Road; go .1 mile. The mill is on the right (north) side of the road.

Brookhaven gave Adam Smith, the son of Richard "Bull" Smith, two acres of land if he would build, maintain, and operate a mill at Stony Brook. (See also Town of Smithtown/Nissequogue/Grave of Richard Smythe/Richard "Bull" Smith.) Smith built Stony Brook's first mill at this location in 1699. Subsequent boundary changes have placed the mill in the Town of Smithtown, Village of Head of the Harbor. It remained in operation until it was destroyed by a flood in 1751. The present mill was built on the same site in 1751. The millstones, which are five feet in diameter and weigh nearly one ton, were shipped from France and are capable of grinding eight bushels of grain an hour. In 1885 Edward Kane, a German immigrant, bought the mill with its surrounding land and transformed it into a winery using the mill to press the grapes that he harvested from his land.

The mill, which is just inside the Town of Smithtown line, was purchased by Ward Melville who subsequently donated it to The Long Island Museum of American Art, History and Carriages at Stony Brook. It has been fully restored to an operating mill. Milling techniques are demonstrated by trained volunteers.

KINGS PARK

Governor Alfred E. Smith / Sunken Meadow State Park
Sunken Meadow Parkway, Kings Park
(631) 269-4333

Take the Long Island Expressway to Exit #53 north (Sagtikos Parkway/Sunken Meadow Parkway). Take Sagtikos Parkway north for 7.3 miles to the park entrance.

This 1,266-acre park has three nine-hole golf courses, picnic areas with barbecues, a bathhouse, restrooms, bike paths, food stands, a boardwalk, athletic fields, and playfields. Facilities are available for swimming in Long Island Sound, saltwater fishing, and hiking. Cross-country skiing is permitted in the winter.

Nissequogue River State Park
St. Johnland Road, Kings Park
(631) 269-4927

Take the Long Island Expressway to Exit #53 north (Sagtikos Parkway/Sunken Meadow Parkway). Go north on Sagtikos Parkway/Sunken Meadow Parkway to Exit #SM4. Go east on Pulaski Road (which becomes Old Dock Road). At the 5th traffic light turn right onto St. Johnland Road. Go .5 mile. The park is on the left side of the road.

This 527-acre park, located on a bluff at the mouth of the Nissequogue River, has outstanding views of the river and Long Island Sound. Primarily a New York State bird conservation area, it offers fishing, hiking, birding, soccer fields, environmental programs, and canoe, kayak, and bicycle rentals. In the winter, cross-country skiing is permitted.

NISSEQUOGUE

David Weld Sanctuary

(Long Island Chapter: The Nature Conservancy)
Boney Lane, Nissequogue
(631) 367-3225

Open with prior permission.

From the village green located at the intersection of Route 25/Jericho Turnpike/ Main Street and Route 111 in Smithtown (Village of the Branch) go north on Route 25A/North Country Road for 2.7 miles. Turn left (west) onto Moriches Road which becomes Horse Race Lane; go 3.2 miles. Turn right (east) onto Boney Lane; go .3 mile. The sanctuary is on the left (north) side of the road.

This 114-acre sanctuary consists of beach front, a hardwood forest, a kettlehole, a woodland swamp, and an overgrown field. It has a wide variety of shrubs, vines, ferns, wildflowers, and trees including the largest tulip tree, *Liriodendron tulip-ifera*, on Long Island.

Please call the Conservancy at the telephone number above to obtain permission to visit the sanctuary as you will need the combination to the gate to enter this Conservancy property.

Grave of Richard Smythe (Richard "Bull" Smith)

Moriches Road, Nissequogue

From the village green located at the intersection of Route 25/Jericho Turnpike/ Main Street and Route 111 in Smithtown (Village of the Branch) go north on Route 25A/North Country Road for 2.7 miles. Turn left (west) onto Moriches Road and go 2.7 miles. The grave is on the right (north) side of Moriches Road about 50 feet west of the intersection with Nissequogue River Road. Look for the cleared narrow path next to a residential driveway; follow the path to the grave site which is at the top of the hill and not visible from the road.

Among the graves in this circa 1680 cemetery are those of Richard "Bull" Smith, the patentee of Smithtown, who died on March 7, 1692, and other members of the family including that of Obadiah, Smith's fifth son who drowned in the Nissequogue River in 1680. (See also Town of Smithtown/Head of the Harbor/ Stony Brook Grist Mill; Town of Smithtown/San Remo/Obadiah Smith House; and Town of Smithtown/Smithtown/Statue of Smithtown Bull.) Also to be found are graves of the Floyds and Brewsters with whom the early Smiths intermarried. (See also Town of Brookhaven/East Setauket/Brewster House; Town of Brookhaven/ Mastic Beach/William Floyd Estate; Town of Brookhaven/Mastic Beach/Woodhull Cemetery/Grave of Nathaniel Woodhull; and Town of Brookhaven/Setauket/Patriot's Rock.) A particularly touching poem is on the grave of Elizabeth Smith, the only daughter of Daniel and Tabitha Smith, who died on March 4, 1789, at age nineteen.

> *Nor virtue, youth or piety could save*
> *The Parents future prospects from the grave*
> *Croped like a Rose before tis fully blown*
> *She ended Life not half her worth was known*

The cemetery site is maintained by the Town of Smithtown and the path leading to the cemetery was cleared by and is maintained by a local Boy Scout troop.

Vail–Blydenburgh Sanctuary
(Long Island Chapter: The Nature Conservancy)
Somerset Drive, Nissequogue
(631) 979-6344 (Environmental Centers of Setauket–Smithtown)
or (631) 367-3225 (The Conservancy)

Open with prior permission.

From the village green located at the intersection of Route 25/Jericho Turnpike/ Main Street and Route 111 in Smithtown (Village of the Branch) go west on Route 25/Jericho Turnpike/Main Street for .9 mile. Turn right (north) onto Edgewood Avenue; go .5 mile. Turn left (west) onto Landing Avenue; go .6 mile. Turn left (south) onto Eckernkamp Road; go .4 mile. Turn left (south) onto Everit Place; go .2 mile. Turn left (east) onto Somerset Drive. Park in the cul-de-sac.

This twenty-seven-acre sanctuary is managed jointly by the Environmental Centers of Setauket–Smithtown and the Long Island Chapter: The Nature Conservancy. It consists of 1,000 feet along the bank of the Nissequogue River, an open field, sloping woods, a marshy field, and one of the few freshwater marshes on Long Island. The woodland area consists of dogwood, black cherry, red maple, red cedar, birch, sassafras, and American chestnut trees. The freshwater marsh has phragmites, cattails, marsh marigolds, blue flag, and jewelweed.

Please call either the Conservancy or the environmental center at the above telephone numbers to obtain permission to use the sanctuary. Groups are asked to call at least ten days prior to their visits.

SAINT JAMES

Butler–Huntington Woods
(Long Island Chapter: The Nature Conservancy)
Fifty Acre Road, Saint James
(631) 367-3225

Open with prior permission.

From the village green located at the intersection of Route 25/Jericho Turnpike/Main Street and Route 111 in Smithtown (Village of the Branch) go north on Route 25A/North Country Road for 1.6 miles. Turn left (west) onto Edgewood Avenue; go .1 mile. Turn right (north) onto Fifty Acre Road; go .7 mile. The preserve is on the left (west) side of the road.

This sixty-six-acre preserve consists of dry woodlands. Mountain laurels, American, black, and red chestnuts, and oaks can be found. There is also an abundance of ferns and lichens making it an ideal place for botanical study of these species. Animal life abounds with towhees, wood pewees, wood thrushes, white-throated sparrows, juncos, chickadees, raccoons, opossums, woodchucks, red foxes, and gray squirrels.

Please telephone the Conservancy at the above telephone number to obtain permission to visit the preserve.

Deepwells Farm – Estate of William Jay Gaynor – Deepwells
Route 25A, Saint James
(631) 854-3719

From the village green located at the intersection of Route 25/Jericho Turnpike/Main Street and Route 111 in Smithtown (Village of the Branch) go north on Route 25A/North Country Road for 2.5 miles The house is on the left (west) side of the road.

The c. 1845 Greek Revival-style mansion was built by Joel Lewis Griffing Smith, a descendant of the town's founder Richard "Bull" Smith, as a wedding gift for his bride. The estate's property was designed to be a working farm. After its sale by Smith in 1851, the property went through several owners until it was purchased in 1909 by William Jay Gaynor.

Gaynor was a New York City politician who had served as a judge in the Second District of the New York Supreme Court (1893–1907) and as Mayor of New York City (1907–1913). The estate's name Deepwells is derived from the presence of two 125-foot wells that Gaynor had had drilled on the property. Seeking refuge from the pressures of office, Gaynor spent many enjoyable days basking in the peacefulness and solitude of his St. James farm.

In 1910, as he was boarding the liner *SS Kaiser Wilhelm der Grosse* at a Hoboken, NJ, pier, Gaynor was the victim of an assassination attempt. After a long, painful recovery at Deepwells, Gaynor succumbed in 1913 to complications from his wound. (One of his attending physicians was Dr. George David Stewart, whose estate Appin House was located in Great River, Long Island.) He was interred at Greenwood Cemetery in Brooklyn.

In 1924 Deepwells was purchased by attorney Winthrop Taylor. After his death in 1970, the farm experienced a steady decline until it was purchased in 1989 by Suffolk County.

The restoration, begun by the county in 1990, is now completed. The house, which is on the National Register of Historic Places, is furnished with historic pieces and is open to the public.

The estate often hosts special events. Check local newspapers for times and dates.

Saint James Episcopal Church

490 North Country Road/Route 25A, Saint James
(631) 584-5560

From the village green located at the intersection of Route 25/Jericho Turnpike/ Main Street and Route 111 in Smithtown (Village of the Branch) go north on Route 25A/North Country Road for 2.4 miles. The church is on the right (east) side of the road. To reach the cemetery, enter from parking lot on Northern Boulevard which is located on the south side of the church. Go .1 mile on the carriage road. The grave of Stanford White is on the left (north) side of the carriage road under a two-story pine tree.

The church, which is on the National Register of Historic Places, was built in 1853. Its tower and narthex were added between 1878 and 1879. Incorporated into the elegant simplicity of its interior are stained-glass windows of great beauty with examples of the stained-glass work of the two most important American artists in that field.

The only documented Tiffany window is the Miller Memorial window on the south wall signed "TIFFANY, NEW YORK." The robes in this *Good Shepherd,* a commonly executed theme by Louis Comfort Tiffany and Tiffany Studios, are of bright red drapery glass. A highlighting or cellar lighting effect, usually achieved by painting a thin layer of pure gold between the plating layers, has been used instead of a halo. A considerable amount of painting was used in this memorial window.

Also on the south wall, signed "TIFFANY STVDIOS, N.Y." is a bronze memorial plaque which is not documented in surviving Tiffany Studios' records. It is dedicated to "James Ely Miller, Captain 1st Reserve Aero Squadron U.S.A., Born March 24, 1883, Killed in combat in France March 9, 1918."

On the north wall the Minott Memorial window portrays an angel in lavenders, pinks, and pearl white opalescence with heavy drapery glass forming the angel's robes—especially the sleeves—very similar to the window called *The Annunciation* in Saint John's Episcopal Church in Cold Spring Harbor. (See also Town of Oyster Bay/Cold Spring Harbor/Saint John's Episcopal Church.) The wings are again formed in small sections as in the *Angel of Resurrection* in the same Cold Spring

166

Harbor church—again in shades of lavender, pink, and white. The same leaves and opalescence, almost a trademark of Tiffany, are seen. Fractured or confetti glass is used in the trees. An ornate Crown of Heaven with small glass jewels emerges from the clouds, each a single-plated, blue and pearl rounded, cloud-like section. This effect is similar to the dove emerging from the clouds in the Cold Spring Harbor *Annunciation*. The only painting on it is that of the face, hands, and arms of the angel. We would have suspected that this too was created by Tiffany Studios if it were not for the partially obliterated signature "Lederle–Geissler, New York." A search of available information on those employed by Tiffany does not reveal either name so it is impossible for us to speculate as to how they might have learned the very specialized techniques which they have employed so well in this window.

Several windows in this church were designed by Stanford White and executed by John LaFarge, who originally adapted glassmaking processes to the making of windows for which Tiffany eventually became famous. The Nicoll Clinch Memorial window, on the south wall, has architectural features. Dedicated to the memory of Bessie Smith White's brother James Clinch Smith, a lieutenant in the Third Cavalry, United States Army, who died on April 15, 1912, on board the *Titanic*. Architectural in style, it features a helmet, sword, and oak leaves, conveying both strength and the military theme. The helmet and sword are recessed while the grave marker comes coldly to the foreground. Also on the south wall, but at the back of the church, partially obscured by the choir loft, is the James and Ann T. Clinch Memorial, dedicated to the maternal grandparents of Mrs. White. Lovely red roses can be seen at the top if you peek under the choir loft; glass jewels were used by LaFarge in the border and considerable plating was used in the areas of dark blue to give depth of color. Although unsigned, both windows have been documented as works of John LaFarge.

The Frederick Barrett Memorial window, on the south wall at the back of the church and also partially obscured by the choir loft, bears the words from the 1861 J. B. Dykes hymn "O hear us when we cry to thee for those in peril on the sea." Christ and fishermen are pictured on a violently stormy sea in this dramatically exciting contemporary window executed in 1967. Additionally, a very contemporary, but pleasing, stained-glass window with a musical theme is in the chancel behind the organ.

Through the doorway on the south wall in the front of the church is the John Lawrence Smith and Sarah Nicoll [Clinch] Memorial window. The theme is the *Tree of Life* with lilies symbolizing the Resurrection. This theme was often used by Louis Tiffany, however the extensive internal plating suggests an artist other than Tiffany. The dark blues were frequently used by John LaFarge and compare favorably to that in the James and Ann T. Clinch Memorial on the north wall in this church, although it is not known if the Smith/Nicoll Memorial was indeed executed by LaFarge.

Located in the cemetery, behind the church, is the grave of Stanford White, the noted architect who was murdered in Manhattan. Judge J. Lawrence Smith, descendant of Richard "Bull" Smith, the patentee of Smithtown, and his wife Sarah Nicoll Clinch Smith are also buried here. They were the parents of Mrs. Stanford White. The cemetery is also on the National Register of Historic Places.

Some years ago, in preparation for restoration work, it was confirmed that the church had originally been painted pumpkin. The present color was chosen from the paint samples uncovered during the restoration research project and was considered more harmonious with its present-day surroundings

(See also Town of Smithtown/Head of the Harbor/Stanford White Estate–Box Hill; Town of Smithtown/Head of the Harbor/Stanford White House; and Town of Smithtown/Village of the Branch/Judge J. Lawrence Smith House–The Homestead.)

Saint James General Store

516 Moriches Road, Saint James
(631) 854-3740

From the village green located at the intersection of Route 25/Jericho Turnpike/Main Street and Route 111 in Smithtown (Village of the Branch) go north on Route 25A/North Country Road for 2.7 miles. Turn left (west) onto Moriches Road; go .2 mile. The store is on the right (north) side of the road.

This store, which is on the National Register of Historic Places, was built in 1857 and has been in continuous use as a general store. The names in the store's ledgers show such notable customers as the entertainers Lionel, Ethel, and John Barrymore, Virginia Lee, Joe Flynn, Lillian Russell, Buster Keaton, Myrna Loy, Irving Berlin, and Ruth Roman. Heavyweight boxing champion Jim Corbett also visited the store.

It is now owned by Suffolk County and features crockery, glassware, woodenware, groceries, dry goods, syrups, cheese, candy sticks, home baked goods, and a wonderful selection of dolls, books, and stuffed toys. It is truly a taste of early America.

Saint James Railroad Station

Lake Avenue, Saint James

From the village green located at the intersection of Route 25/Jericho Turnpike/Main Street and Route 111 in Smithtown (Village of the Branch) go north on Route 25A/North Country Road for 2.7 miles. Turn right (east) onto Moriches Road. Make another right immediately onto Lake Avenue; go .2 mile to the railroad station which is on the right (west) side of the road.

The station, which is listed on the National Register of Historic Places, has been fully restored by the Long Island Rail Road. It was built in 1873 and is a fine example of Victorian-style architecture. The gingerbread trim, however, is typical of the earlier Gothic Revival period.

(See also Town of Babylon/Lindenhurst/1901 Depot Restoration and Town of Southold/Greenport/Railroad Museum of Long Island.)

SAN REMO

Obadiah Smith House

Saint Johnland Road, San Remo
(631) 265-6768

*From the village green located at the intersection of Route 25/Jericho Turnpike/
Main Street and Route 111 in Smithtown (Village of the Branch) go west on Route
25/Jericho Turnpike/Main Street for 1.3 miles. Turn right (north) onto Route 25A/
Saint Johnland Road; go 3 miles. The house is on the right (east) side of the road.*

This circa 1725 house was built by Obadiah Smith, a grandson of Richard
Smith. (See also Town of Smithtown/Nissequogue/Grave of Richard Smythe
(Richard "Bull" Smith.) Of particular interest is the manner in which the house
is built into the side of a hill and the two second-floor rear door exits which are,
in reality, bridges; one is covered. Also of interest is the winding staircase to the
second floor, the kitchen's large stone fireplace, and an external oven.

Ownership of the house was transferred through marriage to the Harned family
where it remained until 1940. Since 1960 the house has been owned by the Smithtown Historical Society and is fully restored. It is on the National Register of Historic Places.

SMITHTOWN

Caleb Smith State Park – Wyandanch Club

Route 25/Jericho Turnpike, Smithtown
(631) 265-1054

*From the village green located at the intersection of Route 25/Jericho Turnpike/
Main Street and Route 111 in Smithtown (Village of the Branch) go west on Route
25/Jericho Turnpike/Main Street for 2.2 miles. The park entrance is on the right
(north) side of the road.*

This 543-acre park encompasses the Caleb Smith I house, a portion of which is
circa 1750, and a mill built in 1795. A descendant of the town's founder, Caleb was
a dedicated patriot who, despite frequent lashings by British soldiers, refused to
swear an oath of allegiance to the Crown. Look for the scar on one of the outside
doors; the damage was done by an angry Tory's sword as he slashed at, but missed,
Caleb. The property was acquired by the Wyandanch Club (formerly the Brooklyn
Gun Club) in 1880 and used as a hunting preserve for its members. Ownership of
the property ultimately passed to the State of New York which has converted it into
an environmental park.

Caleb's house is now a museum containing old farm equipment, a fly fishing display, an owl collection, and displays of seasonal dried flower arrangements.

The park has nature trails. There are provisions also for both hiking, fishing, and guided nature walks. Cross-country skiing is permitted in the winter.

Environmental Centers of Setauket – Smithtown
Sweetbriar Farm
Landing Avenue, Smithtown
(631) 979-6344

From the village green located at the intersection of Route 25/Jericho Turnpike/ Main Street and Route 111 in Smithtown (Village of the Branch) go west on Route 25/Jericho Turnpike/Main Street for .3 mile. Turn right (north) onto Landing Avenue; go .9 mile. The entrance is on the left (west) side of the road.

Overlooking the Nissequogue River, this nature museum has snakes, chickens, goats, opossums, raccoons, and a "deflowered" skunk as well as an exhibit of avian taxidermy. An extensive schedule of varied environmental programs is presented throughout the year.

Explorer Scout Nature Museum
Blydenburgh County Park Mill Road, Smithtown
(631) 854-4949

From the village green located at the intersection of Route 25/Jericho Turnpike/ Main Street and Route 111 in Smithtown (Village of the Branch) go west on Route 25/Jericho Turnpike/Main Street for .9 mile. Turn left (south) onto Brooksite Drive; go .2 mile. Turn right (west) onto New Mill Road; go 1.2 miles to the end of the road and the Smithtown entrance of Blydenburgh County Park.

This small animal museum is located in Blydenburgh County Park and is operated and maintained by a local Boy Scout troop. It contains turtles, mice, snakes, and frogs.

First Presbyterian Church of Smithtown
175 East Main Street, Smithtown
(631) 265-5151

Located opposite the village green at the intersection of Route 25/Jericho Turnpike/Main Street and Route 111 in Smithtown (Village of the Branch).

The original church was founded in 1675 near the intersection of Moriches Road and River Road in Nissequogue. In 1827 the church was dismantled and moved to Stump Pond where it was converted into a watermill. (See also Town of Smithtown/Smithtown/The Mill House, Stump Pond, and New Mill.) The present church structure, which has been on the National Register of Historic Places since 1978, was built at this site in 1827. It is a mixture of Greek Revival, Gothic, and Federal styles of architecture. The interior of the church, with its simple yet beautiful lines and a choir balcony that surrounds the entire congregation, is well worth a visit.

The Mill House, Stump Pond, and New Mill
New Mill Road, Smithtown
(631) 360-0753

From the village green located at the intersection of Route 25/Jericho Turnpike/ Main Street and Route 111 in Smithtown (Village of the Branch) go west on Route 25/Jericho Turnpike/Main Street for .9 mile. Turn left (south) onto Brookside Drive; go .2 mile. Turn right (west) onto New Mill Road; go 1.2 miles to the end of the road and the Smithtown entrance of Blydenburgh County Park. Take the dirt trail to Stump Pond. The house and mill are located next to the pond and in front of the rowboat rental booth.

In 1798 two Smith cousins, Caleb II and Joshua II, entered into an agreement with Isaac Blydenburgh to construct a dam, pond, and grist mill at this site. The trees were cut down but their stumps were left in the ground. The dam was constructed so that the water flooded the area where the tree stumps remained, thus the name Stump Pond. The New Mill is actually the old Presbyterian Church which in 1827 was moved from Moriches Road and remodeled into a mill. (See also Town of Smithtown/Smithtown/First Presbyterian Church of Smithtown.) The circa 1801 Mill House was built by the tenant mill operator. The Mill and the Mill House have been on the National Register of Historic Places since 1983 as part of the Blydenburgh Park Historic District. An appointment to see the Mill House may be made by telephoning the office at the above number.

Please note that these sites provide no special access for people with disabilities and are difficult to reach.

Also found in the park is the Blydenburgh–Weld House which was built in 1821. In that same year the house was blown off plumb during the "great September gale" and has remained so to this day. The house, which contains the headquarters of the Long Island Greenbelt Trail Conference, also has a small museum and a gift shop.

Riverside Conservation Area County Park
Main Street, Smithtown
(631) 854-4949

Suffolk County Resident Pass is required for admission.

From the village green located at the intersection of Route 25/Jericho Turnpike/ Main Street and Route 111 in Smithtown (Village of the Branch) go west on Route 25/Jericho Turnpike/Main Street for 1.1 miles. The park entrance is on the left (south) side of the road.

The thirty-five-acre Nissequogue River wetland and woodland preserve consists of several different parcels of land. The most conveniently located and accessible section is the Riverside Conservation Area which is located on Main Street in Smithtown. The park offers guided nature walks by environmental specialists, fishing, and canoeing in the Nissequogue River.

There are no facilities and use of the park is limited to the above activities.

Statue of Smithtown Bull
Route 25/Jericho Turnpike, Smithtown

From the village green located at the intersection of Route 25/Jericho Turnpike/ Main Street and Route 111 in Smithtown (Village of the Branch) go west on Route 25/Jericho Turnpike/Main Street for 1.3 miles. The statue is on the right (north) side of the road.

The Town of Smithtown was founded by Richard "Bull" Smith. (See also Town of Smithtown/Nissequogue/Grave of Richard Smythe (Richard "Bull" Smith.) A legend has persisted that he obtained from the Indians all the land that he traversed in one day while riding his bull. The statue commemorates his historic, but alas fictitious, ride. In reality Smith purchased the land from Lion Gardiner.

The statue was designed in 1917 by a Long Islander, Charles Cary Rumsey Sr. in his Paris studio in collaboration with Lawrence Smith Butler, a descendant of Smith and a classmate of the sculptor. Although initially designed for Smithtown, the town did not actually acquire the bronze statue of the bull until 1941. For years it stood at the entrance to the Brooklyn Museum. The sculptor's obvious comment about the "Bull" Smith story may have been part of the reason for the delay in the procurement of the statue.

Rumsey also created the hunt frieze on the Manhattan Bridge. In 1922 Rumsey, who was returning to his Brookville estate from polo practice, was killed at the intersection of Jericho Turnpike and Tulip Avenue in Floral Park when the convertible in which he was a passenger over-turned.

VILLAGE OF THE BRANCH

Village Green
Route 25/Jericho Turnpike/Main Street, Village of the Branch

Take the Long Island Expressway to Exit #56 north (Route 111/Smithtown/Islip). Go north on Route 111. At 1.7 miles bear left continuing north on Route 111 for a total of 4.1 miles. The village green is on the right (east) side of the road in front of The Smithtown Library.

This is the site of the 1688 Widow Blydenburgh's house, the first house built in the Village of the Branch. In 1790 George Washington stayed at the house and tethered his horse near what is now the parking lot of The Smithtown Library. Over the years the house fell into disrepair and was demolished in 1907.

Caleb Smith II House

Route 25A/North Country Road, Village of the Branch
(631) 265-6768

From the village green located at the intersection of Route 25/Jericho Turnpike/ Main Street and Route 111 in Smithtown (Village of the Branch) go north on Route 25A/North Country Road for .2 mile. The house is on the right (east) side of the road behind The Smithtown Library.

The house was built in 1819 at the present site of the Mayfair housing development on the north side of Jericho Turnpike in Commack. Found in the attic was a land grant dated July 14, 1659, through which the Indian Sachem Wyandanch transferred ownership of "all his Nissequogue land" to Lion Gardiner. On October 15, 1664, David Gardiner, Lion's son, endorsed the deed transferring the land to Richard "Bull" Smith. (See also Town of Smithtown/Nissequogue/Grave of Richard Smythe (Richard "Bull" Smith.) The deed is presently in the collection of the Brooklyn Historical Society.

The house was moved to its present site in 1955 and is the headquarters of the Smithtown Historical Society. On display are seventeenth- and eighteenth-century furniture, paintings, toys, and a truly fine collection of monogrammed Chinese dinnerware. A reference library is available for research.

Epenetus Smith Tavern

Route 25/East Main Street, Village of the Branch
(631) 265-6768

From the village green located at the intersection of Route 25/Jericho Turnpike/ Main Street and Route 111 in Smithtown (Village of the Branch) go east on Route 25/Jericho Turnpike/Main Street/East Main Street for .2 mile. The inn is on the left (north) side of the road.

This circa 1750 tavern, which was owned by Epenetus Smith, a great-grandson of the town's patentee, became a stopover for the Fulton Ferry, Brooklyn to Sag Harbor stage route. In 1911 the tavern became part of the estate of David J. Ely and was moved from its original location on Main Street just west of the Presbyterian church to the east side of Route 111 just south of the present Smithtown post office. It was later moved to the west side of Route 111 on the present site of the Hillside Village Plaza. In 1972 it was acquired by the historical society and moved to its present location. The tavern was placed on the National Register of Historic Places in 1986.

An extensive educational program for school children is available at the tavern sponsored by the Smithtown Historical Society.

Franklin O. Arthur House
265 Route 25/East Main Street, Village of the Branch
(631) 265-6768

From the village green located at the intersection of Route 25/Jericho Turnpike/ Main Street and Route 111 in Smithtown (Village of the Branch) go east on Route 25/Jericho Turnpike/Main Street/East Main Street for .3 mile. The house is on the left (north) side of the road.

The original owner of this circa 1730 house, which was placed on the National Register of Historic Places in 1986, is unknown. It was eventually owned by Franklin O. Arthur, a blacksmith who later became a dentist. Of particular interest is the beehive oven. The barn, located at the rear of the property, contains a buggy and old farm equipment.

Judge J. Lawrence Smith House – The Homestead
205 Route 25/East Main Street, Village of the Branch
(631) 265-6768

From the village green located at the intersection of Route 25/Jericho Turnpike/ Main Street and Route 111 in Smithtown (Village of the Branch) go east on Route 25/Jericho Turnpike/Main Street/East Main Street for .2 mile. The house is located on the left (north) side of the road.

This circa 1760 house was built by William Blydenburgh I. It was acquired in 1845 by Judge J. Lawrence Smith, a descendant of Richard "Bull" Smith, the town's patentee. Judge Smith was born in Nissequogue in 1816 and attended the Clinton Academy in East Hampton, Yale College (Yale University), and graduated from Princeton University in 1837. He wrote "History of Smithtown," a chapter in Munsell's *History of Suffolk County* published in 1882. Bessie, daughter of Judge Smith and his wife, Sarah Nicoll Clinch Smith, married the famed architect Stanford White and lived in Head of the Harbor at Box Hill. (See also Town of Smithtown/Head of the Harbor/Stanford White Estate–Box Hill; Town of Smithtown/Head of the Harbor/Stanford White House; and Town of Smithtown/Saint James/Saint James Episcopal Church.) Bessie later inherited The Homestead.

The house, which is owned by the Smithtown Historical Society and has been on the National Register of Historic Places since 1986, is open to the public.

Old Schoolhouse
Singer Lane, Village of the Branch

From the village green located at the intersection of Route 25/Jericho Turnpike/ Main Street and Route 111 in Smithtown (Village of the Branch) go south on Route 111 for .1 mile. Turn right onto Singer Lane; go .1 mile. The school is on the right (east) side of the road.

Built in 1802, and moved to its present site in 1868, this building was the first schoolhouse in Smithtown. It was originally built on land belonging to Epenetus Smith II next to his tavern. (See also Town of Smithtown/Village of the Branch/ Epenetus Smith Tavern.) During the winter of 1837–1838 Walt Whitman taught in this schoolhouse. (See also Town of Huntington/Huntington Station/Walt Whitman House.) Presently a commercial establishment, it is nevertheless still open to the public.

The Richard H. Handley Collection – Long Island History Room
The Smithtown Library
1 North Country Road, Village of the Branch
(631) 265-2072

Located on the village green at the intersection of Route 25/Jericho Turnpike/Main Street and Route 111 in Smithtown (Village of the Branch).

The Handley Collection comprises an extensive collection of books, maps, charts, pamphlets, and pictures dealing with the history of Long Island and Smithtown. The collection was begun with a large initial contribution of materials of historical significance by Mrs. Richard H. Handley.

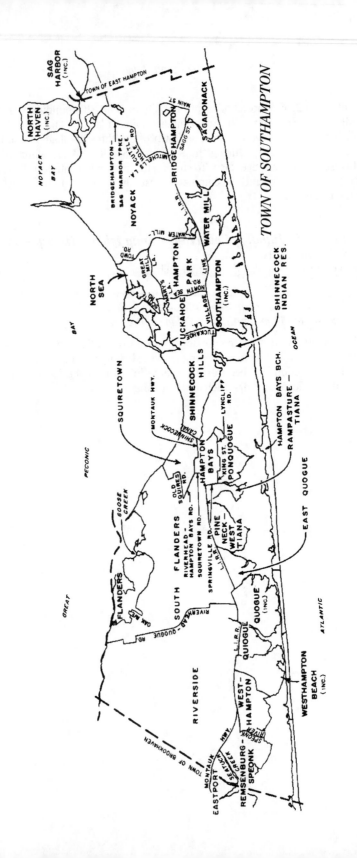

TOWN OF SOUTHAMPTON

TOWN OF SOUTHAMPTON

PARKS AND PRESERVES

Federal Parks and Preserves

Conscience Point National Wildlife Refuge (60 acres), North Sea
Morton National Wildlife Refuge (187 acres), Sag Harbor

State Parks and Preserves

Barcelona Neck Natural Resource Management Area (341 acres), Sag Harbor
   (undeveloped)
Quogue Wildlife Refuge (300 acres), Quogue *(undeveloped)*
Sag Harbor State Golf Course (49 acres), Sag Harbor
Westhampton Management Area (277 acres), Westhampton *(undeveloped)*

County Parks and Preserves

Cranberry Bog County Preserve (460 acres), Riverhead
Hubbard County Park (1,620 acres), Flanders *(undeveloped)*
Meschutt Beach County Park (7 acres), Shinnecock Hills
Poxabogue Pond Preserve (26 acres), Bridgehampton
Sears Bellow County Park (693 acres), Flanders
Shinnecock Beach County Park (East and West) (407 acres), Shinnecock Inlet
Shinnecock Canal County Marina (5 acres), Shinnecock Hills

Long Island Chapter: The Nature Conservancy

Griffith Preserve (17 acres), Quogue
Stuyvesant Wainwright Memorial Refuge (15 acres), Southport
Zoe B. de Ropp Sanctuary (9 acres), East Quogue

South Fork – Shelter Island Chapter: The Nature Conservancy

Sagg Swamp Preserve (84 acres), Bridgehampton
Scallop Pond Preserve (55 acres), North Sea

Arboretums and Gardens

Bridgehampton

Beebe Windmill
Ocean Road, Bridgehampton

From the war memorial at the intersection of Route 27/Montauk Highway and Ocean Road in Bridgehampton go south on Ocean Road for .3 mile. The windmill is on the left (east) side of the road.

This smock-type windmill, which has been on the National Register of Historic Places since 1978, was built in 1820 by Samuel Schellinger for Captain Lester Beebe, a retired sea captain. (See also Town of East Hampton/Amagansett/Miss Amelia's Cottage; Town of East Hampton/East Hampton/Pantigo Mill; and Town of East Hampton/Amagansett/Commercial Fisherman's Museum.) Originally located in Sag Harbor, this was the first windmill in the United States to use cast iron machinery instead of wood, as well as the first in the country to use a fantail rather than manpower to aim the sails into the wind. Captain Beebe died in 1832. In 1837 the windmill was sold to Judge Abraham T. Rose and Richard Gelston and moved by them to the Bridgehampton commons. After passing through a succession of owners and being moved to another location north of the railroad tracks in Bridgehampton, the windmill was finally purchased in 1914 by John E. Berwind, a Pennsylvania industrialist, and moved to its present location on his estate. The Beebe Windmill has the distinction of being the only surviving iron-geared windmill in the United States and the last windmill built on Long Island. Ownership of the windmill was ultimately transferred to the Town of Southampton. In 1984 it was completely restored with 66 percent of its superstructure replaced. At the base of the windmill is a time capsule to be opened on July 4, 2076.

Bridgehampton Historical Society Complex
Main Street, Bridgehampton
(631) 537-1088

From the war memorial at the intersection of Route 27/Montauk Highway and Ocean Road in Bridgehampton go west on Route 27/Montauk Highway for .3 mile. The museum is on the right (north) side of the road.

The Corwith House
(part of Bridgehampton Historical Society Complex)
Main Street, Bridgehampton

The Corwith House is a circa 1800 Greek Revival-style house built by Henry Corwith. It remained in the Corwith family until 1961 when it was acquired by the Bridgehampton Historical Society. The house is presently a museum depicting life in Bridgehampton during the 1800s. There is a splendid Victorian parlor with a circa 1860 organ. Also on display in the house are collections of clothes, toys, looms, and grain bags from the Beebe Windmill.

The Hildrith–Simmons Machine Shop
(part of the Bridgehampton Historical Society Complex)
Main Street, Bridgehampton

The machine shop is located on the grounds of the complex behind the Corwith House. It contains antique engines and farm machines. Perhaps its most unusual item is an engine that operates using garbage as fuel. The entire collection is displayed and operated during the Annual Bridgehampton Antiques Engine Run.

The Wheelwright Shop
(part of the Bridgehampton Historical Society Complex)
Main Street, Bridgehampton

This circa 1870 shop is also located at the complex behind the Corwith House. It was built by George W. Strong and was originally located at the corner of Town Line Road and Parsonage Lane in Bridgehampton. It was donated to the historical society and moved to the complex. The shop contains carpenter tools, and diverse equipment necessary for the making and repairing of wagons, sleds, farm tools, and machinery.

The Hampton Classic Horse Show
Snake Hollow Road, Bridgehampton

From the war memorial on Route 27/Montauk Highway and Ocean Road in Bridgehampton go west on Route 27/Montauk Highway for .7 mile. Turn right (north) onto Snake Hollow Road; go .5 mile. The entrance for the horse show is on the left (west) side of the road.

In August, the week-long Hampton Classic Horse Show, with its 1,000 entries and approximately 20,000 spectators, is one of the major equestrian events in the country. It culminates with the qualifying events for the World Cup finals. Check local newspapers for exact date.

Poxabogue Pond Preserve
Old Farm Road, Bridgehampton
(631) 854-4949

Suffolk County Resident Pass is required for admission.

From the war memorial on Route 27/Montauk Highway and Ocean Road in Bridgehampton go east on Route 27/Montauk Highway for 1 mile to Poxabogue Lane. Turn left (north); go .3 mile. Turn left (west) onto Old Farm Road/Crooked Pond Road; go .4 mile. The preserve is on the left (south) side of the road.

This twenty-six-acre Suffolk County preserve is located at the northeastern end of Poxabogue Pond. The preserve consists of fields, freshwater marshes, and a woodland. The habitat supports a variety of vegetation such as dwarf cinquefoil, wild carrot, sassafras, and both red oak and white oak trees.

Presbyterian Church of Bridgehampton
Main Street, Bridgehampton
(631) 537-0863

From the war memorial at the intersection of Route 27/Montauk Highway and Ocean Road in Bridgehampton go west on Route 27/Montauk Highway for .2 mile. The church is on the left (south) side of road.

The congregation was established in 1670. In 1843 the present Greek Revival-style building with its Ionic columns was built. During the summer the church hosts concerts of both classical and popular music.

Queen of the Most Holy Rosary Church
Main Street, Bridgehampton
(631) 537-0156

From the war memorial at the intersection of Route 27/Montauk Highway and Ocean Road in Bridgehampton go west on Route 27/Montauk Highway for .5 mile. The church is on the right (north) side of the road.

The church's exterior has a Federal-style center entrance with Federal details around the stained-glass windows. There is also a Federal-style door on the church's west side. The interior is unusual with a vaulted ceiling and exposed beams decorated with colorful folk-pattern stenciling reminiscent of Bavaria.

Sagg Swamp Preserve
(South Fork – Shelter Island Chapter: The Nature Conservancy)
Sagg Road/Sagaponak Road, Bridgehampton
(631) 329-7689

Open with prior permission.

From the war memorial at the intersection of Route 27/Montauk Highway and Ocean Road in Bridgehampton turn right (south) onto Ocean Road; go .4 mile. Turn left (east) onto Sagg Road/Sagaponak Road; go .7 mile. The preserve is on the left (north) side of the road. Look for the small sign and narrow footpath.

This eighty-four-acre preserve was acquired by the Conservancy in 1970. It is a mature red maple swamp containing streams, ponds, and bogs. There are ninety-two rare plant species and a diversity of wildlife including long-tailed weasels, red-tailed hawks, and red foxes.

Please call the Conservancy at the above telephone number to obtain permission to visit the preserve.

Saint Ann's Episcopal Church
Main Street, Bridgehampton
(631) 537-1527

From the war memorial at the intersection of Route 27/Montauk Highway and Ocean Road in Bridgehampton go west on Route 27/Montauk Highway for .1 mile. The church is on the left (south) side of the road.

Originally built as a golf course clubhouse in Wainscott, the building was moved over the frozen Sagaponak Pond to its present location in 1909. The contemporary, but perfectly complimentary, bell tower was added in 1983.

EAST QUOGUE

Zoe B. de Ropp Sanctuary
(Long Island Chapter: The Nature Conservancy)
East Quogue
(631) 367-3225

Open with prior permission.

Take the Long Island Expressway to Exit #70 south (Eastport Manor Road/Manorville/Eastport). Go south on Port Jefferson–Westhampton Road/County Road 111/Captain Daniel Roe Blvd. for 4.7 miles. Go east on Sunrise Highway/Route 27 for 5.7 miles to Exit #64 south (County Road 104/Quogue/Riverhead). Go south on County Road 104/Quogue–Riverhead Road for 3.5 miles. Turn left (east) onto Montauk Highway/County Road 80; go 2.2 miles to Josiah Foster Path. Since you must go through private property to enter the sanctuary, please call the Conservancy at the above telephone number for directions beyond this point.

The area on which this nine-acre salt marsh sanctuary is located was probably used by the Shinnecock Indians to harvest fish and shellfish. Later the seaweed from the marsh was collected for fertilizer while its drier regions were used for cattle grazing. The land had been owned by the de Ropp family since 1894. It was donated to the Conservancy by Mrs. Zoe B. de Ropp in 1972.

EASTPORT

Shrine of Our Lady of the Island

Eastport Manor Road, Eastport
(631) 325-0661

Take the Long Island Expressway to Exit #70 south (Eastport Manor Road/Manor-ville/Eastport). Go south on Port Jefferson–Westhampton Road/County Road 111/ Captain Daniel Roe Blvd. for 1.9 miles. Turn right (west) onto Eastport Manor Road/County Road 55; go .6 mile. The entrance to the shrine is on the right side of the road.

Attended to by the Monfort missionaries, the shrine is located on a seventy-acre site overlooking Moriches Bay. Found here are a rosary walk, stations of the cross, a huge statue of Our Lady of the Island situated on a very large glacial boulder, facilities for outdoor masses, a chapel, a meeting hall, a gift shop, a snack bar, picnic tables, and restrooms. It is a marvelous place for those seeking quiet and solitude.

FLANDERS

The Big Duck

Hampton Bays Road/Route 24, Flanders
(631) 852-8292

Take the Long Island Expressway to Exit #71 south. Turn south onto Route 24/ Nugent Drive/Hampton Bays Road and follow it through the traffic circle in Riv-erhead. The Big Duck is on the left (east) side of the road.

The Big Duck, which is twenty-feet-high, measures thirty feet from beak to tail and fifteen feet from wing to wing. It was built by Martin and Jeulee Mauer in 1931 as a roadside stand in which to sell Peking ducks to passing motorists. Originally located on West Main Street in Riverhead, it was moved to Route 24 in Flanders in 1936.

In 1987 it was donated to Suffolk County by Kai and Pouran Eshghi. The county moved it to the edge of Sears Bellow County Park. In 2007 it was moved to its present site.

An excellent example of roadside architecture, the duck is listed on the National Register of Historic Places and serves as an information center for the Long Island Convention and Visitors Bureau. Its gift shop offers an unusual array of "duck-a-bila."

Sears Bellows County Park – The Flanders Club
Pond Road, Flanders
(631) 852-8290

Suffolk County Resident Pass is required for admission.

Take the Long Island Expressway to Exit #70 south (Eastport Manor Road/Manorville/Eastport). Go south on Port Jefferson–Westhampton Road/County Road 111/ Captain Daniel Roe Blvd. for 4.7 miles. Go east on Sunrise Highway/Route 27 for 9.9 miles to Exit #65 north (County Road 24/Hampton Bays/Riverhead). Go north on County Road 24 for 1.4 miles to Bellows Pond Road. Turn left (west) onto Bellows Pond Road; go .6 mile to the campground's administrative office which is on the right (north) side of the road.

This 693-acre park was originally known as The Flanders Club, a private organization devoted to hunting waterfowl. The park offers facilities for a variety of activities such as freshwater swimming, rowboating, horseback riding, fishing, picnicking, hunting, and ice skating. There are bike hostel facilities and a campground. Water and sanitary provisions for trailer and tenters are at the campsite but there are no hook ups.

NORTH SEA

Conscience Point
North Sea Road, North Sea

From the intersection of Route 27/County Road 39 and North Sea in Southampton turn north onto County Road 39. Continue for 2.8 miles to where County Road 39 angles east. Go straight on North Sea Road/County Road 38. Go .5 mile more to Conscience Point which is on the right (east) side of the road.

Located on a peninsula jutting out into North Sea Harbor is a boulder with a bronze plaque commemorating the June 12, 1640, landing of the first English settlers in New York State. The colonists came from Lynn, MA, and had originally tried to land at Manhasset but found that the area was controlled by the Dutch with whom England was at war. They immediately set sail and eventually landed near the site of the Conscience Point boulder. Befriended by the Shinnecock Indians, the colonists migrated south and established the colony of Southampton. The date of their landing is celebrated by Southampton as Founders' Day.

(See also Town of Southampton/Southampton/Old Halsey Homestead and Town of Southampton/Southampton/Southampton Museum Complex.)

Scallop Pond Preserve
(South Fork – Shelter Island Chapter: The Nature Conservancy)
Scott Road, North Sea
(631) 329-7689

Open with prior permission.

Just west of Exit #4 on Sunrise Highway/Route 27/County Road 39 go north onto North Magee Street for 1.7 miles. Turn right (east) onto Scott Road (Scott's Road); go .8 mile. The preserve is on the left (north) side of the road.

This fifty-five-acre tidal wetland is a major spawning and nursery area for Long Island's coastal fish. The habitat supports more than thirty-five different species of invertebrates and has one of the largest white-tailed deer herds on Long Island.

QUOGUE

Church of the Atonement Episcopal Church
Quogue–Main Street, Quogue
(631) 653-6798

Take the Long Island Expressway to Exit #70 south (Eastport Manor Road/Manorville/Eastport). Go south on Port Jefferson–Westhampton Road/County Road 111/ Captain Daniel Roe Blvd. for 4.7 miles. Go east on Sunrise Highway/Route 27 for 5.7 miles to Exit #64 south (County Road 104/Quogue/Riverhead). Go south on County Road 104/Quogue–Riverhead Road for 3.5 miles. Turn right (west) onto Montauk Highway/County Road 80; go 1.5 miles. Turn left (south) onto Quogue–Main Street; go .3 mile. The church is on the right (west) side of the road.

The church celebrated its centennial in 1984, having served the congregation in Quogue continuously every summer since July 13, 1884. Its unusual architecture, unchanged since 1884, is said to be a blend of styles found in Brittany, Italy, and Switzerland, although your imagination may well carry you further east than Europe for comparison. The Flag of the Resurrection has been dramatically incorporated into the weathervane and tops this elaborately shingled structure. Its unusual design is highlighted by the interior wainscotting of both the ceiling and walls with small wooden shingles, like scales of a fish, continuing from the exterior into a most unique and beautiful interior. The interior is graced by some of the most beautiful stained-glass windows on Long Island.

Over the altar, on the north wall, are three fine English stained and painted windows signed "Cox, Buckley & Co., London" and dated 1884 and 1885. They depict Saint Paul and convey messages from both his Epistle to the Romans and his Epistle to the Apostle Timothy. These are complimented by the Samuel Davis Craig (1856) and Helen Kortright Brashear Craig (1853) Memorial windows on the east wall near the main entrance signed "Cox, Sons, Buckley & Co., London, Youghal, & New York 1888."

The jewel glass cross hanging in the chancel is most likely of Tiffany design.

To the right of the altar in the organ alcove is the Benjamin D. K. Craig (1879) and Ann Wagstaff Craig (1855) Memorial window. This dramatic ocean scene in heavy drapery glass, which incidentally was invented by Louis Tiffany, has jewel glass borders, a heavy jewel glass medallion, and early turtle-back tile and floral effects. It features a large white bull's eye or crown glass rondure full moon. The dove winging across the water, eclipsing the full moon, is an artistic interpretation one would find in early Tiffany windows where he eschewed any painting effects in a rejection of European techniques and colors. Plating is more obvious than in later Tiffany work, but this, although unsigned, would be in keeping with his style and technique of the very early period. The large amount of solder used to set jewel glass suggests that this was completed before 1900.

Of a slightly later period and also perhaps an unsigned Tiffany, is the jewel glass composite in the back of the church on the east wall, the Roswell Park Cullen MD (1891) Memorial window. Many decorative details are similar to those found on the Craig/Wagstaff window but are of a more refined quality suggesting the Tiffany period closer to 1900. However, the jewel glass in this window also is set in large amounts of solder dating the work prior to 1900. It includes a beautifully composed Celtic cross and is decorated with Celtic knots.

To the left as you enter the church, on the south wall, is the Henrietta Craig Colgate (1901) Memorial window. Also unsigned, this elegant window portrays a kneeling figure in intense red/violet robes with a raised lighted lamp and book on his knee; it is inscribed "The Lord my God will lighten my darkness" (Psalms 18:28). If there is drapery glass, it is not heavy and is therefore not discernible through the protective plate glass which does obscure the revealing techniques which might lead us to the artist. There is no fractured or confetti glass and plating techniques are fine, as in other work done during the middle years by Tiffany Studios. The landscape work is subtle in both colors and technique with leaves on bushes and trees carefully detailed. The subtlety of the landscape background and the rich blue sky serve to highlight the figure in the artistic style of Louis C. Tiffany. This too may be by the prolific artist in glass.

At the back of the church on the south wall are three unsigned panels listed in the incomplete records of Tiffany Studios. The central *Angel of Praise* is an exquisite angel, holding music, created in pearl opalescent drapery glass. The ribbed wings are finely done. On either side are *Adoring Angels* which have pillars on the sides as framing devices. These window are referred to in Tiffany lists simply as "Craig Memorial window." Each angel is kneeling in adoration with the phrases "In Remembrance of Past Worshippers" on the left and "The Souls of the Righteous are in the Hands of God" on the right. Flowers were such a beautiful signature of Louis C. Tiffany. In these panels we see lilies symbolizing the Resurrection on the left and irises symbolizing remembrance on the right, interestingly on alternate panels from the corresponding message. The sky in each of the three panels, mottled glass in blues, light gold, and apricot, is alike, suggesting that they were indeed executed at the same time. Fractured or mottled glass can be seen at the knees of the kneeling angels and is clearly illustrative of this technique. Of note is the unusual greenish tone of the heavy drapery glass on these kneeling figures. Above are two rose windows with faces of cherubim and geometric patterns.

At the most southern end of the west wall is the Edith Beckwith Smith (1929) Memorial window. This window has previously not been attributed to Tiffany, but we feel that it is possible that this might be a Tiffany creation. If you look carefully in the lower right hand corner, you will see that a molding obscures what appears to be a script signature with the tops of three letters just barely discernible, a signature configuration consistent with the late period of Tiffany Studios. This would have been a commission undertaken after the Tiffany furnaces were closed. A seated angel, whose robes are formed from very heavy drapery glass in opalescent bluish lavender, holds a palm frond, symbolic of the martyr's triumph in death. The wings are interestingly in disarray. The seated position of the angel, the position of the palm frond, and the pinks and lavenders of these wings are most reminiscent of the Minott Memorial window in Saint James Episcopal Church in Saint James, a window from the studios of Lederle–Geissler, New York. (See also Town of Smithtown/Saint James/Saint James Episcopal Church.) Lilies are included to the right. Although lilies, symbolizing the Resurrection, became almost a trademark of Tiffany commissions, these are also seen in the Lederle–Geissler window in Saint James.

In the center of the west wall is the Katharine Van Wyck (1911) Memorial window signed "TIFFANY STVDIOS, NEW YORK." It pictures a landscape at sunset with poplar trees and flowers and is beautifully, yet simply, symbolic. Poppies in the foreground representing sleep, a thought further suggested by the sunset theme, are counterbalanced by the lilies, with further Resurrection symbolism in the form of crosses in the hemispheric portion of the window above. Both mottled glass and fractured or confetti glass are used magnificently in this peaceful scene.

The northernmost window on the west wall, the Mary Livingston Austin Poor (1913) Memorial window, is entitled *Saint Cecilia* and is signed "TIFFANY STVDIOS, N.Y." Saint Cecilia (Cecily), the patroness of musicians, is often portrayed at the organ, although this appears to be artistic license since no organ or other musical experience seems to have been a part of her short life. Lavender heavy drapery glass robes with a rose-red robe over the shoulders adorn the haloed figure. A jewel glass cross is attached to a necklace which is painted on the neck. The head, hands, and halo are the only painted portions. An exquisite single rose lies across the keys of the lower organ keyboard. The organ is represented in brown mottled glass and is an unusual technique in our experience although architectural details in the Aldrich Memorial window in Christ Church in Sag Harbor are also done in mottled glass. (See also Town of Southampton/Sag Harbor/Christ Episcopal Church.) The pipes of the organ are bright yellow and rise across the molding to the top of the lancet window from which emanates downward a lighting effect which perhaps might be suggestive of a "light from heaven." Although this window is not documented in the records of Tiffany Studios, the Bold Memorial window, identical except for the divided organ pipe motif at the top of the lancet, may be seen in the east transept in Christ Episcopal Church in Charlottesville, VA, and is documented in Tiffany Studios' records as *Saint Cecelia*.

Each of these last three windows on the west wall, the Smith, Van Wyck, and Poor Memorials, is actually a lancet window in two sections separated by heavy wooden molding. The top portion of each represents sky in shades of blue and pink mottled glass. There is a lemon brick border around the top hemispheres of both the Van Wyck and Poor windows. Further, the Poor window has painted cherubim, executed in outline only, peering down upon the *Saint Cecelia.* The pipes of the organ extend into the lancet hemisphere giving a sense of continuity to the divided window. The Van Wyck window shows outlined crosses emerging from the sky in the hemisphere portion of that window. It is probable that these too were done by Tiffany Studios and that the Van Wyck and Poor windows were executed at about the same time. The top portion of the Smith lancet is not outlined and is composed of fitted pieces rather than a single large piece of glass. Also, it does not continue the theme of the lower portion, further suggesting that this window was not completed at the same time as the other two lancet hemispheres and that it may not have been the work of the same artist.

Two windows on the east wall by the organ are memorials to a young boy, James Lindsay Fowler (1901). These carry through the sea-oriented theme which prevails in this church. One depicts an angel standing above the stormy sea, and the other depicts Christ aboard ship during a violent storm—perhaps suggesting that we are never alone in the storms of this life. Plexiglas covers the inside of these unsigned windows making artist identification next to impossible. Only the hands and faces are painted. Blues and lavenders predominate with beautiful lavender wings on the angel and a dark purple robe on the Christ figure. Mottled glass is clearly in evidence in the depth of color as is the use of plating. No drapery glass can be seen. These appear to be more contemporary in style than 1901 and we are sure that they are not the work of Tiffany Studios. They are beautifully executed.

Just one small historical note: this entire building was moved a considerable distance from its site by the force of the September 1938 hurricane and subsequent tidal wave. It is said that not a single one of its beautiful windows was broken. Thankfully, they are all here today for us to enjoy and marvel over.

Griffith Preserve
(Long Island Chapter: The Nature Conservancy)
Montauk Highway, Quogue
(631) 367-3225

Open with prior permission.

Take the Long Island Expressway to Exit #70 south (Eastport Manor Road/Manorville/Eastport). Go south on Port Jefferson–Westhampton Road/County Road 111/ Captain Daniel Roe Blvd. for 4.7 miles. Go east on Sunrise Highway/Route 27 for 5.7 miles to Exit #64 south (County Road 104/Quogue/Riverhead). Go south on County Road 104/Quogue–Riverhead Road for 3.5 miles. Turn right (west) onto Montauk Highway/County Road 80; go .1 mile. The entrance is on the left side of the road between two large brick markers.

Eighty percent of this seventeen-acre preserve is an oak and hickory forest with the remainder being a tidal marsh. Early settlers cut salt hay here to feed their livestock during the winter. During the summer months they pastured their animals on the flat grassy areas along the Shinnecock Bay. The preserve was donated to the Conservancy by Eleanor B. Griffith. Visitors to the preserve should take note that there are large sections of greenbrier and poison ivy in the undergrowth.

Please call the Conservancy at the above telephone number to obtain permission to visit the preserve.

Quogue Cemetery Association Inc.

Lamb Avenue, Quogue
(631) 653-5220

Take the Long Island Expressway to Exit #70 south (Eastport Manor Road/Manorville/Eastport). Go south on Port Jefferson–Westhampton Road/County Road 111/Captain Daniel Roe Blvd. for 4.7 miles. Go east on Sunrise Highway/Route 27 for 5.7 miles to Exit #64 south (County Road 104/Quogue/Riverhead). Go south on County Road 104/Quogue–Riverhead Road for 3.5 miles. Turn right (west) onto Montauk Highway/County Road 80; go 1 mile. Turn left (south) onto Lamb Avenue; go .4 mile to the center entrance to the cemetery.

Grave of Admiral Alfred Thayer Mahan (1840–1914)

Follow the carriage road to third carriage road on left. The family plot is on the east corner of the two intersecting carriage roads.

Mahan was born at West Point, where his father was a professor of engineering and noted authority on fortifications and siege warfare. At the age of sixteen he entered the United States Naval Academy and was granted one year advanced standing, a highly unusual honor. He graduated in 1859 and spent the better part of his military career in routine sea and shore duty. His spare time was consumed with writing historical and tactical naval books.

In 1886 he delivered a series of lectures at the War College. So impressive were they that he was made president of the college the same year. In 1890 the lectures were published as a book entitled *The Influences of Sea Power Upon History 1660–1783*. The book quickly became a classic and greatly influenced his friend Theodore Roosevelt, under whom he later served as a naval advisor. Kaiser Wilhelm II of Germany was so impressed by Mahan's book that he ordered it be placed in Germany's naval school libraries. Mahan was a prolific writer whose works were translated into many languages and were closely studied, especially by the Japanese.

He retired from the navy in 1906 and returned to Quogue which, since 1896, had been his principal home.

Quogue Refuge and the Charles Banks Belt Nature Center

3 Old Country Road, Quogue
(631) 653-4771

Take the Long Island Expressway to Exit #70 south (Eastport Manor Road/Manor-ville/Eastport). Go south on Port Jefferson–Westhampton Road/County Road 111/ Captain Daniel Roe Blvd. for 4.7 miles. Go east on Sunrise Highway/Route 27 for 5.7 miles to Exit #64 south (County Road 104/Quogue/Riverhead). Go south on County Road 104/Quogue–Riverhead Road for 3.5 miles. Turn right (west) onto Montauk Highway/County Road 80; go 1.5 miles. Turn right (north) onto Old Main Street; go .8 mile. The refuge is on the left side of the road.

This two-hundred-acre refuge was founded in 1934 by the Southampton Township [sic] Wildfowl Assoc. The association built the Nature Center building in 1970 and is responsible for underwriting the expenses of the refuge while the New York State Department of Environmental Conservation, Division of Fish and Wildlife has the responsibility for maintaining the refuge for the association. The main trail through the refuge is well marked and takes approximately twenty minutes to walk. Also located at the refuge is a wildlife complex where injured birds and animals are cared for until they are ready to be returned to the wild.

Please call for schedules and information about field ecology classes, guided tours, and evening programs.

Quogue Schoolhouse Museum

90 Quogue–Main Street, Quogue
(631) 653-4224

Take the Long Island Expressway to Exit #70 south (Eastport Manor Road/Manor-ville/Eastport). Go south on Port Jefferson–Westhampton Road/County Road 111/ Captain Daniel Roe Blvd. for 4.7 miles. Go east on Sunrise Highway/Route 27 for 5.7 miles to Exit #64 south (County Road 104/Quogue/Riverhead). Go south on County Road 104/Quogue–Riverhead Road for 3.5 miles. Turn right (west) onto Montauk Highway/County Road 80; go 1.5 miles. Turn left (south) onto Quogue–Main Street; go 1.3 miles. The museum is on the left side of the road.

This building was completed in 1882 for use as a schoolhouse. Now, as a museum, it is still a place of learning, with changing exhibits of memorabilia, photographs, and artifacts relevant to local history.

(See also Town of Riverhead/Riverhead/Fresh Pond Schoolhouse; Town of Southold/Cutchogue/Old Schoolhouse; and Town of Southold/Orient/Old Point Schoolhouse.)

REMSENBURG

Remsenburg Community Chapel Presbyterian Cemetery
Basket Neck Lane, Remsenburg

Take the Long Island Expressway to Exit #70 south (Eastport Manor Road/Manorville/Eastport). Go south on the Port Jefferson–Westhampton Road/County Road 111/Captain Daniel Roe Blvd. for 4.7 miles. Go east on Sunrise Highway/Route 27 for 4.1 miles to Exit #63 south (County Road 31/Westhampton Beach). Go south on County Road 31 for 3.7 miles. Turn right (west) onto Montauk Highway/ County Road 80; go 3.3 miles. Turn left (south) onto South Phillips Avenue; go .6 mile. Turn left onto South Road/Main Street; go .1 mile. Turn right onto Basket Neck Lane. The cemetery entrance is on the right side of the road behind the Remsenburg Community Chapel.

Grave of P. G. Wodehouse (1881–1975)

Take the carriage road to the back of the cemetery. The grave site is on the left side of the carriage road about .1 mile from the entrance gate.

A British-born humorist, Wodehouse wrote over ninety novels depicting the lighthearted and raucous life of the English gentry. The most famous of his characters are Bertie Wooster, whom Wodehouse referred to as a "stage dude," Jeeves, his unflappable valet, and, of course Lord Emsworth of Blandings Castle, and his pig, the Empress of Blandings. The writings of Wodehouse have over the years evoked a variety of assessments. Sean O'Casey referred to him as "English literature's performing flea" while Wilfred Sheed called him a "genre hack." However, Halaire Belloc said he was "the best writer of English now alive" and Evelyn Waugh stated that, "He satisfies the most sophisticated taste and the simplest."

After World War II Wodehouse moved to the United States where, in 1952, he purchased a ten-acre estate, on Basket Neck Lane in Remsenburg, which he named Blandings Castle. (See also Town of North Hempstead/Kings Point/P. G. Wodehouse's House.) In 1975 he was made a Knight Commander of the Order of the British Empire, despite his expatriation.

His grave is marked by a large gravestone topped by a granite book in which are carved the titles of four of his books: *Jeeves*; *Blandings Castle*; *Leave It to P. Smith*; and *Meet Mister Mulliner*, and the inscription "He gave joy to countless people."

RIVERHEAD

Cranberry Bog County Preserve
Riverhead–Moriches Road, Riverhead
(631) 854-4949

Suffolk County Resident Pass is required for admission.

Take the Long Island Expressway to Exit #72 south (Riverhead/Calverton). Go south on Route 24 for 4.4 miles to the Riverhead traffic circle. From the circle take Riverhead–Moriches Road/County Road 63 southwest for .9 mile to paths leading to the park.

This 460-acre bog was originally a cranberry farm owned by S. H. Woodhull. Now owned by Suffolk County, this limited use park is a favorite of naturalists and botanists. Guided walks describing the park's various fauna and flora are given year round by environmental specialists.

For further information about the walks, telephone the above number.

SAGAPONACK

Crooked Pond – Final Resting Place of Truman Capote (1924–1984) and Jack Dunphy (1914–1992)
Widow Gavits Road, Sagaponack

From Montauk Highway/Route 27 turn north onto Sagg Road. After the railroad tracks, bear left at the fork in the road onto Topping Path. Continue north on Topping Path to Widow Gavits Road. Go 1 mile on Widow Gavits Road to the pond.

As an author and film/television personality, Capote's celebrity gave him entree to the elite members of society. Openly gay in an era when homosexuality was rarely mentioned, Capote flaunted his flamboyant lifestyle and reveled in being a celebrity. Among his major works were *The Grass Harp, Other Voices Other Rooms, In Cold Blood, Breakfast at Tiffany's,* and *A Christmas Memory.*

Capote's life began its downward spiral into alcoholism and drugs after his ill-fated attempt at writing an exposé of his society friends. Portions of the never completed book *Answered Prayers* were printed in *Esquire* and *New York* magazines and resulted in a label of *persona non gratta* among society's upper strata.

Capote died in Hollywood, CA, of a drug overdose in the home of Johnny Carson's ex-wife Joanne, who arranged for cremation and interment of half of Capote's ashes near the graves of Marilyn Monroe and that of Paris Hilton's goat in Westwood Village Memorial Park in Los Angeles, CA. The other half of Capote's ashes were returned to Sagaponack where they remained on a shelf in the home on Daniels Lane of Capote's life-long companion Jack Dunphy. With Dunphy's death in

1992, his ashes and those of Capote were sprinkled into Crooked Pond. A granite bolder with a bronze plaque commemorates the occasion.

Evergreen Cemetery

Sagaponack–Main Street/Sagg Main Street, Sagaponack

From the war memorial at the intersection of Route 27/Montauk Highway and Ocean Road in Bridgehampton go east on Route 27/Montauk Highway for 1.2 miles. The cemetery is on the right (south) side of the road.

Grave of James Jones (1921–1977)

The grave site is in the southeastern corner of the cemetery. To the left of the simple military-style gravestone is an American flag and the insignia of the 25th Infantry Division ("The Lightning Division").

Jones graduated from high school in 1939 and immediately left Robinson, IL, to enlist in the army serving until 1944. It was his military experiences prior to and during World War II that became the subjects of many of his books. A prolific writer, he began writing in the army but it was not until his first novel, *From Here to Eternity*, was published in 1951 that he achieved fame. Its themes, like so many of his other books, dealt with army life.

After living in Paris for sixteen years, Jones and his family returned to the United States and in 1975 settled in Sagaponak. He died in Southampton Hospital of a massive coronary attack but not before completing his last book, *Whistle*, while in the hospital; literally dictating the last few chapters from his bed in the coronary care unit.

SAG HARBOR

The Annie Cooper Boyd House

Main Street, Sag Harbor
(631) 725-3241

The house is located in the center of Sag Harbor's business district.

This eighteenth-century house is the headquarters of the Sag Harbor Historical Society. Featured are the paintings of Annie Cooper Boyd and a reference library of over five hundred books, letters, documents, pictures, and postcards relating to the history of the village. The house, which is currently undergoing a restoration, is open to the public.

Windmill
Junction of Route 114 and Main Street, Sag Harbor

Located at the eastern end of Main Street at the intersection of Route 114.

The windmill was erected in 1966 approximately fifty feet from the location of the original 1760 mill. The new mill is used as a tourist information center. This is an excellent starting point for touring Sag Harbor. The center has maps, pamphlets, books, postcards, and a walking tour guide to the village's numerous historical houses.

Bay Street Theatre
Main Street and Bay Street, Sag Harbor
(631) 725-9500

The theater is located on the wharf opposite the windmill.

Featured are first-time performances of plays, many of which are adaptations of motion pictures. Also offered are classes in acting and playwriting.

Chester A. Arthur's Summer White House
Union Street, Sag Harbor

Not open to the public.

From the windmill information booth located at the junction of Route 114 and Main Street in Sag Harbor go .4 mile on Main Street through the town bearing right at the fork in the road. Turn left (east) onto Union Street; go .1 mile. The house is on the right (south) side of the road.

Chester Allan Arthur (1830–1886) was born in Fairfield, VT. After graduating in 1848 from Union College in Schenectady, NY, Arthur practiced law in New York City. During the Civil War he served as New York State Quartermaster General. As such, he was responsible for receiving and equipping army volunteers. In 1871 he was rewarded for his loyal service to the Republican Party by President Grant with the position of Collector of the Port of New York. In this post he handled most of the country's customs' revenue as well as the political patronage of one thousand government employees. Arthur was not convicted of wrong doing by a federal investigation of the New York City Custom House but he was removed from his appointed position by President Hayes.

At the 1880 Republican National Convention delegates from New York succeeded in having Arthur placed on the Garfield ticket as the vice-presidential candidate. With the election of Garfield and his assassination in 1881, Arthur became the twenty-first President of the United States. Expected to implement New York State's free-wheeling spoils system on a national level, Arthur surprised everyone by establishing the Federal Civil Service System whereby a person's advancement was based on competitive examinations rather than political influence.

An avid fisherman, Arthur summered at least once during his presidency (1881–1885) at the Sag Harbor home of his close friend Stephan French, a former New York City police commissioner. The large circa 1865–1875 Italianate-style home was remodeled from an earlier structure, possibly an eighteenth-century house. The house is readily identified by its distinctive colonnaded porch and entrance way.

President Chester A. Arthur is buried in Albany Rural Cemetery in Albany, NY. His gravesite is marked by a stunning sarcophagus guarded by a standing angel sculpted in metal.

Christ Episcopal Church
Route 114, Sag Harbor
(631) 725-0128

From Route 27/Main Street/Montauk Highway turn north opposite the village green in East Hampton onto Buell Lane/Route 114 (which becomes Sag Harbor Turnpike); go 6.4 miles to Sag Harbor. The church is on the right (east) side of the road.

The Christ Episcopal Church parish, founded in 1845, met in the town arsenal for forty years before constructing the present building. An unusual covered portico, of later construction, descending the stairs from the church to the sidewalk, greets you as you explore this white frame 1885 slate-roofed church.

A prized Tiffany window, the Belknap (1893) Memorial window, *Cross*, is found on the north wall in the baptistery. It is a stunning pastel glass jewel composite lancet window with a gold glass jewel cross on a gold background clearly illustrating both the plating technique and mottled glass used by Tiffany Studios. The border is a medallion pattern done in glass jewels and worth seeing since few of the medallion windows executed by Tiffany have survived, especially on Long Island. Unsigned, this window is documented in Tiffany Studios' records.

On the west wall is a very large Tiffany commission signed "TIFFANY STVDIOS, N.Y. 1917," the James Herman Aldrich Memorial window based on a painting by Johann Heinrich Hofman. This window, to our knowledge, has not previously been identified in the literature as a documented Tiffany window. It presents the boy Jesus in the temple with the elders (Luke 2:46-50). Jesus is represented in white opalescent drapery glass with gold trim and a gold girdle or belt, the latter symbolizing great wisdom. The spotlighting or cellar lighting effect focuses eyes always, no matter what the time of day or the amount of outside lighting, upon the central figure of Christ, a small figure in relationship to the size of the window, but of incredible dominance. Christ's garments and the facial features of three of the five elders are virtually identical to those in the window depicting the same theme in Christ Episcopal Church in Williamsport, PA. The amount of architectural detail is unusual for a Tiffany window—austere but impressive in glass with a plating effect that gives texture and substance to the gray pillars and walls, an effect similar to that used for the organ in the window *Saint Cecilia* in Church of the Atonement in Quogue. (See also Town of Southampton/Quogue/Church

194

of the Atonement.) Fractured or confetti glass has been beautifully used in trim and borders in subdued colors. Under the window is a 1917 mosaic with Luke 2:46 explaining the window above. This is done in the same subdued colors and is also credited to Tiffany Studios.

Custom House
Garden Street, Sag Harbor
(631) 692-4664

From the windmill information booth located at the intersection of Route 114 and Main Street in Sag Harbor go .4 mile on Main Street through the town bearing right at the fork in the road. The Custom House is on the right side of the road next to the Sag Harbor Whaling and Historical Museum and across the street from the John Jermain Memorial Library.

In 1789 Henry Packing Dering, the son of Mary Sylvester of the Shelter Island Sylvesters, was chosen as Sag Harbor's first custom master and the first postmaster on Long Island. His house, which has been restored by the Society for the Preservation of Long Island Antiquities and has been on the National Register of Historic Places since 1973, contains many original Dering pieces including a custom book, a portable desk, an office desk, an 1817 mailbag, twin iron sleigh beds, a cane made from shark vertebrae, and four Dominy pieces: a clock, a chair, a bullet mold, and a paper weight.

Eastville Heritage House
139 Hampton Street/Route 114, Sag Harbor
(631) 725-4711

From Route 27/Montauk Highway turn north onto Route 114/East Hampton Road/Sag Harbor Turnpike/Hampton Street. Go north on Route 114/Hampton Road. The house is at the intersection of Route 114/Hampton Road and Liberty Street.

This one-story house is sometimes referred to as the Mail Order House or a Sears Modern House. Sears Roebuck and Company sold homes through its catalog from 1908 to 1940. Its 1908 specialty catalog "Book of Modern Homes and Building Plans" featured twenty-two different houses priced from $650 to $2,500. The entire house kit, which was shipped to the customer by railroad, weighed twenty-five tons and consisted of over 30,000 parts. Everything was pre-cut to size and labeled so that the house could be assembled by one carpenter, thereby cutting labor costs. The only items not included were the heating system and plumbing and electrical fixtures. Over the years Sears expanded its program to include 447 different models. To facilitate sales, Sears even offered mortgages.

In 1925 Lippman and Rose Johnson purchased their catalog home. By then prices ranged from under $1,000 to almost $4,400. The Johnsons resided in their home until the 1980s.

Restored by the Eastville Community Historical Society, the house, which serves as the society's headquarters, contains letters, photographs, journals, and furniture dating from the nineteenth century. Exhibits are rotated twice-a-year.

John Jermain Memorial Library

Main Street, Sag Harbor
(631) 725-0049

From the windmill information booth located at the junction of Route 114 and Main Street in Sag Harbor go .4 mile on Main Street through the town bearing right at the fork in the road. The library is on the left side of the road opposite the Sag Harbor Whaling and Historical Museum.

Built in 1910 by Mrs. Russell Sage, the building has a Christopher Wren-type domed ceiling with a round decorative skylight. The dome was constructed of out-sized red bricks in a herringbone pattern. The building houses the public library, a special collection of old documents as well as a museum offering changing exhibits. It has been on the National Register of Historic Places since 1973.

Morton National Wildlife Refuge

Noyac Road, Sag Harbor
(631) 286-0485

Take the Long Island Expressway to Exit #71 south. Go south on Route 24 for 12 miles to Route 27/Montauk Highway. Go east on Route 27/Montauk Highway for 7.1 miles. Turn left (north) onto Sandy Hollow Road/County Road 52. Go .9 mile to North Sea Road/County Road 38. Continue north on County Road 38/North Sea Road and then on Noyac Road as the name changes. Go a total of 6.5 miles on County Road 38. The refuge is on the left side of the road.

The area was originally called Farrington Point after the founder of Southampton, John Farrington. It eventually became known by its present name, Jessup's Neck, when John Jessup obtained ownership of the property in 1679. The grave of Jessup's daughter Abigail, with its distinctive headstone, is on a wooded bluff in the refuge. In 1800 Isaac Osborn purchased the land and introduced the growing of mulberry bushes, and apple and Bartlett pear trees to the area as well as the raising of silkworms, merino sheep, and short-horned cattle. In 1954 the land was donated by Elizabeth Morton to the United States Fish and Wildlife Service.

The 187-acre refuge which has an 120-year-old red maple, believed to be Long Island's oldest, is dedicated to the protection of wildlife. There is a one-mile nature trail which takes approximately one hour to walk. Swimming and picnicking on the extensive beach is permitted, but the building of fires is forbidden.

Oakland Cemetery
Jermain Avenue and Suffolk Street, Sag Harbor

From the windmill information booth located at the junction of Route 114 and Main Street in Sag Harbor go .2 mile through the town, bearing left at fork onto Madison Street. Go .6 mile to Jermain Avenue. Turn right (west); follow Jermain Avenue to the cemetery.

Broken Mast Monument

Go down the main carriage road for .1 mile to the second carriage road. Turn right onto the second carriage road.

This unique monument is a marble shaft shaped like a splintered ship's mast and is dedicated to six local ship masters who died at sea. The dedication on the monument reads: "To commemorate that noble enterprise The Whale Fishery and a tribute to lasting respect to those bold and enterprising ship masters, Sons of Southampton, who periled their lives in a daring profession and perished in actual encounter with the Monsters of the deep, entombed in the ocean. They live in our memory."

Grave of Nelson Algren (1909–1981)

Go down the main carriage road for 50 yards. Turn left (east) onto the first carriage road; go to carriage road number 9. Turn left (north); go 45 yards towards Jermain Avenue. The grave site is on the left (west) side of the carriage road.

Prior to becoming a prolific and successful writer, Algren held a number of jobs during the Depression. He worked as a migrant worker in the South and Southwest, a gas station attendant in Texas, and a salesman selling coffee door to door. He was employed by the WPA writers' project and edited, with Jack Conroy, the *New Anvil*, a magazine devoted to experimental and leftist writing. He won national recognition for his book *The Man With the Golden Arm*, for which he was awarded the National Book Award in 1950. Algren, born Nelson Ahlgren Abraham in Detroit, MI, like James Farrel and Richard Wright, was a realist writer whose books more often than not stressed the seedier aspects of the Chicago slums and tenements. Hemingway referred to him as the best contemporary American writer after Faulkner.

Grave of George Balanchine (1904–1983)

Go down the main carriage road .1 mile to the second carriage road. Turn right onto the second carriage road; go about 50 feet. The grave is on the left side of the road.

A Russian immigrant, Balanchine was the founder of the New York City Ballet and is considered the master ballet choreographer of the twentieth century. While still in Russia he studied both music and ballet and was considered a thorough musician, functioning as both composer and choreographer in the early days of his career.

His gravestone reads "George Balanchine, 1904–1983, Ballet Master" and is adorned with the Russian Orthodox cross and a lyre, the latter being the symbol of the New York City Ballet.

(See also Town of Babylon/Pinelawn/Pinelawn Memorial Park and Cemetery/ Grave of Andre Eglevsky.)

Grave of Alexander Brook (1898–1980)

Go down the main carriage road for 50 yards. Turn left (east) onto the first carriage road; go to carriage road number 10. Turn right (south); go .1 mile. The grave site is on the left (east) side of the carriage road.

At the age of twelve Brook contracted poliomyelitis. During the long recuperation period, a neighbor, who was an artist, bought Brook his first set of paints and canvases. Brook instantly knew that he wanted to make his livelihood as an artist. He studied at Pratt Institute and at the Art Students League. In 1927 he became the assistant director of the Whitney Studio Club. By the age of thirty he had become a successful artist, painting portraits of such Hollywood stars as Katharine Hepburn. Never affected by the Abstract Expressionism of modern artists, he remained a representative of the Realist School. His work is exhibited in the collections of some twenty-one museums.

Old Burying Ground
Union Street, Sag Harbor

From the windmill information booth located at the intersection of Route 114 and Main Street in Sag Harbor go .5 mile on Main Street through the town bearing right at the fork. Turn left (east) onto Union Street opposite the Sag Harbor Whaling and Historical Museum; go .2 mile. The Burying Ground is on the right (south) side of the road next to the Whaler's First Presbyterian Church.

Adjacent to the Whaler's First Presbyterian Church, this cemetery is the final resting place of Revolutionary War soldiers and sailors. William Havens, the captain of three privateers, is also buried here. The cemetery has been on the National Register of Historic Places since 1973.

The Old Sag Harbor Jail House
Division Street, Sag Harbor
(631) 725-3241

The jail is located next to the Sag Harbor police station.

This c. 1910 jail has been restored by the Sag Harbor Historical Society and is open to the public as a period prison museum.

Sag Harbor Fireman's Museum
Sage Street and Church Street, Sag Harbor
(631) 725-3241

From the windmill information booth at the intersection of Route 114 and Main Street in Sag Harbor go .2 mile on Main Street through the town, bearing left at the fork onto Madison Street. Go .1 mile to the museum which is on the corner of Sage Street and Church Street.

The museum contains memorabilia of Sag Harbor's 175-year-old fire department. Since it is often not open when it is supposed to be open, reportedly because of the lack of volunteers, it is best to call the number listed above if you plan to visit.

Sag Harbor State Golf Course
Barcelona Point Road, Sag Harbor
(631) 725-2503

The golf course is on the east side of Route 114.

The nine-hole golf course is situated in the middle of the 341-acre Barcelona Neck Natural Resources Management Area. The course, which may be played as nine or eighteen holes, offers a putting green, golf lessons, electric or pull carts, a clubhouse, and a snack bar.

Sag Harbor Whaling and Historical Museum
Main Street, Sag Harbor
(631) 725-0770

From the windmill information booth located at the junction of Route 114 and Main Street in Sag Harbor go .4 mile on Main Street through the town bearing right at the fork in the road. The museum is on the right (west) side of the road.

This Greek Revival-style building, which has been on the National Register of Historic Places since 1973, was designed in 1845 by Minard Lefever as a home for the wealthy Sag Harbor whaling ship owner, Benjamin Huntting. Of particular interest is the building's Corinthian columns and the roof ornamentation of carved wood representing harpoons and blubber spades. The museum itself contains a treasure of Sag Harbor memorabilia and represents the village's heyday when it was the largest whaling community in New York State and the fourth largest in the world. There are collections of scrimshaw, children's toys, silverware, china, model ships, walking sticks with carved whalebone handles, guns, whaling equipment, carpenter's tools, ships' logs, personal letters, sea shells, shoes from Japan with inlaid mother of pearl, and a circa 1700 kitchen. The most unusual item of all is an eighty-four key "giraffe" piano of which only twenty-six were manufactured and of which only three remain in the United States. (See also Town of Islip/West Bay Shore/Sagtikos Manor.)

Whaler's First Presbyterian Church
44 Union Street, Sag Harbor
(631) 725-0894

From the windmill information booth located at the intersection of Route 114 and Main Street in Sag Harbor go .5 mile on Main Street through the town bearing right at the fork. Turn left (east) onto Union Street opposite the Sag Harbor Whaling and Historical Museum; go .2 mile. The church is on the right side of the road next to the Old Burying Ground.

Designed by Minard Lefever and built by shipwrights in 1844, the church was designed in the Egyptian Revival-style evoking association with the Temple of Solomon. The steeple, which was ornamented with carved wooden harpoons and blubber spades, was tall enough that it could be seen by returning seamen as they rounded Montauk Point. The force of the 1938 hurricane was so great that the 94-year-old steeple, whose main support timbers were embedded approximately thirty feet into the church's structure, was torn from its superstructure and blown thirty feet into the air, landing in the church's graveyard. The church has remained without a steeple as a reminder to its parishioners of the perils faced by mariners. The church is on the National Register of Historic Places.

SHINNECOCK HILLS

Meschutt Beach County Park
Old North Highway, Shinnecock Hills
(631) 852-8205

Suffolk County Resident Pass is required for admission.

From Route 27/Sunrise Highway just east of the Shinnecock Canal go north on North Road for 1.2 miles. Bear right onto Old North Highway; go .3 mile. The beach is on the right side of the road.

This seven-acre park is located next to the Shinnecock Canal County Marina. The park offers protected swimming in Peconic Bay, playgrounds, and a snack bar. Restrooms are provided.

Mill Hill Windmill
Route 27, Shinnecock Hills

Not open to the public.

Take the Long Island Expressway to Exit #70 south (Eastport Manor Road/Manorville/Eastport). Go south on Port Jefferson–Westhampton Road/County Road 111/Captain Daniel Roe Blvd. for 4.7 miles. Go east on Sunrise Highway/Route 27 (which becomes County Road 39) for 15.2 miles to Exit #7. Turn right (south) onto the campus grounds.

This smock-type mill, which is located on the campus of Stony Brook Southampton College, originally was built with wooden machinery but in subsequent years cast-iron machinery was installed. The mill remained in operation until 1889 when it was moved to its present site by Mrs. William Hoyt. The mill and adjacent land became the estate of Arthur B. Claflin who had most of the mill's machinery as well as its fantail removed. It was then converted by him into a tearoom and playhouse. The windmill has been considerably altered over the years and is presently being used as living quarters. It is rumored that the playwright Tennessee Williams summered here.

(See also Town of Southampton/Shinnecock Hills/Stony Brook Southampton College–Arthur B. Claflin Estate.)

Shinnecock Canal County Marina
Old North Highway, Shinnecock Hills
(631) 852-8291

Not restricted to Suffolk County residents.

From Route 27/Sunrise Highway just east of the Shinnecock Canal go north on North Road for 1.2 miles. Bear right onto Old North Highway; go .3 mile. The marina is on the left (west) side of the road.

This five-acre marina is located at the northeastern terminus of the Shinnecock Canal next to Meschutt Beach County Park. It is a transient facility accommodating fifty vessels; allowing dockage for up to seven days. The marina offers a sewerage pump-out station, showers, restrooms, and both water and electrical hook ups. Coupled with the Shinnecock Canal County Park, this is an ideal vacation spot.

Shinnecock Indian Reservation
Route 27A, Shinnecock Hills
(631) 287-4923

The reservation extends south from Route 27A/Montauk Highway. Its perimeters are clearly posted.

The ancestral lands of the Shinnecock Indians included all the land from Westhampton east to East Hampton as well as several tracts of land along the south shore of Peconic Bay. Only about three hundred Shinnecock Indians presently live on the reservation. Located on the reservation is a trading post, a burial ground dating from about 1600, and the Shinnecock Nation Cultural Center and Museum. The Shinnecock Pow Wow is held on the reservation annually around Labor Day. Check newspapers for dates and the schedule of events.

Shinnecock Nation Cultural Center and Museum
100 Montauk Highway, Shinnecock Hills
(631) 287-4923

The cultural center is located at the intersection of Montauk Highway and Westgate Road.

The museum, which is the only Native American owned and operated museum on the Island, depicts the history of the Shinnecock Nation. Included are a whaling exhibit, a wigwam, an ancient birch bark canoe, a large collection of Algonquian bronze sculptures, murals, tools, jewelry, totems, and photographs.
(See also Town of East Hampton/Montauk/The Pharaoh Museum and Town of Southold/Southold/Indian Museum.)

Stony Brook Southampton College – Arthur B. Claflin Estate
Route 27, Shinnecock Hills
(631) 283-4000

Take the Long Island Expressway to Exit #70 south (Eastport Manor Road/Manorville/Eastport). Go south on Port Jefferson–Westhampton Road/County Road 111/Captain Daniel Roe Blvd. for 4.7 miles. Go east on Sunrise Highway/Route 27 (which becomes County Road 39) for 15.2 miles to Exit #7. Turn right (south) onto the campus grounds.

The main house of the estate was designed for Claflin by the noted Beaux-Arts architect Grosvenor Atterbury and built in 1898 on a hill overlooking Shinnecock Bay and the Atlantic Ocean. Claflin, a textile manufacturer from Lakewood, NJ, maintained the estate as his summer residence until the 1930s. In 1949 it was converted into the Tucker Mill Inn. The Mill Hill Windmill, which had been moved to its present site in the 1890s, became the inn's guest house. (See also Town of Southampton/Shinnecock Hills/Mill Hill Windmill.) In 1963 the property was acquired by Long Island University for the site of its Southampton College. In 2006 the eighty-one-acre campus was purchased by the State University at Stony Brook and renamed Stony Brook Southampton College. The interior of the estate's main house, which has been altered considerably over the years, is being used to house the college's administrative offices.

William Merritt Chase's Studio
Canoe Place Road, Shinnecock Hills

Not open to the public.

Take the Long Island Expressway to Exit #70 south (Eastport Manor Road/Manorville/Eastport). Go south on Port Jefferson–Westhampton Road/County Road 111/ Captain Daniel Roe Blvd. for 4.7 miles. Go east on Sunrise Highway/Route 27 for 12.3 miles to Exit #66 (North Road/Shinnecock). Go south on North Road/County Road 39 for .3 mile. Turn left (east) onto Montauk Highway/County Road 80 (at the Shinnecock Canal); go 1.4 miles. Turn left (north) onto Canoe Place Road; go .2 mile. The house is on the right (east) side of the road.

William Merritt Chase (1849–1916), the famous American impressionistic painter and art teacher was born in Williamsburg, IN. His artistic potential became apparent at an early age. After studying still-life painting with Barton S. Hays, Chase entered the National Academy of Design in New York City. In 1872 he enrolled in Munich's Royal Academy, at which he studied for six years. By the time he returned to New York City in 1878, to assume a teaching position at the Arts Students League, he had already attained considerable fame as a portrait and still-life painter. In 1880 he was elected president of the Society of American Artists, a position he held for ten years.

Chase began summering in Shinnecock Hills in 1890. By 1891 he was conducting classes for aspiring artists at The Summer Art School in Shinnecock. The school's popularity grew rapidly and it was not unusual for classes to be comprised of one hundred students.

Chase's colonial-style studio was designed by Stanford White, not for Chase but for Charles L. Atterbury. For reasons that are to this day unknown, the house was subsequently built for Chase rather than for Atterbury. Chase used the large white-columned house as his summer home and studio from 1881 to 1902. The house is on the National Register of Historic Places.

SHINNECOCK INLET

Shinnecock Beach County Park (East and West)
Beach Road, Shinnecock Inlet
(631) 854-4949

Suffolk County Resident Pass is required for admission.

Take Route 27/Sunrise Highway to Canoe Place Road. Turn south onto Canoe Place Road (which becomes Argonne Road). Go .6 mile on Canoe Place/Argonne Road. Turn left onto Lynn Avenue; go 1.8 miles. Turn right onto Shinnecock Avenue; go .1 mile. Turn left onto Forster Avenue (which becomes Lighthouse Road). Go across the drawbridge for a total of 7.5 miles. Turn left onto Beach Road and go 1 mile to Shinnecock Inlet.

This 407-acre undeveloped park is located at the juncture of the Shinnecock Inlet and the Atlantic Ocean. A favorite of sunbathers and fishermen, Shinnecock Beach East is accessible only by four-wheel drive vehicles. An outer beach permit must be obtained in advance for use of a vehicle. Shinnecock Beach West, at the eastern end of Dune Road, has limited parking with no fee. Neither beach has any facilities.

SOUTHAMPTON

British Fort
Windmill Lane, Southampton

From the intersection of Route 27/County Road 39 and North Sea Road in Southampton turn south onto North Sea Road/Main Street; go .5 mile. Bear right onto Windmill Lane; go .1 mile. The fort is on the right (west) side of the road.

The earthenworks fort, which was never given a name, was built by the British on this site during their occupation of Southampton, 1777–1778. A period redoubt has been reconstructed and the area turned into a pleasant park.

Elias Pelletreau Silver Shop
78 Main Street, Southampton
(631) 283-2494

From the intersection of Route 27/County Road 39 and North Sea Road in Southampton turn south onto North Sea Road/Main Street and continue .9 mile. The shop is on the left (east) side of the road next to the Chamber of Commerce.

Built in 1686 by Stephen Boyer, the shop was acquired by Captain Elias Pelletreau in 1748 shortly after the latter had completed his apprenticeship as a silversmith. Pelletreau's son John and grandson William continued the family silversmith business at the same location. The shop was originally turned with the long side facing the road and was attached to the Pelletreau house. The house was demolished to make way for a driveway and the shop was pivoted to its present position. Today items made by the Pelletreaus are avidly sought by collectors of colonial silverware.

The Good Ground Windmill
Dune Road, Southampton

Not open to the public.

From the intersection of Route 27/County Road 39 and North Sea Road in Southampton turn south onto North Sea Road/Main Street and continue for 1 mile. Turn right (west) onto Jobs Lane (which becomes Hill Street/Route 27A); go .4 mile. Turn left (south) onto First Neck Lane; go 1.1 miles. Turn left (east) onto Dune Road; go .3 mile to St. Andrew's Dune Church. The windmill is visible by looking northwest.

This smock-type windmill was built in 1807 by Nathaniel Dominy V and was originally located on Shelter Island. In the 1860s it was moved to Good Ground in Hampton Bays and remained in operation until 1880 when C. Wyllys Betts purchased the windmill and moved it to Southampton. Betts removed the machinery and converted it into a cottage. Over the years the windmill has been considerably altered and incorporated into a much larger home, but its distinctive Ogee Cap with its stalk and ball finial remain untouched and can easily be seen from the lawn of St. Andrew's Dune Church.

North End Graveyard
North Sea Road, Southampton

From the intersection of Route 27/County Road 39 and North Sea Road in Southampton turn south onto North Sea Road/Main Street and continue for .7 mile. The cemetery is on the right (west) side of the road.

The cemetery is located opposite the Herrick home, which was the headquarters of the British General Erskine from 1777–1778 during the occupation of Southampton. The first interment was in 1717 and the last in 1940. The cemetery has historical significance because it contains the graves of many soldiers of the Continental Army.

Old Burying Ground
Little Plains Road, Southampton

From the intersection of Route 27/County Road 39 and North Sea Road in South-ampton turn south onto North Sea Road/Main Street; go 1 mile. Turn left (east) onto Meeting House Lane; go .3 mile. Turn right (south) onto Little Plains Road; go .2 mile. The cemetery is on the right (west) side of the road.

Located in a quiet section of the village this cemetery is the final resting place of many of Southampton's early settlers. The first known burial was in 1649.

Old Halsey Homestead
249 South Main Street, Southampton
(631) 283-2494

From the intersection of Route 27/County Road 39 and North Sea Road in South-ampton turn south onto North Sea Road/Main Street; go 1.5 miles. The house is on the right (west) side of the road.

This house was built in 1648 by Thomas Halsey, one of the first English settlers who landed at Conscience Point in 1640. (See also Town of Southampton/North Sea/Conscience Point.) The house is the earliest English-type frame house in New York State and is furnished with period pieces. Of particular interest are the English-style leaded casement windows in the original section of the house and the "12 over 12" and "8 over 12" double-hung windows found in the newer circa 1800 addition. There is an extremely large country kitchen which Halsey built for his wife Phebe, who was later murdered in the house by marauding Pequot Indians from Connecticut. A circa 1700 man's shaving kit and an 1820 Dominy clock are particularly fascinating. The herb and flower gardens have been reconstructed by the Southampton Colonial Society to correspond to Phebe Halsey's inventory of English bulbs and seeds brought with her from Lynn, MA, and ultimately from England.

Parrish Art Museum
25 Jobs Lane, Southampton
(631) 283-2118

From the intersection of Route 27/County Road 39 and North Sea Road in South-ampton turn south onto North Sea Road/Main Street; go 1 mile. Turn right (west) onto Jobs Lane; go .1 mile. The museum is on the right (north) side of the road.

Samuel Longstreth Parrish was born in Philadelphia, PA, in 1849. His family, who were Quakers, was among the colony's first settlers having arrived in Penn-sylvania with William Penn. Parrish was a Harvard graduate, successful New York lawyer, and avid collector of Renaissance paintings and sculpture. After becoming a permanent resident of Southampton, he decided to establish an art museum in the community with his own personal art collection as its base. Established in 1898, the museum has expanded beyond Parrish's original Renaissance contribution to include an impressive representation of nineteenth- and twentieth-century American painters. The museum has three galleries, an 160-seat auditorium, and an exquisite sculpture garden. Like its counterpart, the Guild Hall in East Hampton, the museum offers changing art exhibits, lectures, popular and classical concerts, and European and American film classics.

In 2009 the museum plans to relocate to a new museum facility in Water Mill.

(See also Town of Southampton/Southampton/Southampton Historical Museum Complex.)

Sacred Hearts of Jesus and Mary Cemetery
Route 27, Southampton

From the intersection of Route 27/County Road 39 and North Sea Road in South-ampton go west on Route 27/County Road 39 for .4 mile. Turn right (north) into the most western cemetery entrance.

Grave of Gary Cooper (1901–1961)

Make an immediate left (west) onto the first carriage road; go .1 mile. The grave is on the right (north) side of the road just before the curve. The grave site is marked by a large pink rock.

Gary Cooper (1901–1961) was born Frank James Cooper in Helena, MT. His father, who was a cattleman and a judge in the Montana Supreme Court, had been born in Bedfordshire, England. Gary attended public school in England for a short period but was dismissed for ungentlemanly behavior; he had a fight with a newsboy. He returned to the United States and attended Wesleyan College in Helena and Grinnell College in Iowa, graduating from neither institution. After trying unsuccessfully to make a living as a cartoonist in Chicago he decided to move to Los Angeles, claiming it was easier to starve in a warm climate. Cooper began his film career as an extra and progressed to bit parts in "horse operas." His first big role was that of the second male lead opposite Ronald Colman in *Winning of Barbara Worth*. He was still "type cast" as a western actor until his role in Paramount's production of *Wings*. He went on to win Academy Awards for his roles in *Sergeant York* (1941) and *High Noon* (1952) and was given a special academy citation in 1961.

When Cooper learned that he had cancer, he remarked to Ernest Hemingway, "Papa, I bet I beat you back to the barn." Gary Cooper died May 13, 1961; Ernest Hemingway committed suicide on July 2nd of the same year. Originally buried in Los Angeles, CA, Cooper was moved to Southampton thirteen years later by his wife who had subsequently married a Southampton physician.

Saint Andrew's Dune Church
12 Gin Lane, Southampton
(631) 283-3015

Closed during the winter.

From the intersection of Route 27/County Road 39 and North Sea Road in South-ampton turn south onto North Sea Road/Main Street; go 1 mile. Turn right (west) onto Jobs Lane (which becomes Hill Street/Route 27A); go .4 mile. Turn left (south) onto First Neck Lane; go 1.1 miles. Turn left (east) onto Gin Road; go .3 mile. The church is on the right (south) side of the road.

Built in 1851 by the federal government as a life saving station, the building was acquired by Dr. Theodore Gaillard Thomas, donated as a church in 1879, and moved to its present site. Originally called Saint Andrews-by-the-Sea, the name was changed in 1884 to Saint Andrew's Dune Church. While not a member of the Episcopal Diocese of Long Island it does have close ties to the diocese and its services are usually conducted by visiting Episcopalian clergy. The additions of the north and south transepts were made in 1883; the choir and aisles were added in 1887–1888 and enlarged in 1894. The church was severely damaged by the 1938 hurricane and had to be completely rebuilt.

Its interior has such treasures as a thirteenth-century Purbect marble base credence table from Netley Abbey in Southampton, England; two English chancel chairs made in 1681; an English Bible and Prayer Book printed in 1639; oak corbels from the fifteenth-century Blythburg Church in Suffolk, England; and molding head and finial from York Minster, England. As if these were not enough, the church has an incredibly impressive list of Tiffany windows.

In the north transept is the Mary E. Holbrook (1890) Memorial window. Although unsigned, it is listed in Tiffany Studios' records as "Holbrook Memorial Window. Ornamental" and no other Holbrook Memorial is listed in the church records. It is a uniquely fascinating marine mosaic with rough-hewn jewel glass, pebbles, and sea shells. Tiffany did many jewel glass and pebble windows but this is the only one that we have found on Long Island which includes shells. Other artists in glass did use this unique technique, however. (See also Town of Shelter Island/Shelter Island/Chapel in the Grove–Union Chapel and Town of Shelter Island/Shelter Island/Saint Mary's Episcopal Church.) The Holbrook window was restored by the Betts family after being severely damaged by the unnamed hurricane of September 1938, during which the following documented Tiffany windows were destroyed beyond repair:

1. Ismay Memorial window, *Queen of Heaven* (east of the door in south transept; matched Trevor Memorial window);
2. Russell Memorial window, *Christ Blessing Child* (south wall of nave; replaced by window in European style);
3. Trevor Memorial window, *Good Shepherd* (south wall in south transept; original matched Ismay Memorial window; replaced by window in European style);
4. Stephens (Stevens) Memorial window, *Lead Kindly Light* (south wall of nave);
5. DeLuze Memorial window, ornamental (in south transept).

In the north transept on the west wall is the Ogdon Cryder (1902) Memorial window, listed in the records of Tiffany Studios and signed simply "TIFFANY STVDIOS." It is entitled *Sir Galahad* and shows a young knight in beautifully detailed silver/blue armor with his horse represented in pearl opalescent drapery glass over a painted horse's head. It is a stunning effect. There is extensive use of fractured or confetti glass in the trees and an unusual use of dark purple drapery glass in the tree trunks. To further understand the plating technique used by Louis C. Tiffany and his employees, go outside the church and look at the back of this window. You will be able to see clearly the use of layered colors to achieve depth of color and dimension. Note especially the layer of red glass on the back which intensifies both whiteness in the horse and the silvery effect in the armor.

On the north wall is the Louise Holbrook Betts (1925) Memorial window. This landscape from the late period, and therefore not included in the records of Tiffany Studios, is signed "LOUIS C. TIFFANY, N. Y." and is executed in vibrant colors clearly demonstrating the experimental landscape work produced by Tiffany Studios during these later years. There is extensive use of both mottled glass and fractured glass with neither figures nor flowers giving it a clearly contemporary look. Plating effects are dramatic.

Also in the north transept, but on the east wall, is the Theodore Gaillard Thomas (1903) Memorial window signed "TIFFANY STVDIOS, NEW YORK" and entitled *Christ Blessing the Children*. If this window was not signed and listed in the Tiffany Studios' surviving partial list of commissions, no one would suspect this to be a Tiffany commission. Robes, faces, and border patterns are painted in the European style making it enormously compatible with the many later windows which are clearly in the European style, such as those by Wilbur Herber Burnham, Boston, MA, but less compatible with other Tiffany commissions in this church.

Directly to the left of the Theodore Gaillard Thomas Memorial is the Howard Lapsley Thomas (1897) Memorial window depicting an angel warrior executed in bright yellow, red, and bright green with lavender wings. The plating work is disturbingly obvious and suggests the early, experimental years of this technique. Although unsigned, we would suggest that it had been done by artists other than Louis C. Tiffany and his studio. The garish colors and the glassing-over of painted areas, as in the Moses in Trinity Episcopal Church in Roslyn, are techniques which would not suggest Tiffany Studios as the source of the work. (See also Town of Oyster Bay/Roslyn/Trinity Episcopal Church.)

The Josephine Churchill Nicoll (1915) Memorial window in the north transept opposite the choir depicts an angel holding aloft the beatitude "Blessed are the pure in heart" (Matthew 5:8). This window, listed nowhere else in the literature, is clearly signed "TIFFANY STVDIOS, N.Y. 1915." The angel is formed from heavy drapery glass which appears to be thicker in the center of the panel giving a beautiful third dimension to the figure. Blue swirled mottled glass and plating have been used in the background to represent sky.

In the south transept is the Margaret H. Schieffelin (1892) Memorial window. Although unsigned, records of Tiffany Studios do list this commission of *Saint Margaret*. She is shown holding a smooth cross in her hands. Her robes are in yellow-gold drapery glass with a single jewel glass at her neck. Vine-like flowers frame the single figure. The face of the saint is painted in a more European style than usually seen in Tiffany windows. This window also was damaged by the 1938 hurricane and later restored.

In pictures showing the south side of the badly damaged church after the 1938 hurricane, the C. Wyllys Betts (1887) Memorial window can be seen miraculously undamaged. It is a most beautiful window depicting a cross, surrounded by lilies symbolizing the Resurrection, emerging from a remarkably dark sky formed from dark blue, red, and purple glass. All the colors in this window are vibrant; boldly announcing the Resurrection theme "He asked life. Thou gavest him a long life; even for ever and ever." Although unsigned and undocumented, there is ample reason to believe that this may have been executed by Louis C. Tiffany. Mr. Betts' brother, Frederic Henry Betts, gave the memorial to the church; both men were among the founders of Saint Andrew's.

Also in the south transept on the west wall is the George G. Dewitt (1912) Memorial window. This window has not been documented in the lists of Tiffany commissions, but it is clearly signed "TIFFANY STVDIOS, NEW YORK," a signature used from about 1900–1915. This *Angel of Resurrection* is positioned in a large, beautiful field of lilies with blue bells in the foreground, a flower not often included by Tiffany. The angel's robes are formed from heavy drapery glass as are the lavender wings. Lavender, blues, and an almost aqua sky give this *Angel of Resurrection* an unique appearance.

The Frederic Henry Betts (1906) Memorial window is perfectly situated on the west wall of the nave since its sunset color tones are even more beautiful when intensified at sunset. Signed "TIFFANY STVDIOS, NEW YORK" and documented in the records of Tiffany Studios, this dramatic landscape, so different from the 1925 Louise Holbrook Betts Memorial in the north transept of this same church, clearly displays the artistic talent of Louis C. Tiffany and his designers when undertaking floral themes, most of which were commissioned for homes and are therefore rarely viewed by the public. Trellised creamy yellow roses frame the sunset landscape with deep pink poppies in the foreground, the latter generally symbolizing sleep. There is clearly a feeling of peace, quiet, and gentle beauty.

Two unsigned windows made by John LaFarge have been documented—the Louisa Miller Howland Memorial (1884) window, *The Harpist*, in the north transept; and the Julia White Howland Memorial (1898) window, *Madonna and Child*, on the south wall of the baptistery. The latter window was destroyed during the 1938 hurricane and the 1947 replacement considerably alters LaFarge's original concept.

Southampton Cemetery Association

Route 27, Southampton

From the intersection of Route 27/County Road 39 and North Sea Road in South-ampton go west on Route 27/County Road 39 for .3 mile. Turn right (north) into the cemetery.

Grave of Jack Dempsey (1895–1983)

Go north on the carriage road for .2 mile. Turn left (west); go .1 mile to the Hart mausoleum which is located on the right (north) side of the carriage road. Walk north for six plots and east for two plots. The grave site is on the right directly behind the Hart mausoleum.

William Harrison Dempsey (Jack) was born in Manassa, CO. Determined to become a boxer, he trained endlessly. The turning point in his career came in 1919 when, at twenty-four, the six-foot, 180-pound Dempsey knocked out the six-foot-six-inch, 270-pound Jess Willard in the fourth round to become the heavy-weight champion of the world. Known as the "Manassa Mauler," Dempsey went on to defend his title five times before losing by decision to Gene Tunney in 1926. Dempsey was elected to the Boxing Hall of Fame in 1954. After his boxing days were over he became a popular New York City restauranteur.

On his gravestone are carved boxing gloves and the inscription,

Heavyweight champion of the world 1919–1926
A gentle man and a gentleman.

Southampton Historical Museum Complex

17 Meeting House Lane, Southampton
(631) 283-2494

From the intersection of Route 27/County Road 39 and North Sea Road in South-ampton turn south onto North Sea Road/Main Street; go 1 mile. Turn left (east) onto Meeting House Lane; go .1 mile. The complex is on the left (north) side of the road.

The Rodgers family owned the present site of the complex as early as 1645. The house was built in 1843 by Albert Rodgers, a whaling captain. In 1899 ownership eventually passed to Samuel L. Parrish, who modified the house adding two wings and moving it further back on the property in 1927. (See also Town of South-ampton/Southampton/Parrish Art Museum.) In 1943 the Village of Southampton purchased the house from the Parrish estate and used it as a community center and office for the Red Cross.

In 1951 the Southampton Colonial Society obtained it for use as a museum. The museum complex consists of the house, a blacksmith shop, a drug store, a one-room schoolhouse, a carriage shed, a carpenters shop, and a cobblers and har-ness shop. It contains a veritable treasure trove with collections of china, clothes, dolls, dollhouses, doll carriages, Indian artifacts, fans, whaling equipment, sleds, wagons, period furniture, and even a steam thresher. Perhaps the most unusual article is the dining room table. Originally a rectangular grand piano forte, it was cut down to create a table. If you look closely at the table top, you can see where the holes in the wood, from the piano's hinges, were filled.

SOUTHPORT

Stuyvesant Wainwright Memorial Refuge
(Long Island Chapter: The Nature Conservancy)
Upper Red Creek Road, Southport
(631) 367-3225

Open with prior permission.

Take the Long Island Expressway to Exit #70 south (Eastport Manor Road/Manor-ville/Eastport). Go south on Port Jefferson–Westhampton Road/County Road 111/ Captain Daniel Roe Blvd. for 4.7 miles. Go east on Sunrise Highway/Route 27 for 9.9 miles to Exit #65 south (Route 24/Hampton Bays/Riverhead). Go north on County Road 24 for 2.4 miles. Turn right (east) onto Red Creek Road. Take either Upper or Lower Red Creek Road for 1.4 miles until both roads rejoin. The entrance is off Upper Red Creek Road just north of the junction and down a private road the entrance to which is marked by stone markers labeled "RCPA."

This fifteen-acre preserve consists of a pine oak forest, a freshwater swamp, and a tidal marsh. The Wainwright family purchased the land in 1934. At that time it was predominantly fields used for growing Christmas trees and for the raising of ducks and pheasants. In 1976 the Wainwright family donated the land to the Conservancy.

Please call the Conservancy at the above telephone number to obtain permission to visit the preserve.

WATER MILL

The Water Mill Museum

41 Old Mill Road, Water Mill
(631) 726-4625

Opposite the village green on Route 27/Montauk Highway in Water Mill turn north onto Old Mill Road; go .1 mile. The mill is on the left (west) side of the road.

The Village of Water Mill was named after this mill which was built in 1644. Edward Howell, the first miller, was given a grant of forty acres by the village for his services. He retained possession of the mill until it was bought by William Ludlam in 1653. The Ludlam family ground grain at this site until 1748 when William Ludlam sold the mill to Elias Petty. Petty used the structure as a textile factory. Over the years the mill has been used as a post office, an ice cream factory, an ice house, a boys' club, a tea house, and a shop. In 1942 The Ladies Auxiliary of Water Mill, Inc. purchased and restored the mill. It has been on the National Register of Historic Places since 1983.

Among the more unusual items found upstairs in the museum are an eel trap, a button collection, an 1820 barn frame loom, a Wedgewood ironstone collection, and an 1861 American flag with thirty-four stars, issued when Kansas became a state and used until 1863 when West Virginia entered the Union. There is also a gift shop and changing art exhibit of local artists on the premises. The mill is functional and demonstrations are given of the entire process of grain milling.

Water Mill Windmill

Halsey Lane, Water Mill

Located at the intersection of Route 27/Montauk Highway and Halsey Lane on the village green in Water Mill.

Originally located at Hog Neck in Sag Harbor, this smock-type windmill was built in 1800 making it the second oldest of Long Island's eleven remaining windmills; the one on Gardiner's Island, built in 1795, being the oldest. The Water Mill Windmill did not have many innovations but rather retained many of the features of the older post-type windmills such as the use of a long pole located at the rear of the cap to rotate the cap and sails into the wind, and a single set of millstones driven directly from the brake wheel. In 1813 the mill was purchased by James Corwith, modernized, and moved to its present site on the Water Mill Village Commons where it remained in operation until 1888. The mill was forced to cease operations when a large mansion, which cut off the wind, was built on Mecox Bay. The owners of the estate eventually purchased the windmill, but didn't move it as their property adjoined the village commons. In 1931 the estate became a convent for the Order of Saint Dominic. The windmill was deeded by the order to the Water Mill Improvement Association in 1934. In 1985 work began on its restoration by the association and was completed in 1987. The windmill is the best surviving example of an early smock-type windmill on Long Island and has been on the National Register of Historic Places since 1978.

WESTHAMPTON BEACH

106th Rescue Wing – New York Air National Guard
Gabreski Airport, Westhampton Beach
(631) 723-7339

Take the Long Island Expressway to Exit #70 south (Eastport Manor Road/Manorville/Eastport). Go south on Port Jefferson–Westhampton Road/County Road 111/ Captain Daniel Roe Blvd. for 4.7 miles. Go east on Sunrise Highway/Route 27 for 4.1 miles to Exit #63 south (County Road 31/Westhampton Beach). Go south on County Road 31 for 2.7 miles. The entrance for the 106th Rescue Group is on the left (east) side of the road.

The 106th Rescue Wing's motto is "That others may live." The unit has a long history of service to the state and country. It traces its roots to the 1st Aero Company, which was formed in 1915 as a unit of the 1st Battalion Signal Corps. After World War I the unit was renamed the 102nd Observation Squadron of the New York Guard.

Known today as the 106th Rescue Wing of the New York Air National Guard, it flies air-refueling and air search and rescue missions in its HC-130P "Hercules" and search and rescue missions in its Sikorsky HH-60 "Pave Hawk" planes. It operates and maintains the only air rescue aircraft in the northeastern United States capable of aerial refueling.

To tour their facilities, call the above telephone number for arrangements.

(See also Town of Babylon/East Farmingdale/American Airpower Museum; Town of Islip/Bayport/Bayport Aerodrome; and Town of Hempstead/Garden City/ The Cradle of Aviation Museum.)

Sky Sailors Glider Flights
Rust Avenue, Building 313
Gabreski Airport, Westhampton Beach
(631) 288-5858

Take the Long Island Expressway to Exit #70 south (Eastport Manor Road/Manor-ville/Eastport). Go south on Port Jefferson–Westhampton Road/County Road 111/ Captain Daniel Roe Blvd. for 4.7 miles. Go east on Sunrise Highway/Route 27 for 4.1 miles to Exit #63 south (County Road 31/Westhampton Beach). Go south on County Road 31 for 2.2 miles. The entrance to the airport is on the left (east) side of the road. Turn left (east) into the airport; go .2 mile. Turn right (south) onto Rust Avenue; go .3 mile. The office is on the left (east) side of the road.

If you wish to become a licensed glider pilot or simply want to experience the thrill of being a passenger on a glider flight, Sky Sailors offers you the opportunity to either solo or to be a passenger on a glider flown by a qualified FAA pilot. Also offered are aerial advertising, sky-diving, sightseeing flights, and hot-air-balloon and bi-plane rides.

(See also Town of Riverhead/Calverton/Skydive Long Island.)

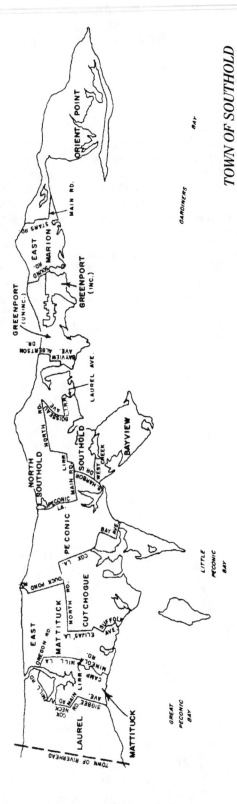

TOWN OF SOUTHOLD

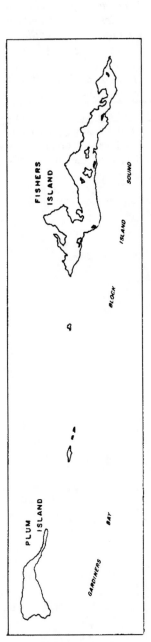

TOWN OF SOUTHOLD

PARKS AND PRESERVES

Federal Parks and Preserves
none

State Parks and Preserves
Camp Hero State Park (415 acres), Orient *(undeveloped)*
Orient Beach State Park (357 acres), Orient

County Parks and Preserves
Cedar Beach County Park (63 acres), Cedar Beach
Goldsmith's Inlet County Park (60 acres), Peconic
Inlet Point County Park (39 acres), Stirling *(undeveloped)*
Orient Point County Park (48 acres), Orient *(undeveloped)*
Peconic Dunes County Park (37 acres), Peconic

Long Island Chapter: The Nature Conservancy
Howell Meadow Preserve (5 acres), Southold
Husing Pond Preserve (21 acres), Mattituck
Margolin Marsh Preserve (25 acres), Orient
Marratooka Lake Preserve (11 acres), Mattituck
Meadow Beach Preserve (12 acres), Cutchogue
Mud Creek Preserve (6 acres), Cutchogue
Whitcom Marsh Preserve (17 acres), Orient

Arboretums and Gardens

Cedar Beach

Cedar Beach County Park
Cedar Beach Road, Cedar Beach
(631) 854-4949

Suffolk County Resident Pass is required for admission.

From the village green in Southold at the intersection of Route 25/Main Road and Young's Avenue go west on Route 25/Main Road for .9 mile to Bayview Road. Turn left (south) onto Bayview Road/Main–Bayview Road; go 2.9 miles. Turn left (east) onto Cedar Beach Road; go 1.5 miles to the park.

This sixty-three-acre park is limited to swimming during the summer months. It should be noted that there are neither facilities nor lifeguard protection.

Cutchogue

Cutchogue Cemetery
Route 25/Main Road, Cutchogue

From the village green in Cutchogue go east on Route 25/Main Road for .6 mile. The cemetery is on the left (north) side of the road.

Grave of Douglas Stuart Moore (1893–1969)

From the cemetery entrance go north on the carriage road for .1 mile. Turn left (west) onto the first carriage road that intersects from the left; go .1 mile. The grave site is on the right (east) side of the carriage road. There is a large black granite family plot marker.

Moore, a noted musicologist and composer, was born in Cutchogue and raised in Brooklyn. His ancestors include Thomas Moore, who settled in Southold in 1640, and the noted colonial leaders Miles Standish and John Alden. (See also Town of Southold/Southold/Southold Historical Society Complex/Thomas Moore House.) Moore received his undergraduate degree from Yale University and his doctorate from the Cincinnati Conservatory of Music. In Paris, he studied music under the tutelage of Vincent D'Indy and Nadia Boulanger and here in the United States with Ernest Bloch. He served as the curator of the Cleveland Museum of Art before joining Columbia University's faculty, where he remained for thirty-six years eventually becoming chairman of the music department. Moore authored several books on music theory but his greatest contributions to music were his compositions which include several symphonies, numerous chamber works, and several American folk operas. In 1951 he was awarded the Pulitzer Prize for his opera *Giants in the Earth* and in 1958 his opera *The Ballad of Baby Doe* received the New York Music Critics Circle Award.

Moore always considered himself to be a Long Islander and summered regularly in Cutchogue where he held annual drama and music summer workshops for the area's youth. In his honor, annual concerts are given in August on the Cutchogue Village Green.

Fort Corchaug
New Suffolk Avenue, Cutchogue

From the village green in Cutchogue on Route 25/Main Road go west on Route 25/Main Road for .3 mile. Turn left (south) onto Moores Lane; go 1 mile through the golf course. Turn right (west) onto New Suffolk Avenue; go .3 mile. The fort is on the right side of the road (north) half way up Downs Creek in the direction of Route 25/Main Road.

Nothing remains of the impressive Indian fort that was located on the west bank of Downs Creek in Cutchogue. Built by the Corchaug Indians long before the Europeans arrived, the fortress, which was built of logs with walls measuring 210 feet by 160 feet, enclosed approximately three-quarters of an acre. It was a defensive position against the marauding attacks of the Pequot Indians of Connecticut.

In 1973 the archaeological research of Dr. Ralph Solecki helped place the site on the National Register of Historic Places in 1974. Dr. Solecki, who grew up in Cutchogue and later became the curator of the Smithsonian Institute in Washington, DC, has determined that the English and Dutch traded with the Indians long before the founding of Southold in 1640. Among the many artifacts he found at the site are nails, flatblades, part of a sword, two jew's-harps, and part of an iron kettle. These items are now part of the Smithsonian's collection.

Meadow Beach Preserve
(Long Island Chapter: The Nature Conservancy)
Nassau Point Road, Cutchogue
(631) 367-3225

Open with prior permission.

From the village green in Cutchogue go east on Route 25/Main Road for 1 mile. Turn right (south) onto Eugene's Road; go .7 mile. Turn right (west) onto Bay Avenue (which becomes Nassau Point Road); go 1.5 miles. Park at the causeway and walk along the shore to the preserve.

This twelve-acre salt marsh is an excellent vantage point from which to observe migrating shorebirds and waterfowl. Cord grass, sea lavender, sea rocket, and seaside

219

knotweed can be found. The preserve is host to a variety of marine life such as fiddler crabs, mussels, scallops, and numerous other mollusks.

Please call the Conservancy at the above telephone number to obtain permission to visit the preserve.

Mud Creek Preserve
(Long Island Chapter: The Nature Conservancy)
Skunk Lane, Cutchogue
(631) 367-3225

Open with prior permission.

From the village green in Cutchogue go east on Route 25/Main Road for 1.1 miles. Turn right (south) onto Eugene's Road; go .8 mile. Turn right (west) onto Skunk Lane; go .3 mile. The preserve is on the right (west) side of the road.

This six-acre preserve is primarily a lush salt meadow with an oak and hickory forest located on a narrow strip of its eastern border. An abundance of salt grass, salt hay, and cord grass, as well as fiddler crabs and blue crabs, are found there. Numerous birds such as snowy egrets, green heron, great blue heron, and clapper rail are attracted to the preserve by the abundant food. The area around the preserve was probably used by the Corchaug Indians to gather fish and shellfish. During colonial times the salt grasses were used as animal feed. The preserve was donated to the Conservancy by several people over a period of time from 1975 through 1981.

Please call the Conservancy at the above number to obtain permission to visit the preserve.

Old Burying Ground
Route 25/Main Road, Cutchogue

From the village green in Cutchogue go east on Route 25/Main Road for 1 mile. The cemetery is on the right (south) side of the road.

Many second generation founders of Southold, the oldest English town in New York State, are buried in this cemetery. The earliest marked grave is dated 1717 but it is believed that there are several earlier unmarked graves.

Cutchogue Historic Complex
Village Green, Route 25/Main Road and Cases Lane, Cutchogue
(631) 734-7122

Old House
(part of Cutchogue Historic Complex)
Village Green, Route 25/Main Road and Cases Lane, Cutchogue

The Old House was built in 1649 by John Budd, the great-grandson of the Earl of Warwick. The massive ancestral castle of the Warwicks is located in Warwick, England, not far from Stratford-upon-Avon. Budd gave the house to his daughter Anna and her husband Benjamin Horton as a wedding present. (See also Town of Southold/Cutchogue Historic Complex/The Wickham Farmhouse and Town of Southold/Southold/Horton Lighthouse.)

The newly married couple had it moved from Southold to Cutchogue. It was eventually sold to the Wickham family who retained ownership until it was confiscated by New York State because of the family's loyalist sympathies during the Revolution. It was purchased by Jared Landon in 1784 and sold to William Harrison Case, whose heirs transferred ownership to the Congregational Society of Cutchogue. The house, which is large for its era, has two floors and a full attic which is reached by "good-morning-style" stairs. There are two large fireplaces, one in the kitchen and the other in the "setting room" or "hall." They measure nine-feet-five-inches-long by three-feet-deep by five-feet-high. Of particular interest are the casement windows and closets, both extremely unusual features in this era of Colonial-style architecture. The string latch on the front door is also intriguing. The house is sparingly furnished but among the personal items found here, the 1776 formal gown is especially beautiful. The house, which is the oldest English-style house in New York State, was placed on the National Register of Historic Places in 1966.

Old Schoolhouse
(part of Cutchogue Historic Complex)
Village Green, Route 25/Main Road and Cases Lane, Cutchogue

The Old Schoolhouse was built in 1840 on the other side of Route 25 just east of the Old Presbyterian Church. In 1903 the school was closed and moved to a field behind the Old Presbyterian Church where it was used to house farm workers. It was donated to the Cutchogue–New Suffolk Historical Council and moved to its present site on the village green in 1961. It is furnished as a period schoolhouse and even has an original desk as well as an arrowhead collection and local memorabilia. Of particular interest are a 13-star flag used between 1777 and 1795 and a 45-star flag issued in 1896 when Utah became a state and which remained in use until 1907 when Oklahoma entered the Union.

The Wickham Farmhouse
(part of Cutchogue Historic Complex)
Village Green, Route 25/Main Road and Cases Lane, Cutchogue

The circa 1740 farmhouse, which is on the National Register of Historic Places, was built on Route 25 just west of Cutchogue by Caleb Horton, who is reputed to be the first white child born in Southold. (See also Town of Southold/Cutchogue/ Cutchogue Historic Complex/Old House and Town of Southold/Southold/Horton Lighthouse.) In 1780 Caleb's grandson David sold the farm to John Wickham. The Wickhams moved the house twice, once in the early 1900s and again in 1913 when it was used to house tenant farmers. Threatened with destruction by a road widening project, the Wickham family donated the house to the Cutchogue–New Suffolk Historical Council which moved it to its present location on the village green in 1965. The house is furnished with period furniture.

EAST MARION

East Marion Cemetery
Cemetery Road, East Marion

From Route 25/Main Road in East Marion turn south onto Cemetery Road; go .1 mile. Turn left (east) onto a dirt road which leads into the cemetery.

Grave of Mark Rothko (1903–1970)

Go straight on the cemetery's main carriage road for about 50 feet. The grave is on the right side of the carriage road just north of a large cross gravestone. It is marked by a simple rock monument.

Mark Rothko was born in Dvinsk, Russia, but immigrated to Portland, OR, with his family in 1913. After attending Yale, he began a career which brought him recognition as a pioneer in American Abstract Expressionist and Surrealistic painting which characteristically included rectangular shapes suspended in space. He was a member of The Ten, a group of expressionist painters who held annual shows. (See also Town of East Hampton/East Hampton/Childe Hassam's Grave.) Despondent, Rothko committed suicide by slashing his elbows. After a six-year battle over the custody of his paintings, his daughter was able to obtain a portion of the estate. At the time of publication, a court action was in progress to exhume Rothko's remains from East Marion Cemetery and to rebury him in a cemetery in Westchester County, New York.

FISHERS ISLAND

Saint John's Episcopal Church
Alpine Avenue, Fishers Island
(631) 788-7497 (church rectory)

To reach Fishers Island, take the ferry from Orient Point, New York, to New London, Connecticut, and then take the ferry from New London to Fishers Island, New York. The New London docks for these two ferries are about 600 yards apart. The church is at least a twenty- to thirty-minute walk from the dock on Fishers Island. It might be prudent to take a bicycle or car onto the ferry.

This lovely white clapboard 1881 church with blue shutters serves a small summer community on this idyllic outpost of Suffolk County. The cool and serene color scheme is continued inside even to the individually created needlepoint kneeling pillows hung in each pew.

Over the carved white altar is the Bowers (1891) Memorial window. No signature is visible on this lancet window, documented in the surviving records of Tiffany Studios as *Our Savior.* Christ is pictured with hands extended. He is clothed in dark red and deep blue drapery glass robes with the blue robe draped over his left arm. This drapery glass composition is fashioned from smaller pieces of the heavy glass than would be seen in works of Tiffany's later period. The neckline is outlined with gold. Light is dramatically focused through the cruciform halo formed from light gold opalescent glass much in the same manner as that seen in the Bowne Memorial window in Saint George's Episcopal Church in Flushing, NY, and in the Hamilton/Messenger Memorial window which can be viewed in All Saints Episcopal Church in Great Neck. (See also Town of North Hempstead/Great Neck/All Saints Episcopal Church.) Its spotlighting effect draws the viewers attention immediately to the well-painted face of Christ. Christ stands on mauve-colored rocks at the shore. A blue sky with lavender and pink fades to a pure light lavender at the horizon which is absolutely horizontal, a most unusual technique, for Tiffany. The lavender abuts directly against the dark blue water formed of a pebbly glass. This pebbly glass, a type and quality not often used by Tiffany Studios, appears also in green at the left of the foreground. We question whether this Kokomo-style glass may have been replaced original glass during a repair process.

This window has undergone some dramatic and unfortunately obvious repair. Both horizontal and vertical support bars have been installed. Additionally, and very sadly in our view, an attempt to repair the small brick-like border has resulted in the loss of Tiffany glass which was replaced with painted glass. Perhaps because the color could not even be approximated, the entire border has been painted a rust color. The lower right hand corner is part of the repaired area. Any signature which might have been there is no longer verifiable.

GREENPORT

Greek Orthodox Church of Saints Anargyroi and Taxiarhis
702 Route 25/Main Street, Greenport
(631) 477-1801

From the war memorial at the intersection of Route 25/Main Street and First Street in Greenport go west on Route 25/Main Street for .2 mile. The church is on the left side of the road.

The Greek Orthodox Church of Saints Anargyroi and Taxiarhis now occupies the structure that once was the Presbyterian Church of Greenport, dedicated in 1835. The Greek Orthodox church was established in 1981. Its interior is adorned with both new and old icons of enormous beauty.

Margaret Ireland House
319 Main Street, Greenport
(631) 477-3026

From the war memorial at the intersection of Route 25/Main Street and First Street in Greenport go west on Route 25/Main Street for .5 mile. The museum is on the right side of the road.

Originally this site was occupied by the Clark House which was also known as the Old Inn. Built in 1831, it hosted such famous celebrities as President John Quincy Adams, General Winfield Scott, Admiral George Dewey, and Mr. and Mrs. David Gelston Floyd. Floyd's grandfather was William Floyd who lived in Mastic Beach and was a signer of the Declaration of Independence. It was in this inn that a vote was taken changing the town's name from Greenhill to Green Port. (Later it became Greenport.) The inn remained in business for nearly one hundred years prior to its demolition.

The Margaret Ireland House, which was also built in 1831, has had some thirty-one owners and was originally located across the street from the Old Inn. In 1973 the house was donated to the Sterling Historical Society by Mr. and Mrs. Fred Preston and moved by the historical society to its present site in 1976. The house features Victorian furniture, a small doll and toy collection, and pictures made from human hair. Relics from the 72-gun battleship *USS Ohio* are also on display. The ship was built in Brooklyn in 1817 and literally blown up for scrap iron in Greenport after it was decommissioned. The figurehead from the *USS Ohio* is displayed in a pavilion on the village green in Stony Brook. (See also Town of Brookhaven/Stony Brook/The Hercules Pavilion.) A unique exhibit is a barometer, broken by and showing the barometric pressure at the center of the 1938 hurricane.

Railroad Museum of Long Island
440 Fourth Street, Greenport
(631) 477-0439

The museum is located in the center of the village's business district.

The museum is in a restored 1890 Long Island Rail Road freight station. Featured are photographs, uniforms, a control tower, a gift shop, and a railroad model of Greenport.

Outside the building is a 1907 railroad snowplow and a restored 1925 wooden caboose. Additional rolling stock can be found at the museum's restoration site in Riverhead.

(See also Town of Riverhead/Riverhead/Railroad Museum of Long Island.)

MATTITUCK

Husing Pond Preserve
(Long Island Chapter: The Nature Conservancy)
Great Peconic Bay Boulevard, Mattituck
(631) 367-3225

Open with prior permission.

From the Mattituck Historical Society on Route 25/Main Road in Mattituck go 1.4 miles west on Route 25/Main Road. Turn left (south) onto Bay Avenue; go .6 mile. Turn right (west) onto Great Peconic Bay Boulevard; go .5 mile. The preserve is on the right (north) side of the road opposite the town beach and Mattituck Yacht Club.

This twenty-one-acre preserve consists of a freshwater lake, a wetland, and a woodland with trails through all three sections. The woodlands contain oak, hickory, and red swamp maple trees. Due to the diversity of the habitat, much variety of wildlife is found in the preserve such as ospreys, great blue herons, green herons, black-crowned night herons, ducks, red foxes, squirrels, raccoons, and cottontail rabbits.

Please telephone the Conservancy at the above number to obtain permission to visit the preserve.

Marratooka Lake Preserve
(Long Island Chapter: The Nature Conservancy)
Route 25/Main Road, Mattituck
(631) 367-3225

Open with prior permission.

From the Mattituck Historical Society on Route 25/Main Road in Mattituck go .4 mile west on Route 25/Main Road. The preserve is on the left (south) side of the road.

This eleven-acre preserve consists of one of the Island's few undisturbed kettle-hole areas. It has an abundance of aquatic plants such as pickerelweed, water-milfoil, and swamp loosestrife. The protected woodland area contains stands of black cherry and black locust trees, and a field of open grass. Wildlife, such as ospreys, herons, ducks, opossums, masked shrews, eastern cottontail rabbits, white-footed mice, and red foxes are also found. There are diverse populations of amphibians and reptiles.

Please telephone the Conservancy at the above number to obtain permission to visit the preserve.

Mattituck–Laurel Historical Society and Museums
Route 25/Main Road, Mattituck
(631) 298-5248

Located on Route 25/Main Road.

The museum complex consists of a 1799 house, an 1840 house, an 1840 school-house, an 1846 milk house, and a circa 1850 barn. The 1799 house was built by Jesse Tuthill. It contains period furnishings, collections of clothes, quilts, and arrowheads. Of particular interest is an oversized 34-star flag which came into use in 1861 with the admission of Kansas into the Union and remained in official use for only two years.

ORIENT

Buttonwood Tree
Young's Road and Route 25/Main Road, Orient

Located opposite the Civil War Memorial in Orient at the junction of Route 25/ Main Road and Young's Road.

The tree, which is an American sycamore, was planted during colonial times and is the oldest existing landmark in the Orient Historic District. According to legend the tree was the local rallying point for patriots after the signing of the Declaration of Independence. Located in the middle of Young's Road, the tree and the corner encompassing the Civil War Memorial are listed on the National Register of Historic Places.

Indian Memorial Rock Carvings
Long Island Sound, Orient

From the Civil War Memorial in Orient at the intersection of Route 25/Main Road and Young's Road go north on Young's Road for .4 mile to the end of the road and to the edge of Long Island Sound. Walk east (to the right) for about one mile on the beach and over the glacial boulders around the point to the carvings.

In 1933 Elliot A. Brooks, a native of Orient, did more than twenty rock carvings to commemorate the Poquatuck and Montauk Indians. They have been carved on glacial erratics, the name given to the often very large boulders deposited by the retreating glacier. The best time to view the carvings is during low tide. Wear sneakers or similar shoes as you will have to climb some boulders. This is not something people with disabilities should attempt. The carvings can also be reached by boat as they are along the shoreline of Long Island Sound. Photographs of the carvings may be seen in the Oyster Ponds Historical Society Museum on Village Lane in Orient. (See also Town of Southold/Orient/Oysterponds Historical Society Museum Complex/The Village House.)

Margolin Marsh Preserve
(Long Island Chapter: The Nature Conservancy)
Route 25/Main Road, Orient
(631) 367-3225

Open with prior permission.

From the Civil War Memorial on Route 25/Main Road in Orient go east on Route 25/Main Road for 1.8 miles. The preserve is on the right (south) side of the road.

The preserve consists of twenty-five acres of salt marsh separated from uplands by a dike built after the 1938 hurricane. An osprey nesting platform has been extremely active in recent years. Recent archeological work done on this preserve has revealed that the earliest Indians who settled in this area have no hereditary link with later Indian tribes who settled here in about 100 B.C.

Please call the Conservancy at the telephone number above to obtain permission to visit the preserve.

Orient Beach State Park
Route 25/Main Road, Orient
(631) 323-2440

From the Civil War Memorial on Route 25/Main Road in Orient go east on Route 25/Main Road for 3.4 miles. The park is on the right (south) side of the road.

This 357-acre park offers facilities for picnicking, swimming, fishing, and ball-playing. There is a food stand. Restrooms are provided.

Oysterponds Historical Society Museum Complex
Village Lane, Orient
(631) 323-2480

From the Civil War Memorial on Route 25/Main Road in Orient turn south onto Village Lane; go .4 mile. The museum complex is on the left (east) side of the road.

The Village House
(part of the Oysterponds Historical Society Museum Complex)
Village Lane, Orient

Built in 1790 as the home of Augustus Griffin, a local teacher, innkeeper, and historian, it has been known as The Village House throughout its history. Enlarged several times, Griffin's home became an inn and the second stop westward on the stage line from the Orient Point Inn to New York City. Since 1944 The Village House has been the home of the Oysterponds Historical Society. It is on the National Register of Historic Places as are all the buildings included in the Oysterponds Historical Society Museum Complex.

Upon entering the house the visitor is greeted by music from an 1890 Olympia music box. The beautifully appointed Victorian front parlor has an antique organ, an antique accordion collection, an Edison phonograph (1896–1901), and a melodeon among its more prized possessions. A separate room contains Indian artifacts, the most outstanding of which are a Clovis point and the skeleton of a young Indian male in the burial position used by Long Island Indian tribes.

The Revolutionary and Civil War Room contains guns, swords, posters, powder horns, and other memorabilia of those two early struggles.

The Orient Room has memorabilia from the Orient Point Inn including a guest book and china. Shell, butterfly, clothes, quilt, and photograph collections are also displayed. Of particular interest in the photograph collection are the pictures of Elliot A. Brooks' Indian Memorial Rock Carvings. (See also Town of Southold/Orient/Indian Memorial Rock Carvings.) There is even an 1889 39-star American flag, denoting North Dakota's entrance into the Union.

On the second floor there are doll and toy collections. The model locomotive, tender, and passenger car were built by Orren F. Payne of Southold. He started the project in 1858 at the age of eleven and completed it in 1881. It is truly a work of art and must be seen.

Webb House
(part of Oysterponds Historical Society Museum Complex)
Village Lane, Orient

This building was built in 1720 by Captain William Booth as an inn and was located at the junction of Sterling Creek and Main Street in Greenport. After a succession of owners the inn fell on hard times. In 1810 the inn was moved by forty yoke of oxen to North Road. This journey, which took two days, was accomplished by the new owners, the Youngs, thus saving the inn from the previous owners' creditors. In 1954 the building was about to be demolished when it was purchased by Mr. and Mrs. George R. Latham and moved by barge five miles to its present location in Orient.

Upon entering the Webb House the visitor is greeted by music from a circa 1800 music box. The house is furnished in period furniture and has collections of flowing blue china and clothes. The early eighteenth-century piano made by Astor and Co., London, is one of the earliest pianos made. The attic defies description. It has everything imaginable in it including a coffin which, incidentally, is not empty.

Old Point Schoolhouse
(part of Oysterponds Historical Society Museum Complex)
Village Lane, Orient

The schoolhouse was built in 1888 and originally stood about one mile from Orient Point. It was moved to its present location by the Oysterponds Historical Society and houses the society's impressive genealogical and archival library. It is opened to scholars and students by appointment.

Red Barn
(part of Oysterponds Historical Society Museum Complex)
Village Lane, Orient

Originally built as a grain market on Village Wharf, Red Barn was later used by local fishermen to repair and store nets. It was acquired by the Oysterponds Historical Society and moved to its present site. On display are a myriad of objects including the first chemical spraying wagon, sleds, ice harvesting equipment, and wagons, as well as an old country store with penny candy for sale.

Hallock Building
(part of Oysterponds Historical Society Museum Complex)
Village Lane, Orient

Built in 1891 one mile east of its present location, the Hallock Building was the cookhouse and dormitory of the Halyoake Farm. It was acquired by the Oysterponds Historical Society and moved to its present site. It presently houses collections of paintings, ship models, farm implements, marine objects, and looms, as well as special exhibits.

Shinbone Alley
(part of Oysterponds Historical Society Museum Complex)
Vincent Street, Orient

Shinbone Alley is the former home of an Orient fisherman. It now serves as the home of the director of the historical society and is not open to the public.

Amanda Brown Schoolhouse
(part of Oysterponds Historical Society Museum Complex)
Village Lane, Orient

The schoolhouse, which was built in 1862, was originally located just east of the Congregational church on Main Road in Orient. It was acquired by the Oysterponds Historical Society and moved to its present location on Village Lane. It is presently being used for craft workshops and demonstrations.

Slave Burying Ground
Narrow River Road, Orient

From the Civil War Memorial on Route 25/Main Road in Orient go south on Village Road (which becomes King Street) for 1.2 miles. Turn right onto Narrow River Road; go .1 mile. The cemetery is on the left side of the road.

Slavery persisted in the Orient area until 1830. The cemetery consists of the graves of about twenty slaves and their owners, Dr. Seth Tuthill and his wife Maria. The Tuthills were owners of Hog Pond Farm and wished to be buried with their former slaves.

Whitcom Marsh Preserve
(Long Island Chapter: The Nature Conservancy)
Route 25/Main Road, Orient
(631) 367-3225

Open with prior permission.

From the Civil War Memorial on Route 25/Main Road in Orient go east on Route 25/Main Road for 1.7 miles. The preserve is on the left (north) side of the road.

This seventeen-acre preserve has the only freshwater marshland in Orient. It is primarily a bird sanctuary with nesting osprey and black-crowned night herons.

Please call the Conservancy at the telephone number above to obtain permission to visit the preserve.

PECONIC

Goldsmith's Inlet County Park
Mill Pond Road, Peconic
(631) 854-4949

Suffolk County Resident Pass is required for admission.

From the village green in Cutchogue go east on Route 25/Main Road for 2.9 miles. Turn left (north) onto Peconic Lane (which becomes Mill Road); go 1.4 miles to the park which is located on Long Island Sound.

This sixty-acre nature park boarders Long Island Sound and supports a variety of animal life including deer, Canada geese, small hawks, and numerous wetland animals. For guided tours contact the environmental specialist at the above telephone number.

Peconic Dunes County Park
Sound View Avenue, Peconic
(631) 854-4949

Suffolk County Resident Pass is required for admission.

From the village green in Southold at the intersection of Route 25/Main Road and Young's Avenue turn north onto Young's Avenue; go 1.1 miles. Turn right onto North Road; go about 50 feet. Turn left (north) onto Lighthouse Road; go .5 mile. Turn left (west) onto Sound View Avenue; go 1.8 miles. The park is on the right (north) side of the road.

During the summer this thirty-seven-acre park is a co-educational camp for Suffolk County youths between the ages of seven and twelve. Activities include sailing, sports, arts, and crafts. For applications call the above telephone number. During other times of the year educational organizations may rent the facilities for ecological, environmental, and conservation studies.

SOUTHOLD

Custer Institute
Bayview Road, Southold
(631) 765-2626

From the village green in Southold at the intersection of Route 25/Main Road and Young's Avenue go west on Route 25/Main Road for .9 mile to Bayview Road. (Bayview Road forks south off Route 25/Main Road.) Go .2 mile on Bayview Road. The museum is on the left side of the road.

The Custer Institute and observatory evolved from a series of meetings held by amateur astronomers at the Cedar Beach home of Charles W. Elmer. By the early 1930s the organization formally adopted a charter and its present name, which honors General George A. Custer, whose niece was married to Elmer.

Its present site was acquired and the north section of the structure erected. The southern section of the observatory, with its three refracting telescopes, was built in 1961.

The use of the facility is not restricted to members. Activities open to the general public include stargazing, films, concerts, art exhibits, field trips, and lectures on a myriad of topics. Their brochure states that "no area of the human experience is exempt from discussion." For their year-round calendar of events call the above telephone number. (See also Town of Huntington/Centerport/Suffolk County Vanderbilt Museum and Planetarium–William Kissam Vanderbilt Jr. Estate–Eagle's Nest.)

Horton Lighthouse

Lighthouse Road, Southold
(631) 765-2101

From the village green in Southold at the intersection of Route 25/Main Road and Young's Avenue turn north onto Young's Avenue; go 1.1 miles. Turn right (east) onto North Road; go less than 50 feet. Turn left (north) onto Lighthouse Road; go .7 mile to the lighthouse.

The Horton family owned Cliff Lots, the site of the lighthouse, since 1640 when Barnabas Horton settled in Southold, and established his farm. (See also Town of Southold/Cutchogue/Cutchogue Historic Complex/Old House.) In 1757 Colonel George Washington, then a young army surveyor, recognized the need for a lighthouse at this site. In 1790, during his presidency, he actually commissioned one to be built. In 1855, with the failure of the Horton family to pay property taxes, Cliff Lots was sold for $500 at a sheriff's auction to Charles H. Payne, who in turn sold it to the United States government for $600. The lighthouse was finally built in 1857. Its light was originally fueled by whale oil and kerosene as the building did not have electricity until the twentieth century. In 1933 it was abandoned by the Coast Guard, acquired by Southold Park District, and turned into a museum with local memorabilia and Indian artifacts. During World War II the Coast Guard again occupied the lighthouse using it as an air watch station; it was abandoned after the war.

In 1976 the Southold Park District restored the lighthouse. A marine museum was established there by the Southold Historical Society. In the museum collection are a captain's sword made from a swordfish saw, an 1812 cannon ball taken from the cliffs near Montauk Lighthouse, a small scrimshaw collection, ship models, a lighthouse log, pictures of local shipwrecks, and nautical paintings. The lighthouse is located on a seven-acre park with picnic tables overlooking Long Island Sound.

Howell Meadow Preserve

(Long Island Chapter: The Nature Conservancy)
Off Clearview Avenue, Southold
(631) 367-3225

Open with prior permission.

From the village green in Southold at the intersection of Route 25/Main Road and Young's Avenue go west on Route 25/Main Road for .4 mile. Turn left (south) onto Oaklawn Avenue; go 1 mile. Turn right (west) onto Clearview Avenue; go .1 mile. Turn left (south) onto a short dead-end, unnamed street. The preserve is to the left and directly ahead.

This five-acre combination of oak woodland and tidal salt marsh contains salt hay, spike grass, sea lavender, cord grass, marsh elder, and phragmites. Black ducks, yellow egrets, herons, and terns are attracted by the diversity of the habitat. There are no trails. It is advisable to obtain parking permission from the local police.

Please call the Conservancy at the above telephone number to obtain permission to visit the preserve.

Indian Museum
1080 Bayview Road, Southold
(631) 765-5577

From the village green in Southold at the intersection of Route 25/Main Road and Young's Avenue go west on Route 25/Main Road for .9 mile to Bayview Road. (Bayview Road forks south off Route 25/Main Road.) Go .2 mile on Bayview Road. The museum is on the right side of the road.

The museum, which is owned and operated by the Long Island Chapter of New York State Archeological Association, has the largest collection of Algonquin ceramic pottery in the country. It also has an impressive collection of Indian carved soapstone pots and bowls, spears, arrowheads, knife blades, hammers, drills, hoes, children's toys, fishing tackle, jewelry, clothes, and religious relics. Of particular interest is the collection of Indian pots dating from 3,000 B.C. and the cremation urns which were intentionally broken by the Indians so that their spirit could escape. Lectures are given by an extremely knowledgeable staff. The Mott Memorial Library, located in the museum, is available for research.

Old Burying Ground
Route 25/Main Road, Southold

From the village green in Southold at the intersection of Route 25/Main Road and Young's Avenue go west on Route 25/Main Road for .3 mile. The cemetery is located on the left (south) side of the road.

This is the site of the oldest English meetinghouse in New York State dating from 1640. The structure served as a church, fort, court, and prison. The burial ground, which dates from 1640, is the oldest English burying ground in New York State.

First Presbyterian Church of Southold
53100 Route 25/Main Road, Southold
(631) 765-2597

From the village green in Southold at the intersection of Route 25/Main Road and Young's Avenue go west on Route 25/Main Road for .3 mile. The church if located on the left (south) side of the road adjacent to the Old Burying Ground.

Founded October 21, 1640, this is the oldest English church in New York State. The cornerstone of the present building, the parish's third, was laid in 1803 by Ezra L'Hommedieu. (See also Town of East Hampton/Montauk/Montauk Lighthouse.) On display at the church are historic documents relevant to its past history.

Southold Historical Society Complex
Route 25/Main Road, Southold
(631) 765-5500

From the village green in Southold at the intersection of Route 25/Main Road and Young's Avenue go east on Route 25/Main Road for .2 mile. The historical society is on the right (south) side of the road.

Thomas Moore House
(part of Southold Historical Society Complex)
Route 25/Main Road, Southold

This circa 1790 house, which is owned by the Southold Historical Society, has some rooms dating from before 1653. One of these rooms has three walls with original paneling. Of interest are the exposed beams which have been coded in Roman numerals by the carpenter who rebuilt the house on the present site. The house is furnished in period furniture and contains a chair that originally belonged to Thomas Moore, two Dominy Chippendale-style side chairs, a Ben Cleveland clock, a barn loom, as well as collections of flowing blue, Willow, and Canton china.

Ann Hallock Currie–Bell House
(part of Southold Historical Society Complex)
Route 25/Main Road, Southold

Built in 1895, the interior of the house is a marvelous example of Victorian architecture. Its ornate solid mahogany staircase, beamed ceilings, ornate plasterwork, and ceiling paintings epitomize the Victorian era. In addition to the Victorian furnishings, there are extensive collections of sandwich, pressed, carnival, and cranberry glass, as well as silverware made by Tiffany. There is a large and appealing collection of paintings by Thomas Currie–Bell. Among the many items offered for sale by the Southold Historical Society in the gift shop are reproductions of antique glassware made from the original molds.

Pine Neck Barn
(part of Southold Historical Society Complex)
Route 25/Main Road, Southold

This eighteenth-century barn contains early farm tools, wagons, sleds, carpenter tools, a reaper, and a nineteenth-century printing press.

Down Carriage House
(part of Southold Historical Society Complex)
Route 25/Main Road, Southold

This 1845 carriage house is located behind the Hallock Currie–Bell House. On display are old farm tools, carriages, and sleighs.

Cleveland Glover Gagen Blacksmith Shop
(part of Southold Historical Society Complex)
Route 25/Main Road, Southold

This circa 1845 blacksmith shop was moved by the Southold Historical Society from its original location at the western end of Main Road in Southold. The blacksmith shop is fully equipped with a functional forge.

Whitaker Historical Collection
Southold Free Library
Route 25/Main Road, Southold
(631) 765-2077

From the village green in Southold at the intersection of Route 25/Main Road and Young's Avenue go west on Route 25/Main Road for .2 mile. The library is on the right (north) side of the road.

The historical collection, which is predominately genealogical in nature, is located in the Southold Free Library. The library is situated on what in colonial times was called Feather Hill and which was the site of the home of the Quaker Captain John Underhill. It was Underhill's merciless campaigns against the Indians that secured Long Island and much of the land between the Hudson River and Narragansett Bay for the colonists. (See also Town of North Hempstead/Manhasset/Manhasset Friends Meeting House; Town of Oyster Bay/Jericho/Jericho Friends Meeting House; Town of Oyster Bay/Matinecock/Matinecock Friends Meeting House; Town of Oyster Bay/Mill Neck/Underhill Burying Ground/Grave of Captain John Underhill; Town of Oyster Bay/Oyster Bay/Council Rock; and Town of Shelter Island/Shelter Island/Cemetery and Monument to Quaker Martyrs.)

The current structure was designed in 1891 by G. H. Skidmore, a Riverhead architect, for the Southold Savings Bank; thus, its rather formidable appearance. In 1927 the bank moved to a new location and the building was acquired by Mr. and Mrs. Edward Cahoon who presented it as a gift to the library in 1928.

NASSAU COUNTY

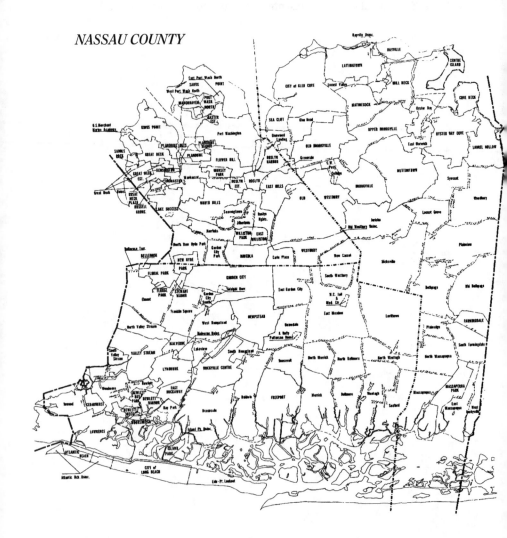

Nassau County

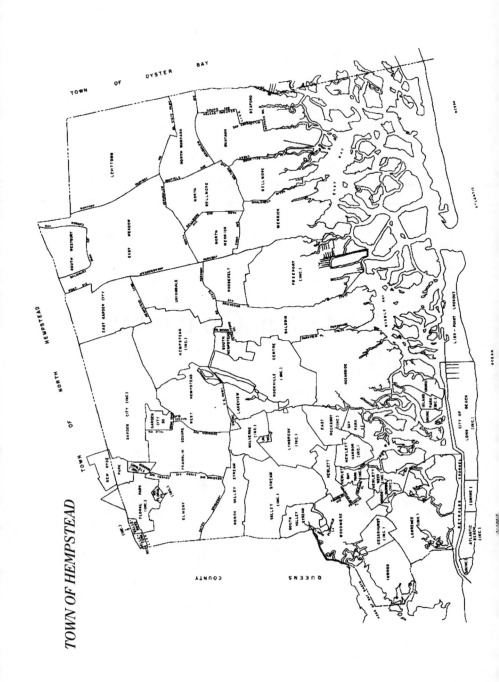

TOWN OF HEMPSTEAD

TOWN OF HEMPSTEAD

PARKS AND PRESERVES

Federal Parks and Preserves
Lido Beach National Wildlife Refuge, Lido Beach

State Parks and Preserves
Hempstead Lake State Park (775 acres), Hempstead
Jones Beach State Park (2,413 acres), Wantagh
Valley Stream State Park (97 acres), Valley Stream

County Parks and Preserves
Bay County Park (96 acres), Bay Park
Brookside Preserve (22 acres), Freeport *(undeveloped)*
Camman's Pond Park (8 acres), Merrick *(undeveloped)*
Cedar Creek County Park (260 acres), Seaford
Cow Meadow County Park and Preserve (178 acres), Freeport
Eisenhower County Park (930 acres), East Meadow
Eugene Nickerson Beach County Park (121 acres), Lido Beach
Grant County Park (35 acres), Hewlett
Halls Pond Park (11 acres), West Hempstead
Inwood County Park (16 acres), Inwood
Lofts Pond Park (14 acres), Baldwin *(undeveloped)*
Merokee Preserve (25 acres), Bellmore *(undeveloped)*
Milburn Pond Park (24 acres), Freeport *(undeveloped)*
Mill Pond County Park (54 acres), Bellmore *(undeveloped)*
Mitchel Athletic Complex (49 acres), Uniondale
North Woodmere County Park (150 acres), North Woodmere
Reverend Arthur Mackey Sr. Park (27 acres), Roosevelt
Silver Lake Park (9 acres), Baldwin *(undeveloped)*
Tackapausha Preserve (84 acres), Seaford
Tanglewood Park Preserve (11 acres), Lakeview
Wantagh County Park (111 acres), Wantagh
Washington Avenue Park (4 acres), Seaford

Arboretums and Gardens
Hofstra University (238 acres), Hempstead

Baldwin

Baldwin Historical Society Museum

1980 Grand Avenue, Baldwin
(516) 223-6900

Take Meadowbrook Parkway to Exit #M8W (Sunrise Highway/Freeport). Go west on Sunrise Highway for 2.4 miles. Turn right (north) onto Grand Avenue; go .8 mile. The museum is on the left (west) side of the road.

This small museum has changing exhibits and memorabilia of particular relevance to the history of Baldwin. Their collection includes postcards, photographs, documents, and artifacts.

Bay Park

Bay County Park

First Avenue, Bay Park
(516) 571-7245

Nassau County Leisure Pass is required for admission.

Take Meadowbrook Parkway to Exit #M10 (Loop Parkway/Point Lookout/Lido Beach/Long Beach). Go 2.9 miles on Loop Parkway. Turn right (west) onto Lido Blvd.; go 3.8 miles. Turn right (north) onto Long Beach Blvd. (which becomes Austin Blvd. and then becomes Long Beach Road); go 2.4 miles. Turn left (west) onto Daly Blvd.; go .5 mile. Turn right (north) onto Lawson Blvd.; go 1.4 miles. Turn left (west) onto Atlantic Avenue; go .2 mile. Turn left (south) onto Ocean Avenue; go .1 mile. Turn left continuing south onto Front Street; go .2 mile. Turn left onto Morton Avenue (which becomes Fifth Avenue). Follow it to Compton Avenue and to the park entrance.

This ninety-six-acre park has limited campsites, baseball fields, soccer fields, softball fields, basketball courts, cricket fields, jogging paths, boat launching ramps, a roller skating rink, an ice skating rink, tennis courts, volleyball courts, cross-country skiing trails, picnic facilities, a playground, a nine-hole golf course, a pro shop, meeting/community/activity rooms, restrooms, and a first-aid station. Some of the athletic fields and courts are lighted.

BELLMORE

Mill Pond County Park
Merrick Road and Abby Court, Bellmore
(516) 572-0218

Take the Long Island Expressway to Exit #44 south (N.Y. 135/Seaford–Oyster Bay Expressway). Go south on the Seaford–Oyster Bay Expressway for 9.8 miles to Exit #1W (Merrick Road/Freeport). Go west on Merrick Road for 1.5 miles. The preserve is on the right (north) side of the road.

This fifty-four-acre preserve is predominately a lake surrounded by nature walks. Ice skating is allowed during the winter, weather permitting.

EAST MEADOW

Eisenhower County Park
Hempstead Turnpike, East Meadow
(516) 572-0348

Nassau County Leisure Pass is required for admission.

Take Meadowbrook Parkway to Exit #M5E (Hempstead Turnpike/East Meadow/ Levittown). Go east on Hempstead Turnpike/Route 24 for .7 mile. Turn left (north) into the park.

This 930-acre park offers an unbelievable array of activities: baseball fields, football fields, lacrosse fields, cricket fields, hockey fields, soccer fields, softball fields, basketball courts, croquet courts, shuffleboard courts, horseshoe courts, paddle tennis courts (no nets), tennis courts, volleyball courts, bicycle paths, bicycle rentals, roller hockey, skate rentals, jogging paths, lawn bowling courts, model boating pond, three eighteen-hole golf courses, a driving range, picnic areas, playgrounds, a senior citizen area, a puppet theater, an indoor activities center with games for people with disabilities and for senior citizens, boat rentals, an ice skating rink, sledding hills, cross-country skiing trails, a restaurant, restrooms, the Harry Chapin Lakeside Theatre, and the county's aquatic center, which was built in 1998 for the Goodwill Games.

EAST ROCKAWAY

The Grist Mill Museum
Woods Avenue, East Rockaway
(516) 599-2278

Take Meadowbrook Parkway to Exit #M8W (Sunrise Highway/Freeport/Baldwin). Go west on Sunrise Highway for 5 miles. Turn left (south) onto Rocklyn Avenue; go .6 mile. Turn left (south) onto Atlantic Avenue; go .2 mile. Turn left (east) onto Woods Avenue; go .1 mile. The mill is on the right (south) side of the road.

This grist mill, which was built in 1688 by Joseph Haviland, is the oldest surviving building in Nassau County. Originally located on Mill River, it was purchased in 1818 by Alexander Davidson whose family operated it until the 1920s. In 1962 the Village of East Rockaway saved the mill from demolition, moved it to its present site, and restored it for use as a museum.

The mill's interior is divided into several rooms each depicting a different theme. On display are a barber shop, a dental office, a dry goods store, a blacksmith shop, a schoolroom, antique tools, antique gowns, an 1893 fire fighting pumper, as well as exhibits on wildlife, Long Island Indians, home life, and shipwrecks.

Also featured are three American flags: a 35-star flag issued in 1863 when West Virginia became a state, used only until 1864 when Nevada became a state; a 45-star flag issued in 1896 when Utah became a state and used until 1907 when Oklahoma became a state; and a 48-star flag issued in 1912 when Arizona and New Mexico achieved statehood and used until 1959 when Alaska became a state.

(See also Town of Islip/Oakdale/Connetquot River State Park and Preserve–Southside Sportsmen's Club; Town of Smithtown/Head of the Harbor/Stony Brook Grist Mill; and Town of Southampton/Water Mill/The Water Mill Museum.)

ELMONT

Belmont Park Race Track
2150 Hempstead Turnpike, Elmont
(718) 641-4700

Take the Long Island Expressway to Exit #30 south (Cross Island Parkway/Kennedy Airport). Go south on Cross Island Parkway for 3 miles to Exit #26D (Belmont Race Track).

In 1905 August Belmont II opened the race track named after his father, who had died in 1890. The senior Belmont was a devout breeder of thoroughbreds, lover of horse racing, and president of the American Jockey Club. (See also Town of Babylon/North Babylon/Belmont Lake State Park–August Belmont Sr. Estate–Nursery

Stud Farm; Town of Brookhaven/Yaphank/Southaven County Park–Suffolk Club; and Town of Islip/Oakdale/Connetquot River State Park and Preserve–Southside Sportsmen's Club.)

In addition to flat racing, the track offers "Breakfast at Belmont" where visitors may watch thoroughbreds working out while dining at the trackside cafe. During breakfast, New York Racing Authority commentators present informative interviews with trainers, jockeys, and other racing personalities. Tours of the race track are available after breakfast. Telephone the track at the above number for specific times and dates of breakfasts and tours.

FREEPORT

Cow Meadow County Park and Preserve
Main Street, Freeport
(516) 571-8685

Nassau County Leisure Pass is required for admission.

Take Meadowbrook Parkway to Exit #M9W (Merrick Road/Freeport). Go west on Merrick Road for .6 mile. Turn left (south) onto Henry Street/South Main Street; go 1.3 miles to the park entrance.

This 178-acre park has a marina, a landing pier, a fishing pier, a spray pool, an ice skating rink, basketball courts, handball courts, horseshoe courts, paddleball courts, shuffleboard courts, tennis courts, lighted soccer fields, lighted softball fields, baseball fields, areas for chess and checkers, jogging paths, nature walks, picnic areas, a playground, restrooms, and first-aid facilities. Some courts are lighted for night play.

Freeport Historical Museum
350 South Main Street, Freeport
(516) 623-9632

Take Meadowbrook Parkway to Exit #M9W (Merrick Road/Freeport). Go west on Merrick Road for .6 mile. Turn left (south) onto Henry Street/South Main Street; go .6 mile. The museum is on the right (west) side of the road.

Located in a circa 1910 house, the museum has a children's room with antique dolls, toys, games, and trains, Civil War memorabilia, antique clothes and parasols, vaudeville memorabilia from the Long Island Good Hearted Thesbian Society (LIGHTS), a 1900 kitchen, and extensive collections of antique tools, antique photographic equipment, and tools for making equestrian paraphernalia. Of special interest is the collection of American flags which includes a 13-star flag made in 1777 along with 37-, 38-, 39-, 40-, 44-, 45-, 46-, and 48-star flags.

Long Island Collection
Freeport Memorial Library
144 West Merrick Road, Freeport
(516) 379-3274

Take Meadowbrook Parkway to Exit #M9W (Merrick Road/Freeport). Go west on Merrick Road for 1 mile. The library is on the right (north) side of the road.

This collection specializes in genealogical and historical information relevant to Long Island. In addition to books, old documents, papers, and maps are available.

(See also Town of North Hempstead/Roslyn/The Bryant Library; Town of Riverhead/Suffolk County Historical Society Museum; and Town of Smithtown/Village of the Branch/The Richard H. Handley Collection/The Smithtown Library.)

Nautical Cruise Lines
395 Woodcleft Avenue, Freeport
(516) 623-5712

Reservations required.

Take Meadowbrook Parkway to Exit #M9W (Merrick Road/Freeport). Go west on Merrick Road for 1 mile. Turn left (south) onto Guy Lombardo Avenue; go 1 mile. Turn right (west) onto Front Street; go .1 mile. Turn left (south) onto Woodcleft Avenue. Parking is on the left (east) side of the road.

The Nautical Cruise Lines operates the 100-foot, 300-passenger *Nautical Princess* as well as the 160-foot, 600-passenger *Nautical Empress*. Both ships, which are fully climate-controlled for year-round sailing, feature enclosed dining rooms and offer dinner, brunch, and holiday cruises, as well as charters for private occasions.

GARDEN CITY

Cathedral of the Incarnation
50 Cathedral Avenue, Garden City
(516) 746-2955

Take the Long Island Expressway to Exit #34 south (New Hyde Park Road). Go south on New Hyde Park Road for 3.2 miles. Turn left (east) onto Stewart Avenue; go 1.9 miles to where it becomes Cathedral Avenue. Go .2 mile on Cathedral Avenue. The Cathedral is on the right (west) side of the road.

In 1869 Alexander Turney Stewart, a Manhattan merchant, purchased 7,170 acres of land on the Hempstead Plains for the then exorbitant price of $55-an-acre. His intent was to create a totally planned residential community for select upper-middle class families. Stewart supervised the design of the community's streets, water supply system, gas works, and landscaping as well as the construction of the original Garden City Hotel and his own line of the Long Island Rail Road.

After his death in 1876, his widow Cornelia decided to build a cathedral as a memorial to her husband. The Episcopal Diocese of Long Island accepted her offer and agreed to move the seat of the Diocese from Brooklyn to Garden City. The building was designed by Henry S. Harrison and built by James L'Hommedieu. Construction was started in 1876 and was completed in 1885. Bishop Abram Newkirk Littlejohn became the first Bishop of Long Island. (See also Town of North Hempstead/Great Neck/All Saints Episcopal Church.)

Prior to completion of the Cathedral, Stewart's remains were stolen from the graveyard of Saint Marks-in-the-Bowery and held for ransom. A body was eventually recovered after the ransom was paid but there seems to be some uncertainty as to whether it was, indeed, that of Stewart. Nevertheless, it was buried in a crypt under the chancel. Legend says that the crypt was wired so that anyone tampering with the crypt would set off an alarm causing the thirteen bells in the tower to ring.

The cathedral is an imposing sight with its steeple rising 180 feet above the Hempstead Plains. Its more than seventy stained-glass windows were designed and executed by the English firm of Clayton and Bell with the exception of those in the Chapel of the Resurrection in the undercroft which were designed and executed by the English firm of Heaton, Butler, and Bayne. One is immediately awed by the impressive fan-vaulting over the nave, the extensive use of Italian and Greek marble, the hand-carved solid mahogany woodwork in the sanctuary and choir, the hand-carved oak pulpit and canopy, the 5,676-pipe organ, the largest on Long Island, and the free-standing high altar made in Antwerp, Belgium.

The Chapel of the Resurrection, which is located at the east end of the undercroft, has finely ribbed fan-vaulting extending gracefully from twelve marble columns surrounding a rotunda. Its stained-glass windows are considered to be the finest in the cathedral. The large alabaster urn on the right of the rotunda originally stood in the middle directly over the final resting place of Alexander and Cornelia M. Stewart. The cathedral stands today as one of the finest, if not the finest, examples of thirteenth-century Gothic Revival architecture in the eastern United States. It has been on the National Register of Historic Places since 1978.

(See also Town of Hempstead/Garden City/Saint Paul's School.)

The Cradle of Aviation Museum
Charles Lindbergh Boulevard, Garden City
(516) 572-4111

Take Meadowbrook Parkway to Exit #M5W (Hempstead Turnpike/Route 24). Go west on Hempstead Turnpike/Route 24 for .6 mile. Turn right (north) onto Earle Ovington Boulevard; go .5 mile. Turn left (west) onto Charles Lindbergh Drive and proceed to museum.

Just east of Garden City's residential area and a bit further east of Camp Mills where Douglas MacArthur trained the Rainbow Division, the Army Air Corps established Field #2, an army airfield later called Hazelhurst Field in honor of the first noncommissioned officer killed in an aviation accident. One year later, in 1918, the field was renamed Mitchel Field in honor of New York City Mayor John Purroy Mitchel. Early in his career, as a city special investigator, he earned the nickname "Torquemada," a reference to the leader of the Spanish Inquisition, because of his relentless pursuit of corruption. In 1914, at the age of thirty-four, Mitchel became the fusion party candidate for mayor of New York City and managed to defeat the Tammany Hall machine, becoming the city's youngest mayor. During his term as mayor he was accused by many of favoring the rich and was handily defeated in his 1917 reelection bid. An advocate of military service, Mitchel joined the Army Air Corps on July 6, 1918. While training at Gerstner Field in Lake Charles, LA, his seatbelt became unfastened and he fell five hundred feet to his death from his single-seater, open-cockpit plane.

Mitchel Field remained in operation until after the Korean War. Today it serves as the site of the Cradle of Aviation Museum. It is impossible to do justice to this world-class museum in the space of this text. Here is a partial listing of the planes found at the museum: a full scale replica of the Wright brothers' first plane; a 1903 Wright Flyer #1; a 1911 Wright EX "Vin Fiz"; the only known 1918 Breese Penguin in existence; Lindbergh's 1918 Curtiss JN4 "Jenny" which he bought for $500 and used for barnstorming; a 1928 Ryan B-l Brougham, the sister ship of the *Spirit of Saint Louis* and the plane personally flown by Jimmy Stewart in the movie; a 1941 Curtiss P40E; a 1943 Fairchild PT-26 Cornell; a 1945 Grumman F6F-5 Hellcat; a 1945 Republic P47N Thunderbolt; a 1946 Aeronca 7 Champion; a 1946 Stinson 108 Voyager; a 1950 Lockheed TV2 Seastar; a 1952 Grumman F9F Cougar; a 1954 North American F86H Sabre fighter; a 1955 Grumman F11A Tiger; a 1956 Republic F84F Thunderstreak; a 1959 F105B Thunderchief; a Grumman Lunar Module; a Grumman Lunar Land Rover; and an Apollo Command Module.

The 130,000-square-foot museum also features a Mars Virtual Voyage, an IMAX Dome Theatre with a five-story-tall, seventy-foot, wrap-around screen, a gift shop, and the Red Planet Café.

(See also Town of Babylon/East Farmingdale/American Airpower Museum; Town of Islip/Bayport/Bayport Aerodrome; and Town of Southampton/Westhampton Beach/106th Rescue Wing–New York Air National Guard.)

Garden City Historical Society Museum
109 Eleventh Street, Garden City
(516) 456-0433

The Museum is located near the center of the village's residential section.

The Victorian-style house was donated to the historical society in 1977 by The Episcopal Diocese of Long Island which had used it as part of their complex at the Cathedral School of Saint Mary.

Known locally as one of the "Apostle Houses," the 1872 house, which is one of the original houses built by Garden City's founder Alexander Turney Stewart, stood at 89 Fifth Avenue in the village. In 1988 the historical society moved it to its present site and began an extensive seventeen-year restoration for use as its museum.

Now open to the public and on the National Register of Historic Places, the museum, which is accessible to people with disabilities, features an exhibit room with changing exhibits and a permanent exhibit of the village's Episcopalian schools, Saint Mary's and Saint Paul's. The museum also has period furniture, clothing, and paintings. Its research library has over 150 archival photographs of Garden City and Hempstead, wood-prints of Long Island scenes, and about two hundred books.

The historical society sponsors a children's program and lecture series. A building survey of the village's pre-1935 structures is currently being developed.

Long Island Children's Museum
11 Davis Avenue, Garden City
(516) 224-5800

Take the Meadowbrook Parkway to Exit #M4W. Make the first right onto Charles Lindbergh Blvd. The museum is at the intersection of Charles Lindbergh Blvd. and Davis Avenue.

Located in a 40,000-square-foot converted airplane hangar, the museum is designed as a learning laboratory for children ages two through twelve. It utilizes twelve galleries of interactive exhibits to stimulate the learning process.

Nassau County Firefighters Museum
1 Davis Avenue, Garden City
(516) 572-4177

Take the Meadowbrook Parkway to Exit #M4W. Make the first right onto Charles Lindbergh Blvd. The museum is at the intersection of Charles Lindbergh Blvd. and Davis Avenue.

The 5,000-square-foot museum, which opened in 2006, is located next to The Cradle of Aviation. Visitors will learn how 911 calls are routed and how firefighters position themselves to battle blazes. Through interactive displays, the visitor is able to experience a fire while historical exhibits trace the evolution of fire boxes and firefighting apparatus. The tour of the museum culminates in the Fire Safe Theater where viewers learn how to prevent a devastating fire.

(See also Town of Brookhaven/Ridge/Brookhaven Volunteer Firefighters' Museum.)

Nassau County Police Museum
1490 Franklin Avenue, Garden City
(516) 573-7620

Take the Long Island Expressway to Exit #39 south (Glen Cove Road/Hempstead). Go south on Glen Cove Road for 2.9 miles. Turn right (west) onto Old Country Road; go 1.2 miles. Turn left (south) onto Franklin Avenue; go .1 mile.

The museum is on the right (west) side of the road in the Nassau County Police Headquarters.

This small museum displays uniforms, medals, microscopes, and cameras used by the police force. A picture collection is also displayed.

(See also Town of Brookhaven/Yaphank/Suffolk County Police Museum.)

Old Nassau County Courthouse
1550 Franklin Avenue, Garden City

Take the Long Island Expressway to Exit #39 south (Glen Cove Road/Hempstead). Go south on Glen Cove Road for 2.9 miles. Turn right (west) onto Old Country Road; go 1.2 miles. The courthouse is on the left (south) side of the road facing Franklin Avenue.

In 1898 the Towns of Oyster Bay, North Hempstead, and South Hempstead voted to secede from Queens County and form a new county called Nassau. The first county courthouse located on Main Street in Mineola was quickly outgrown by the rapidly growing county. While searching for a site for a new courthouse, the county was approached by The Garden City Company and offered the present site free of charge. Thus arose the anomaly of the county seat being Mineola, but the county courthouse being geographically located in the Village of Garden City. On July 13, 1900, Governor Theodore Roosevelt laid the cornerstone of the new courthouse.

Of particular interest is the rotunda with murals on its stairway depicting scenes from the history of Long Island. The building has been on the National Register of Historic Places since 1978.

Saint Paul's School
295 Stewart Avenue, Garden City
(516) 465-4000 (Village Hall)

Take the Long Island Expressway to Exit #34 south (New Hyde Park Road). Go south on New Hyde Park Road for 3.2 miles. Turn left (east) onto Stewart Avenue; go 1.6 miles. The school is on the left (north) side of the road.

The school, built in 1877, was donated to The Episcopal Diocese of Long Island along with the Cathedral School of Saint Mary (demolished), a see house, the Cathedral of the Incarnation, and sixty acres of land by Cornelia Stewart as a memorial to her husband Alexander Turney Stewart, the founder of Garden City. In 1993 the Village of Garden City purchased the school. In 2004 the school's forty-eight-acre campus was dedicated as a park by the village. To date, the fate of the Neo-Gothic-style building is undetermined as is the fate of the beautiful Tiffany window in the former student chapel.

Tiffany records confirm that the unsigned Thomas Newcomb Memorial window, Conversion of Saint Paul on the Road to Damascus (Acts 9:1-9), on the west wall

Town of Hempstead

in the second-floor chapel in the main building, is indeed by the famous artist in glass. There are two large panels in the window with six figures, three of which are soldiers. A most unusual aspect of this window is the intense blackness of uniforms, helmets, shields, and spear points of the soldiers. Except for a bit of blue, no portion of the white light spectrum is emitted through the smooth glass. It has an astounding effect which we have never seen used to this extent. The kneeling Saul of Tarsus is seen on the right with the City of Damascus in the background. His gold drapery glass robes are so finely formed that, from a distance, they actually look like fine velvet. Paul's wealthy origins are also suggested in the perfectly matched jewel glass neckline of his robe. The "blinding light from heaven" emerges at the left of the window. Light and shadow effects on those who stand beside the blinded Saul, neither seeing the light nor hearing the voice from heaven, are extremely well done. Mottled glass has been used effectively in both the blue-green sky and hillside suggesting that this was executed during Tiffany Studios' middle-to-late period. Extensive plating is apparent.

The decorations above this window are reminiscent of the arches of the Cathedral of the Incarnation on Cathedral Avenue in Garden City. (See also Town of Hempstead/Garden City/Cathedral of the Incarnation.) The small rose window above contains a gold, jewel glass Greek cross set in a blue-green floral background with Greek lettering. The decoratives below do not appear to be Tiffany's. These have been broken and repaired and replaced so that color patterns and techniques make it difficult to assign origin.

On the east wall is a window with two panels depicting the Annunciation and the Magnificat. These are European etched and painted glass, probably French. Carved pews and a lovely brass altar rail reflect the Gothic motif of the chapel. The building has been on the National Register of Historic Places since 1978.

Vanderbilt Motor Parkway Toll House
Seventh Street, Garden City
(516) 746-7724

Take the Long Island Expressway to Exit #34 south (New Hyde Park Road). Go south on New Hyde Park Road for 3.2 miles. Turn left (east) onto Stewart Avenue; go 1.9 miles to where it becomes Cathedral Avenue. Go .1 mile on Cathedral Avenue. Turn left (east) onto Seventh Street; go .6 mile. The toll house is in Garden City Parking Field 6E on the right (south) side of the road.

The Vanderbilt Motor Parkway extended from Great Neck to Ronkonkoma. Completed in 1914 at a cost of $2.5 million, the approximately forty-five-mile-long, twenty-two-feet-wide parkway was the first to utilize concrete pavement, banked turns, guardrails, and landscaping. Traffic was monitored by its own special police force, although "scorching" was permitted. Tolls were collected at each of the twelve toll houses. A one-way trip originally cost the motorist $2.00; it was later reduced to $1.00 and ultimately to $.40. The parkway was officially closed in 1938 due to competition from the newly completed Northern State Parkway. Only 15.2 miles, all of which are in Suffolk County, remain of the Vanderbilt Motor Parkway

251

extending from Half Hollow Road in Dix Hills to Rosevale Avenue in Ronkonkoma. To our knowledge, this is the only surviving toll house of the twelve original toll houses, all of which were designed by John Russell Pope who also designed the Museum of Natural History in New York City and the National Gallery of Art in Washington, DC. In addition, at the terminus of the parkway in Ronkonkoma, Vanderbilt constructed a hotel which was also designed by John Russell Pope. It was built in a style reminiscent of French architecture and, although not an exact copy, it was called *Le Petit Trianon* after a restaurant in Versailles, France. Managed by the former manager of the Hotel Astor, it became a popular stopping place for those who used the Motor Parkway.

The circa 1909 toll house, previously a private residence, today houses the Garden City Chamber of Commerce. It was moved to the present site in 1989 from its original location on Vanderbilt Court, which is off Clinton Avenue just north of Stewart Avenue in Garden City.

(See also Town of Babylon/North Babylon/Belmont Lake State Park–August Belmont Sr. Estate–Nursery Stud Farm; Town of Brookhaven/Yaphank/Southaven County Park–Suffolk Club; Town of Hempstead/Elmont/Belmont Park Race Track; Town of Huntington/Centerport/Suffolk County Vanderbilt Museum and Planetarium–William Kissam Vanderbilt Jr. Estate–Eagle's Nest; Town of Islip/Islip/Saint Mark's Episcopal Church; Town of Islip/Oakdale/Connetquot River State Park and Preserve–Southside Sportsmen's Club; and Town of Islip/Oakdale/Dowling College–William Kissam Vanderbilt Sr. Estate–Idlehour.)

HEMPSTEAD

African American Museum
110 North Franklin Street, Hempstead
(516) 572-0730

From the Denton Village Green in Hempstead go west on Fulton Avenue/Route 24 for .3 mile. Turn right (north) onto Franklin Street; go .1 mile. The museum is on the right (east) side of the road.

The museum is dedicated to the history of Long Island's African-American community who have made a significant contribution on both local and national levels. Dioramas, films, lectures, and special events provide a multi-faceted approach to the interpretation of Afro-American heritage.

The museum also houses the African Atlantic Genealogical Society Inc., which provides workshops in genealogical research.

Christ's First Presbyterian Church of Hempstead
353 Fulton Avenue, Hempstead
(516) 292-1644

Located on the east end of the Denton Village Green.

In 1644 The Reverend Richard Denton and his followers came from Halifax, England, by way of Plymouth Colony and Stanford, CT, in the hope of securing civil and religious freedom. The first church was built within a stockade for protection from Indians on what is now the Denton Village Green.

During the Revolutionary War the fourth church to be built on the site was used by British soldiers as a storehouse and barracks. The fifth building was erected on the same site in 1803 and remained in use until 1846 when it was moved to the corner of Fulton Avenue and Washington Street and converted into the manse. The sixth building to be erected on the site was built in 1846 and remodeled in 1908. It was demolished in 1969.

The present building, which was built in 1969, is just east of the site of the first six churches and is designed in the octagonal style of the 1800s but with the clean contemporary lines of modern architecture. The large avant-garde stained-glass windows over the altar were designed by Willet Studios of Philadelphia. This church serves the oldest Presbyterian congregation in continuous existence in the United States.

(See also Town of Hempstead/Hempstead/Denton Village Green.)

Denton Village Green
Fulton Avenue, Hempstead

Take the Long Island Expressway to Exit #39 south (Glen Cove Road/Hempstead). Go south on Glen Cove Road/Clinton Road for 5.2 miles. Turn right (west) onto Fulton Avenue/Route 24; go .2 mile. The village green is on the right (north) side of the road.

The village green is named after The Reverend Richard Denton, the founder of Hempstead and leader of the colonists who settled in the area in 1644. Christ's First Presbyterian Church of Hempstead, now at the intersection of Fulton Avenue and Washington Street, was first built on the green. (See previous entry.) There are several Revolutionary War soldiers and early settlers buried on the green as is The Reverend Zachariah Green who, as a Continental soldier, was part of the contingent that rescued the Presbyterian Church of Setauket from British soldiers. He later became a minister serving both the Setauket and Hempstead Presbyterian churches. (See also Town of Brookhaven/Setauket/Presbyterian Church of Setauket and Town of Hempstead/Hempstead/Christ's First Presbyterian Church of Hempstead.) His son-in-law was Benjamin F. Thompson, the noted historian and author of *History of Long Island.*

Hempstead Lake State Park
Southern State Parkway, Hempstead
(516) 766-1029

Located at Exit #18 on Southern State Parkway.

This 775-acre state park has food stands, picnic areas, bridle paths, bike paths, hiking trails, an archery range, paddle tennis courts, clay tennis courts, all-weather tennis courts, horseshoe courts, athletic fields, a model boat basin, an ice skating rink, restrooms, a playground, and an antique carousel. The thirty-six wooden-horse carousel with calliope music was donated by August Heckscher Sr.

Hofstra Arboretum
Hofstra University
Hempstead Turnpike, Hempstead
(516) 463-6623

Take Meadowbrook Parkway to Exit #M4W (Nassau Coliseum/Hempstead Turnpike). Go west on Hempstead Turnpike/Route 24. The university is on the left (south) side of the road.

The grounds of Hofstra's 238-acre campus have been officially designated as an arboretum. Featured are over one hundred clearly labeled trees and shrubs, a knot garden, a sensory garden for people with visual impairment, a garden of easily-cared-for perennials and ornamental grasses, and a bird sanctuary with a songbird study garden.

Each spring the university hosts a garden show and a tulip festival. Call the above telephone number or check the local newspapers for the dates of these events.

Long Island Collection
Hempstead Public Library
115 Nichols Court, Hempstead
(516) 481-6990

Located on the east end of the Denton Village Green.

Included in this special collection are original manuscripts and a photograph collection specific to Long Island. There is also a Walt Whitman collection.

Saint George's Episcopal Church
319 Front Street, Hempstead
(516) 483-2771

From the Denton Village Green in Hempstead take Fulton Avenue/Route 24 east for .1 mile. Turn right (south) onto Washington Avenue; go .1 mile. Turn right (west) onto Front Street; go .1 mile. The church is on the right (north) side of the road.

The first meetinghouse was built within a wooden stockade in 1648 by the town. In 1673 it was replaced, at public expense, by a second larger meetinghouse. Religious services held in both early buildings were not limited to one particular religious denomination but rather limited only to the "Word of God."

In 1702 Saint George's Episcopal Church of Hempstead was founded. That same year Queen Anne of England presented a silver chalice, paten, and prayer book to the church, but their delivery was intercepted by pirates who used the chalice and paten as a cup and plate. Indeed it was not until 1706 that they were recovered and presented to the church. The scratches on the silver from this unfortunate episode are still readily visible. The church was finally granted a charter by King George II of England in 1735. This charter, which is in the church's possession, still governs church functions today.

During the Revolutionary War, Continental soldiers, under the command of Colonel Cornell, converted the church into a storehouse and used the church's golden cock weather vane, which had been on the church's steeple since 1725, for target practice. The weather vane still has sixteen bullet holes from this incident. Continental soldiers even went so far as to use the church's communion table as an eating table.

The church did not suffer indignities solely at the hands of the patriots. During the British occupation of Long Island British soldiers desecrated the church's cemetery by using the headstones as hearthstones.

The present church, which has been on the National Register of Historic Places since 1973, was constructed in 1822. It was extended in 1856 and remodeled in 1893 and again in 1906 but it has still maintained its pure Federal-style of architecture. The hand-wound, six-day clock was made in Sag Harbor in 1854 by the company of Sherry and Bryon.

The interior is elegant in its simplicity with its wooden carving of Saint George and the Dragon in the vestibule, the crest of King George in front of the choir loft, the pine cone symbol of colonial America's welcome over the top of the canopy of the pulpit, and its English, French, and American stained-glass windows.

The small, centrally-placed Henry Van Rensselaer Kennedy Memorial (March 17, 1863–July 13, 1912) window on the east wall features a single male figure with right hand raised. It is signed "J. A. Holzer MCMXVII." Mr. Holzer was a designer for Tiffany Studios. Whether this was a commission of Tiffany Studios or a privately executed commission, prior to his joining the Tiffany firm, is not known since it is not noted in the surviving records of Tiffany Studios. Instead of drapery glass to give deep dimensional effects, chunks of glass are placed in relief, much of it fractured and mottled especially for landscape effect. The lack of continuity of these pieces of glass suggests that perhaps this is composed of refuse glass left over from larger commissions—some of it quite possibly was drapery glass. The plating technique, so typical of Tiffany designs, is used in the sky and in the figure whose hands, legs, and face are painted. Autumn leaves, frequently used in Tiffany designs, are depicted across the top. The figured panel is surrounded by clear and lightly colored framing glass in a geometric configuration.

Directly to the left of the Holzer design is the Bessie Morgan Belmont Memorial, dated September 27, 1898, and given by Marion K. Kennedy. Again, this is a small panel enclosed in plain framing glass. This memorial also displays the chunk glass relief technique, seen in the Holzer design, with no drapery glass. It too has plating especially in the background. The Virgin is depicted holding a small bouquet of lilies, a flower associated with Virgin Mary symbolism and extensively used by Tiffany and his designers to symbolize the Resurrection. The painted portions of this panel are of rather poor quality. Dark blue and dark pink chunks of glass have been incorporated to give a three-dimensional effect. It is unsigned and also not listed in Tiffany records but is similar in design to the one beside it, raising questions as to its designer. It has been repaired and extensively releaded obscuring its origins.

The noted Loyalist Josiah Martin and his son Samuel are buried under the chancel. (See also Town of Hempstead/Lawrence/Rock Hall Museum.) The cemetery which surrounds the church is the final resting place of such notable colonial families as Baldwin, Conklin, Gardiner, Hewlett, Hicks, Raynor, Sammis, Seaman, Townsend, Van Nostrand, and Van Wyck. Buried in plot A99 is The Reverend Samuel Seabury, the third rector of Saint George's Church and the father of the first bishop of the Episcopal Church of America. (See also Town of Huntington/Huntington/Saint John's Episcopal Church and Town of Huntington/Huntington/Kissam House.)

Saint Paul's Greek Orthodox Church
110 Cathedral Avenue, Hempstead
(516) 483-5700

From the Denton Village Green in Hempstead go west on Fulton Avenue/Route 24 for .6 mile. Turn right (north) onto Cathedral Avenue; go .3 mile. The church is on the right (east) side of the road.

Saint Paul's was established in 1951 in the Village of Roosevelt. The groundbreaking for the church's present building was held during the summer of 1957. This beautiful Byzantine-style church is truly worth a visit. Magnificent mosaic murals, depicting events in the life of Christ among other subjects, cover the walls with intense gold, blue, and red. Many of these are re-creations of thirteenth- and fourteenth-century Byzantine murals and some are translations into mosaic of iconographic subjects. They are unquestionably among the most beautiful examples of this art form in the world. The forty-eight standing figures in the dome represent, in glorious mosaic, the Biblical genealogy extending in time from Adam to Christ.

The exquisite chandeliers incorporate meaningful symbolism: twelve votives representing the twelve disciples; four support chains representing the four apostles who authored the Gospels; the golden crown signifying that Christ is King; and the single chain to the ceiling representing monotheism. They are beautiful and of traditional Byzantine design. The carved white onyx bishop's chair is ornately decorated with fine bronze work. Note the elegant marble pillars and the carved marble pulpit. Some of the stained-glass windows are translations of icons into stained glass; an artistic triumph of no small difficulty.

Of special interest is the *Tearing Ikon of the Sorrowful Mother of God* found in the Virgin's chapel with its exquisite thirteenth-century styled mosaic. The golden mosaic background is breathtaking. The icon has been declared by the Holy Synod of the Ecumenical Patriarchate to be a Sign of Divine Providence.

The beauty and harmony of this church make it, in our experience, one of the most beautiful in the world. No matter how short your stay on Long Island, do try to include Saint Paul's in your itinerary.

United Methodist Church of Hempstead
40 Washington Avenue, Hempstead
(516) 485-6363

From the Denton Village Green in Hempstead take Fulton Avenue/Route 24 east for .1 mile. Turn right (south) onto Washington Avenue; go .1 mile. The church is on the left (east) side of the road at the intersection of Washington Avenue and Front Street.

The 158-foot spire of this church has risen above the Hempstead Plains since 1852 when the present church replaced an 1820 church building which the congregation had outgrown. Its Italian Renaissance ceiling, from which hang eight massive brass lamps, is spectacularly beautiful. The carved altar and choir loft are flanked by matching ranks of organ pipes; the organ dates from 1947. Pews, also handsomely carved, are elegant.

The Thorne Memorial on the east wall is a truly beautiful Tiffany window signed "TIFFANY GLASS DECORATING COMPANY NEW YORK," a signature used from 1890–1899. Although listed in the Tiffany Studios' records as *Resurrection*, this two-paneled window is an unusual Resurrection window in that it does not picture Christ but instead features an angel standing on a rock at the tomb telling the two Marys, "He is not here for he is risen, as He said" (Matthew 28:6); "Because I live, ye shall live also" (John 14:19). The angel, in robes composed of heavy pearl white opalescent drapery glass with multicolored wings extending dramatically straight up, is positioned to capture the morning sun. Her right arm is raised and her left hand carries a palm frond, symbolic of victory. The spotlighting effect, so often used by Tiffany, is dramatic here and is in sharp contrast to the deep blue sky and to the dark colors emitted through the drapery glass used to fashion the women's robes. The Virgin Mary is in green while Mary Magdalene appears in blue and dark red. The combination of colors used here in the robes of Mary Magdalene are exactly as they appear in the Bigelow Memorial window, *Resurrection*, in Christ Episcopal Church in Corning, NY. Palm trees, as seen here, were also included in the Corning window. In an unusual touch, a bouquet of lilies, symbolizing Resurrection, has been "laid on the ground" in the foreground extending across the two panels. Both external and internal plating are apparent.

The large round window above features a blue opalescent glass-jeweled cross surrounded by flowers. It is edged in a pink brick effect which surrounds petals fashioned in mottled dark blue glass. Suspended from the arms of the cross, in a scale-like manner, are an alpha and an omega symbolizing the perfect balance of the beginning and the end through Christ's sacrifice on the cross. Although we have seen the alpha and the omega used in other windows by Tiffany Studios, we have never seen these Greek letters used in quite the symbolic way that they are used in this window.

Other decorative, non-figure windows have the colors and American technique favored by Tiffany and are, therefore, perfectly harmonious.

HEWLETT

Grant County Park
Broadway and Sheridan Avenue, Hewlett
(516) 571-7821

Nassau County Leisure Pass is required for admission.

Take Meadowbrook Parkway to Exit #M6W (Southern State Parkway). Go west on Southern State Parkway for 3.1 miles to Exit #19S. (Peninsula Blvd./Rockville Centre). Go south on Peninsula Blvd. for 5.4 miles. Turn left (east) onto Mill Road; go .4 mile. Turn left (north) onto West Broadway; go .1 mile. Turn left onto Broadway; go .8 mile. The park is on the right side of the road.

This thirty-five-acre park has baseball fields, softball fields, basketball courts, handball courts, horseshoe courts, paddleball courts, shuffleboard courts, tennis courts, a roller skating rink, an ice skating rink, sledding hills, lake fishing, pedal boat rentals, an area for chess and checkers, a picnic area, restrooms, playgrounds, a swimming pool, and a wading pool. These facilities are located adjacent to an eighteen-acre lake.

Saint Joseph's Roman Catholic Church
Broadway, Hewlett
(516) 374-0290

Take Meadowbrook Parkway to Exit #M6W (Southern State Parkway). Go west on Southern State Parkway for 3.1 miles to Exit #19S (Peninsula Blvd./Rockville Centre). Go south on Peninsula Blvd. for 5.4 miles. Turn left (east) onto Mill Road; go .4 mile. Turn left (north) onto West Broadway; go .1 mile. Turn left (north) onto Broadway; go .2 mile. The church is on the left (west) side of the road.

The parish, established in 1872 as a mission of Saint Joachim's of Lawrence, built this Spanish Mission-styled church in 1929. It is easily recognizable by its tile roof, twin copper-roofed turrets, and "turned" exterior columnar decorations. Its interior is highlighted by fine quality grisaille-style, stained-glass windows depicting the family life of Jesus, Mary, and Joseph and by three extraordinarily beautiful large rose windows. The wainscotted ceiling is accented by stone beams crossed by stenciled beams. The arches in front of the chancel of the main altar and the alcoves of the small side chapels are ornately outlined and beautifully painted. In addition, there are carved wooden canopies suspended over the side chapels. Museum quality paintings mark the stations of the cross.

In 1946 the relics of Saint Pia were placed in the altar. He was a second century North African saint from the Roman province of Numidia, now Algeria, about whom nothing else is known. His martyrdom is celebrated on January 19th.

INWOOD

Inwood County Park
Bayview Avenue, Inwood
(516) 571-7894

Nassau County Leisure Pass is required for admission.

Take Meadowbrook Parkway to Exit #M6W (Southern State Parkway). Go west on Southern State Parkway for 3.1 miles to Exit #19S (Peninsula Blvd./Rockville Centre). Go south on Peninsula Blvd. for 5.4 miles. Turn left (east) onto Mill Road; go .4 mile. Turn left (north) onto West Broadway; go .1 mile. Turn right (south) onto Broadway; go 3.1 miles. Turn right (west) onto Doughty Blvd.; go .5 mile. Turn left (south) onto Bayview Avenue and go .8 mile to the park entrance.

This sixteen-acre park has boat launching ramps, basketball courts, bocce courts, paddle tennis courts, volleyball courts, an area for chess and checkers, playgrounds, an ice skating rink, and pier fishing facilities.

FAR ROCKAWAY, QUEENS

First Presbyterian Church
13-24 Beach 9th Street (Central Avenue and Sage Street), Far Rockaway
(718) 327-2440

Although this entry takes you a few streets out of Nassau County and into Queens County, the First Presbyterian Church of Far Rockaway is well worth a visit and, years ago, it all used to be the same county anyway.

Take Meadowbrook Parkway to Exit #M6W (Southern State Parkway). Go west on Southern State Parkway for 3.1 miles to Exit #19S (Peninsula Blvd./Rockville Centre). Go south on Peninsula Blvd. for 7.5 miles. Turn left (east) onto Rockaway Turnpike; go .8 mile. Turn right (south) onto Central Avenue; go 1 mile. The church is on the right (east) side of the road.

This small, beautifully designed and appointed church was a gift to the congregation of the First Presbyterian Church of Far Rockaway by Margaret Olivia Slocum Sage in 1908 as a memorial to her husband Russell, the financier who was reputed to be worth $80 million at his death in 1906. The gift also included the Sunday school building and the manse.

At the end of the nave, on the southeast wall, is a large window designed by Louis Comfort Tiffany, reported to have cost $35,000 in 1909. Although unsigned, it is documented in records of Tiffany Studios. This twenty-five-foot-high by twenty-one-foot-wide *Tree of Life* landscape is one of the largest of Tiffany's landscapes. It is not a single window but instead a composite of variously sized trefoil panels topped by many smaller windows which complete the landscape and contribute to the impressionistic quality of the piece, achieving a unique and beautiful effect. This memorial within its Gothic-style framing is nothing less than spectacular.

Fractured or confetti glass is used superbly in this window. It was at about the time this window was made that Tiffany began to use this technique extensively. The tree is pictured as firmly rooted in the earth. The trunk, gnarled with age, and the leaves, showing the colors of the autumn of life, reach heavenward. The sky is in tones of rose, lavender, and aqua. This aqua, an unusual color for Tiffany, is also seen in the 1912 Dewitt Memorial window *Angel of Resurrection* in Saint Andrew's Dune Church in Southampton (see also Town of Southampton/Southampton/Saint Andrew's Dune Church) and in the altar piece in All Saints Episcopal Church in Bayside. A bright natural area at the horizon utilizes natural sunlight from the southeast to divide sky from earth as would a prism, a most interesting technique which not only delineates the horizon but also prevents the numerous horizontal bands of color from becoming a confusion of patterns. The southeastern exposure limits the glaring that an eastern exposure would have presented in the morning or that a western exposure would have given in the evening. It will be noted that there is less extensive plating used in this landscape than would be found in figure windows of the same period.

Positioned in this pristinely white interior surrounded by rich woods, Tiffany's artistry is perfectly shown.

An interesting footnote concerning this window is that Ralph Adams Cram had planned Gothic windows for this wall to complete the Gothic design of the chapel. The frames were in place when he went to Europe. While he was abroad, Mrs. Sage commissioned Tiffany to design and install the window which we see today. Cram later revenged this act by changing the Cathedral of Saint John the Divine from Romanesque to Gothic architecture. In the course of the changes Tiffany's exquisitely beautiful Byzantine-style chapel was boarded up and forgotten, to be destroyed over the years by neglect and the ravages of water leakage and mold growth. Remnants of this chapel were salvaged and installed in the garden chapel at Tiffany's estate Laurelton Hall. It too was forgotten and totally destroyed by the elements after the devastating 1957 fire which destroyed Tiffany's Long Island home and so much of his work. Remnants of the chapel, recovered from Laurelton Hall, are now on display at the Hosmer–Morse Museum in Winter Park, FL.

Surviving Tiffany records list ornamental windows in the First Presbyterian Church in Far Rockaway. However, a booklet available from the church states that all other windows were made and designed by Mary Tillinghast except for the *Christ and Apostle* window over the chancel which she made from designs by Cram, Goodhue, and Ferguson.

LAWRENCE

Rock Hall Museum
199 Broadway, Lawrence
(516) 239-1157

Take Meadowbrook Parkway to Exit #M6W (Southern State Parkway). Go west on Southern State Parkway for 3.1 miles to Exit #19S (Peninsula Blvd./Rockville Centre). Go south on Peninsula Blvd. for 6.2 miles. Turn left (east) onto Woodmere Blvd.; go .7 mile. Turn right (south) onto Broadway; go 1.9 miles. The entrance is on the left (east) side of the road.

Rock Hall, which is on the National Register of Historic Places, was built in 1767 by Josiah Martin, a prosperous trader from Antigua, West Indies. Martin's land holdings consisted of six hundred acres extending from Rock Hall to the ocean front at Far Rockaway. During the Revolutionary War Martin was an active Loyalist whose ships were used to transport British soldiers to the area while the house became a haven for his daughter Elizabeth and her Loyalist husband who was the last colonial governor of North Carolina. In 1824 Thomas Hewlett purchased the house and its remaining 125 acres. The Hewlett family presented the house to the Town of Hempstead for use as a museum.

Both Josiah Martin and his son Samuel are buried under the chancel of Saint George's Episcopal Church in Hempstead. (See also Town of Hempstead/Hempstead/Saint George's Episcopal Church.)

The house is decorated in period furnishings. Of particular interest are the 400-year-old ivory chess set, the circa 1790 Hepplewhite sofa, original Dutch tiles around the bedroom fireplace, a harp, a piano forte, and the dress in which Elizabeth Martin was presented at the Court of Saint James.

(See also Town of Brookhaven/Mastic Beach/The Manor of St. George; Town of Brookhaven/Mastic Beach/William Floyd Estate; Town of Huntington/Lloyd Harbor/Henry Lloyd Manor; Town of Huntington/Lloyd Harbor/Joseph Lloyd Manor; and Town of Oyster Bay/Oyster Bay/Raynham Hall.)

Levittown

Levittown Historical Museum
Levittown Memorial Education Center
150 Abby Lane, Levittown
(516) 731-5728

From Gardiner's Avenue turn east onto Reed Lane. Make a right onto Abby Lane and proceed to the Levittown Memorial Education Center.

In 1951 William Jaird Levitt Sr. completed his 17,500 single-family community of Levittown on land that had previously been potato fields.

Located on the lower floor of the center, the museum is dedicated to preserving the community's history. It offers photographs, memorabilia of the era, and a small gift shop. Of special interest is the reproduction of several rooms that would have been typical of the early Levitt houses.

(See also Town of Babylon/Pinelawn/Mount Ararat Cemetery/Grave of William Jaird Levitt Sr. and Town of Oyster Bay/Mill Neck/William Jaird Levitt Sr. House–La Colline.)

Lido Beach

Eugene Nickerson Beach County Park
Lido Boulevard, Lido Beach
(516) 571-7724

Nassau County Leisure Pass is required for admission.

Take Meadowbrook Parkway to Exit #M10 (Loop Parkway/Point Lookout/Lido Beach/Long Beach). Go 2.9 miles on the Loop Parkway. Turn right (west) onto Lido Boulevard; go .1 mile. The park is on the left (south) side of the road.

This 121-acre park stretches 3,500 feet along the Atlantic Ocean shoreline. It has campsites with a dump station, ocean swimming, cabana rentals, cabinette rentals, surf fishing, a swimming pool, a kiddy pool, swimming programs for people with disabilities, basketball courts, handball courts, paddleball courts, tennis courts, volleyball courts, lockers, steam rooms, soccer fields, snack concessions, senior citizen activities, a game room, and restrooms.

LONG BEACH

Long Beach Historical Society Museum
226 West Penn Street, Long Beach
(516) 432-1192

West Penn Street is located one street south of and parallel to West Beech Street.

The Museum is located in a 1908 Spanish-style house built for Kate Goldner. In 1921 it was purchased from Goldner by the Barret family. In 1997 the Barrets sold the house to the historical society. Much of its interior remained unchanged over the years. The house still has its original wood paneling, stained-glass windows, lighting, and wallpaper.

Their reference collection includes maps of Reynolds' original community. There is also a small gift shop.

MALVERNE

Malverne Historical and Preservation Society
369 Ocean Avenue, Malverne
(516) 887-9727

The house is located at the intersection of Ocean Avenue and Church Street.

Featured in a restored 1854 house, which serves as the society's headquarters, are photographs and memorabilia pertinent to Malverne's history, clothing, tools, and a room featuring famous people from the village.

NORTH WOODMERE

North Woodmere County Park
Branch Boulevard and Hungry Harbor Road, North Woodmere
(516) 571-7801

Nassau County Leisure Pass is required for admission.

Take Meadowbrook Parkway to Exit #M6W (Southern State Parkway). Go west on Southern State Parkway for 3.1 miles to Exit #19S (Peninsula Blvd./Rockville Centre). Go south on Peninsula Blvd. for 5.4 miles. Turn right (west) onto Mill Road; go .5 mile. Turn left (south) onto Hungry Harbor Road; go 1.4 miles. The park entrance is on the right side of the road.

This 150-acre park offers a picnic area, a playground, lighted baseball fields, softball fields, soccer fields, lighted football fields, an olympic-sized swimming pool, a kiddy pool, a diving pool, a nine-hole par-thirty-one golf course, a clubhouse, a driving range, bay fishing, bicycle paths, shuffleboard courts, paddleball courts, tennis courts, volleyball courts, jogging paths, basketball courts, handball courts, horseshoe courts, a fieldhouse, lockers, showers, restrooms, food concessions, and a boathouse for boat rentals. Sailing instructions are available. Concerts are held in the park during the summer months while cross-country skiing is permitted in the winter.

OCEANSIDE

Marine Nature Study Area
Slice Drive, Oceanside
(516) 766-1580

Take Meadowbrook Parkway to Exit #M8W (Sunrise Highway/Freeport). Go west on Sunrise Highway for 2.4 miles. Turn left (south) onto Grand Avenue; go 1.3 miles. Turn right (west) onto Atlantic Avenue; go .4 mile. Turn left (south) onto Waukena Avenue; go .7 mile. Turn left (east) onto Park Avenue; go .3 mile. Turn left (north) onto Gulf Drive (which becomes Bunker Drive); go .4 mile. Turn left onto Slice Drive; go .1 mile to park entrance.

Owned by the Town of Hempstead, this fifty-two-acre preserve is devoted to environmental and natural history education. It comprises eight different habitats and instructional areas with visual aids at each site. Subjects covered at these sites are tides, Long Island's glacial geology, barrier beach and estuarine formations, ecology of the estuary, micro and macro algae, bird life, migration, bay community, and barrier beach plant and animal life. There are several boardwalks and a nature trail transversing the preserve. Because of its diverse habitats, over 199 species of birds have been recorded in the preserve. Guided tours are conducted by trained environmental staff.

ROCKVILLE CENTRE

Phillips House Museum
28 Hempstead Avenue, Rockville Centre
(516) 764-7459

Take Meadowbrook Parkway to Exit #M8W (Sunrise Highway/Freeport/Baldwin). Go west on Sunrise Highway for 4.3 miles. Turn right (north) onto North Village

Avenue; go .3 mile. Turn right (east) onto Hempstead Avenue; go .1 mile. The museum is on the left (north) side of the road.

This circa 1882 house, the last of the captains' homes in the Rockville Centre area, was the home of Captain Samuel F. Phillips. It was moved to its present site in 1974 and opened as a museum in 1976. A beautifully appointed Victorian parlor is on permanent exhibit. Other rooms are utilized for three major exhibit changes a year.

SEAFORD

Cedar Creek County Park
Merrick Road, Seaford
(516) 571-7470

Nassau County Leisure Pass is required for admission.

Take the Long Island Expressway to Exit #44 south (N.Y. 135/Seaford–Oyster Bay Expressway). Go south on the Seaford–Oyster Bay Expressway for 9.8 miles to Exit #1W (Merrick Road/Freeport). Go west on Merrick Road for .7 mile. The park is on the left (south) side of the road.

This 260-acre park has a lighted roller skating rink, skate rentals, jogging paths, a spray pool, an ice skating rink, an archery range, basketball courts, tennis courts, handball courts, paddleball courts, a playground, soccer fields, softball fields, an aerodrome for radio-controlled airplanes, sledding hills, and restrooms.

Seaford Historical Museum
3890 Waverly Avenue, Seaford
(516) 850-9188

Take the Long Island Expressway to Exit #44 south (N.Y. 135/Seaford–Oyster Bay Expressway) for 9.8 miles to Exit #1E (Merrick Road/Amityville). Go east on Merrick Road for .4 mile. Turn left (north) onto Southard Avenue; go .2 mile. Turn right (east) onto Waverly Avenue and make an immediate right into the parking lot.

The museum, located in an 1893 schoolhouse and operated by the Seaford Historical Society, preserves the history of Seaford through photographs, memorabilia, and exhibits. There are collections of typewriters, cameras, musical instruments, clothes, and antique tools. Displayed is a 1907 46-star American flag which was issued when Oklahoma became a state and which remained in use until 1912 when New Mexico and Arizona became states. Of particular interest is a 1906 Seaford skiff, unique in its design to allow for navigation in the shallow local waters.

Tackapausha Museum and Preserve
Washington Avenue, Seaford
(516) 571-7443

Take the Long Island Expressway to Exit #44 south (N.Y. 135/Seaford–Oyster Bay Expressway). Go south on the Seaford–Oyster Bay Expressway for 9.8 miles to Exit #1E (Merrick Road/Amityville). Go east on Merrick Road for .6 mile. Turn left (north) onto Washington Avenue; go .1 mile. The museum is on the right (east) side of the road.

Nassau County's eighty-four-acre Tackapausha Preserve, named after a sachem of the Massapequa Indians, is maintained as a wildlife sanctuary devoted to education and nature. It boasts the largest white cedar stand on Long Island. The adjacent museum maintains collections of native animals and plants which are available for research. It also offers programs for both children and adults emphasizing concern for animals and the environment. Ice skating and cross-country skiing are permitted during the winter; nature walks and a small zoo are available year round.

UNIONDALE

Mitchel Athletic Complex
Charles Lindbergh Boulevard, Uniondale
(516) 572-0400

Nassau County Leisure Pass is required for use.

Take Meadowbrook Parkway to Exit #M5W (Hempstead Turnpike/Route 24). Go west on Hempstead Turnpike/Route 24 for .6 mile. Turn right (north) onto Earle Ovington Boulevard; go .5 mile. Turn left (west) onto Charles Lindbergh Drive; go .3 mile. Turn left (south) into parking lot and follow signs to the athletic complex and the rifle and pistol range.

The forty-nine-acre complex has four softball fields, one baseball field, and seven soccer fields. Also found in the park is an indoor rifle and pistol range.

Mitchel Complex Rifle and Pistol Range
(part of the Mitchel Athletic Complex)
Charles Lindbergh Boulevard, Uniondale
(516) 572-0420

The range has six soundproof bays with five firing points in each bay. It can accommodate competition, training, and practice using rifles, pistols, and revolvers of all caliber. There are classrooms, storage rooms, lockers, maintenance shops, and storage areas for ammunition.

Nassau County Veterans' Memorial Coliseum

1255 Hempstead Turnpike, Uniondale
(516) 794-9303

Take Meadowbrook Parkway to Exit #M4W (Nassau Coliseum/Hempstead Turnpike). Go .4 mile west on Hempstead Turnpike. The entrance is on the right (north) side of the road.

This sports arena, which seats 16,500 people, hosts boxing bouts, concerts, track and field events, wrestling matches, conventions, ice shows, boat shows, horse shows, dog shows, trade shows, and the circus. It is also the home of the Long Islanders hockey team.

VALLEY STREAM

Pagan–Fletcher Restoration

143 Hendrickson Avenue, Valley Stream
(516) 872-4159

The museum is located on Hendrickson Avenue between Fletcher and Corona Avenues.

In 1977 the c. 1840 Colonial Revival-style house was purchased by the Village of Valley Stream. After a fifteen-year restoration the house, which is on the National Register of Historic Places, is operated as a museum by the Valley Stream Historical Society. Featured are three floors of rooms furnished in the style of the Victorian era while its basement contains artifacts from Curtis Airfield (now the site of Green Acres Mall).

On the museum's grounds are found artifacts from the historic Raustein Gas Station, a Columbia Aircraft Hangar emblem, and a period herb garden.

Valley Stream State Park

Southern State Parkway, Valley Stream
(516) 825-4128

Located on Southern State Parkway between Exits #14 and #15.

This ninety-seven-acre state park has horseshoe courts, basketball courts, athletic fields, bike paths, hiking trails, a playground, food stands, restrooms, and a picnic area.

WANTAGH

Grave of Checkers
Bide-A-Wee Pet Memorial Park
3300 Beltagh Avenue, Wantagh
(516) 785-6153

Take the Long Island Expressway to Exit #44 south (N.Y. 135/Seaford–Oyster Bay Expressway). Go south for 7.9 miles to Exit #3 (N.Y. 105/Massapequa/Hempstead). Turn left onto the service road; go .1 mile. Turn right (west) onto Jerusalem Avenue; go .7 mile. Turn left (south) onto Wantagh Avenue; go .4 mile. Turn right (west) onto Beltagh Avenue; go .2 mile. The cemetery is on the left (south) directly across from the office and in line with the flag pole. Section 5, Grave A38D

In 1952 Richard Nixon was chosen as the vice-presidential candidate on the Eisenhower ticket. During the campaign the issue of $18,000 raised by Nixon supporters in California became an issue. The money had been raised in 1950 to enable Nixon to campaign for Republican programs and candidates during election and non-election years. Even though Nixon had been able to show that the funds were used only for political expenses, Democrats raised the spectre of a secret slush fund. Republican leaders, fearing that Eisenhower's chances for election would be jeopardized, encouraged Nixon to resign from the ticket. On September 23, 1952, Nixon went on national television and radio and emotionally discussed his personal finances showing that he had not personally profited from the fund. He went on to say of his wife, "Pat doesn't have a mink coat. But she does have a respectable Republican cloth coat." As to the cocker spaniel Checkers, given as a gift to his daughters, he vowed to keep it. After the speech, Eisenhower gave Nixon his full support declaring, "You're my boy!" They went on to defeat their Democratic opponents, Governor Adlai E. Stevenson of Illinois and Senator John J. Sparkman of Alabama, and the Nixon speech was dubbed the "Checkers Speech."

Checkers' grave is marked by a pink marble headstone inscribed "Checkers 1952–1964 Nixon."

Jones Beach State Park
Ocean Drive, Wantagh
(516) 785-1600

Take the Long Island Expressway to Exit #44 south (N.Y. 135/Seaford–Oyster Bay Expressway for 7 miles. Go west on Southern State Parkway for 1.5 miles to Exit #27S (Wantagh Parkway/Jones Beach State Park).

In 1692 Thomas Jones came to Long Island by way of Ireland and France and became a privateer preying on ships in the Atlantic and Caribbean. Because of these very lucrative endeavors, he was able to purchase 6,000 acres of marshland and ocean front in the vicinity of what is now known as Jones Beach. In 1700 he established a whaling station on an uninhabited section of the outer beach. By the time he died in 1713 the outer beach area was already known as Jones Beach.

The 2,413-acre Jones Beach State Park was opened in 1929. It was the creation of Robert Moses, the master architect of many of Long Island's roads and parks. The park offers facilities for an unbelievable array of activities. There is a restaurant, cafeterias, food stands, picnic areas, a boat basin, a roller skating rink, a miniature golf course, pitch and putt golf, shuffleboard courts, paddle tennis courts, basketball courts, an archery range, an outdoor theater, an outdoor dance floor, exercise trails, fishing piers, surf fishing, a bait station, a boardwalk, bathhouses, restrooms, and ocean, bay, and pool swimming.

It is interesting to note that the two-hundred-foot water tower, which rises above a one-thousand-foot-deep freshwater well, was inspired by the campanile in Saint Mark's Square in Venice. Its storage tanks hold 315,000 gallons of water.

Castles in the Sand Museum
(part of the Jones State Park Complex)
East Bathhouse
(516) 785-1600

The museum chronicles the history of Jones Beach. Featured are photographs, maps, and plans of the park's construction, old uniforms worn by the park's employees, vintage video's of the park in the 1940s and 1950s, and other memorabilia of the park's early days.

Nikon At Jones Beach Theater
(part of the Jones Beach Complex)
Parking Field #5
(516) 221-1000

The first outdoor amphitheater on the site was a wooden structure that was razed in 1945. It was replaced with a 8,200-person capacity concrete structure with a 104-foot-wide stage, in which is installed a 76-foot revolving center and an underwater tunnel connecting the shore to the stage. In 1992 seating capacity was increased to 11,200. Today's amphitheater, enlarged in 1998, has a seating capacity of 15,000.

Originally presenting operettas, Broadway musicals, and classical concerts, the theater's offerings have been undated to appeal to current trends in entertainment.

(See also Town of Brookhaven/Farmingville/Bald Hill Cultural Park.)

Theodore Roosevelt Nature Center
(part of the Jones Beach Complex)
West End Field #1
(516) 679-7254

Children are introduced to the seashore and dune environments, emphasized in this nature center, through hands-on, feel-and-learn activities with live marine animals and microscopic examination of tiny life forms. There is a also a Discovery Bone Cove, where children can dig up whale bones, a butterfly walk, a "shipwreck" viewing area, and an environment boardwalk that allows you to walk out into the dunes and view the plants and animals in their unique marine habitats without damaging the fragile dune environment.

Limited activities are available for people with disabilities.

Trump On The Ocean
(part of the Jones Beach Complex)
Parking Field #4

Manhattan real estate mogul Donald Trump is in the process of constructing a $40 million, three-story, 36,000-square-foot, 1,400-person capacity facility adjacent to the boardwalk. Scheduled to open in 2009, it will house a restaurant, catering facility, and nightclub.

West End Boat Basin
(part of the Jones Beach Complex)
Parking Field West End #1

This section of the park features a bird sanctuary to host migratory birds, and the aforementioned Theodore Roosevelt Nature Center. It is a multi-purpose area, providing also a boat basin with seventy-six free slips for the use of day visitors.

Wantagh County Park
Merrick Road, Wantagh
(516) 571-7460

Nassau County Leisure Pass is required for admission.

Take the Long Island Expressway to Exit #44 south (N.Y. 135/Seaford–Oyster Bay Expressway). Go south on the Seaford–Oyster Bay Expressway for 9.8 miles to Exit #1W (Merrick Road/Freeport). Go west on Merrick Road for 1.1 miles. Turn left (south) onto Woodland Avenue. The park is on the left side of the road.

This 111-acre park has baseball fields, softball fields, hockey fields, soccer fields, lacrosse fields, football fields, an olympic-sized swimming pool, a diving pool, a kiddy pool, lockers, showers, restrooms, basketball courts, bocce courts, horseshoe courts, shuffleboard courts, tennis courts, volleyball courts, bicycle paths, bicycle rentals, jogging paths, an area for chess and checkers, a picnic area, a playground, a fishing pier, a boat launching ramp, a 136-slip-marina with electricity, water, and a pump-out station, refreshment stands, and an amphitheater. There are tent camping facilities for organized youth groups available from Labor Day through June 15th.

The sensory garden, which contains vegetation which appeals to the sense of touch, smell, and sound, is the most unusual attraction. It is designed for the enjoyment of both people with and without visual needs.

Wantagh Preservation Society Museum
Wantagh Avenue, Wantagh
(516) 826-8767

Take the Long Island Expressway to Exit #44 south (N.Y. 135/Seaford–Oyster Bay Expressway). Go south on the Seaford–Oyster Bay Expressway for 7.9 miles to Exit #3 (N.Y. 105/Massapequa/Hempstead). Turn left onto the service road; go .1 mile. Turn right (west) onto Jerusalem Avenue; go .7 mile. Turn left (south) onto Wantagh Avenue; go 1 mile. The museum is on the right (west) side of the road.

The museum comprises the original 1885 Ridgewood Long Island Rail Road Station—the name Wantagh was not adopted by the community until 1891—and the *Jamaica* railroad car which was built for the Long Island Rail Road in 1912 as a parlor car. The *Jamaica,* which was donated by the railroad to the society in 1972, included a solarium, cooking facilities, and an ice-cooled air conditioner. The station was originally located on Railroad Avenue just east of Wantagh Avenue. In 1966 it was donated by the railroad to the society and moved to its present site for use as a museum. Restored to its 1904 appearance, it houses railroad memorabilia and early pictures of Wantagh. The *Jamaica* is still in the process of being restored but the complex has been on the National Register of Historic Places since 1983.

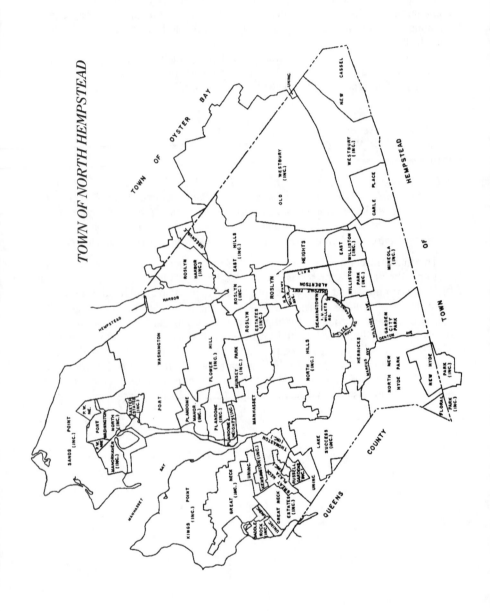

TOWN OF NORTH HEMPSTEAD

TOWN OF NORTH HEMPSTEAD

PARKS AND PRESERVES

Federal Parks and Preserves
none

State Parks and Preserves
none

County Parks and Preserves
Barbara Johnson Park and Preserve (5 acres), Port Washington *(undeveloped)*
Christopher Morley County Park (98 acres), Roslyn Estates
Flower Hill County Park (10 acres), Flower Hill
Garvies Point Museum and Preserve (62 acres), Glen Cove
Hempstead Harbor County Park (60 acres), Port Washington
Herricks Pond Park (4 acres), Herricks *(undeveloped)*
Leeds Pond Preserve (35 acres), Plandome Manor
Sands Point County Park and Preserve (216 acres), Sands Point
Stannard Brook Park (3 acres), Port Washington *(undeveloped)*
William Cullen Bryant Preserve (141 acres), Roslyn Harbor *(undeveloped)*

Long Island Chapter: The Nature Conservancy
Harbor Hill Sanctuary (4 acres), Lake Success
Kings Point Preserve (14 acres), Kings Point

Arboretums and Gardens
Clark Botanic Garden (12 acres), Albertson
Old Westbury Gardens (160 acres), Old Westbury

ALBERTSON

Clark Botanic Garden – Grenville Clark Sr. Estate
193 I. U. Willets Road, Albertson
(516) 484-8600

Take the Long Island Expressway to Exit #37 south (Willis Avenue/Mineola/ Roslyn). Go south on Willis Avenue for 1.1 miles. Turn left (east) onto I. U. Willets Road; go .4 mile. The botanical garden is on the left (north) side of the road.

This twelve-acre botanical garden has carefully planned and labeled displays of shrubs, exotic trees, native trees, spring bulbs, perennial flowers, annual flowers, daylilies, herbs, wildflowers, roses, and a children's garden, all of which are set in a gently rolling landscape. During June and July there are evening classical music programs as well as lectures. Restrooms are provided.

Searing–Roslyn United Methodist Church
134 I. U. Willets Road, Albertson
(516) 621-1837

Take the Long Island Expressway to Exit #37 south (Willis Avenue/Mineola/ Roslyn). Go south on Willis Avenue for 1.1 miles. Turn right (west) onto I. U. Willets Road; go .5 mile. The church is on the right (north) side of the road.

In 1785 the Searing Methodist Society was organized by The Reverend Philip Cox. Three years later in 1788 Jacob Searing donated a fifty-foot by sixty-foot plot of land and within a short time $750 had been raised to construct a church. Measuring thirty by thirty-four feet, the church did not have windows and seated only ninety-six people. In 1834 it was enlarged to accommodate 230 parishioners with the original structure becoming the front section of the new building. The hand wrought nails and original shingles of the first church are still visible on the north side of the building. This church, with its small cemetery located on the east side, is the oldest Methodist church on Long Island.

FLOWER HILL

Flower Hill County Park
Port Washington Boulevard, Flower Hill
(516) 572-0200

Take the Long Island Expressway to Exit #36 north (Searingtown Road/Shelter Rock Road/Port Washington/Manhasset). Go north on Searingtown Road (which becomes Port Washington Boulevard) for 2.4 miles. The park is on the left (west) side of the road.

This ten-acre park offers nature walks through wooded areas with a pond.

GREAT NECK

All Saints Episcopal Church
855 Middle Neck Road, Great Neck
(516) 482-5392

Take the Long Island Expressway to Exit #33 north (Community Drive/Lakeville Road/Great Neck). Go north on Lakeville Road (which becomes Middle Neck Road) for 3.4 miles. The church is on the right (east) side of the road.

All Saints Episcopal Church, built in 1886, is a lovely English-style field stone church with red trim, a slate roof, and cloisters. It is said that one Scottish craftsman carved the exquisite oak chancel, choir, pulpit, and altar. They are breathtakingly beautiful. In addition, the church has three stained-glass windows documented in Tiffany records. According to church members, Tiffany's work was spurned on several occasions in favor of English windows in keeping with the style of the church. The apse windows and those in the back of the nave, as well as others in the church, are English and, for their genre, are beautiful.

The Farnham Memorial window on the north wall, entitled *Angel with Landscape,* is clearly signed Edward P. Sperry and dated 1907. Mr. Sperry was a designer for Louis C. Tiffany and this commission is listed in the surviving records of Tiffany Studios. This four-paneled window with trefoil-arching pictures an angel in an autumn landscape. The passage "I will lift mine eyes onto the hills from whence cometh my help" (Psalms 121:1) explains the attitude of the haloed, but wingless angel. Look closely and you will see that the halo is a light effect created by plating. It is a beautiful example of the technique. Also demonstrative of this plating technique are the hillsides where both internal and external plating are clearly in evidence and allow for the illusion of enormous depth of field. Much fractured or confetti glass was used to make the hillsides but there is virtually no drapery glass. The book is brilliantly composed of bright pearl white opalescent glass while the angel's robes are of pearl/green to lavender opalescent glass. It is a strikingly serene and inspiring window.

The Hamilton/Messenger Memorial window, *Sermon on the Mount,* is also on the north wall. This is also a four-paneled, trefoil-arched window of extraordinary composition and continuity. Fractured or confetti glass has been used effectively in landscape details, especially in the effort to represent rocks. Very heavy pure white opalescent drapery glass is used in the robes of the seated Christ whose left arm appears to be around a small child and whose right arm is raised. Christ is pictured with a cruciform halo, symbolizing His divinity. An unusual lemon opalescent glass robe is seen on one of the kneeling female figures to the right. Three-dimensional opalescent lilies have been included. This window, which is recorded in Tiffany Studios' lists as the Hamilton Memorial, is unsigned.

On the south wall is the Child's Memorial window, a four-paneled, trefoil-arched window. Entitled *Angel of Praise*, a common title used by Tiffany Studios, it portrays a scene quite different from others having the same title. In the two center panels two golden-haloed angels with unusually colorful rose to purple wings, composed of small leaded pieces, are each playing an instrument. One, in green robes, is playing a violin which looks like a mandolin. The other, in dark blue-green robes, plays a guitar. Very heavy drapery glass is used. Decorative side panels have the turtleback tiles used in geometric windows for which Tiffany became quite famous. These are in shades of brown and are rather primitive when compared to others of this type. This memorial is listed in the incomplete records of Tiffany Studios but is also unsigned.

Behind the parish is a cemetery in which is buried Bishop Abram Newkirk Littlejohn, the first Episcopalian Bishop of Long Island who died in 1901. His grave is marked by a horizontally positioned Celtic cross. To find his grave, go .1 mile into the cemetery. It is on the left (north) side of the road just before the parking lot. (See also Town of Hempstead/Garden City/Cathedral of the Incarnation.)

Ellery Queen's House
91 Old Mill Road, Great Neck

Not open to the public.

Take the Long Island Expressway to Exit #33 north (Community Drive/Lakeville Road/Great Neck). Go north on Lakeville Road (which becomes Middle Neck Road) for 2.5 miles. Turn left (west) onto Old Mill Road; go .3 mile. The house is on the right (north) side of the road.

In 1929 Frederic Dannay (1905–1982) and his cousin, Manfred Lee, collaborated under the pseudonym Ellery Queen. Within three years their books had become so popular that they were able to devote their full time to writing and ultimately published over forty mystery books. They wrote separately but met in their secret Fifth Avenue office to consolidate their material. The location of the Manhattan hideout was unknown even to their wives. For ten years Dannay was able to conceal the identity of Ellery Queen by wearing a mask at public appearances. The subterfuge was shattered when their publisher inadvertently mentioned their names at a cocktail party. The Ellery Queen character went on to become famous not only in books but also on television, on radio, and in motion pictures.

The collection of Ellery Queen papers, which comprise more than 25,000 items including manuscripts, drafts, and correspondence with other well-known authors, is located at Columbia University.

GREAT NECK ESTATES

F. Scott Fitzgerald's House

6 Gateway Drive, Great Neck Estates

Not open to the public.

Take the Long Island Expressway to Exit #33 north (Community Drive/Lakeville Road/Great Neck). Go north on Lakeville Road (which becomes Middle Neck Road) for 1.9 miles. Turn left (west) onto Cedar Drive; go .1 mile. Turn right (north) onto Gateway Drive; go .1 mile. The house is on the left side of the road.

F. Scott Fitzgerald and his wife Zelda were no strangers to Long Island. During the 1920s they rented the Spanish tile-roofed stucco house on Gateway Drive for nineteen months. During this time they attended the sumptuous Gold Coast parties with such notables as Lillian Russell, Groucho Marx, Leslie Howard, Ariel and Will Durant, P. G. Wodehouse, George S. Kaufman, Oscar Hammerstein II, and Ring Lardner. Fitzgerald's book *The Great Gatsby* was written during his stay in Great Neck and is a profile of life in Sands Point during this era. The house is privately owned.

Frank Lloyd Wright House

9A Myrtle Drive, Great Neck Estates

Not open to the public.

Take the Long Island Expressway to Exit #33 north (Community Drive/Lakeville Road/Great Neck). Go north on Lakeville Road (which becomes Middle Neck Road) for 1.9 miles. Turn left (west) onto Cedar Drive; go .5 mile to the stop sign on the corner of Magnolia Drive and Myrtle Drive. Turn right (north) onto Myrtle Drive; go 50 feet. The house is on the left corner.

Frank Lloyd Wright (1867–1959) was born in Richland Center, WI. After studying engineering briefly at the University of Wisconsin, Wright moved to Chicago and became a draftsman at the architectural firm of Joseph Lyman Silsbee. It was while working for Silsbee that Wright designed his first building. During his career, which spanned almost seventy years, Wright was one of America's most influential and imaginative architects.

This seven-room house, designed by Wright, was built in 1936–1937 for Mr. and Mrs. Benjamin Rehbuhn. During the construction there were problems with laborers who were accustomed to building traditionally designed homes and didn't understand Wright's plans for windows, doors, trims, skylights, the two-story glass living room, walls paneled in cypress wood, a radiant-heating system, or for an existing tree to protrude through the dining room floor. Due to excessive heat, the tree died within the first year after construction of the house was completed.

The house was furnished with a combination of pieces designed by Wright and pieces chosen by Mrs. Rehbuhn. Although Mr. Rehbuhn died in 1966, his wife elected to remain in the house until a fire in 1970 caused her to move to Florida and to place the house up for sale. Although there was extensive smoke damage, there was no structural damage, but the house remained unsold for two years. In 1972 restoration began and in 1974 Roland Rehbuhn, the Rehbuhn's son, moved into the house with his family and continued the restoration until the house was sold in 1979. It is interesting to note that this house, which is the only Frank Lloyd Wright house on Long Island, was not truly innovative but rather a direct descendant of the homes he built in the beginning of the century. It was, in fact, a mélange of his prairie style.

Will and Ariel Durant's House

51 Deepdale Drive, Great Neck Estates

Not open to the public.

Take the Long Island Expressway to Exit #33 north (Community Drive/Lakeville Road/Great Neck). Go north on Lakeville Road (which becomes Middle Neck Road) for 1.9 miles. Turn left (west) onto Cedar Drive; go .1 mile. Turn right (northwest); follow the circuitous Deepdale Drive for .6 mile. The house is on the right side of the road.

William James Durant (1885–1981) was born in Adams, MA. He received his undergraduate degree in 1907 from Saint Peter's College in Jersey City, NJ, before entering Seton Hall Seminary to become a priest. In 1911 he left the seminary before taking his final vows and took a teaching position at the Ferrer Modern School. It was during his two-year stay at this school that he met and married his pupil Ada Kaufman (Ariel) of Prosurov, Russia. In 1917 Durant received his doctorate degree in philosophy from Columbia University where he also spent one semester teaching. His students were so impressed with his lectures that they encouraged him to publish them. The resulting book, *The Story of Philosophy*, was published in 1926. It has since become a standard, selling over two and a half million copies. In 1935 the Durants moved to Los Angeles and began writing their eleven-volume *Story of Civilization*. They worked a fifty-six-hour, seven-day week, reading some 500 volumes for each volume written. They were awarded the 1967 Pulitzer Prize for Volume 10 of the set, *Rousseau and the Revolution*, and the Presidential Medal of Freedom in 1977.

When asked for his view of the world and civilization, Durant said, "The world situation is all fouled up. It always has been. It always will be. I see no reason for change. . . . Civilization is a stream with banks. The stream is sometimes filled with blood from people killing, stealing, shouting, and doing the things historians usually record, while on the banks, unnoticed, people build homes, make love, raise children, sing songs, write poetry and even whittle statues. The story of civilization is the story of what happened on the banks."

The Durants lived in this house in 1935. They also lived in two other houses in the Great Neck area—44 North Drive, Kensington (1928) and 2 Henry Street, Great Neck (1932). All three houses are privately owned and not open to the public.

GREAT NECK PLAZA

Marx Brothers' House
21 Lincoln Road, Great Neck Plaza

Not open to the public.

Take the Long Island Expressway to Exit #33 north (Community Drive/Lakeville Road/Great Neck). Go north on Lakeville Road (which becomes Middle Neck Road) for 1.4 miles. Turn right (east) onto Shenck Avenue; go .5 mile. Turn left (north) onto Highland Avenue; go .1 mile. Turn right (east) onto Shoreward Drive; go .1 mile. Turn right (south) onto Lincoln Road; go about 50 feet. The house is on the left (east) side of the road.

The Marx brothers chronologically from oldest to youngest were: Julius (Groucho), Leonard (Chico), Arthur (Harpo), Milton (Gummo), and Herbert (Zeppo). Their mother immigrated to the United States from Alsace, France, and their father from Germany. Groucho, Chico, Harpo, and Zeppo began in vaude- ville with a singing act called The Four Nightingales. As their adolescent voices changed, the singing act was transformed into a comedy act. By 1919 their act had become a success. Their first musical, *I'll Say She Is*, was a smash hit. It was followed on Broadway by *The Cocoanuts* (1925) and *Animal Crackers* (1928). Groucho was so accomplished at ad-libbing that each night was virtually an entirely different show. Their first two films, *The Cocoanuts* (1929) and *Animal Crackers* (1930), were filmed at Paramount's Long Island studios.

It was during the 1920s and in the early 1930s that the Marx brothers lived in this large three-story, ten-room stucco house. They moved to Hollywood in 1931, where they continued making movies: *Monkey Business* (1931); *Horsefeathers* (1932); *Duck Soup* (1933); *A Night at the Opera* (1935); Groucho's favorite *A Day at the Races* (1933); *Room Service* (1938); *A Night in Casablanca* (1946); and *Love Happy* (1949), their last film together.

GREENVALE

Roslyn Cemetery

Route 25A, Greenvale

Take the Long Island Expressway to Exit #39 north (Glen Cove Road/Glen Cove). Go north on Glen Cove Road/Guinea Woods Road for 1.8 miles. Turn left (west) onto Route 25A/Northern Boulevard; go .3 mile. The cemetery is on the right (north) side of the road.

East Toll–Gate House

From Route 25A/Northern Boulevard go through the main gate of the cemetery. Make an immediate right (east) onto the carriage road; go .1 mile.

Located in the cemetery is a nineteenth-century toll house from the Flushing North Hempstead Toll Road Company which operated a road (modern-day Northern Boulevard) that connected North Hempstead to New York City. Known as the East Toll-Gate, the one-and-a-half-story, board-and-batten building is the company's only surviving toll house.

Grave of William Cullen Bryant (1794–1878)

From Route 25A/Northern Boulevard go straight on the main carriage road for .2 mile. The family plot is at the fork in the carriage road.

Bryant was born in Cummington, MA. At the age of thirteen he published his first poem "The Embargo" which ridiculed the policies of President Thomas Jefferson. In 1817 his most famous poem "Thanatopis," a meditation on the meaning of death, was published. By 1825 he was recognized as one of America's finest romantic poets. His poetry tends to describe landscapes, finding moral and spiritual significance in nature. In 1826 he joined the staff of the *Evening Post,* a Manhattan daily newspaper noted as a leading voice of the Democratic Party. An outspoken opponent of slavery, Bryant later joined the Republican Party because of its opposition to slavery.

(See also Town of North Hempstead/Roslyn/William Cullen Bryant and Christopher Morley Collection–The Bryant Library and Town of North Hempstead/Roslyn Harbor/William Cullen Bryant Estate–Cedarmere.)

Grave of Frances Eliza Hodgson Burnett (1849–1924)

From Route 25A/Northern Boulevard go through the main gate of the cemetery. Make an immediate right (east) onto the carriage road; go .1 mile. There is a statue of Lionel facing the grave.

280

Born in Manchester, England, Burnett immigrated with her parents to Knoxville, TN. Her first literary success was *That Lass O' Lowrie's* (1877) which centered on life in Lancashire, England. She is best remembered today for *Little Lord Fauntleroy* (1886), who many believe was modeled after her son Lionel. The book relates the youth of an insufferable, mollycoddled, priggish boy whose dress, conduct, and curls made a generation of boys in the 1880s and 1890s very uncomfortable.

Burnett's estate Fairseat was in Plandome Manor as was Bentleigh, the estate of her son Vivian.

Grave of Christopher Morley (1890–1957)

From Route 25A/Northern Boulevard go straight (north) on the main carriage road for .1 mile. The grave is on the left (west) side of the carriage road about six rows west of the Ketcham family marker.

Christopher Morley was born in Haverford, PA. His father was a distinguished mathematician and his mother was both a poet and a musician. He graduated from Haverford College after being elected to the Phi Beta Kappa Society in 1910 and subsequently attended New College, Oxford, as a Rhodes Scholar. In 1913 he returned to America and began a career as a novelist and essayist publishing eighteen volumes of fiction, sixteen volumes of poetry, and thirteen collections of essays during his lifetime. His house and writing studio are located in Roslyn.

(See also Town of North Hempstead/Roslyn/William Cullen Bryant and Christopher Morley Collections–The Bryant Library and Town of North Hempstead/Roslyn Estates/Christopher Morley County Park–Griswald/Ryan Estate.)

KINGS POINT

George M. Cohan's House
100 Kings Point Road, Kings Point

Not open to the public.

Take the Long Island Expressway to Exit #33 north (Community Drive/Lakeville Road/Great Neck). Go north on Lakeville Road (which becomes Middle Neck Road) for 3.3 miles. Turn left (west) onto Steamboat Road; go 1.2 miles. Turn right (east) onto Kings Point Road; go .4 mile. The house is on the left (north) side of the road on the corner of Steppingstone Lane.

George Michael Cohen, the noted actor, playwright, composer, lyricist, and producer, lived in this large Mediterranean villa-style house overlooking Long Island Sound from 1914 to 1927. Born in Providence, RI, to a vaudevillian family, he made his stage debut as a baby in his father's vaudeville act and had his first speaking part

281

at the age of eight. At eleven he wrote his first play and published his first song at age sixteen. As a member of The Four Cohans, he traveled throughout America performing with his family and perfecting his unique style of song and dance. By 1900 The Four Cohans had become vaudevillian stars playing the major theaters of New York and Chicago. In 1901 George's first major play was performed on Broadway. It received poor reviews as did his second. In 1904 Cohan formed a partnership with Sam H. Harris, who also resided in Great Neck. It was through this association with Harris that George was to produce many of his subsequent Broadway successes. During this era he wrote *Give My Regards to Broadway* (1904), *Yankee Doodle Boy* (1904), *You're a Grand Old Flag* (1906), and *Over There* (1917). Embittered by the 1919 Actors' Equity Association strike, Cohan dissolved his partnership with Harris and withdrew from show business.

In the later years of his life he was known for his acting in plays written by other authors rather than as the producer and playwright whose plays were noted for their flag-waving patriotism. In 1940 he was presented a Presidential Medal by President Roosevelt for his contributions to the American patriotic spirit as embodied in his song "Over There." During the course of his career Cohan wrote approximately forty plays, collaborated on untold others, produced one hundred and fifty plays, and composed over five hundred songs. He died in 1942 believing that he had outlived his usefulness to the American theater. He is buried with his family, The Four Cohans, in a mausoleum in Woodlawn Cemetery in The Bronx. Incidentally, the mausoleum has a Tiffany stained-glass window.

Herman Wouk's House
16 Dock Lane, Kings Point

Not open to the public.

Take the Long Island Expressway to Exit #33 north (Community Drive/Lakeville Road/Great Neck). Go north on Lakeville Road (which becomes Middle Neck Road) for 3.5 miles. Turn left (west) onto Redbrook Road; go 1 mile. Turn right (north) onto Kings Point Road; go .8 mile. Turn right (east) onto Dock Lane; go .2 mile bearing right at the fork. The house is on the left side of the road.

Wouk was born in Manhattan in 1915. He received his undergraduate degree from Columbia University in 1934. Upon graduation, he worked as a scriptwriter for comedian Fred Allen. With the advent of World War II, Wouk enlisted in the navy and served as a lieutenant aboard the destroyer-minesweeper *USS Southard* in the Pacific. During the war he wrote his first novel *Aurora Dawn* and received the Pulitzer Prize in 1951 for his second novel, *The Caine Mutiny*.

It was during the 1950s that Wouk lived in this house. Active in local affairs, he was one of the founders of the Great Neck Synagogue.

Kings Point Preserve

(Long Island Chapter: The Nature Conservancy)
Kings Point Road, Kings Point
(516) 367-3225

Open with prior permission.

Take the Long Island Expressway to Exit #33 north (Community Drive/Lakeville Road/Great Neck). Go north on Lakeville Road (which becomes Middle Neck Road) for 3.3 miles. Turn left (west) onto Steamboat Road; go 1.2 miles. Turn right (north) onto Kings Point Road; go 1.5 miles. The preserve is located on the left (west) side of the road.

This fourteen-acre preserve is predominately a tidal pond controlled by a tidal gate. Since most of the shoreline is privately owned and there are no parking facilities, it must be observed from your car. Wildlife includes both water fowl and shorebirds such as ducks, Canada geese, yellowlegs, sandpipers, egrets, and herons.

Please call the Conservancy at the above telephone number to obtain permission to visit the park and to notify the Kings Point police.

Martha Raye's House

7 Turtle Cove Lane, Kings Point

Not open to the public.

Take the Long Island Expressway to Exit #33 north (Community Drive/Lakeville Road/Great Neck). Go north on Community Drive (which becomes East Shore Road) for 3 miles. Turn right continuing north on East Shore Road for an additional .9 mile. Turn right onto Turtle Cove Lane; go .1 mile. The house is on the right side of the road overlooking Manhasset Bay.

Margie Yvonne Reed was born in Butte, MT, in 1916. Her parents were performers in the carnival and vaudeville circuit. At the age of three Margie joined her parents' song and dance act. She changed her name to Martha Raye, a name she picked out of the phone book in her early teens. By that time she was touring the Loew's circuit with her own act. Raye became a star almost overnight after her 1936 movie with Bing Crosby, *Rhythm on the Range*. Noted for her rowdy slapstick style of comedy in movies, Broadway, radio, and television, Raye was proclaimed the country's leading comedienne for the 1953–1954 television season and given the title "queen of buffoons."

The large Tudor-style house in which she lived is easily visible from the road.

Oscar Hammerstein II's House
40 Shore Drive, Kings Point

Not open to the public.

Take the Long Island Expressway to Exit #33 north (Community Drive/Lakeville Road/Great Neck). Go north on Lakeville Road (which becomes Middle Neck Road) for 4.1 miles. Continue straight onto Wildwood Drive; go .3 mile. Turn right (northeast) onto Mitchell Drive; go .3 mile. Turn right (east) onto Shore Drive; go .1 mile. The house is on the left side of the road overlooking Manhasset Bay.

Hammerstein (1895–1960) was born in New York City. He received his undergraduate and law degrees from Columbia University. After practicing law for one year he realized that his first love, like that of his grandfather and father, was music. His grandfather, Oscar Hammerstein Sr., after whom he was named, owned and operated the Manhattan Opera House, while his father, William, was a theatrical manager. His uncle, Young Hammerstein, a Broadway producer, advised Oscar to learn all aspects of theatrical production before writing musicals. Following his uncle's advice, Oscar began his career as a stage hand, eventually working his way up to stage manager. His first hit show *Wildflower* (1923) was followed by *Rose Marie* (1924), *Desert Song* (1925), and *Show Boat* (1927). In 1940 Richard Rogers and Oscar Hammerstein collaborated on *Pal Joey*. This collaboration was followed by *Oklahoma* (1943), *I Remember Mama* (1944), *Carousel* (1945), *Allegro* (1947), *South Pacific* (1950), for which they received the Pulitzer Prize, and *The King and I* (1951).

This house, in which Hammerstein lived from 1926 to 1960, was subsequently owned by comedian Alan King. Hammerstein also lived at 13 Grace Avenue (1923–1924) in Great Neck Plaza. Both houses are privately owned and not open to the public.

P. G. Wodehouse's Home
121 Arrandale Avenue, Kings Point

Not open to the public.

Take the Long Island Expressway to Exit #33 north (Community Drive/Lakeville Road/Great Neck). Go north on Lakeville Road (which becomes Middle Neck Road) for 3.1 miles. Turn left (west) onto Arrandale Avenue; go .7 mile. The house is on the right (north) side of the road and is called High Hedges.

P. G. Wodehouse (1881–1975), the British-born writer and humorist, lived in this large expanded Cape Cod-style house from 1918 to 1921. He also lived at 17 North Drive in Kensington, just south of Great Neck Gardens, periodically from 1922 to 1924. Both houses are privately owned and not open to the public. (See also Town of Southampton/Remsenburg/Remsenburg Community Chapel Presbyterian Cemetery/Grave of P. G. Wodehouse.)

Ring Lardner's House – The Mange

325 East Shore Road, Kings Point

Not open to the public.

Take the Long Island Expressway to Exit #33 north (Community Drive/Lakeville Road/Great Neck). Go north on Community Drive (which becomes East Shore Road) for 2.5 miles. The house is on the left (west) side of the road.

Ringgold Wilmer Lardner (1885–1933), the noted journalist, short-story writer, and playwright, was born in Niles, MI. His college education consisted of one semester as a mechanical engineering student at the Armour Institute in Chicago. After a series of odd jobs, which included being a handyman in a gas station, Lardner was employed at *The Times* in South Bend, IN, as a court and police reporter. Two years later he joined the staff of *The Examiner* as a sports reporter covering the White Sox baseball club. By 1913 he was reporting sports events for *The Chicago Tribune.* During this time Lardner became an established short-story writer and playwright, collaborating on plays with George M. Cohan and George S. Kaufman.

Lardner lived in this house from 1921 to 1928.

(See also Town of East Hampton/Apaquogue/Ring Lardner's House–Still Pond and Town of North Hempstead/Kings Point/George M. Cohan's House.)

United States Merchant Marine Academy – Walter P. Chrysler Estate – Forker House

Steamboat Road, Kings Point

(516) 773-5515 (museum)

Take the Long Island Expressway to Exit #33 north (Community Drive/Lakeville Road/Great Neck). Go north on Lakeville Road (which becomes Middle Neck Road) for 3.3 miles. Turn left (west) onto Steamboat Road; go 1.3 miles to the academy's entrance.

The academy is located on the former Henri Bendel/Walter P. Chrysler and William S. Barstow estates. Henri Bendel (1867–1936) was a prominent Manhattan milliner. In 1916 Bendel built a Beaux-Arts French Renaissance-style main house for his estate in Kings Point. In 1923 Walter P. Chrysler (1875–1940) purchased the estate as his summer home. Chrysler, who began his working career as a machinist's apprentice, eventually became president of the Buick Motor Company. In 1920 he created the Chrysler Motor Company by combining Maxwell Motor Company and Dodge Brothers.

In 1924 Chrysler's daughter Thelma married Byron Cecil Foy and resided at Foy Farm in Matinecock. Foy would eventually become a vice-president in the Chrysler Corporation.

On the eve of World War II, Chrysler sold his estate to the federal government for $100,000 for the establishment of a merchant marine academy. With the advent of war, the academy's enrollment reached its highest level: 2,471 students. Because of the wartime need for manpower, the academy's training program was reduced from four years to eighteen months then to twelve months and finally to eight months. Classes were held anywhere suitable or even unsuitable—in the mansion, stables, woodsheds, and greenhouses. After the war, Congress established Kings Point as one of the five service academies. Its present enrollment is 1,000, of whom 8 percent are women. The Chrysler mansion, now known as Wiley Hall, has become the administration center.

The academy continued its growth with the purchase in 1975 of the Beaux-Arts Italian Renaissance-style residence of the inventor and electrical engineer William S. Barstow. The Barstow mansion is now known as Lundy House and serves as the American Merchant Marine Museum. Open weekends, it houses displays of, rare and antique navigational instruments, photographs, maritime paintings, and ship models including sixteen-foot models of Washington and Liberty ships, and changing exhibits of marine memorabilia.

Long Island was also the site of three secondary military academies—Saint Paul's School in Garden City; Eastern Military Academy in Cold Spring Harbor; and LaSalle Military Academy in Oakdale. Unfortunately, all three no longer exist.

LAKE SUCCESS

Harbor Hill Sanctuary
(Long Island Chapter: The Nature Conservancy)
Lake Road, Lake Success
(516) 367-3225

Open with prior permission.

Take the Long Island Expressway to Exit #33 south (Community Drive/Lakeville Road/Great Neck). Go south on Lakeville Road for .5 mile. Turn right (west) onto Lake Road and make an immediate left into the first driveway. Park in the small paved area on the left, some 50 yards from the entrance.

The four-acre woodland sanctuary is located one mile outside of New York City. It consists of tulip, sweetgum, Norway maple, oak, cherry, and dogwood trees. Viburnum, bramble, jewelweed, Virginia creeper, poison ivy, English ivy, snowdrop, conifers, and varieties of fern abound. Also found are Virginia bluebell and white trillium, both of which are protected species. The sanctuary is used as a bird-banding station, providing information on bird migration.

Please call the Conservancy at the above telephone number to obtain permission to visit the sanctuary.

MANHASSET

Christ Episcopal Church
1355 Northern Boulevard, Manhasset
(516) 627-2184

Take the Long Island Expressway to Exit #33 north (Community Drive/Lakeville Road/Great Neck). Go north on Community Drive for 1.3 miles. Turn right (east) onto Route 25A/Northern Boulevard; go .6 mile. The church is on the left (north) side of the road.

Established in 1803 as a mission of Saint George's of Hempstead and built in much the same Colonial-style as its parent church (See also Town of Hempstead/Hempstead/Saint George's Episcopal Church), Christ Church was built on land purchased from George Onderdonk for $195.47, according to church records. (See also Town of North Hempstead/Manhasset/Onderdonk House.) The first church burned in 1912 after being struck by lightning and was replaced by the present structure in 1914. However, again in January 1935, fire struck and the new structure was severely damaged. The church was further modified in 1938 when the cupola was blown off by the September hurricane; it was not replaced.

Fortunately, only one panel of the elegant grisaille-styled Skidmore Memorial window over the altar, *The Redemption,* was damaged in the fire of 1935. This window was designed by Henry Wynd Young and dedicated in 1929. Both the east and west walls are graced by vibrantly-colored, multi-paneled, grisaille-styled lancet windows.

The Linkletter window, *The Judgment,* on the south wall is considerably more recent. It is a complicated design but interesting.

On the west wall is the 3-foot by 2½-foot Payne Whitney Memorial window presented to the church in 1934. It depicts the *Appearance of Christ in the Upper Room after the Resurrection* in a flat two-dimensional style. A combination of stained-glass and French etching work, it is a treasure. A postcard from the church lists this window as being from the Church of Saint Denis, France, and of the twelfth century but the curator of The Cloisters verifies that it is a restoration of a window from the Virgin's Chapel of the Church of Saint Germaine des Pres in Paris dating from about 1240 (i.e., thirteenth century). A current survey has traced most of the windows from the French church. It lists many in the United States and throughout Europe in museums and in private collections. Three other windows from this church are close by at The Cloisters; at the Metropolitan Museum of Art; and at the Baltimore Museum of Fine Art.

Manhasset Friends Meeting House
1421 Northern Boulevard, Manhasset
(516) 365-5142

Take the Long Island Expressway to Exit #33 north (Community Drive/Lakeville Road/Great Neck). Go north on Community Drive for 1.3 miles. Turn right (east) onto Route 25A/Northern Boulevard; go .8 mile. The house is on the left (north) side of the road.

The Manhasset Society of Friends was organized in 1702. They purchased their first meetinghouse in 1737 which became known as the Cow Neck Meeting House, later to be called the Manhasset Meeting House. The building was in continuous use except for a short period during the Revolutionary War when it was occupied by British and Hessian soldiers. The present meetinghouse was built in 1812 on the same site. It incorporates the benches and timbers of the original structure. The large oak tree in front is one of the oldest on Long Island.

(See also Town of Oyster Bay/Jericho/Jericho Friends Meeting House; Town of Oyster Bay/Matinecock/Matinecock Friends Meeting House; Town of Oyster Bay/ Mill Neck/Underhill Burying Ground/Grave of Captain John Underhill; Town of Oyster Bay/Oyster Bay/Council Rock; Town of Shelter Island/Shelter Island/Cemetery and Monument to Quaker Martyrs; and Town of Southold/Southold/Whitaker Historical Collection–Southold Free Library.)

North Hempstead Historical Collection
Town Hall
220 Plandome Road, Manhasset
(516) 627-0590 Extension 371

Take the Long Island Expressway to Exit #33 north (Community Drive/Lakeville Road/Great Neck). Go north on Community Drive for 1.3 miles. Turn right (east) onto Route 25A/Northern Boulevard; go .6 mile. Turn left (north) onto Plandome Road; go .2 mile. The Town Hall is on the right (east) side of the road.

There are changing displays of pictures and artifacts pertaining to local history. Also located on the premises is a reference library.

Onderdonk House
1471 Northern Boulevard, Manhasset
(516) 627-2703 (for necessary appointment)

Take the Long Island Expressway to Exit #33 north (Community Drive/Lakeville Road/Great Neck). Go north on Community Drive for 1.3 miles. Turn right (east) onto Route 25A/Northern Boulevard; go .9 mile. The house is on the left (north) side of the road.

Horatio Gates Onderdonk (1808–1886), a descendant of one of the first Dutch families to settle on Long Island, was born in Manhasset. After graduating from

288

Columbia College in 1829, he entered the mercantile trade in New York City prior to entering law school. After graduating, he practiced law in Manhasset for fifty years and was appointed a judge of Kings County in 1848. Married twice, he had eight children which necessitated the building of a large home. The circa 1836 Onderdonk House, which is one of the finest examples of Greek Revival-style architecture on Long Island, has been listed on the National Register of Historic Places since 1980. Onderdonk is buried in the family plot in Wood Cemetery behind the Community Reformed Church at 90 Plandome Road in Manhasset.

Whitney Pond County Park – Mitchell Homestead
Northern Boulevard and Community Drive, Manhasset
(516) 571-8300

Nassau County Leisure Pass is required for admission.

Take the Long Island Expressway to Exit #33 north (Community Drive/Lakeville Road/Great Neck). Go north on Community Drive for 1.3 miles. The park is on the right (east) side of the road.

This twenty-four-acre park is built on the site of the Mitchell Homestead which was destroyed by fire in 1979. The park offers pond fishing, pedal boat rentals, model boat sailing, stoopball courts, handball courts, tennis courts, basketball courts, a swimming pool, a diving pool, a wading pool, showers, lockers, jogging paths, pond ice skating, and a playground. Both picnic and refreshment facilities are provided.

The transfer of this park to the Town of North Hempstead is being considered.

NORTH HILLS

Saint Ignatius Retreat House – Nicholas Brady Estate – Inisfada
Searingtown Road, North Hills
(516) 621-8300

Open when retreats are not in progress.

Take the Long Island Expressway to Exit #36 north (Searingtown Road/Shelter Rock Road/Port Washington/Manhasset). Go north on Searingtown Road for .6 mile. The house is on the left (west) side of the road.

Nicholas Anthony Brady (1843–1913) was born in Lille, France, of Irish parentage and immigrated to the United States with his family while still a young child. His formal education never went beyond the elementary school he attended in Troy, NY. At the age of nineteen he opened a tea store in Albany which was so successful that it became one of the earliest examples of chain store planning in the United States. Over the years his business enterprises extended into granite quarries, gas, oil, and transportation. He was one of the principal organizers of the Boston Rapid Transit Company and president of New York Edison Company. At the time of his death he was a director of more than twenty corporations and had amassed a fortune estimated at $70 million.

His son Nicholas, a graduate of Yale, succeeded him in business, and in 1916 built his 300-acre estate *Inisfada*, which is the Gaelic name for Long Island. In 1937 Nicholas' wife Genevieve donated the estate to the New York Provence of the Society of Jesus which operates the estate as a retreat house.

The Tudor-style mansion has thirty-seven chimneys, carved granite nursery rhyme characters on either side of the *porte-cochere*, and twelve signs of the zodiac over the main door. When touring the interior of the mansion, pay particular attention to the seventeenth-century Italian Renaissance refectory table, Raphael's paintings *Madonna, The Assumption of Our Lady, Christ Taken Down from the Cross,* and *The Adoration of the Shepherds,* as well as the hand-wrought copper doors leading to the solarium.

OLD WESTBURY

Old Westbury Gardens – John S. Phipps Estate – Westbury House
71 Old Westbury Road, Old Westbury
(516) 333-0048

Take the Long Island Expressway to Exit #39 north (Glen Cove Road/Glen Cove). Go east on the eastbound expressway service road (which is called Old Westbury Road) for 1 mile. Turn right (south) continuing on Old Westbury Road for an additional .4 mile. The entrance to Old Westbury Gardens is on the left (east) side of the road.

John Shaffer Phipps' father, Henry, was Andrew Carnegie's partner in the Carnegie Steel Company, which became U.S. Steel and is now known as USX. John married Margarita Grace of the Grace Shipping Lines. Their Beaux-Arts Georgian-style residence was built in 1906, three years after their marriage. Among the facilities on the estate were a dairy farm, an orchard, a golf course, indoor tennis courts, a polo field, and a large stable complex.

In 1958 the Old Westbury Gardens Foundation, a nonprofit organization, acquired one hundred acres of the estate and established an arboretum and horticulture center. The seventy-room mansion is furnished as it was during the family's occupancy with paintings by such noted artists as Sargent, Constable, Reynolds, and Gainsborough; and furniture by Chippendale. In 1978 the mansion was placed on the National Register of Historic Places.

Surrounding the house are five eighteenth-century-style botanical gardens with walkways and reflecting pools. During the summer special events and concerts are held on the grounds. Picnic facilities are available.

(See also Town of Oyster Bay/Brookville/DeSeversky Conference Center of New York Institute of Technology–du Pont/Guest Estate.)

PLANDOME MANOR

Leeds Pond Preserve
1526 North Plandome Road, Plandome Manor
(516) 627-9400

Take the Long Island Expressway to Exit #33 north (Community Drive/Lakeville Road/Great Neck). Go north on Community Drive for 1.3 miles. Turn right (east) onto Route 25A/Northern Boulevard; go .6 mile. Turn left (north) onto Plandome Road; go 1.7 miles. Turn left continuing north on North Plandome Road for an additional .3 mile. The museum is on the right (south) side of the road.

This thirty-five-acre county preserve has a large pond surrounded by nature trails. Also located in the preserve is the Science Museum of Long Island.

Science Museum of Long Island – Herman Goldman Estate
(part of the Leeds Pond Preserve)
1526 North Plandome Road, Plandome Manor
(516) 627-9400

This is not a museum in the normal meaning of the word but rather it is a facility that offers workshops, lectures, and seminars on virtually all topics in the scientific field. Call the telephone number above for a detailed schedule of events.

PORT WASHINGTON

Hempstead Harbor County Park
West Shore Road, Port Washington
(516) 571-7930

Nassau County Leisure Pass is required for admission.

Take the Long Island Expressway to Exit #36 north (Searingtown Road/Shelter Rock Road/Port Washington/Manhasset). Go north on Searingtown Road/Port Washington Road/Route 101 for 4 miles. Turn right (east) onto Beacon Hill Road; go 2.3 miles. Make a U-turn; go back .4 mile. The park is on the right (east) side of the road.

This sixty-acre park spans 2,400 feet of beach in Hempstead Harbor with a raised paved promenade running the entire length of the beach. The park offers camping sites for self-contained units, bay swimming, a sailing program, a minia-ture golf course, a lighted eighteen-hole astroturf par-two and par-three course, a two level fishing pier, basketball courts, handball courts, horseshoe courts, paddle-ball courts, shuffleboard courts, volleyball courts, badminton courts, jogging paths, sled hills, a playground, and a senior citizen area. Picnic facilities are provided.

Summer evening entertainment programs are held in an open air arena. Please call the park office for the schedule of events.

The transfer of this park to the Town of North Hempstead is being considered.

Nassau Knolls Cemetery and Memorial Park
500 Port Washington Boulevard, Port Washington

Take the Long Island Expressway to Exit #36 north (Searingtown Road/Shelter Rock Road/Port Washington/Manhasset). Go north on Searingtown Road/Port Washington Boulevard/Route 101 for 3.3 miles. Turn left (west) into the cemetery entrance.

Grave of Henry Stanley Lomax (1899–1987)

Follow the carriage road to the right for .1 mile. Turn left (south) on carriage road. Bear right at fork. Then make an immediate left. Keep right following road to east side of red brick carillon tower. Stop at flagstone path opposite door of tower on Chimes Hill. Walk up flagstone path for 55 feet. The grave site is on the left (south) side of path.

Henry Stanley Lomax was born in Pittsburgh, PA. He moved to Long Island and attended high school at Saint Paul's School in Garden City. (See also Town of Hempstead/Garden City/Saint Paul's School.) After graduating from Cornell University, he became a reporter for the *New York Journal American* before joining WOR Radio in 1936 as a sports announcer. His nightly fifteen minute sports programs became an event that no true sports fan would miss. His retirement from WOR in 1976 saddened his fans who remember his strong support of local amateur teams.

The Polish Museum
16 Belleview Avenue, Port Washington
(516) 883-6542

Take the Long Island Expressway to Exit #36 north (Searingtown Road/Shelter Rock Road/Port Washington/Manhasset). Go north on Searingtown Road/Port Washington Road/Route 101 for 4 miles. Turn left (west) onto Main Street; go .3 mile. Turn left (south) onto Belleview Avenue; go .1 mile. The museum is on the right (west) side of the road.

Located in the old Port Washington Public Library, this museum is devoted to the accomplishments of the Polish people. It contains collections of dolls, folk costumes, and pictures, as well as memorabilia, World War II artifacts, and icons. A large reference library can be utilized for research. It contains books, historical documents, and maps dealing with Polish history, culture, and genealogy. (See also Town of Riverhead/Riverhead/Polish Festival.)

Sands–Willets House

336 Port Washington Boulevard, Port Washington
(516) 365-9074

Take the Long Island Expressway to Exit #36 north (Searingtown Road/Shelter Rock Road/Port Washington/Manhasset). Go north on Searingtown Road/Port Washington Boulevard/Route 101 for 2.9 miles. The house is on the left (west) side of the road.

The house is owned and operated by the Cow Neck Peninsula Historical Society which acquired it in 1967. The circa 1735 original portion of the house was built by the Sands family while the Greek Revival east wing was added in 1848 by Edmund Willets. The house which is furnished in period furniture also contains a reference library.

Located at the rear of the property is the seventeenth-century, Dutch-style Sands' barn which was moved to its present location in 1979 from Sands Point. It houses a collection of tools and farm implements. Of particular interest are the hand-hewn beams and siding on the barn.

The house has been on the National Register of Historic Places since 1985.

ROSLYN

Roslyn Clock Tower

Main Street and Old Northern Boulevard, Roslyn

Take the Long Island Expressway to Exit #39 north (Glen Cove Road/Glen Cove). Go north on Glen Cove Road/Guinea Woods Road for 2.4 miles. Turn left (west) onto Back Road; go .1 mile. Turn left (south) onto Bryant Avenue; go 2.1 miles. Turn left (west) onto Old Northern Boulevard; go .2 mile. The tower is on the left (south) side of the road.

The tower was designed by the firm of Lamb and Rich, the same architects who executed Theodore Roosevelt's residence Sagamore Hill in Cove Neck. The forty-four-foot tower was built in 1895 of granite and red sandstone and contains a 2,700-pound bell above its clock. The interior of the tower is not open to the public.

George Washington Manor
1305 Old Northern Boulevard, Roslyn
(516) 621-1200

The Manor is located on the north side of the road directly opposite the Roslyn Clock Tower.

Henry Onderdonk settled on Main Street in Roslyn in 1752. He was immediately appointed supervisor of highways and later supervisor of the Town of Hempstead. With the defeat of the Continental Army at the Battle of Long Island, British and Hessian soldiers settled into the relative peace afforded by the occupation of Long Island. Onderdonk's house was used to quarter them and his wagons and horses were pressed into service for their use. After the war he found time to resume his active role in local politics and still operated his grist mill and two paper mills.

While making his grand tour of Long Island in 1790, George Washington breakfasted at Onderdonk's and wrote in his diary ". . . breakfasted at a Mr. Onderdonk's here we were kindly received and well entertained." Today Onderdonk's house is the George Washington Manor Restaurant and follows in Onderdonk's tradition of hospitality.

(See also Town of North Hempstead/Manhasset/Onderdonk House.)

Trinity Episcopal Church
1579 Northern Boulevard, Roslyn
(516) 621-7925

From the Roslyn Clock Tower go east on Old Northern Boulevard for .2 mile. Turn left (north) continuing on Old Northern Boulevard for a total of .5 mile. Turn right (east) onto Witte Lane; go .1 mile. Turn left (north) onto Church Street. The church is on the right (east) side of the road.

Easily recognized by its Mission-styled bell tower, this lovely 1906 English-style church, designed by McKim, Mead, and White, was erected through the generosity of Katherine Mackay, reportedly for about $50,000 as a memorial to her father William Alexander Duer. Its beautifully beamed ceiling is adorned with a carved angel choir similar to that which can be seen in Saint John's of Lattingtown in Locust Valley. (See also Town of Oyster Bay/Locust Valley/Saint John's of Lattingtown.)

The southernmost window in the west transept, the Hooper Memorial window, is signed "LOUIS C. TIFFANY, N.Y." The enameled signature usually indicates that the commission was completed between 1915 and 1920. However, the dates on this window suggest that it was completed after 1927. The style in which the drapery glass has been employed also indicates that this was a product of Tiffany's late period, after the Tiffany Furnaces in Corona, Queens, were closed in 1924 and just prior to the bankruptcy of Tiffany Studios in 1932. Windows of this late period of Tiffany Studios are not in the surviving records and, to our knowledge, this window has not been previously described. In the left panel Christ is seen preaching, presumably the words of Matthew 25:40, as noted at the bottom of the window. His robes are splendid drapery glass in colors ranging from opalescent pearl to pale blue and pink. The seated female figure with the golden urn in her hands in the right panel is clothed in very colorful robes, yet, not for a minute, does this display of color detract from the standing figure of Christ. Irises, symbolizing remembrance, and lilies, symbolizing the Resurrection, are seen in the foreground. These flowers appear so often in Tiffany designs that they are almost trademarks and can be useful in the identification of unsigned Tiffany windows. There is extensive use of fractured glass and mottled glass in the landscaping effects in the background with much use of purple. Although extensive plating has been used, it is not obvious and painting is limited only to faces, hands, and feet.

The parish has attributed several other windows to Tiffany by tradition, none of which are listed in the surviving records of Tiffany Studios. We are not convinced that these are indeed by Tiffany Studios. Directly to the north of the signed Hooper Memorial is the William Collins Whitney Memorial entitled *Moses Viewing the Promised Land* (Deuteronomy 34:1). (See also Town of Oyster Bay/Old Westbury/New York Institute of Technology–William C. Whitney Estate.) Moses, in bright yellow-gold outer robes emblazoned with a purple stripe, is seen at the left receiving the vision of the Promised Land from God, the Promised Land in which he would never set foot. The pearl robe underneath shows obvious plating but no drapery glass. The lack of drapery glass and the color of the robes lend credence to the probability that these were designed by someone other than Tiffany or his staff. The covering of the face, hands, and feet with clear glass again raises question of Tiffany's involvement. The landscaping technique in dark green and brown mottled glass and fractured glass with a stream flowing down the center is, however, reminiscent of Tiffany's 1917 Hartwell Memorial in Central Baptist Church in Providence, RI, considered to be the largest Tiffany landscape commission, except that the details of tree leaves and needles and the leaves of ferns are clearly more detailed than in this Moses window. The 1912 Fletcher Dutton Proctor Memorial window in The Union Church in Proctor, VT, also comes to mind. This again contains proportionately larger amounts of fractured or confetti glass than most Tiffany landscapes. However, in the Proctor Memorial flowers in the foreground refine the landscape and clearly place Tiffany's artistic signature upon it. There are no flowers here; Tiffany rarely missed an opportunity to include the flowers he had learned to portray so very well.

Above the Moses window is a rose window with eight spokes, all of which are plated in blues and pinks. The center is dominated by a gold glass jeweled cross. The church history states that this was of Tiffany design; a gift of Mrs. Mackay. However, it should be noted that both John LaFarge and Tiffany designed this type of window.

A fourth window, directly to the north of the Moses window, described in the church history as *Jacob's Dream* (Genesis 32:1-2), shows the figure of Jacob in blue robes surrounded by angels. The rock upon which he reclines, Jacob's Pillow, has found a place in British folklore as the Stone of Destiny or Scone upon which kings of Scotland were crowned, now under the Coronation Throne in Westminster Abbey. This window, the Charles Albert Stevens Memorial, also shows clear glass covering of the painted areas and no drapery glass, but instead an illusionary drapery effect with clear glass over, a technique not previously encountered in Tiffany-executed or Tiffany-approved work. Mottled glass used here is also very different from that seen in documented Tiffany windows. A comparison to the mottled glass in the Hooper window will illustrate. There are no flowers in this work either. The angels, their painted faces, their attitude, their multicolored wings, and both the color and designs of their robes, are very reminiscent of angels in several of the windows in Christ Episcopal Church in Corning, NY, made by Lamb and Company. The Corning windows also show the clear glass covering over painted areas and over drapery glass as seen here and in the Moses window.

Over the altar is *The Creation*. It is a beautiful and unusual window depicting God in blue-gray robes with His hand raised in rays of light, "And let there be light" (Genesis 1:3). There is much amplification of the light through the use of yellow, rather than allowing rays of natural light enhanced by plating techniques to complete the effect as in so many Tiffany windows such as the *Resurrection* in the United Methodist Church of Hempstead (See Town of Hempstead/Hempstead/ United Methodist Church of Hempstead) and the *Our Saviour* window over the altar at Trinity Episcopal Church in Northport (See Town of Huntington/Northport/Trinity Episcopal Church). Cloud-shaped pieces in blues, turquoise, and gray form the background. Again there is no drapery glass and plating work is obvious only on the back of this and all the windows in this church traditionally credited to Tiffany, but unsigned. Tiffany figure windows, upon very close examination, show plating applied to the front to diffuse and soften the light and applied to the back to provide perspective in landscapes. Although John LaFarge was really the American inventor of the plating technique, having revived a Venetian glass procedure, he never used it with the skill that Tiffany developed. Tiffany invented the drapery glass technique and he and his designers used it almost exclusively. Others, including LaFarge, never used drapery glass to the extent or with the same dramatic results as did those associated with Tiffany Studios. In combination, these two techniques produce distinctive, recognizable, and truly beautiful artistic results. These technical points together with the subject matter lead us to believe that this window was not created by Louis Comfort Tiffany, who, to our knowledge, only used symbolism to represent God.

The windows on either side of *The Creation* do not reflect the same talent as does the large altar piece.

The remainder of the stained-glass windows in the church proper have been attributed to Wippell and Co., Ltd., of Exeter, England, although only a few are signed. Fine grisaille examples and figure windows of imaginative and pure colors are among these. To the right of the main entrance is one English-designed window that is especially fascinating. Borders of different colors and densities create three-dimensional effects which are best appreciated if the lights of the church are off; if the day is overcast, all the better.

If you ask the clergy, they will gladly arrange for you to see five more, unsigned and undocumented, but undoubtedly, Tiffany-designed windows. These too were first described by the authors. Originally high up on the north wall of a small chapel which is now a hallway at the front of an all-purpose room, the windows are presently mounted on the north wall of the all-purpose room. Please note that these windows must be viewed in bright afternoon sunlight and even then they are not as glorious as they could be. Also note that the intended colors, especially in those panels to the right, are distorted by the obstruction of the hillside and trees outside.

These five rectangular windows, although bordered and separated by wall space, retain the continuity intended by the artist. The adoring angel on the left, the William Travers Duer Memorial, is robed in blue drapery glass and has her hands clasped. Her fine drapery glass wings in brown, gold, and green tones curl around as they touch the ground, giving substance and softness to the glass feathers. The adoring angel on the right, the John William Mackay Memorial, is robed in a green/brown/gold drapery glass and has her hands folded toward her left shoulder. The differing attitudes of the adoring angels is always a clue to a Tiffany design. The robes and wings of this angel are in brown, gold, and green with little contrast apparent. This may, however, be partially caused by the lack of direct sunlight, as previously mentioned.

The three panels in the center, the William Alexander Duer (1906) Memorial, picture two children kneeling beside a young Jesus. The faces of these figures are said to be those of the Mackay children, Katherine, Ellin, and John, a fact confirmed by John Mackay, according to the rector. Ellin Mackay, who died in 1988, was the wife of Irving Berlin. The faces of the children and those of the adoring angels are beautifully painted. The children are pictured kneeling on stones beside a pond or stream with a field of flowers behind them. In the distance, hillsides are visible. A rainbow spans the three central panels against a multicolored sky which picks up the colors of the rainbow.

The child on the left, with hands together in prayer, is robed in pink drapery glass. Flowers are held in the left hand of the second kneeling child to the right of Jesus. Fine drapery glass forms the gold-toned robes. The standing figure of the young Jesus is seen with His hands extended at about waist height, much like the pose chosen for the adult Christ in the apse window in Saint Ann's Episcopal Church. (See also Town of Islip/Sayville/Saint Ann's Episcopal Church.) Although His drapery glass robes here are an unspectacular brown/green/pink combination, the opalescent glass halo focuses light and the viewer's attention immediately on Jesus.

The plating on these windows, both internal and external, is wonderful, giving fine foreground details and a background that carries your eyes into the hillsides beyond.

Trinity Church was placed on the National Register of Historic Places in 1986.

Valentine House
1 Paper Mill Road, Roslyn
(516) 621-2240

From the Roslyn Clock Tower go east on Old Northern Boulevard for .2 mile. Turn right (south) onto East Broadway; go .2 mile. The house is on the right side of the road in Roslyn Park on Paper Mill Road.

This circa 1800 house is now the annex of The Bryant Library, which uses it as its computer training center.

The house also has meeting rooms and a book store operated by the Friends of The Bryant Library, carrying used books.

Van Nostrand–Starkins House
Main Street, Roslyn
(516) 625-4363 (Roslyn Landmark Society)

From the Roslyn Clock Tower go south on Main Street for .4 mile. The house is on the right (west) side of the road.

After passing through a multitude of owners this circa 1680 house was finally acquired by the Roslyn Landmark Society. The society has restored the house to its 1700 appearance and furnished it with period pieces indigenous to Long Island and New York State. Of particular interest are the two-panel, two-drawer cherry blanket chest and the Long Island-style gumwood Dutch cupboard or *kas.*

William Cullen Bryant and Christopher Morley Collections
The Bryant Library
Paper Mill Road, Roslyn
(516) 621-2240

From the Roslyn Clock Tower go east on Old Northern Boulevard for .2 mile. Turn right (south) onto East Broadway; go .2 mile. The library is on the right side of the road in Roslyn Park on Paper Mill Road.

The Bryant Room of the library has an extensive special collection of books, letters, pictures, and historical and critical material relating to William Cullen Bryant and Christopher Morley.

(See also Town of North Hempstead/Greenvale/Roslyn Cemetery; Town of North Hempstead/Roslyn Estates/Christopher Morley County Park–Griswald/Ryan Estate; and Town of North Hempstead/Roslyn Harbor/William Cullen Bryant Estate–Cedarmere.)

ROSLYN ESTATES

Christopher Morley County Park – Griswald/Ryan Estate
Searingtown Road, Roslyn Estates
(516) 571-8113

Nassau County Leisure Pass is required for park admission. Nonresidents may visit the Knothole if special arrangements are made.

Take the Long Island Expressway to Exit #36 north (Searingtown Road/Shelter Rock Road/Port Washington/Manhasset). Go north on Searingtown Road for .4 mile. The park entrance is on the right (east) side of the road.

Mrs. Frank Griswald built a mansion on this site in the early 1900s. It was bought by John Dennis Ryan, an official of Anaconda. Ryan, in turn, built a second mansion on the property for his son John Carlos Ryan. After a heated dispute with his father, John Carlos refused to live in the new house and indeed never did. The first mansion was destroyed by fire and John Carlos' mansion became the clubhouse for the Renaissance Country Club. The country club was converted into condominiums in 1988.

Named for Christopher Morley who lived nearby, this ninety-eight-acre county complex has something for everyone. There is a nine-hole, par-thirty golf course, a practice putting green, a pro shop, a thirty-acre nature area with over a mile of walkways and nature trails, a model boat sailing pond, badminton courts, handball courts, horseshoe courts, volleyball courts, tennis courts, paddle tennis courts, paddleball courts, shuffleboard courts, softball and baseball fields, an olympic-sized swimming pool, a diving pool, a kiddy pool, jogging paths, an ice skating rink, sledding hills, cross-country skiing trails, a picnic area, a playground, restrooms, cafeterias, concert facilities, senior citizen programs, and even an area for checkers.

Also located in the park is the Knothole, the log cabin where the noted American essayist and journalist Christopher Morley did most of his writing. Built in 1934 by Morley on the grounds of his Roslyn Estates house, which he called Green Escape, it served as a studio where he could write in isolation, publishing more than seventy titles. On the lintel above the porch, as you enter the Knothole, is the inscription *Assisdues Sis In Bibliotheca Quae Tibi Pardisi Loco Est*, "Be assiduous in the library because for you it is the place of paradise." Morley's retreat is a small structure with bunks, a fireplace, a desk, and a Dyamarion bathroom, designed by Buckminister Fuller, which is a small self-contained metal bathroom containing a sink, medicine cabinets, a tub, a shower, and a toilet. Found in the Knothole are Morley's books, letters, and mementos including his sixty-two-and-a-half-minute hourglass, pipe, inkwell, and medals. In 1966 the Knothole was moved to its present site in what Morley called Santa Claus Woods because it is where he walked with his children on Christmas Eve. The studio is operated by the Christopher Morley Knothole Association which holds readings at the studio.

(See also Town of North Hempstead/Greenvale/Roslyn Cemetery/Grave of Christopher Morley and Town of North Hempstead/Roslyn/William Cullen Bryant and Christopher Morley Collections–The Bryant Library.)

ROSLYN HARBOR

Nassau County Museum of Fine Arts – Bryce/Frick Estate
1 Museum Drive, Roslyn Harbor
(516) 484-9337

Take the Long Island Expressway to Exit #39 north (Glen Cove Road/Glen Cove). Go north on Glen Cove Road/Guinea Woods Road for 1.8 miles. Turn left (west) onto Route 25A/Northern Blvd.; go .4 mile. Bear right (north) to the entrance.

The Museum of Fine Arts is located on the former 145-acre Bryce/Frick Estate. Bryce, a noted American author, diplomat, editor, and congressman, purchased land, then known as Upland Farms, from the estate of poet and editor William Cullen Bryant and built a two-story, Beaux-Arts Georgian-style main house. In 1919 the estate was sold to Childs Frick, the son of Henry Clay Frick. The elder Frick was a partner of Andrew Carnegie and chairman of the board of the Carnegie Steel Corporation which later became U.S. Steel and is now known as USX. Childs immediately altered the main house and in subsequent years added additional buildings; a gatehouse (1925) and a laboratory building (1936), called Millstone Lab because of the two huge millstones at its entrance. The laboratory is presently used by Nassau County as an educational center. An avid paleontologist, zoologist, and botanist, Frick also built a monkey house, an aviary, and a bear pit, and established a conifer forest of over four hundred specimens. Indeed he was so committed to the study of natural history that he was the benefactor responsible for the establishment of the American Museum of Natural History in Manhattan.

Frick, who died at the age of eighty-one, remained on the estate for almost fifty years before it was acquired by Nassau County in 1969 for use as its fine arts museum offering concerts, special programs, art exhibitions, and lectures. The estate was placed on the National Register of Historic Places as part of the Cedarmere/Clayton Historic District in 1986.

William Cullen Bryant Estate – Cedarmere

225 Bryant Avenue, Roslyn Harbor
(516) 571-8130

Take the Long Island Expressway to Exit #39 north (Glen Cove Road/Glen Cove). Go north on Glen Cove Road/Guinea Woods Road for 1.8 miles. Turn left (west) onto Route 25A/Northern Boulevard; go 1 mile. Bear right onto Witte Lane; go .1 mile. Turn right (north) onto Bryant Avenue; go .4 mile. The house is on the left (west) side of the road.

William Cullen Bryant (1794–1878), the famed American romantic poet, was originally a lawyer. By 1825 he had given up his law practice to become a New York journalist and, later, editor and part owner of the *Evening Post*, a Manhattan daily newspaper which at that time was noted for its free trade and antislavery positions.

At the age of fifty Bryant became a first-time homeowner when in 1843 he purchased land in Roslyn Harbor for a summer home which he named Cedarmere. The name seeks to convey the image of the cedar trees so prevalent in the area and the nearness to the sea (*mere*). The original clapboard farmhouse was rebuilt into its present style by Bryant's grandson Harold Godwin in 1902 after a fire had severely damaged the second and third floors. It remained in the Bryant family until 1975 when Elizabeth Love Godwin, Bryant's great-granddaughter, bequeathed the house along with seven of the original two hundred acres to Nassau County along with a trust fund of $100,000 for its maintenance.

The county is presently in the process of restoring Cedarmere's impressive gardens, Bryant's first floor library, a small boathouse, a duck house, and a mill, all of which will be open to the public. The house will also be available as a conference center. Cedarmere was placed on the National Register of Historic Places as part of the Cedarmere/Clayton Historic District in 1986.

(See also Town of North Hempstead/Greenvale/Roslyn Cemetery/Grave of William Cullen Bryant and Town of North Hempstead/Roslyn/William Cullen Bryant and Christopher Morley Collections–The Bryant Library.)

William Joseph Casey Jr.'s House – Mayknoll
10 Glenwood Road, Roslyn Harbor

Not open to the public.

Take the Long Island Expressway to Exit #39 north (Glen Cove Road/Glen Cove). Go north on Glen Cove Road/Guinea Woods Road for 1.8 miles. Turn left (west) onto Route 25A/Northern Boulevard; go 1 mile. Bear right onto Witte Lane; go .1 mile. Turn right (north) onto Bryant Avenue; go .9 mile. Turn left (continuing north) onto Glenwood Road; go .2 mile. The house is on the left (west) side of the road.

In 1948 Casey, the controversial head of the Central Intelligence Agency in the Reagan administration, purchased Mayknoll. It is a Victorian-style house, surrounded by a large piece of property and service buildings, which overlooks Hempstead Harbor. Casey was residing at Mayknoll at the time of his death.

(See also Town of North Hempstead/Westbury/Cemetery of the Holy Rood/Grave of William Joseph Casey Jr.)

Rosyln Heights

Temple Beth Shalom Judaica Museum
401 Roslyn Road, Roslyn Heights
(516) 621-2288

Take the Long Island Expressway to Exit # 37 (Willis Avenue/Mineola/Roslyn). Go north on Willis Avenue/Mineola Avenue to Garden Street. Turn right (south) onto Roslyn Road. Proceed to Temple Beth Shalom.

The museum has artifacts and exhibits of art, photographs, and paintings that depict Jewish heritage around the world.

(See also Town of Huntington/Commack/Jewish Sports Hall of Fame and Long Island Jewish Discovery Center and Town of Oyster Bay/Glen Cove/Holocaust Memorial and Educational Center of Nassau County.)

RUSSELL GARDENS

W. C. Fields' House
Darley Road and Melbourne Road, Russell Gardens

Not open to the public.

Take the Long Island Expressway to Exit #33 north (Community Drive/Lakeville Road/Great Neck). Go north on Lakeville Road (which becomes Middle Neck Road) for 1.3 miles. Turn left (west) onto Darley Road; go .2 mile. The house is at the corner of Melbourne and Darley Roads.

Born William Claude Dukenfield in Philadelphia, PA, W. C. Fields (1879–1946), began his show business career in 1897 as a tramp juggler. It was during his appearance in the *Ziegfeld Follies* (1915–1921) that Fields abandoned juggling and developed the cantankerous, amoral, cynical stage character who abhorred children, animals, suckers, and teetotalers. He continued performing on Broadway and in vaudeville until 1930 but abandoned these areas of performing in the 1930s to appear regularly on radio and to make several films which have over the years become cult classics.

It was while performing on Broadway that Fields rented this house. He delighted in shocking his neighbors by practicing his golf stroke on the front lawn.

SADDLE ROCK

Richard Tucker's House
10 Melville Lane, Saddle Rock

Not open to the public.

Take the Long Island Expressway to Exit #33 north (Community Drive/Lakeville Road/Great Neck). Go north on Lakeville Road (which becomes Middle Neck Road) for 2.5 miles. Turn left (west) onto Old Mill Road; go .6 mile. Continue across Bayview Avenue onto Emerson Drive for an additional .2 mile. Turn right (north) onto Melville Lane. The house is the first house on the left (west) side of the road.

Richard Tucker (1913–1975) was born Reuben Ticker in Brooklyn. After graduating from New Utrecht High School, he worked days as a runner for a Wall Street brokerage firm, as an errand boy in the garment district, and later opened his own garment business while continuing to study voice at night. Despite the absence of a substantial operatic background, he entered the Metropolitan Opera's Auditions of the Air and won second place. In 1945, with limited operatic experience, he made his debut as Enzo Grimaldo in *La Gioconda* and rapidly became an internationally famous star whose voice quality was compared to that of Enrico Caruso.

Tucker died in Kalamazoo, MI, in 1975 while on tour. He was the first singer to have his funeral service in the Metropolitan Opera House and the first member of the Jewish faith to have a memorial mass at Saint Patrick's Cathedral. He is buried in Mount Lebanon Cemetery in Glendale, Queens, NY.

The Saddle Rock Grist Mill

Grist Mill Lane, Saddle Rock
(516) 571-7900

Take the Long Island Expressway to Exit #33 north (Community Drive/Lakeville Road/Great Neck). Go north on Lakeville Road (which becomes Middle Neck Road) for 2.5 miles. Turn left (west) onto Old Mill Road; go .6 mile. Turn right (north) onto Bayview Avenue; go .3 mile. Turn left (west) onto Grist Mill Lane; go .2 mile. The mill is on the right (north) side of the road.

Madnan's Neck (the original name of Great Neck) derived its name from Nan Heatherton, who in the mid-1600s settled in the area with a contingent from Lynn, MA. Landing at Kings Point, she laid claim to the entire area and for ten years vigorously defended her claim, earning the nickname "Mad Nan." Thus accounting for the original name Madnan's Neck.

Records indicate the existence of the Saddle Rock Grist Mill as early as 1702 when its owner Robert Hubbs Jr. sold his share in the mill to Henry Allen. In subsequent years Allen, a prosperous farmer and merchant, acquired complete ownership of the mill. It remained in the family until the early 1830s when it was sold to John Tredwell who, in turn, sold it to Richard Udall in 1833. The mill remained in the Udall family until 1950 when it was transferred to the Nassau County Historical Society. In 1955 it was deeded to Nassau County which has completely restored it to its 1700s appearance. The mill has the distinction of being one of the few remaining operating tidal grist mills of this era in America and is on the National Register of Historic Places.

SANDS POINT

Sands Point County Park and Preserve
Howard Gould/Daniel Guggenheim Estate – Hempstead House
Harry Guggenheim Estate – Falaise

Middle Neck Road, Sands Point
(516) 571-7900

Take the Long Island Expressway to Exit #36 north (Searingtown Road/Shelter Rock Road/Port Washington/Manhasset). Go north on Searingtown Road/Shelter Rock Road/Route 101/Middle Neck Road for 6 miles. The park is on the right (east) side of the road.

Located in the 216-acre preserve are three fine examples of turn-of-the-century Beaux-Arts architecture that reflect the grandeur of Long Island's Gold Coast.

Castlegould, the estate's stable and carriage house patterned after Ireland's Kilkenny Castle, was built by Howard Gould, the heir of railroad magnate Jay Gould. The building now houses the visitors' reception center.

Hempstead House, the estate's main residence, was built in 1910–1912 incorporating many of the features of Tudor architecture. At present the house, which is in the midst of restoration, is closed except for special exhibits.

Daniel Guggenheim acquired the estate in 1917. In 1923 he deeded ninety acres of it to his son Harry Frank Guggenheim in order that Harry might build his house which would be named Falaise. Now open to the public, Falaise features the Guggenheim's furnishings and their collections of modern and primitive paintings and sculpture. It is in this Beaux-Arts Normandy-style manor house that Charles Lindbergh wrote his book *We* and it was also to this house that the Lindberghs retreated after the tragic death of their son.

In addition to the three buildings, you might want to explore the five nature trails, three of which are self-guided. There is also tent camping year round for organized youth groups exploring conservation projects. Supervision must be provided.

The annual Medieval Festival, with its costumed re-creation of a fourteenth-century medieval fair including jousting, tournaments, music, crafts, food, and children's games, is an event worth seeing.

John Philip Sousa's House – Wildbank

14 Hicks Lane, Sands Point

Not open to the public.

Take the Long Island Expressway to Exit #36 north (Searingtown Road/Shelter Rock Road/Port Washington/Manhasset). Go north on Searingtown Road/Shelter Rock Road/Route 101/Middle Neck Road for 6.5 miles. Turn left (west) onto Cow Neck Road; go .5 mile. Turn right (north) onto Barkers Point Road; go 1.2 miles. Turn right (east) onto Hicks Lane; go .1 mile. The house is on the left (north) side of the road.

John Philip Sousa (1854–1932), the "March King," noted composer, and bandmaster was born in Washington, DC, to parents of Portuguese, Spanish, and German extraction. His love of music became apparent when at age six he entered a conservatory to study violin and, later, band instruments. He was thirteen when, with the encouragement of his father, he enlisted in the United States Marine Band. Sousa left the band after five years to study violin, theory, and harmony with George Felix Benkert. During the 1870s he played violin at Ford's Opera House, Kerman's Theatre Comique, and with Jacques Offenbach's orchestra at the Philadelphia Centennial Exhibition. In 1880, at age twenty-six, Sousa became the conductor of the United State Marine Band, a position he retained for twelve years. It was during this time that he composed some of his most famous marches:

"Semper Fidelis" (1888); "The Washington Post March" (1889); "Hands Across the Sea" (1899); and "The High School Cadets" (1890). Sousa left the Marine Corps and, with his own band, toured the United States, visited Europe four times, and made one round-the-world trip between 1892 and 1912. He became wealthy as a result of his compositions. Royalties from his march "Stars and Stripes Forever" (1897) alone amounted to $300,000. This remarkably prolific composer wrote one hundred and forty military marches, more than fifty songs, six waltzes, two overtures, twelve suites, numerous miscellaneous compositions, three novels, and an autobiography, *Walking the March*.

Wildbank, which has been on the National Register of Historic Places since 1966, was Sousa's last home. He lived here from 1914 to 1932. The 1907, three-story, red-tile-roofed mansion is located on three acres overlooking Long Island Sound. It remained in the Sousa family until 1965. Only the garage complex is readily visible from the road.

Sousa is buried in Arlington National Cemetery.

WESTBURY

Cemetery of the Holy Rood
Old Country Road, Westbury
(516) 334-7990

Take the Long Island Expressway to Exit #39 south (Glen Cove Road/Hempstead). Go south on Glen Cove Road for 2.8 miles. Turn left (east) onto Old Country Road; go 1.9 miles. The cemetery is on the left (north) side of the road.

Grave of Margaret "Molly" Brown (1867–1932)

Margaret was born in Hannibal, MO. The daughter of Irish immigrants John and Johanna Collins Tobin, Margaret was one of six children. At the age of nineteen she left Hannibal to join her brother in Leadville, CO, where she worked in a store. That same year she met and married James Joseph Brown, a thirty-one-year-old mining engineer. When Brown devised an efficient method of extracting gold from mines, they became millionaires almost overnight.

The new-found wealth enabled Margaret to embark on her life-long dedication to improving conditions for the poor, children, women, and mine workers. To this end Margaret helped establish soup kitchens, lobbied for improved working conditions, raised money for the construction of hospitals, and became an advocate for women's rights.

While returning to the United States aboard the *Titanic*, Margaret earned the nickname "The Unsinkable Molly Brown" because of her courageous efforts to rescue her fellow passengers as the ship was sinking.

Grave of Oleg Cassini (1913-2006)

Born in Paris, France, Cassini was the son of a Russian diplomat and an Italian countess. With the advent of the Russian Revolution and the subsequent loss of his father's family fortune and status, his father adopted the more prestigious surname of his wife, that is, Cassini.

After studying art in France, Oleg immigrated to the United States in 1936. During the 1940s and early 1950s he worked as a clothing designer for Paramount Pictures. Some of his more notable films were *The Shanghai Gesture* (1941), *The Razor's Edge* (1946), *The Ghost and Mrs. Muir* (1947), *The Wonderful Urge* (1948), *Whirlpool* (1949), *Where the Sidewalk Ends* (1950), *The Mating Season* (1951), and *On the Riviera* (1951).

During his Hollywood years Cassini was married two times and unofficially engaged once. His first wife Mary Fahrney was the daughter of a Chicago industrialist. Cassini's second wife was actress Gene Tierney with whom he fathered two daughters, one of whom was born with a hearing and visual impairment and a cognitive disability because of Tierney's exposure to German measles during her pregnancy. After his eight-year marriage to Tierney ended, Cassini was unofficially engaged to actress Grace Kelly.

Cassini relocated to Manhattan and began designing "off the rack" clothes. In the 1960s he was catapulted to fame when First Lady Jacqueline Kennedy chose him as her personal designer. Cassini would subsequently become the first clothing designer to franchise his name.

Grave of William Joseph Casey Jr. (1913–1987)

Go north for .1 mile on the main carriage road. The grave site is on the right (east) side of the road. Section 7, Range AA, Plot 12

Casey was born in Elmhurst, Queens, and raised in Bellmore, Long Island. He received his undergraduate degree from Fordham University in 1934 and his law degree from Saint John's University in 1937. During World War II he helped organize and coordinate the activities of the French Resistance for the Office of Strategic Services (O.S.S.), the predecessor of the Central Intelligence Agency (C.I.A.), and eventually became O.S.S. Chief of Operations in the European theater. After the war Casey embarked on several careers. He taught and practiced law, wrote or edited some thirty financial books, was a financier, and held several government posts. In 1971 he was appointed chairman of the Securities and Exchange Commission. He also served in the Nixon administration as undersecretary of Economic Affairs and later as chairman of the Export-Import Bank. In 1980 Casey was chosen as director of the C.I.A. by President Reagan. During his tenure in the agency Casey is credited with restoring its power and morale.

Most of his governmental life was cloaked in secrecy and controversy whether it was his testimony before Congress, his involvement in the mining of Nicaraguan harbors, or his role in the Iran-Contra Affair. He died of a malignant brain tumor in the midst of the Iran-Contra Congressional Hearing. Casey remains an enigma in death as he was in life.

(See also Town of North Hempstead/Roslyn Harbor/William Joseph Casey Jr.'s House–Mayknoll.)

North Fork Theatre at Westbury
960 Brush Hollow Road, Westbury
(516) 334-0800

Take the Long Island Expressway to Exit #40 west (Route 25 west/Westbury). Exit and follow signs to Brush Hollow Road. Turn left onto Brush Hollow Road; go .7 mile. The theater entrance is on the left (east) side of the road.

This theater in the round, formerly known as Westbury Music Fair, presents plays and musicals as well as classical, jazz, rock, pop, and country-western concerts with top-name performers.

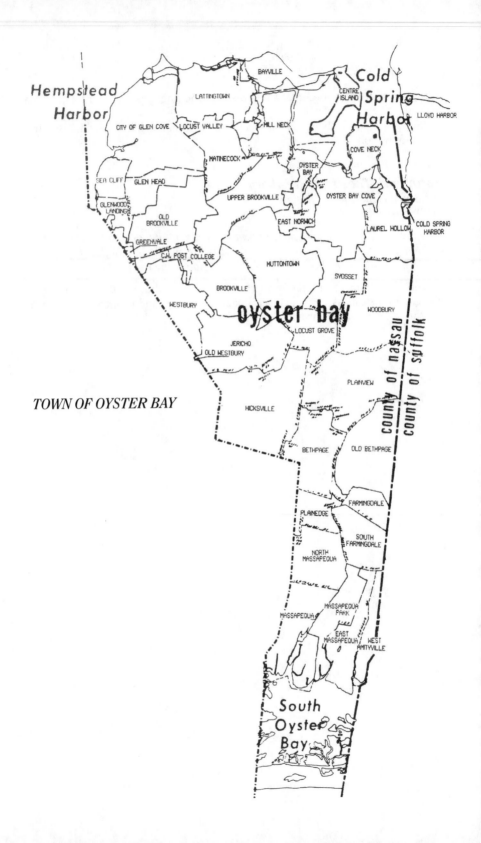

TOWN OF OYSTER BAY

TOWN OF OYSTER BAY

Parks and Preserves

Federal Parks and Preserves
Sagamore Hill National Historic Site (83 acres), Cove Neck

State Parks and Preserves
Bethpage State Park (1,475 acres), Farmingdale
Massapequa State Park (596 acres), Massapequa
Trail View State Park (453 acres), Old Bethpage *(undeveloped)*

County Parks and Preserves
Battle Row County Park and Campground (44 acres), Old Bethpage
Cantiague County Park (127 acres), Hicksville
Garvies Point Museum and Preserve (62 acres), Glen Cove
Massapequa Preserve (423 acres), Massapequa
Muttontown Preserve (550 acres), East Norwich
Tiffany Creek Preserve (197 acres), Oyster Bay Cove
Welwyn Preserve (204 acres), Glen Cove

Long Island Chapter: The Nature Conservancy
Bertha and Reginald Rose Refuge (15 acres), Upper Brookville
Cordelia Hepburn Cushman Preserve (15 acres), Oyster Bay Cove
Davenport Sanctuary (8 acres), Laurel Hollow
Fox Hollow Preserve (26 acres), Laurel Hollow
Franklin Pond Preserve (14 acres), Cold Spring Harbor
Hope Goddard Iselin Preserve (42 acres), Upper Brookville
Louis C. Clark Sanctuary (8 acres), Old Brookville
Oaces Sanctuary (26 acres), East Norwich
Saint John's Preserve (14 acres), Cold Spring Harbor

Arboretums and Gardens
Bailey Arboretum (42 acres), Lattingtown
C. W. Post Community Arboretum (20 acres), Brookville
J. P. Humes Japanese Stroll Garden (4 acres), Mill Neck
Planting Fields Arboretum State Historic Park (409 acres), Upper Brookville

BAYVILLE

Bayville Historical Museum
34 School Street, Bayville
(516) 628-1720

Take the Long Island Expressway to Exit #41 north (N.Y. 106/N.Y. 107/Jericho). Go north on Route 107 (which becomes Cedar Swamp Road) for 4.2 miles. Turn right (east) onto Route 25A/Northern Blvd.; go .9 mile. Turn left (north) onto Wolver Hollow Road; go 1.5 miles. Turn right (east) onto Chicken Valley Road (which becomes Oyster Bay Road); go 2.6 miles. Turn right onto Bayville Road (which becomes Bayville Avenue); go 3.1 miles. Turn right (south) onto School Street; go .2 mile. The museum is the right (west) side of the road.

This small museum illustrates local history through memorabilia and photographs. There is a collection of farm tools on display.

BROOKVILLE

C. W. Post College – Marjorie Meriweather Post Estate – Hillwood
720 Northern Boulevard, Brookville
(516) 299-2000

Take the Long Island Expressway to Exit #41 north (N.Y. 106/N.Y. 107/Jericho). Go north on Route 107 (which becomes Cedar Swamp Road) for 4.2 miles. Turn left (west) onto Route 25A/Northern Boulevard; go .2 mile. The college is on the left (south) side of the road.

Long Island University established its Brookville campus in 1954 on the four-hundred-acre former estate of Marjorie Meriweather Post. Mrs. Post subsequently donated over one million dollars to the college which was named for her father Charles William Post, the founder of Post Cereals. Post, born in Springfield, IL, established himself in the grain and farm implements business. At the age of thirty-seven, as a result of financial reversals and ill health, he entered a sanitarium in Battle Creek, MI, and quickly recovered on a regimen of nutrition and physical fitness. Subsequently he went into business manufacturing a coffee substitute he originally called Monk's Brew but later named Postum. Then came Grape Nuts and Post Toasties and the establishment of a corporation that was eventually merged into General Foods Corporation.

The Post estate, which was known as Hillwood, was established in 1921 by Marjorie Meriweather Post and added to in 1935 by the purchase of the adjacent Philip Gossler residence. Hillwood consisted of a seventy-room, Beaux-Arts Tudor-style main house, a second but smaller residence for her daughter Eleanore, servants' quarters, a garage complex, a thatched cottage-style playhouse, and a horse farm. The main house has been converted by the college into an administration center, the garage and servants' complex is now the student services center, the horse farm, with its indoor show ring, has become part of an equestrian center, and Eleanore's house is the admissions building and graduate facility.

C. W. Post Arboretum
(part of C. W. Post College)
720 Northern Boulevard, Brookville
(516) 299-2333

Twenty acres of the college's 308-acre campus has been officially designated as an arboretum. It has one hundred and fourteen trees of one hundred different species clearly labeled with interesting horticultural information. In the spring there is a display of some 75,000 tulips and daffodils. The self-guided walking tour takes from 30 to 45 minutes.

Hillwood Art Museum
(part of C. W. Post College)
Hillwood Commons
720 Northern Boulevard, Brookville
(516) 299-4073

The 4,500-square-foot museum houses an impressive array of some 650 artifacts, paintings, textiles, bronzes, sculptures, ceramics, and glass of the pre-Columbian, Persian, Egyptian, Hellenistic, Etruscan, Roman, and Chinese Ming and Han eras. In addition, there is a significant collection of contemporary works of art.

The museum also hosts extensive education programs designed for children in the third through twelfth grades.

Tilles Center
(part of C. W. Post College)
720 Northern Boulevard, Brookville
(516) 299-3100

Ninety percent of the performances at the center are devoted to the classical repertoire and are performed by major national and international orchestras and soloists.

DeSeversky Conference Center of New York Institute of Technology – du Pont/Guest Estate
Northern Boulevard, Brookville
(516) 686-7675

Take the Long Island Expressway to Exit #41 north (N.Y. 106/N.Y. 107/Jericho). Go north on Route 107 (which becomes Cedar Swamp Road) for 4.2 miles. Turn left (west) onto Route 25A/Northern Boulevard; go 1.7 miles. The center is on the left (south) side of the road.

Alfred Irenee du Pont (1864–1935) was the grandson of the founder of E. I. du Pont and Company. At the age of twenty he left Massachusetts Institute of Technology to enter the family business as a chemist. With the death of Eugene du Pont in 1902, he and two cousins, Thomas Coleman du Pont and Pierre S. du Pont, took over the company thus preventing it from being absorbed by their major competitor Laflin and Rand. Alfred's split with the family came in 1907 when he divorced his wife to marry his second cousin Alicia Bradford Maddox. The resulting family bitterness was so intense that Alfred actually sued several members of the family for slander. The sale of Thomas' share of the company to a corporation headed by Pierre resulted in the ouster of Alfred from E. I. du Pont and Company in 1915. Alfred never forgot the incident and when Thomas ran for the United States Senate in 1916, Alfred acquired several of Delaware's local newspapers whose editorial positions subsequently contributed to Thomas' defeat.

In 1916 Alfred began the construction of his Brookville estate White Eagle and in 1918 organized the Nemours Trading Company. His wife Alicia died in 1920. This, coupled with severe financial losses in Europe, induced him to sell the estate and move to Florida in 1926 with his new wife Jessie D. Ball.

The estate was purchased by Mrs. Frederick Guest, the daughter of Henry Phipps. (See also Town of North Hempstead/Old Westbury/Old Westbury Gardens–John Shaffer Phipps Estate–Westbury House.) Her husband Frederick was a member of the British House of Commons, the grandson of the Duke of Marlborough, and, therefore, a first cousin of Sir Winston Churchill. She remained on the estate, which was renamed Templeton, until her death in 1959. The estate was subsequently sold by her son to New York Institute of Technology.

Now known as the DeSeversky Conference Center, it is available for catered affairs.

COLD SPRING HARBOR

Cold Spring Harbor Fish Hatchery
Route 25A, Cold Spring Harbor
(516) 692-6768

Take the Long Island Expressway to Exit #45 north (Manetto Hill Road/Plainview/ Woodbury). Go north on Woodbury Road for 3.4 miles. Turn left (north) onto Route

108/Harbor Road; go 1.6 miles. Turn left (west) onto Route 25A/North Hempstead Turnpike; go .1 mile. The hatchery is on the left (south) side of the road.

The former New York State fish hatchery is now a tourist and educational facility operated by the Village of Cold Spring Harbor. It has eight outdoor ponds and seven aquaria all of which are stocked with various species of freshwater turtles and fish found in New York State. There is also a History of Hatchery Museum which features changing exhibits on aquatic life.

Franklin Pond Preserve
(Long Island Chapter: The Nature Conservancy)
Route 108/Harbor Road, Cold Spring Harbor
(516) 367-3225

Open with prior permission.

Take the Long Island Expressway to Exit #45 north (Manetto Hill Road/Plainview/Woodbury). Go north on Woodbury Road for 3.4 miles. Turn left (north) onto Route 108/Harbor Road; go .8 mile. Turn left (west) onto a dirt road. Go .1 mile to the preserve.

In 1680 the area that encompasses this fourteen-acre preserve had both saw and grist mills established on the banks of the pond. Just prior to the Civil War the mills became unprofitable, the industry declined, and the area became a summer resort. It remained a resort area well into the 1930s.

In 1977 the preserve was donated to the Conservancy. It consists of a pond, mud flats, woodland swamps, red maple swamps, and a moist oak community with pink lady slippers and pinxters. The preserve is host to a wide variety of ducks, herons, sandpipers, gulls, reptiles, and amphibians.

Please telephone the Conservancy at the above number to obtain permission to visit the preserve.

Saint John's Episcopal Church
Route 25A, Cold Spring Harbor
(516) 692-6368

Take the Long Island Expressway to Exit #45 north (Manetto Hill Road/Plainview/Woodbury). Go north on Woodbury Road for 3.4 miles. Turn left (north) onto Route 108/Harbor Road; go 1.6 miles. Turn left (west) onto Route 25A/North Hempstead Turnpike; go .2 mile. Entrance to the church's parking lot is on left (south) side of the road.

The church was built in 1831 with contributions from sixty-eight families on land purchased for $300. In order to pay the salaries of the rector and the sexton, pews were rented to parishioners for as much as $12.50 per year. The rectory was built in 1839 and the chancel was added to the church in 1862. The church was totally remodeled in the 1880s.

Of particular interest are the three magnificent stained-glass windows by Louis Comfort Tiffany on the east wall of the church, all of which are documented in Tiffany Studios' records. The Moore Memorial window, signed "TIFFANY STV-DIOS," is on the far right (south) and is called *Angel of Resurrection*. The angel's pearl white opalescent drapery glass robes, a technique developed by Tiffany, are unusually draped at the waist to give a handsome, fashionable blouson look. Four of the lilies in the field of opalescent lilies, so very typical of Tiffany, are also done in heavy drapery glass and externalized. The angel's wings are a composite of small leaded pieces in white, gray, and pink shades.

The center window, the John Divine Jones Memorial window, is called *Good Shepherd* and represents a common theme used by Tiffany. We have seen this very same *Good Shepherd* in Christ Episcopal Church in Williamsport, PA, and in the Bryn Mawr Presbyterian Church in Bryn Mawr, PA. It differs from these windows primarily in that the sun is seen on the horizon here. We presume that this is a rising sun since the window in on the east wall and gloriously captures the sunrise. Blues and greens dominate this window with lavender/pearl opalescent drapery glass used to form Christ's outer robe; an effective accent over the red robe which has been internally plated with rose drapery glass. A meadow composed of fractured or confetti glass was chosen for the foreground of this window, while rocks and clumps of grass appear in the other two similar windows mentioned. This window is documented in Tiffany records but is unsigned.

At the far left (north), near the choir loft, is the Townsend Jones Memorial (1906) window depicting the *Annunciation,* also unsigned but documented as the Jones/Bleeker Memorial in the surviving partial list of Tiffany commissions. In contrast to the wings of the *Angel of Resurrection,* the wings of the Archangel Gabriel, Angel of the Annunciation, are composed of larger pieces in lavender, pink, and white. The robes of the kneeling Virgin and the angel are in opalescent lavender with touches of pink. On a cloudy day the plating which creates this effect can be clearly seen. Even the sky is lavender with shadings of pink and blue. Mottled glass swirls heavenward. The Holy Ghost, represented by a painted haloed dove, is seen emerging from the clouds. A small clump of lilies has been included to the right of the Virgin. Note also the clear, flat pearl opalescent glass which has been used to form the pages of the book. This is in dramatic contrast to the opalescent drapery glass used elsewhere. There is a striking similarity between this third window and a window by the Lederle–Geissler Company which can be seen on the north wall of Saint James Episcopal Church in Saint James. (See also Town of Smithtown/Saint James/Saint James Episcopal Church.) Each window has a decorative panel on the bottom which can be opened to catch gentle Sunday morning breezes off the lake.

Above the altar is a very lovely crown canopy. The church is simply decorated and painted white both inside and out. Against this simplicity these windows are all the more marvelous.

(See also Town of Oyster Bay/Laurel Hollow/Memorial Cemetery of Saint John's Church.)

Saint John's Pond Preserve
(Long Island Chapter: The Nature Conservancy)
Route 25A, Cold Spring Harbor
(516) 367-3225

Open with prior permission.

Take the Long Island Expressway to Exit #45 north (Manetto Hill Road/Plain-view/Woodbury). Go north on Woodbury Road for 3.4 miles. Turn left (north) onto Route 108/Harbor Road; go 1.6 miles. Turn left (west) onto Route 25A/North Hempstead Turnpike; go .2 mile. The preserve property is on the left (south) side of the road. Parking is available at either the fish hatchery parking lot or near the church.

This fourteen-acre preserve is located next to Saint John's Church along the shoreline of Saint John's Pond. It consists of a woodland swamp, wet woods, and dry woods with tall stands of spotted touch-me-nots, skunk cabbage, cinnamon fern, oaks, mountain laurels, and red maples. Wildlife includes a wide variety of birds, opossums, flying squirrels, red foxes, raccoons, eastern moles, and several species of frogs and turtles. Of particular interest are the endangered osprey that are often found in the preserve.

Please call the Conservancy at the above telephone number and make arrangements to obtain the key to the preserve's gate which is locked due to vandalism.

COVE NECK

Sagamore Hill National Historic Site – Theodore Roosevelt Estate – Sagamore Hill
Cove Neck Road, Cove Neck
(516) 922-4447

Take the Long Island Expressway to Exit #41 north (N.Y. 106/N.Y. 107/Jericho). Go north on Route 106/Oyster Bay Road/Pine Hollow Road for 6.4 miles. Turn right (east) onto East Main Street (which becomes Cove Road); go 1.3 miles. Turn left (north) onto Cove Neck Road; go 1 mile to the entrance.

Theodore Roosevelt (1858–1919) was born in New York City into a prominent New York family. Upon graduating from Harvard College, he entered government service serving as a leader in the New York State legislature (1884), president of the New York Police Board (1895–1897), Assistant Secretary of the Navy (1898), Commander of the Rough Riders (1898), Governor of New York State (1898–1900), Vice-President of the United States (1901), and President of the United States (1901–1909).

In 1884 he built his home in Cove Neck calling his 155-acre estate Sagamore Hill after the Long Island Indian *sachem* Sagamore, who resided in what is now

Cove Neck. During his presidency the house was used as the summer White House. The house along with eighty-three acres is administered by the National Park Service and remains today as it was in Roosevelt's time and reflects, with warmth, the large family that lived there. Completely restored, it is filled with Roosevelt possessions and memorabilia. Of particular interest is the trophy room which served as a presidential reception room for the numerous dignitaries that visited the estate. Sagamore Hill has been on the National Register of Historic Places since 1966.

Also located on the site is Old Orchard, the estate of Theodore Roosevelt Jr. Administered by the National Park Service, it is an exhibition and audio-visual center illustrating the history of the Roosevelt family and their role in United States history.

There is a forty-acre environmental study area of woods, ponds, a beach, and a tidal creek connecting Old Orchard and Cold Spring Harbor which is open to environmental groups. Guided walks are also periodically open to the public. Call the number listed above for information concerning this activity.

(See also Town of East Hampton/Montauk/The Third House; Town of Islip/Sayville/Roosevelt County Park–John Ellis Roosevelt Estate–Meadow Croft; Town of Oyster Bay/Oyster Bay/Christ Episcopal Church; Town of Oyster Bay/Oyster Bay/First Presbyterian Church; and Town of Oyster Bay/Oyster Bay/Young's Memorial Cemetery/Grave of Theodore Roosevelt.)

EAST MASSAPEQUA

Will Rogers' House
425 Clocks Boulevard, East Massapequa

Not open to the public.

Take the Long Island Expressway to Exit #49 south (Route 110/Amityville). Go south on Route 110/Broad Hollow Road/Broadway for 7.8 miles. Turn right (west) onto Route 27A/Merrick Road; go .5 mile. Turn left (south) onto Clocks Boulevard; go .4 mile. The house is on the right (west) side of the road.

William Penn Adair Rogers (1879–1935), the cowboy philosopher, humorist, actor, and news commentator, was born on the frontier lands near the present town of Claremore, OK. Will's formal education was sporadic, culminating in 1897 with one year at Kemper Military School in Boonville, MO. After leaving school he went to the Texas panhandle to become a cowboy. In 1902 he sailed to Argentina; from there he went to South Africa; and then on to Australia before returning to the United States to join a wild west show in New York City. In 1905 he began interspersing caustic political comments to the audience during his rope trick act. He appeared in his first musical in 1912, became a Broadway star by 1915, and reached the height of his Broadway career with the *Ziegfeld Follies* (1916–1918, 1922, 1924–1925).

His motion picture career began in 1918 but silent movies were not suited to his style. With the advent of "talkies" his movie career soared. By 1934 he was receiving $200,000 per picture. This combined with his radio appearances, lectures, and writing gave him an estimated annual income of $600,000, making him the highest-paid performer in show business at the time.

A devotee of air travel, Rogers and Wiley Post died in an airplane crash while en route to the Orient. Rogers is buried in Forest Lawn Memorial Park in Glendale, CA.

This 1890s three-story frame house was rented by Will and his family for one year (1915–1916) while he was performing on Broadway. The house, which has remained essentially unaltered, is privately owned.

EAST NORWICH

Muttontown Preserve – Egerton Winthrop Estate – Benjamin Moore Estate – Chelsea
Muttontown Lane, East Norwich
(516) 571-8500

Not restricted to Nassau County residents.

Take the Long Island Expressway to Exit #41 north (N.Y. 106/N.Y. 107/Jericho). Go north on Route 106 for 4.1 miles to Route 25A/North Hempstead Turnpike. Turn left (west) onto Route 25A/North Hempstead Turnpike; go .2 mile. Turn left (south) onto Muttontown Lane; go .2 mile to the preserve entrance.

This 550-acre county preserve is part of the former estate of lawyer and prominent member of New York society Egerton L. Winthrop (1861–1926). Educated at Columbia University Law School, Winthrop became a partner in the Wall Street law firm of Winthrop and Stimson. Other members of the firm were former Secretary of War Henry Lewis Stimson and former Secretary of State Elihu Root. (See also Town of Huntington/West Huntington/West Hills County Park–Henry Lewis Stimson Estate–Highold and Town of Oyster Bay/Laurel Hollow/Memorial Cemetery of Saint John's Church/Grave of Henry Lewis Stimson.) The circa 1903 Beaux-Arts Federal-style main house was acquired by the county in 1969. It is now known as Nassau Hall and houses the administrative offices of the Nassau County Museum.

Also located in the preserve is Chelsea, the former estate of Benjamin Moore, who was the descendant of Clement Clark Moore, who published the poem "Twas the Night Before Christmas," now confirmed to have been written by Henry Livingston. Built in 1923, it is an unusual combination of Chinese, French Renaissance, and English architecture. The mansion, which is listed on the National Register of Historic Places, is open to the public for special occasions. Check local newspapers for times and dates.

The preserve consists of six distinct habitats, moist woodlands, a field, a pioneer woodland, an upland forest, a conifer stand, and glacially-formed rolling hills and kettle ponds. Because of the diversity of the habitat there is an abundance of wildlife such as opossums, masked shrews, short-tailed shrews, eastern moles, woodchucks, red bats, brown bats, red fox, snapping turtles, eastern box turtles, northern brown snakes, red-backed salamanders, toads, spring peepers, and bullfrogs.

Tent camping is permitted for organized youth groups on conservation projects. Guided nature walks and specialized conservation projects may be arranged with the preserve's environmental staff. During the winter cross-country skiing is permitted on the preserve's four miles of marked trails.

Oaces Sanctuary
(Long Island Chapter: The Nature Conservancy)
Route 25A, East Norwich
(516) 367-3225

Open with prior permission.

Take the Long Island Expressway to Exit #41 north (N.Y. 106/N.Y. 107/Jericho). Go north on Route 106 for 4.1 miles. Turn right (east) onto Route 25A/North Hempstead Turnpike. The preserve is on the left (north) side of Route 25A at the intersection with Route 106.

This twenty-six-acre sanctuary contains red, white, black and pin oaks, pignuts, mackernuts, red maples, sassafras, mountain laurels, and maple-leaved viburnums. Two unusual features of the sanctuary are American chestnut saplings growing from the roots of larger trees that died of chestnut blight at the turn of the century and spikenard, which are not usually found this far north. Wildlife is typical of hardwood forests with nesting woodpeckers, titmice, migrating warblers, grey squirrels, voles, shrews, mice, flying squirrels, opossums, raccoons, cottontail rabbits, and chipmunks.

Please call the Conservancy at the above telephone number to obtain permission to visit the sanctuary.

FARMINGDALE

Bethpage State Park
off Seaford–Oyster Bay Expressway, Farmingdale
(516) 249-0701

Take the Long Island Expressway to Exit #44 south (N.Y. 135/Seaford–Oyster Bay Expressway). Go south on the Seaford–Oyster Bay Expressway for 3.9 miles to Exit #8 Bethpage State Park.

This 1,475-acre park has five eighteen-hole golf courses, electric cart rentals, a clubhouse, a driving range, a restaurant, a cafeteria, food stands, restrooms, bridle paths, polo grounds, a picnic area, hiking paths, sledding hills, skiing trails, tennis courts, and athletic and playing fields.

GLEN COVE

Glen Cove War Memorial
Glen Cove Avenue, Glen Cove

Take the Long Island Expressway to Exit #39 north (Glen Cove Road/Glen Cove). Go north on Glen Cove Road/Guinea Woods Road for 5.1 miles to the intersection of Route 107/Glen Cove Arterial Highway. Bear left and go an additional 1.4 miles to the war memorial which is in front of the Glen Cove Public Library at the intersection of Glen Cove Arterial Highway/Pratt Boulevard and Glen Cove Avenue/Brewster Street.

The memorial is dedicated to the memory of those residents of Glen Cove who were killed during World War I.

Frank Winfield Woolworth Estate – Winfield Hall
77 Crescent Beach Road, Glen Cove

Not open to the public.

From the war memorial located in front of the Glen Cove Public Library at the intersection of Glen Cove Avenue and Glen Cove Arterial Highway/Pratt Boulevard go south on Glen Cove Avenue for .1 mile. Turn right (north) onto Charles Street; go .3 mile. Turn left (west) onto The Place (which becomes Ellwood Street); go .3 mile. Turn right (east) onto Landing Road; go 50 feet. Turn left (north) onto Crescent Beach Road; go .5 mile. The house is on the left (west) side of the road.

Frank Winfield Woolworth (1852–1919) was born in upstate New York and attended business college in Watertown, NY. After graduation he worked for a while as a clerk in a grocery store before opening his first five-and-dime store in Utica, NY, in 1879. From these humble beginnings, the Woolworth Company became an international organization consisting of over one thousand stores in the United States, Great Britain, and Canada.

The fifty-six-room, Beaux-Arts main house of his estate, a combination of Italian and French Renaissance-style architecture, was built between 1916 and 1917. Its main staircase, which is made of marble, cost approximately $2 million and is arguably the most costly staircase ever built. The furnishings of each of the bedroom suites reflected different historic periods. The extensive garden complex was patterned after the Borghese Gardens in Rome. Over the years the estate,

319

which has been on the National Register of Historic Places since 1979, has had many owners and is presently privately owned.

First Presbyterian Church
9 North Lane, Glen Cove
(516) 671-0258

From the war memorial located in front of the Glen Cove Public Library at the intersection of Glen Cove Avenue and Glen Cove Arterial Highway/Pratt Boulevard go east on Glen Cove Avenue (which becomes Brewster Street) for .4 mile. Turn right (south) onto North Lane. The church is on the east side of North Lane at its intersection with Brewster Street.

This church was built in 1905 in the Eastlake decorative style which was in vogue and highly fashionable from 1870 to 1890. Eastlake-style is characterized by carved panels, perforated gables, a profusion of spindles and lattice work, large curved brackets, and scrolls with an exaggerated three-dimensional appearance. The church's interior is circular in shape with a wainscotted ceiling and geometrically designed stained-glass windows.

Garvies Point Museum and Preserve – Dr. Thomas Garvie Estate
50 Barry Drive, Glen Cove
(516) 571-8010
Not restricted to Nassau County residents.

From the war memorial located in front of the Glen Cove Public Library at the intersection of Glen Cove Avenue and Glen Cove Arterial Highway/Pratt Boulevard go south on Glen Cove Avenue for .1 mile. Turn right (north) onto Charles Street; go .3 mile. Turn left (west) onto The Place (which becomes Ellwood Road); go .3 mile. Turn left (west) onto Landing Road; go .6 mile. Turn left (south) onto Germaine Street; go .1 mile. Turn right (west) onto McLoughlin Street; go 50 feet. Turn left (south) onto Barry Drive; go .2 mile to the park entrance.

The sixty-two-acre preserve is located on the former estate of Dr. Thomas Garvie. It is now part of the Nassau County Museum system and consists of glacial moraine covered by forests, thickets, and meadows through which approximately five miles of nature trails traverse.

The adjacent museum specializes in the geology and Indian archaeology of Long Island. It regularly schedules film programs throughout the year as well as special exhibits and workshops. During the winter months the preserve permits cross-country skiing along designated routes.

Paddle Steamer Thomas Jefferson

Glen Cove Marina Shore Road, Glen Cove
(516) 759-4282

Reservations required.

From the war memorial located in front of the Glen Cove Public Library at the intersection of Glen Cove Avenue and Glen Cove Arterial Highway/Pratt Boulevard; go south on Glen Cove Avenue for.4 mile. Turn right (west) onto Shore Road; go .3 mile. The marina is on the right (north) side of the road.

In the mid-1800s travel by steamboat between New York City and Long Island was common. With the influx of vacationers Glen Cove became a thriving resort area. Now, some 150 years later, steamboat travel has returned to Long Island Sound.

The *Thomas Jefferson* is an eighty-foot, ninety-ton replica of an 1850s side-wheel paddle steamer. It has a large, enclosed, and nicely appointed dining room with bar, two levels of decks for taking in the sun, and a truly congenial crew dressed in period costumes. A wide variety of cruises is offered including a gourmet dinner cruise, a champagne brunch cruise, a cocktail cruise, and a sunset cruise.

The boat may be chartered for special occasions such as weddings, parties, or corporate affairs.

Webb Institute of Naval Architecture – Herbert Lee Pratt Sr. Estate – The Braes

298 Crescent Beach Road, Glen Cove
(516) 671-2213

From the war memorial located in front of the Glen Cove Public Library at the intersection of Glen Cove Avenue and Glen Cove Arterial Highway/Pratt Boulevard go south on Glen Cove Avenue for .1 mile. Turn right (north) onto Charles Street; go .3 mile. Turn left (west) onto The Place (which becomes Ellwood Street); go .3 mile. Turn right (east) onto Landing Road; go 50 feet. Turn left (north) onto Crescent Beach Road; go 1.1 miles to the entrance to the college which will be directly ahead of you at the end of the road.

The school was established in 1889 at Fordam Heights in The Bronx by the shipbuilding magnate William H. Webb. With the transition from wooden to iron vessels Webb realized that the increased need for size, speed, and power required by the newer iron vessels necessitated a more formal and detailed education in naval architecture and marine engineering than hitherto known. The institute's admission standards and course work for undergraduates is extremely rigorous but, thanks to the generous endowment established by Mr. Webb, the students are rewarded with a totally tuition-free education.

In 1949 the college moved to its present location on the twenty-six-acre former Herbert Lee Pratt Sr. estate. The Pratt estate was established in 1912 and known as *The Braes,* a Scottish term which refers to sloping banks of a hillside that lead down to the water. The Beaux-Arts main house was built in the seventeenth-century

Jacobean-style. Now known as Stevenson Taylor Hall, it houses the college's recitation rooms, faculty offices, library, dormitory rooms, public rooms, dining hall, science laboratories, computer center, and auditorium.

Welwyn Preserve – Harold Irving Pratt Sr. Estate – Welwyn
100 Crescent Beach Road, Glen Cove
(516) 572-0200

Not restricted to Nassau County residents.

From the war memorial located in front of the Glen Cove Public Library at the intersection of Glen Cove Avenue and Glen Cove Arterial Highway/Pratt Boulevard go south on Glen Cove Avenue for .1 mile. Turn right (north) onto Charles Street; go .3 mile. Turn left (west) onto The Place (which becomes Ellwood Street); go .3 mile. Turn right (east) onto Landing Road; go 50 feet. Turn left (north) onto Crescent Beach Road; go .8 mile. The preserve is on the right (east) side of the road.

This 204-acre preserve is part of the former six-hundred-acre estate of Charles Pratt, who along with John D. Rockefeller was a major stockholder in Standard Oil Company. Pratt divided his property among his six sons who added to the family holdings increasing the compound to two thousand acres. The Manor House, belonged to his son John. It is now Glen Cove Mansion and Conference Center. The *Braes*, which was the home of his son Herbert, is now the Webb Institute of Naval Architecture. Killenworth, the forty-one-room Tudor-style home of his son George, is currently leased to the Russian government and is used by them as a diplomatic residence. His son Frederick's estate is now the Glengariff Nursing Home. Charles Jr.'s home is the only one that no longer exists as it burned down a number of years ago.

Welwyn was the home of his son Harold. It is now owned and operated by Nassau County. The Georgian-style mansion houses the Holocaust Memorial and Educational Center of Nassau County.

The grounds of the estate, with its impressive stand of tulip trees, forests, salt marsh, and swamps, is maintained as a nature preserve. Printed guides are available for self-guided nature walks. Guided nature walks can also be arranged. Special environmental programs may be arranged if advance notice is given.

Holocaust Memorial and Educational Center of Nassau County
(part of Welwyn Preserve complex)
100 Crescent Beach Road, Glen Cove
(516) 571-8040

Located in the former Harold Irving Pratt Sr. mansion in the 204-acre Welwyn Preserve, the museum seeks to instill tolerance by depicting the horrors of the Holocaust through exhibits, lectures, seminars, and its research library.

(See also Town of Huntington/Commack/Jewish Sports Hall of Fame and Long Island Jewish Discovery Museum and Town of North Hempstead/Roslyn Heights/ Temple Beth Shalom Judaica Museum.)

HICKSVILLE

Cantiague County Park
West John Street, Hicksville
(516) 571-7056

Nassau County Leisure Pass is required for admission.

Take the Long Island Expressway to Exit #40 south (N.Y. 25/Jericho/Westbury). Go south on Cantiague Rock Road for 1.3 miles. Turn left (east) onto West John Street; go .3 mile. The park is on the left (north) side of the road.

This 127-acre park offers a nine-hole golf course, a driving range, a year round indoor ice rink, ice hockey, ice skating, skate rentals, an olympic-sized swimming pool, a diving pool, a wading pool, lockers, restrooms, showers, football fields, soccer fields, lighted softball fields, baseball fields, basketball courts, shuffleboard courts, bocce courts, stoopball courts, tennis courts, an area for chess and checkers, jogging paths, sled hills, a picnic area, a playground, and refreshment facilities. Concerts and teen dances are held at the park throughout the year.

Hicksville Gregory Museum – Long Island Earth Science Center
1 Heitz Place, Hicksville
(516) 822-7505

Take the Long Island Expressway to Exit #41 south (N.Y. 106/N.Y. 107/Jericho/ Hicksville). Take Route 106/107 south bearing left at .9 mile onto Route 107/North Broadway for a total of 1.2 miles. Turn left (east) onto East Barclay Street; go .2 mile. Turn right (south) onto Bay Avenue. The museum is about 50 feet from the corner on Heitz Place.

Located in a circa 1895 former courthouse, which is on the National Register of Historic Places, the museum has collections of fossils, minerals, rocks, crystals, butterflies, moths, and fluorescent rocks. The collection of fluorescent rocks displays truly dazzling colors when illuminated with ultra violet light.

The museum also has a gift shop and changing historical exhibits. Workshops are offered on various topics throughout the year. Please telephone the museum at the above number for a schedule of these events.

Trinity Lutheran Church
40 West Nicholai Street, Hicksville
(516) 931-2225

Take the Long Island Expressway to Exit #41 south (N.Y. 106/N.Y. 107/Jericho/ Hicksville). Take Route 106/107 south bearing left at .9 mile onto Route 107/North Broadway for a total of 1.4 miles. Turn right (west) onto West Nicholai Street; go .1 mile. The church is on the right (north) side of the road.

The main door of this church was made by Bruno Bearzi using Ghiberti's technique with molds taken by the Italian government in the 1940s from the original east door at the Baptistery of Florence in Italy. Ghiberti (1378–1455), a goldsmith and painter, produced works which are characterized by grace and smoothness. His famous Gates of Paradise east door at the Baptistery of Florence was referred to by Michelangelo as being "so fine that they might fittingly stand at the Gates of Paradise." The three-dimensional bronze doors are divided into ten sections with each section portraying a biblical event in gilded relief set in a plain molding. An illusion of space was achieved by a combination of pictorial perspective and sculptural means. Thus, buildings are represented by use of the painter's one-point perspective, construction and figures project toward the viewer, while the upper portion of the relief becomes increasingly flatter.

JERICHO

Jericho Friends Meeting House
6 Old Jericho Turnpike, Jericho
(516) 921-2379

Take the Long Island Expressway to Exit #41 north (N.Y. 106/N.Y. 107/Jericho). Go north on Route 106/Oyster Bay Road/Pine Hollow Road for .9 mile. Turn right (east) onto Old Jericho Turnpike; go .3 mile. The house is on the right (south) side of the road.

Elias Hicks, the noted Friends preacher, designed this meetinghouse which was built in 1787 on land purchased from Benjamin and William Wright. It has remained in continuous use with the only major modification being the addition of a porch in 1818.

(See also Town of North Hempstead/Manhasset/Manhasset Friends Meeting House; Town of Oyster Bay/Matinecock/Matinecock Friends Meeting House; Town of Oyster Bay/Mill Neck/Underhill Burying Ground/Grave of Captain John Underhill; Town of Oyster Bay/Oyster Bay/Council Rock; Town of Shelter Island/Shelter Island/Cemetery and Monument to Quaker Martyrs; and Town of Southold/Southold/Whitaker Historical Collection–Southold Free Library.)

LATTINGTOWN

Bailey Arboretum – Frank Bailey Estate – Munnysunk
Bayville Road and Feeks Lane, Lattingtown
(516) 571-8020

Not restricted to Nassau County residents.

Take the Long Island Expressway to Exit #41 north (N.Y. 106/N.Y. 107/Jericho). Go north on Route 107 (which becomes Cedar Swamp Road) for 4.2 miles. Turn right (east) onto Route 25A/Northern Boulevard; go .9 mile. Turn left (north) onto Wolver Hollow Road; go 1.5 miles. Turn right (east) onto Chicken Valley Road (which becomes Oyster Bay Road); go 2.6 miles. Turn right (north) onto Bayville Road; go .6 mile. The arboretum is on the right (east) side of the road.

This forty-two-acre arboretum is located on the bog and woodland sections of the former Bailey estate, Munnysunk. Now a Nassau County arboretum, it contains a large collection of native and exotic trees and shrubs including the largest tricolor beech, striped maple, dawn redwood, and weeping willow trees on Long Island. The main house of the former estate is available for garden club meetings. The nature trail, which meanders through the grounds, is an excellent place from which to observe the area's rich plant, bird, and animal life.

Locust Valley Cemetery
Ryefield Road, Lattingtown

Take the Long Island Expressway to Exit #41 north (N.Y. 106/N.Y. 107/Jericho). Go north on Route 107 (which becomes Cedar Swamp Road) for 4.2 miles. Turn right (east) onto Route 25A/Northern Blvd.; go .9 mile. Turn left (north) onto Wolver Hollow Road; go 1.5 miles. Turn right (east) onto Chicken Valley Road (which becomes Oyster Bay Road); go 2.6 miles. Turn right (north) onto Bayville Road; go .3 mile. Turn left (west) onto Ryefield Road; go .1 mile. The cemetery is on the right (north) side of the road.

Grave of Frank Nelson Doubleday (1889–1949)
Go 100 yards from the main gate on the carriage road to the first path on the left (west). Walk about 100 yards on the path. The grave site is to the right (north) near a large standing cross.

In 1918, at the age of twenty-nine, Doubleday joined his father's company of Doubleday, Page, and Company as a junior partner. In 1928 he became president and later headed the company as chairman of the board after his father's death in 1934. It was not until 1947 that the company became known as Doubleday and Company. By that time it was the largest publishing house in the country, employing over 4,765 people, with thirty-six retail stores, several book clubs, and numerous reprint divisions selling more than thirty million books annually.

Grave of Rocky Graziano (1922–1990)

Go north on the main carriage road (turning right at each intersection) for a total of .3 mile. Go 100 feet north (right) down the flagstone steps to end of the path. The grave is three rows beyond the path and slightly to the right of the path.

Born Thomas Rocco Barbella, Rocky was raised in Manhattan's less-than-fashionable lower East Side. The son of an unsuccessful boxer, Rocky entered the boxing profession and fought his way through the ranks becoming middleweight champion from 1947 to 1948.

After retiring from boxing, he became an actor and television personality appearing in the motion picture *Tony Rome* (1967) and the television program *Miami Undercover*. He also hosted a short-lived television series with comedian Henny Youngman, *The Henny and Rocky Show*. Graziano's best-remembered television appearances were as the perennial guest on the *Martha Raye Show*. (See also Town of North Hempstead/Martha Raye's House and Town of Southampton/ Southampton/Grave of Jack Dempsey.)

Grave of William Robertson Coe (1869–1955)

Go north on the main carriage road (turning right at each intersection) for a total of .3 mile. Go 100 feet south on the path on the left (south) side of the carriage road. The grave site is on the left (east) side of the path. From the grave site the cemetery's office is clearly visible to the southeast.

Born in Worcestershire, England, William Coe completed his undergraduate work at Albion Academy in Cardiff, Wales. He immigrated to the United States in 1883 and in 1884 obtained employment with the insurance firm of Johnson and Higgins, becoming president of the corporation in 1910 and chairman of the board in 1916. His other business interests included being on the boards of directors of Virginian Railway Company, Loup Creek Colliery Company, and the Wyoming Land Company. In later life he returned to school receiving his law degree from the University of Wyoming in 1948, at the age of seventy-nine, and a master's degree from Yale in 1949, at the age of eighty.

(See also Town of Oyster Bay/Oyster Bay/Planting Fields Arboretum–William Robertson Coe Estate–Planting Fields.)

Saint John's of Lattingtown
Lattingtown Road, Lattingtown
(516) 671-3226

Take the Long Island Expressway to Exit #41 north (N.Y. 106/N.Y. 107/Jericho). Go north on Route 107 (which becomes Cedar Swamp Road) for 4.2 miles. Turn right (east) onto Route 25A/Northern Blvd.; go .9 mile. Turn left (north) onto Wolver Hollow Road; go 1.5 miles. Turn right (east) onto Chicken Valley Road (which becomes Oyster Bay Road and then becomes Buckram Road); go 3.3 miles. Continue on when it becomes Forest Avenue for a total of 4.3 miles. Turn right (north) onto Lattingtown Road (which becomes Skunks Misery Road); go .6 mile. Turn left (west) onto Overlook Road; go .7 mile. The church is on the left side of the road at the intersection of Overlook, Old Tappan, and Lattingtown Roads.

Union Chapel, a small frame building built in 1859, was the first place of worship in Lattingtown. It was situated on Lattingtown Road opposite the entrance to what is now Saint Josaphat's Monastery. In 1912 the present English-style field stone church was built on land donated by William D. Guthrie. The church's ornately carved wooden ceiling, choir loft, altar, and pews—the latter two in the linenfold pattern—were donated by Mr. and Mrs. J. P. Morgan. They were designed by Scottish architect Sir Robert Lorimer and made in Scotland. Carved wooden angel choirs, mounted the length of the church on both sides of the aisle on the ceiling, are similar to those found in Trinity Episcopal Church in Roslyn. (See also Town of North Hempstead/Roslyn/Trinity Episcopal Church.) The windows are all painted glass made by Camm Studio: Smethwick: North Birmingham, England. There is a grisaille-styled window above the altar, a gift of Mr. and Mrs. Guthrie, and windows depicting Saints John the Baptist, Christopher, Francis, Paul, Mark, Peter, Luke, John, and Matthew on either side and in the rear of the church.

The rectory and cloister were added in 1919. The cloister has marble pillars with carved stone capitals depicting events in the Bible. The representation of Noah's ark is particularly interesting. In 1954 the final alteration of the church was made with the expansion of the nave on both sides. This church, which is off the beaten track, is well worth a visit.

Seymour Lipton's House
12 Fox Lane, Lattingtown

Not open to the public.

Take the Long Island Expressway to Exit #41 north (N.Y. 106/N.Y. 107/Jericho). Go north on Route 107 (which becomes Cedar Swamp Road) for 4.2 miles. Turn right (east) onto Route 25A/Northern Blvd.; go .9 mile. Turn left (north) onto Wolver Hollow Road; go 1.5 miles. Turn right (east) onto Chicken Valley Road (which becomes Oyster Bay Road); go 2.6 miles. Turn right (north) onto Bayville Road; go .9 mile. Turn right continuing north on Bayville Road for an additional .7 mile. Turn left (west) onto Fox Lane; go .3 mile. The house is on the right (north) side of the road.

Born in Manhattan, Seymour Lipton received his undergraduate degree from Columbia University. It was also from Columbia that he received the degree of Doctor of Dental Surgery in 1927. While continuing in his dental practice, Lipton became a self-taught sculptor, whose works often expressed social struggle and anguish through metaphorical expression, botanical imagery, or the human figure. His art is difficult to classify within the mainstream of the American Abstract Expressionist movement. Many of Lipton's major commissions were for public buildings such as the IBM Building in New York City, Dulles International Airport in Washington, DC, the Golden Gateway Redevelopment Project in San Francisco, CA, and Lincoln Center in New York City. *The Archangel* (1964), in Philharmonic Hall in Lincoln Center, is unseen, but heralded by a compilation of bells, cymbals, and horns. His work can also be seen in the Arboretum at Hofstra University in Hempstead.

Lipton died in 1986.

LAUREL HOLLOW

Davenport Sanctuary
(Long Island Chapter: The Nature Conservancy)
Route 25A, Laurel Hollow
(516) 367-3225

Open with prior permission.

Take the Long Island Expressway to Exit #45 north (Manetto Hill Road/Plainview/Woodbury). Go north on Woodbury Road for 3.4 miles. Turn left (north) onto Route 108/Harbor Road; go 1.6 miles. Turn left (west) onto Route 25A/North Hempstead Turnpike; go .8 mile to Laurel Hollow Road. The preserve property is on the right (north) side of Route 25A.

This eight-acre sanctuary is predominantly a moist woodland with a one-acre kettlehole pond. Vegetation consists of hybrid chestnut trees, black locusts, red maples, red oaks, dogwoods, mountain laurels, rhododendrons, black willows, greenbriers, and wineberries. Because of the diverse nature of the sanctuary, the area abounds with small mammals, woodland birds, and waterfowl.

Please call the Conservancy at the above telephone number to obtain permission to visit the sanctuary and to receive final directions.

Fox Hollow Preserve
(Long Island Chapter: The Nature Conservancy)
White Oak Tree Road, Laurel Hollow
(516) 367-3225

Open with prior permission.

Take the Long Island Expressway to Exit #45 north (Manetto Hill Road/Plain-view/Woodbury). Go north on Woodbury Road for 3.4 miles. Turn left (north) onto Route 108/Harbor Road; go 1.6 miles. Turn left (west) onto Route 25A/North Hempstead Turnpike; go 1.6 miles. Turn left (south) onto White Oak Tree Road (a one lane road); go .1 mile. The path leading into the preserve is on the left (east) side of the road. It is best to park on Route 25A and walk to the entrance.

This twenty-six-acre preserve was once part of a 1,000-acre farm. The preserve is predominantly a mature oak woods dominated by black, white, red, and chestnut oaks. Also found in the preserve are various varieties of hickories, white pines, black birches, red maples, beeches, sassafras, dogwoods, and mountain laurels. Among the wildlife found are horned owls, cardinals, tufted titmice, red-bellied woodpeckers, red fox, flying squirrels, and both red-tailed and broad-winged hawks. There is an extensive trail system throughout this preserve. Please call the Conservancy at the above telephone number to obtain permission to visit the preserve.

Memorial Cemetery of Saint John's Church
Route 25A, Laurel Hollow

Take the Long Island Expressway to Exit #45 north (Manetto Hill Road/Plain-view/Woodbury). Go north on Woodbury Road for 3.4 miles. Turn left onto Route 108/Harbor Road; go 1.6 miles. Turn left (west) onto Route 25A/North Hempstead Turnpike; go 1.6 miles. Turn right (north) onto Cove Road; go .1 mile to the rear entrance of the cemetery. Turn right (east) and follow the carriage road.

Grave of Otto Hermann Kahn (1867–1934)

From the cemetery's rear entrance on Cove Road go west on the carriage road for .2 mile. The grave is on the right (south) side of the carriage road. There is a semi-circular flagstone path and steps ascending to the family plot. The grave is very close to that of Henry Lewis Stimson.

Kahn was born in Mannheim, Germany. His father, a banker, decreed that Otto was to enter the financial world. At age twenty-one he was employed by the Deutsch Bank in Berlin but was presently transferred to England. His love of England blossomed and he became a British citizen. After five years in England he was offered a job with the banking firm of Speyer and Company in Manhattan. He arrived in New York in 1893 and spent two years at Speyer and Company before joining the banking firm of Kuhn, Loeb, and Company. It was not long before he was recognized as the financial genius behind the firm. Indeed it was Kahn who helped Harriman reorganize the nation's railroad system.

Throughout his life Kahn was a connoisseur of the arts. In 1903 he became a stockholder in the Metropolitan Opera Company, eventually owning 84 percent of its stock. He donated money to numerous organizations and projects. In 1921 he was awarded the Legion of Honor for his financial help to the Allied cause during World War I. He also gave large sums for the restoration of the Parthenon in Athens. The full extent of his philanthropy will never be known as many of his gifts were given anonymously. His homes in Manhattan and Cold Spring Harbor were filled with works of art and were compared to the palaces of the Medicis.

After suffering severe losses in the financial crash of 1929, he died suddenly while lunching with partners.

Grave of Alfred Pritchard Sloan Jr. (1875–1966)

From the cemetery's rear entrance on Cove Road go west on the carriage road for .3 mile, bearing right at the curve. The grave is on the left (north) side of the carriage road.

Alfred Sloan was born in New Haven, CT. He was president of the Hyatt Roller Bearing Company for fifteen years and of United Motors Corporation for three years before becoming president (1923-37) and then both president and chairman of the board (1936-56) of General Motors Corporation. He was also chairman of the board of the Sloan–Kettering Institute for Cancer Research in Manhattan.

Grave of Henry Lewis Stimson (1867–1950)

From the cemetery's rear entrance on Cove Road go west on the carriage road for slightly more than .2 mile. The grave is on the right (south) side of the carriage road very close to that of Otto Hermann Kahn.

After graduating from Harvard Law School, Stimson entered the prestigious law firm of Root and Clark. When Root went to Washington to become Secretary of War, Stimson started his own practice with Bronson Winthrop. Stimson's life was devoted to public service. Theodore Roosevelt appointed him attorney for the Southern District of New York State in 1906; he ran unsuccessfully for governor of New York State in 1910; William Howard Taft appointed him Secretary of War in 1911; during World War I he served as a lieutenant colonel in the field artillery; in 1927 Calvin Coolidge sent him to Nicaragua to negotiate peace in their civil war; in 1928 Calvin Coolidge appointed him governor-general of the Philippines; in 1929 he became Secretary of State in Herbert Hoover's cabinet; and in 1940 Franklin Delano Roosevelt appointed him Secretary of War. Stimson retired from public service on his seventy-eighth birthday in 1945 and returned to his home Highold in West Huntington.

(See also Town of Huntington/West Huntington/West Hills County Park–Henry Lewis Stimson Estate–Highold and Town of Oyster Bay/East Norwich/Muttontown Preserve–Egerton Winthrop Estate and Benjamin Moore Estate–Chelsea.)

MASSAPEQUA

Massapequa Preserve
Merrick Road, Massapequa
(516) 571-7443

Not restricted to Nassau County residents.

Take the Long Island Expressway to Exit #44 south (N.Y. 135/Seaford–Oyster Bay Expressway). Go south on the Seaford–Oyster Bay Expressway for 9.8 miles to Exit #1E (Merrick Road/Amityville). Go east on Merrick Road for 1.4 miles. The park is on the left (north) side of the road.

This 423-acre Nassau County preserve consists of freshwater wetlands, red maple swamps, streams, a dry woodland area of oak and red maple trees, and possibly the best pine barrens in Nassau County. There are nature trails throughout the preserve. Guided tours may be arranged by telephoning the above number. No vehicles are permitted in the preserve.

MATINECOCK

Matinecock Friends Meeting House
Duck Pond Road, Matinecock
(516) 676-0393 (Friends Academy School)

Take the Long Island Expressway to Exit #41 north (N.Y. 106/N.Y. 107/Jericho). Go north on Route 107 (which becomes Cedar Swamp Road) for 4.2 miles. Turn right (east) onto Route 25A/Northern Boulevard; go .9 mile. Turn left (north) onto Wolver Hollow Road; go .6 mile. Turn left (continuing north) onto Piping Rock Road; go 2.4 miles to Duck Pond Road. The house is on the northern corner of Duck Pond Road and Piping Rock Road.

Since 1671, when the Society of Friends first settled in the Matinecock area, they have been a dominant influence. Problems arose for the Friends when in 1657 Peter Stuyvesant, the governor of New Amsterdam, instituted a policy of repressing the Meeting. To escape the persecution, many members simply moved to the area of Oyster Bay controlled by the English.

Founded in 1671, this is the oldest officially organized Friends Meeting in the United States. The circa 1725 meetinghouse was in continuous use until its destruction by fire in December 1985. In 1986 the meetinghouse was rebuilt utilizing its original design and as many original bricks and hand-wrought nails and hinges as possible.

(See also Town of North Hempstead/Manhasset/Manhasset Friends Meeting House; Town of Oyster Bay/Jericho/Jericho Friends Meeting House; Town of Oyster

Bay/Mill Neck/Underhill Burying Ground/Captain John Underhill's Grave; Town of Oyster Bay/Oyster Bay/Council Rock; Town of Shelter Island/Shelter Island/Cemetery and Monument to Quaker Martyrs; and Town of Southold/Southold/Whitaker Historical Collection–Southold Free Library.)

MILL NECK

John P. Humes Japanese Stroll Garden
Dogwood Lane, Mill Neck
(516) 676-4486

Take the Long Island Expressway to Exit #41 north (N.Y. 106/N.Y. 107/Jericho). Go north on Route 107 (which becomes Cedar Swamp Road) for 4.2 miles. Turn right (east) onto Route 25A/Northern Blvd.; go .9 mile. Turn left (north) onto Wolver Hollow Road; go 1.5 miles. Turn right (east) onto Chicken Valley Road (which becomes Oyster Bay Road); go 1.9 miles. Turn right (northeast) onto Dogwood Lane; go 20 feet. The entrance is on the right (south) side of the road. The garden is surrounded by a stockade fence with no identifying sign.

Located on a four-acre hillside, this garden oasis was created by John P. Humes, the former United States Ambassador to Austria (1970–1975). On a trip to Japan, Humes became entranced by the beauty and serenity of Japanese gardens. Upon returning to the United States, he engaged a Japanese gardener to create a traditional Japanese garden and tea house on his Mill Neck estate.

In 1980 he donated the garden to the Wild Life Sanctuary which opened the garden to the public in 1987.

Mill Neck Manor School for the Deaf and Early Childhood Center – Robert L. Dodge Estate – Mill Neck Manor
Frost Mill Road, Mill Neck
(516) 922-4100

Take the Long Island Expressway to Exit #41 north (N.Y. 106/N.Y. 107/Jericho). Go north on Route 107 (which becomes Cedar Swamp Road) for 4.2 miles. Turn right (east) onto Route 25A/Northern Blvd.; go .9 mile. Turn left (north) onto Wolver Hollow Road; go 1.5 miles. Turn right (east) onto Chicken Valley Road (which becomes Oyster Bay Road); go 1.8 miles. Turn right (northeast) onto Frost Mill Road; go .4 mile. Turn left continuing on Frost Mill Road for an additional .7 mile. The manor is on the right (east) side of the road.

The Cotswold-style mansion, which has been on the National Register of Historic Places since 1979, was designed by the architectural firm of George Clinton and William Hamilton Russell, who resided in Islip. Built in 1924, it has oak paneling throughout, ornate fireplaces, plaster ceilings of English design, and stained-glass windows by Charles Connick of Boston. A unique feature is the presence of two stained-glass skylights in the hallway of the third floor. Movie buffs may recognize the mansion from the Charles Bronson film *Death Wish* (1982), from *Trading Places* (1983), or from the 1954 film *It's a Woman's World*.

The eighty-six-acre estate, with its formal gardens, has been beautifully preserved by the school.

During the fall, the school opens the estate to the public for its annual Apple Festival. Please call the school at the telephone number listed above or check local newspapers for the exact hours of festival programs.

Underhill Burying Ground
Factory Pond Road, Mill Neck

Not open to the public.

Take the long Island Expressway to Exit #41 north (N.Y. 106/N.Y. 107/Jericho). Go north on Route 107 (which becomes Cedar Swamp Road) for 4.2 miles. Turn right (east) onto Route 25A/Northern Blvd.; go .9 mile. Turn left (north) onto Wolver Hollow Road; go 1.5 miles. Turn right (east) onto Chicken Valley Road (which becomes Oyster Bay Road); go 2.6 miles. Turn right onto Bayville Road, turning right again at .9 mile, and continue north on Bayville Road for a total of 1.4 miles. Turn right (east) onto Factory Pond Road; go .8 mile. The entrance to the cemetery is on the right (south) side of the road on private property.

Grave of Captain John Underhill (1597–1672)

The noted colonial military leader and magistrate John Underhill, the son of John and Honor Pawley Underhill, was born in Kenilworth, Warwickshire, England. The son of a mercenary in the service of the Netherlands, it was expected that he would follow in his father's footsteps. Indeed, he became a cadet in the guard of the Prince of Orange and there married his first wife Helena de Hooch. In 1630 he came to Boston with John Winthrop to help in the organization of the Massachusetts Bay militia and became a representative in the Boston assembly. In 1637 he brutally destroyed the Indian forts at Mystic, CT, breaking the power of the Pequots. (See also Town of East Hampton/East Hampton/Old Cemetery/Grave of Lion Gardiner.) Instead of returning as a hero he was banished from Boston for siding with the Antinomians against the orthodox party in control of Boston. He returned to England in 1637 for one year at which time he wrote an account of the Indian wars. In 1638 he returned to Boston but was forced to flee to Dover, NH, where in 1641 he secured for himself the position of governor of Exeter and Dover. He moved to Connecticut, became an assistant justice, and in 1643 represented Stamford in the New Haven Assembly. Soon afterward he was employed by the Dutch to pacify the Canarsie Indians who had been attacking English and Dutch settlers. As a reward for his success, he was given land on Manhattan and an island in Jamaica Bay. Upon moving to Flushing, he assumed the position of sheriff, a position he held for nine years. In 1653 he was forced to flee from New Netherlands to Southold and then to Setauket because of his denunciation of Peter Stuyvesant's unjust taxation and dealings with the Indians. He reaped his revenge when in 1664 he was instrumental in helping the English gain control of New Netherlands.

With English control of Long Island secure, Underhill was able to move to Matinecock in 1667, not far from where his son had settled in 1664 and where he probably became a Quaker. There he spent his final days as an elder statesman on his estate Killingworth—not to be confused with Killenworth, the Pratt estate in Glen Cove used by the Russian delegation to the United Nations.

(See also Town of North Hempstead/Manhasset/Manhasset Friends Meeting House; Town of Oyster Bay/Jericho/Jericho Friends Meeting House; Town of Oyster Bay/Oyster Bay/Council Rock; Town of Shelter Island/Shelter Island/Cemetery and Monument to Quaker Martyrs; and Town of Southold/Southold/Whitaker Historical Collection–Southold Free Library.)

William Jaird Levitt Sr.'s House – La Colline
Oyster Bay and Glen Cove Road, Mill Neck

Not open to the public.

Take the Long Island Expressway to Exit #41 north (N.Y. 106/N.Y. 107/Jericho). Go north on Route 107 (which becomes Cedar Swamp Road) for 4.2 miles. Turn right (east) onto Route 25A/Northern Blvd.; go .9 mile. Turn left (north) onto Wolver Hollow Road; go 1.5 miles. Turn right (east) onto Chicken Valley Road; go 1.3 miles. Turn right (northeast) onto Beaver Brook Road (which becomes Oyster Bay and Glen Cove Road); go .3 mile. The house is on the left (north) side of the road.

Levitt was born in Brooklyn in 1907. He was a student at New York University for three years but left school in 1927 before receiving his degree. In 1929 he founded Levitt and Sons with his father and brother. From the beginning, William was the president of the firm while his brother Alfred designed the houses and their father was in charge of landscaping. Their two-hundred-house Strathmore development in Manhasset was completed in 1934. During the next seven years the firm built 2,000 more houses; but it was not until the end of World War II that Levitt made his mark on the construction industry by utilizing mass construction techniques. In 1947 he built the 17,500-house development that became known as Levittown, Long Island. This was followed by the 16,000-house Levittown in Bucks County, PA, and a third Levittown in Willingboro Township, NJ. In the latter part of the 1980s, Levitt experienced severe financial setbacks causing the discontinuation of a massive development in Florida.

In 1988 his sixty-eight-acre Mill Neck estate La Colline was sold. The French-inspired, U-shaped, thirty-five-room mansion was built in 1963. It has gilt French paneling from Vanderbilt's Fifth Avenue mansion, a conservatory, an elaborate entertainment pavilion, a marble-floored rotunda, an atrium, a greenhouse, indoor-outdoor tennis courts, and a swimming pool. The gatehouse is a reproduction of his Levittown ranch. During his long career Levitt built over 140,000 houses worldwide.

(See also Town of Babylon/Pinelawn/Mount Ararat Cemetery/Grave of William Jaird Levitt Sr. and Town of Hempstead/Levittown/Levittown Historical Society.)

OLD BETHPAGE

Battle Row County Park and Campground
Claremont Road, Old Bethpage
(516) 572-8690

Take the Long Island Expressway to Exit #48 south (Round Swamp Road/Old Bethpage/Farmingdale/Village Restoration). Go south on Old Country Road for .3 mile. Bear left (continuing south) onto Round Swamp Road; go 1.4 miles. Turn left (east) onto Old Bethpage Road; go .3 mile. Turn right (south) onto Claremont Road. Go 50 feet to the entrance which is on the right (west) side of the road opposite a town dump.

This forty-four-acre campground has sixty campsites with water and sanitary facilities, dumping stations, and electrical hook ups. There are also two rally fields, a recreational field, and a baseball field.

Old Bethpage Village Restoration
Round Swamp Road, Old Bethpage
(516) 572-8400

Take the Long Island Expressway to Exit #48 south (Round Swamp Road/Old Bethpage/Farmingdale/Village Restoration). Go south on Old Country Road for .3 mile. Bear left (continuing south) onto Round Swamp Road; go .5 mile. The restoration is on the left (east) side of the road.

Nassau County's Old Bethpage Village Restoration is a step backward into the Long Island of the eighteenth and nineteenth centuries. Houses, barns, shops, and farms all gently transport you back to a quieter and simpler time. Each month brings new themes to the village such as Thanksgiving, Christmas, and Independence Day celebrations, visiting military units from a by-gone era, harvest time, or needlework demonstrations. It is a fun place for both children and adults.

One word of caution: since it will take at least three hours to tour the village, wear comfortable shoes and clothes. Facilities for picnicking are available. If you prefer, a cafeteria is located in the reception area. Restrooms are provided. Foreign language audio tours are available.

OLD BROOKVILLE

Louis C. Clark Sanctuary

(Long Island Chapter: The Nature Conservancy)
Valentine's Road, Old Brookville
(516) 367-3225

Open with prior permission.

Take the Long Island Expressway to Exit #41 north (N.Y. 106/N.Y. 107/Jericho). Go north on Route 107 (which becomes Cedar Swamp Road) for 4.2 miles. Turn left (west) onto Route 25A/Northern Boulevard); go 1.1 miles. Turn right (north) onto Valentine's Road; go .8 mile. The sanctuary is on the right (east) side of the road.

This eight-acre sanctuary was once part of a larger tract of land known as the Valentine Farm. It consists of a pond, a stream, and a buttonwood/red tupelo swamp. There are over one hundred and fifty wildflower and twenty-five shrub species to be found here. Because of the diversity of habitat, the preserve is a haven for butterflies and moths.

Please call the Conservancy at the above telephone number to obtain permission to visit the sanctuary.

OLD WESTBURY

New York Institute of Technology – William C. Whitney Estate

Northern Boulevard, Old Westbury
1-800-345-6948

Take the Long Island Expressway to Exit #41 north (N.Y. 106/N.Y. 107/Jericho). Go north on Route 107 (which becomes Cedar Swamp Road) for 4.2 miles. Turn left (west) onto Route 25A/Northern Boulevard; go 1.1 miles. The college is on the left (south) side of the road.

The Dorothy Schure Old Westbury campus of New York Institute of Technology is located on a portion of the former 530-acre estate of William C. Whitney, the prominent New York lawyer, politician, and sportsman. The circa 1902 Tudor-style main house was designed by McKim, Mead, and White. It, along with the stable complex, was enlarged by his son Harry Payne Whitney in 1906. The Whitneys were avid horsemen; their stables of over two hundred horses reached its peak between 1924 and 1933. The main house was demolished in 1942 by Harry's son Cornelius Vanderbilt Whitney and a new house was erected on the same site.

The new house is presently the Westbury Golf and Country Club. The exteriors of the original Tudor-style stables (1898–1899) and the Tudor hunting lodge-style gymnasium have remained untouched but their interiors have been completely remodeled by the college for educational use. It is worth a visit to the college campus to see these remnants of the grandeur of Long Island's Gold Coast.

(See also Town of North Hempstead/Roslyn/Trinity Episcopal Church and Town of Islip/Oakdale/Connetquot River State Park and Preserve–Southside Sportsmen's Club.)

OYSTER BAY

Christ Episcopal Church
61 East Main Street, Oyster Bay
(516) 922-6377

Take the Long Island Expressway to Exit #41 north (N.Y. 106/N.Y. 107/Jericho). Go north on Route 106/Oyster Bay Road/Pine Hollow Road for 6.4 miles. Turn right (east) onto East Main Street; go .1 mile. The church is on the left (north) side of the road.

The parish was founded in 1705 but the present field stone church was built in 1878. It was in this church that President Theodore Roosevelt and his family worshiped for thirty years. The church's interior has off-white walls and a beamed ceiling which form an elegant framework for the European painted windows. Memorial plaques on the walls dedicated to Teddy's children, Quentin, Kermit, and Theodore Jr., and to their cousin Eleanor attest to the Roosevelts' active participation in the parish.

(See also Town of East Hampton/Montauk/The Third House; Town of Islip/Sayville/Roosevelt County Park–John Ellis Roosevelt Estate–Meadow Croft; Town of Oyster Bay/Oyster Bay/First Presbyterian Church; Town of Oyster Bay/Oyster Bay/Young's Memorial Cemetery/Grave of Theodore Roosevelt; and Town of Oyster Bay/Cove Neck/Sagamore Hill National Historic Site–Theodore Roosevelt Estate–Sagamore Hill.)

Council Rock
Lake Avenue, Oyster Bay

Take the Long Island Expressway to Exit #41 north (N.Y. 106/N.Y. 107/Jericho). Go north on Route 106/Oyster Bay Road/Pine Hollow Road for 6.3 miles. Turn left (west) onto West Main Street; go .6 mile. Turn left (south) onto Lake Avenue; go .1 mile. The rock is on the right (west) side of the road.

In 1672 George Fox, the founder of the Society of Friends, came to Oyster Bay to preach at a four-day meeting. The event which occurred at this site attracted over two hundred people; witnessing the influence that the Friends had in this

337

sparsely populated area. Fox's pulpit, according to tradition, was a large rock which is located on the west side of the road and bears the inscription:

Council Rock
Here George Fox 1672 met with
Wrights, Underhill and Feeke
at a Quaker Meeting.

(See also Town of North Hempstead/Manhasset/Manhasset Friends Meeting House; Town of Oyster Bay/Jericho/Jericho Friends Meeting House; Town of Oyster Bay/Matinecock/Matinecock Friends Meeting House; Town of Oyster Bay/Mill Neck/Underhill Burying Ground/Grave of Captain John Underhill; Town of Shelter Island/Shelter Island/Cemetery and Monument to Quaker Martyrs; and Town of Southold/Southold/Whitaker Historical Collection–Southold Free Library.)

First Presbyterian Church
60 East Main Street, Oyster Bay
(516) 922-5477

Take the Long Island Expressway to Exit #41 north (N.Y. 106/N.Y. 107/Jericho). Go north on Route 106/Oyster Bay Road/Pine Hollow Road for 6.4 miles. Turn right (east) onto East Main Street; go .1 mile. The church is on the right (south) side of the road.

Built in 1873, this Stick-style clapboard church was designed by Josiah Cleaveland Cady who also designed the Old Metropolitan Opera House and the American Museum of Natural History, both in Manhattan, as well as the Huntington Town Historian's Office and the Huntington Historical Society headquarters. (See also Town of Huntington/Huntington/Huntington Historical Society and Town of Huntington/Huntington/Huntington Town Historian's Office.) The church, which is on the National Register of Historic Places, is one of the few remaining examples of Stick architecture, a style that was popular for a short period of time from 1860–1890. In addition to its architectural importance, the church is historically significant, for it was at this church that President Theodore Roosevelt's father served as an elder and it was here that the young Teddy attended services.

(See also Town of East Hampton/Montauk/The Third House; Town of Islip/Sayville/Roosevelt County Park–John Ellis Roosevelt Estate–Meadow Croft; Town of Oyster Bay/Oyster Bay/Christ Episcopal Church; Town of Oyster Bay/Oyster Bay/Young's Memorial Cemetery/Grave of Theodore Roosevelt; and Town of Oyster Bay/Cove Neck/Sagamore Hill National Historic Site–Theodore Roosevelt Estate–Sagamore Hill.)

Oyster Bay Historical Society Museum – Wightman House
20 Summit Street, Oyster Bay
(516) 922-5032

Take the Long Island Expressway to Exit #41 north (N.Y. 106/N.Y. 107/Jericho). Go north on Route 106/Oyster Bay Road/Pine Hollow Road for 6.2 miles. Turn right (east) onto Summit Street; go .1 mile. The house is on the right (south) side of the road.

Originally located on South Street, this circa 1720 house is named for The Reverend Charles S. Wightman. It served as his home until his death in 1934 when it was bequeathed by him to the Baptist church. Over the years the house has seen many owners and has been used as a gift shop and a law office as well as a residence before being acquired by the Town of Oyster Bay.

Now the home of the Oyster Bay Historical Society, it has several rooms furnished appropriately to the Colonial and Federal periods with artifacts and memorabilia from Oyster Bay.

An addition is planned that will house the society's archives. At present, the reference library is located in the Wightman House and is available for research.

Oyster Bay Railroad Museum
Railroad Avenue, Oyster Bay

The museum is located adjacent to Roosevelt Memorial Park.

In 2005 the Long Island Rail Road formally gifted the historic station house, railway yard, and its turntable to the Town of Oyster Bay.

The turntable has been restored and the station house is in the process of being restored for use as a museum. It should be noted that the Oyster Bay turntable is one of only two remaining turntables on Long Island.

Raynham Hall
20 West Main Street, Oyster Bay
(516) 922-6808

Take the Long Island Expressway to Exit #41 north (N.Y. 106/N.Y. 107/Jericho). Go north on Route 106/Oyster Bay Road/Pine Hollow Road for 6.3 miles. Turn left (west) onto West Main Street; go .1 mile. The house is on the right (north) side of the road.

Raynham Hall was built in 1738 utilizing a traditional salt box-style of architecture. It was the home of Samuel Townsend who served as justice of the peace, town clerk, and delegate to the New York Provincial Congress. A noted patriot, he was arrested in 1776 for his separatist activities. His son Robert, whose codename was "Samuel Culper Jr.," was a member of the famous Long Island spy ring. Following the fall of Long Island, Raynham Hall became the headquarters of the British Lieutenant Colonel Simcoe. It was here that Major Andre and Benedict Arnold's plot to surrender West Point to the British was detected. The information was passed on to Colonel Benjamin Tallmadge who arranged the capture of Major Andre.

The house, which has been fully restored and is furnished with eighteenth-century and Victorian-style pieces, has been on the National Register of Historic Places since 1974. The bull's eye glass in the Dutch-style front door is original.

(See also Town of Brookhaven/East Setauket/Brewster House; Town of Brookhaven/Mastic Beach/The Manor of Saint George; Town of Brookhaven/Setauket/ Presbyterian Church of Setauket; Town of Brookhaven/Setauket/Richard Woodhull House; and Town of Oyster Bay/Oyster Bay/Townsend Burying Ground.)

Theodore Roosevelt Memorial Sanctuary and Trailside Museum
Oyster Bay Cove Road, Oyster Bay
(516) 922-3200

Take the Long Island Expressway to Exit #41 north (N.Y. 106/N.Y. 107/Jericho). Go north on Route 106/Oyster Bay Road/Pine Hollow Road for 6.4 miles. Turn right (east) onto East Main Street (which becomes Cove Road); go 1.3 miles. Park in the cemetery parking lot and walk about 200 feet further east to the sanctuary entrance, which is on the right (south) side of the road.

The plant and animal life of this twelve-acre sanctuary are indigenous to this area. Because of the diverse nature of the habitat, numerous species of birds are attracted to the preserve. The sanctuary, which is affiliated with the National Audubon Society, has a museum with changing exhibits of plants and animals found on Long Island. The grave of President Theodore Roosevelt is in the cemetery adjacent to the sanctuary. (See Young's Memorial Cemetery, page 341.)

Townsend Burying Ground
Simcoe Street, Oyster Bay

Take the Long Island Expressway to Exit #41 north (N.Y. 106/N.Y. 107/Jericho). Go north on Route 106/Oyster Bay Road/Pine Hollow Road for 6.1 miles. Turn left (west) onto Tooker Avenue; go .2 mile. Turn right (north) onto Lexington Avenue; go .1 mile. Turn right (east) onto Simcoe Street and go to the end of the street. Take the dirt path on the right (south) to the cemetery.

Buried here are John Townsend I, who was interred in 1668; Samuel Townsend, who owned Raynham Hall; and his son Robert (1753–1838) and daughter Sally (1761–1842). Robert, a member of the Long Island spy ring, had the codename "Samuel Culper Jr." Robert and possibly his sister Sally were instrumental in foiling Benedict Arnold's plan to surrender West Point.

(See also Town of Brookhaven/East Setauket/Brewster House; Town of Brookhaven/Mastic Beach/The Manor of Saint George; Town of Brookhaven/Setauket/ Presbyterian Church of Setauket; Town of Brookhaven/Setauket/Richard Woodhull House; Town of Oyster Bay/Oyster Bay/Raynham Hall; and Town of Oyster Bay/ Oyster Bay/Townsend Museum.)

Townsend Museum
107 East Main Street, Oyster Bay
(516) 671-0021

Take the Long Island Expressway to Exit #41 north (N.Y. 106/N.Y. 107/Jericho). Go north on Route 106/Oyster Bay Road/Pine Hollow Road for 6.4 miles. Turn right (east) onto East Main Street; go .2 mile. The museum is on the left (north) side of the road.

On display are Townsend family objects, documents, maps, portraits, books, and furniture. There is a reference library available for research.

(See also Town of Brookhaven/East Setauket/Brewster House; Town of Brookhaven/Mastic Beach/The Manor of Saint George; Town of Brookhaven/Setauket/Presbyterian Church of Setauket; Town of Brookhaven/Setauket/Richard Woodhull House; Town of Oyster Bay/Oyster Bay/Raynham Hall; and Town of Oyster Bay/Oyster Bay/Townsend Burying Ground.)

Young's Memorial Cemetery
Cove Road, Oyster Bay

Take the Long Island Expressway to Exit #41 north (N.Y. 106/N.Y. 107/Jericho). Go north on Route 106/Oyster Bay Road/Pine Hollow Road for 6.4 miles. Turn right (east) onto East Main Street (which becomes Cove Road); go 1.3 miles. The cemetery is on the right (south) side of the road.

Grave of Theodore Roosevelt (1858–1919)

To reach Roosevelt's grave walk up the only carriage road to the top of the hill. The grave is on the left (east) side of the carriage road surrounded by a high wrought iron fence.

Born in New York City, Theodore Roosevelt was the twenty-sixth President of the United States and a distant cousin of President Franklin Delano Roosevelt. Throughout his life Teddy was active in both military and governmental affairs. The foreign policy of his administration is best characterized by his motto "Walk softly but carry a big stick" while his domestic policy concentrated on curbing trusts, regulating big businesses, and the conservation of the country's natural resources.

Buried with President Roosevelt is his wife Edith Kermit Roosevelt (1861–1948). Also in the cemetery are the graves of their daughter Edith Roosevelt Derby (1891–1977) and their son Archibald Bulloch Roosevelt Sr. (1894–1979).

(See also Town of East Hampton/Montauk/The Third House; Town of Oyster Bay/Oyster Bay/Christ Episcopal Church; and Town of Oyster Bay/Cove Neck/Sagamore Hill National Historic Site–Theodore Roosevelt Estate–Sagamore Hill.)

OYSTER BAY COVE

Cordelia Hepburn Cushman Preserve
(Long Island Chapter: The Nature Conservancy)
Route 25A, Oyster Bay Cove
(516) 367-3225

Open with prior permission.

Take the Long Island Expressway to Exit #41 north (N.Y. 106/N.Y. 107/Jericho). Go north on Route 106/Oyster Bay Road for 4.1 miles. Turn right (east) onto Route 25A/North Hempstead Turnpike; go 2.1 miles to the Cushman driveway which is located on the right (south) side of the road. The entrance to the preserve is about 250 feet up the driveway.

This fifteen-acre preserve is a mature hardwood forest consisting of chestnuts, white oaks, maples, beeches, mountain laurels, pink lady's slippers, dwarf rattle-snake plantains, trailing arbutus, spotted wintergreens, and woodferns. The preserve attracts a variety of woodland birds especially during migration.

Please call the Conservancy at the above telephone number to obtain permission to visit the preserve.

SEA CLIFF

Church of Our Lady of Kazan
Bryant Avenue, Sea Cliff
(516) 671-6616

Take the Long Island Expressway to Exit #39 north (Glen Cove Road/Glen Cove). Go north on Glen Cove Road/Guinea Woods Road for 1.8 miles. Turn left (west) onto Route 25A/Northern Boulevard; go 1 mile. Bear right onto Witte Lane; go .1 mile. Turn right (north) onto Bryant Avenue; go .9 mile. Turn left (continuing north) onto Glenwood Road; go .6 mile. Bear right (north) as it merges onto Shore Road (which then becomes Prospect Avenue); go 1.3 miles. Turn right (east) onto Bryant Avenue (Note that this is a different Bryant Avenue from the one previously mentioned); go .1 mile. The church is on the left (east) side of the road.

To enter the church's grounds you must pass through a carved wooden arch which is adorned with two icons; *Christ* and *Virgin with Child*. Symbolic carvings on the pillars of the arch are religious with the exception of one, the imperial crest which was adopted by Ivan III (Ivan the Great) in the early 1490s and remained the official crest of tsarist Russia until the Bolshevik overthrow of the Romanov dynasty in 1917. Also exclusively Russian in origin are carved representations of *paskha*, with its XB declaring "Christ Risen," and *kulick*, both traditional Easter food specialties and both symbolic of the joy of the traditional Russian Easter.

Above the church's door is an icon of the Virgin Mary and the Christ Child with His hand raised in benediction. It is flanked on either side by icons of angels and wooden pillars which are carved with the same symbols found on the arch at the entrance to the church's grounds.

The interior of this wooden church is designed in the style of the eighteenth-century country churches of Russia. It has a low ceiling and is ornately decorated with icons. In keeping with the rustic atmosphere of the church, the iconostasis, the screen which divides the main body of the church from the sanctuary, is made of wood upon which are displayed some of the church's more important icons. Also, as is the custom in Russia, there are no pews.

(See also Town of Huntington/Dix Hills/Saint Andrews Orthodox Church.)

Sea Cliff Museum
95 Tenth Avenue, Sea Cliff
(516) 671-0090

Take the Long Island Expressway to Exit #39 north (Glen Cove Road/Glen Cove). Go north on Glen Cove Road/Guinea Woods Road for 4.9 miles. Bear right onto Cedar Swamp Road; go .2 mile. Turn left (west) onto Sea Cliff Avenue; go 1.6 miles. Turn right (west) onto Central Avenue. The museum is on the right (east) side of the road at the intersection of Central Avenue and Tenth Avenue.

This museum has a large collection of historical photographs and over nine hundred postcards pertaining to local sites, a Victorian-era kitchen, and a clothing collection documenting wearing apparel from the Victorian era to the 1930s. There is also a small gift shop.

Upper Brookville

Bertha and Reginald Rose Refuge
(Long Island Chapter: The Nature Conservancy)
Mill River Road, Upper Brookville
(516) 367-3225

Open with prior permission.

Take the Long Island Expressway to Exit #41 north (N.Y. 106/N.Y. 107/Jericho). Go north on Route 106 for 4.1 miles. Turn left (west) onto Route 25A/North Hempstead Turnpike; go .4 mile. Turn right (north) onto Mill River Road; go 1.1 miles to just past the entrance to the Mill River Club. The refuge is on the right (east) side of the road.

This fifteen-acre preserve, which is a typical northern hardwood forest, is one of the few remaining climax woodlands in Nassau County. It consists of scarlet oaks, grey and black birches, black cherries, sassafras, white pines, American chestnuts, and mountain laurels. Wildlife typical of woodlands such as thrushes, vireos, titmice, jays, crows, and woodpeckers are found in the preserve.

Please call the Conservancy at the above telephone number to obtain permission to visit the preserve as access and parking for it are located on private property.

Hope Goddard Iselin Preserve
(Long Island Chapter: The Nature Conservancy)
Chicken Valley Road, Upper Brookville
(516) 367-3225

Open with prior permission.

Take the Long Island Expressway to Exit #41 north (N.Y. 106/N.Y. 107/Jericho). Go north on Route 107 (which becomes Cedar Swamp Road) for 4.2 miles. Turn right (east) onto Route 25A/Northern Blvd.; go .9 mile. Turn left (north) onto Wolver Hollow Road; go 1.5 miles. Turn right onto Chicken Valley Road; go .5 mile. The locked gate is on the right (east) side of the road just before Laurel Woods Drive.

This forty-two-acre field and woodland preserve consists of white pines, oaks, beeches, and mountain laurels. The entire woodland section of the preserve, with the exception of the white pines which were planted in the 1930s, is a second growth woodland. The wildlife consists of typical woodland species of birds and mammals although some great horned owls have been sighted in the preserve.

Please call the Conservancy at the above telephone number to obtain permission to visit the preserve and to make arrangements to obtain the key to the gate lock.

Planting Fields Arboretum – William Robertson Coe Estate – Planting Fields
1395 Planting Fields Road, Upper Brookville
(516) 922-9200

Take the Long Island Expressway to Exit #41 north (N.Y. 106/N.Y. 107/Jericho). Go north on Route 106. Turn left (west) onto Route 25A/Northern Boulevard. Make the first right (north) turn onto Mill River Road. Follow the green and white signs to the arboretum.

William Robertson Coe immigrated to America from England in 1883 and made his fortune in marine insurance. In 1919 he built a sixty-five-room house in a combination of English medieval-style and Elizabethan-style architecture incorporating many aspects of Beaux-Arts design. Named Planting Fields, the original Indian name for the area, the house is faced in Indiana limestone. The hand-glazed terracotta tiles, stained-glass windows, and wood and stone carvings all came from fifteenth- and sixteenth-century English Tudor homes. Take particular notice of the stained-glass windows as they came from Hever Castle where Ann Boleyn, the wife of Henry VIII, once lived. Also of interest is the 1723 wrought-iron Carshalton gate at the main entrance, which also was imported from England. (See also Town of Oyster Bay/Lattingtown/Locust Valley Cemetery/Grave of William Robertson Coe.)

The arboretum offers guided tours, meeting rooms, and reference library facilities. Nature trails go through a profusion of labeled azalea and rhododendron varieties, as well as other plant, tree, and shrub collections. The greenhouse features a large selection of tropical plants, annuals, and special seasonal displays.

During the warmer months concerts are held on the arboretum's lawns. The arboretum has been on the National Register of Historic Places since 1979.

In 2007 the arboretum became the depository for the Long Island State Parks Commission. Included in the collection are 80,000 negatives, 25,000 photographs, 65,000 slides, 100,000 architectural and engineering drawings, and 49 motion picture reels collectively documenting the creation of the Island's state park system.

Appendix I
CATERING IN GOLD COAST MANSIONS

Estates, which may be rented for catered affairs,
are identified below by the original owner.

Bailey Arboretum
(516) 571-8020

Frank Bailey estate,
Munnysunk, Lattingtown

Coindre Hall
(631) 581-0022

George McKesson Brown estate,
West Neck Farm, Lloyd Harbor

DeSeversky Center
(516) 686-7675

Alfred Irene du Pont estate,
White Eagle, Brookville

Dowling College
(631) 244-3131

William K. Vanderbilt Sr. estate,
Idlehour, Oakdale

Glen Cove Mansion and
Conference Center
(516) 671-6400

John Teele Pratt Sr. estate,
Manor House, Glen Cove

Indian Neck Hall
(631) 277-7800

Frederick Gilbert Bourne estate,
Indian Neck Hall, Oakdale

Leeds Pond Preserve
(516) 484-7431

Herman Goldman estate,
Plandome Manor

Nassau County Museum of Art
(516) 484-9337

Lloyd Stephens Bryce estate,
Bryce House, Roslyn Harbor

Oheka Castle Catering
(631) 692-2707

Otto Hermann Kahn estate,
Oheka, Cold Spring Harbor

Sands Point Park and Preserve
(516) 571-7900

Howard Gould estate,
Castlegould, Sands Point

Suffolk Vanderbilt Museum
(631) 854-5555

William Kissam Vanderbilt Jr. estate,
Eagle's Nest, Centerport

Swan Club
(516) 621-7600

Arthur Williams estate,
Brook Corners, Glen Head

Timber Point County Country Club
(631) 581-0022

William Laurence Breese estate,
Timber Point, Great River

Town of Oyster Bay Golf Course
(516) 921-5707

Victor Morawetz estate,
Three Ponds, Woodbury

The Unitarian Church
(516) 627-6560

Charles Shipman Payson estate,
Manhasset

West Sayville County Golf Course
(631) 589-0022

Anson Wales Hard Jr. estate,
Meadow Edge, West Sayville

APPENDIX II
GOLD COAST MANSIONS THAT CAN BE VISITED

Estates are identified by the original owner.

SUFFOLK COUNTY

Bayard Cutting Arboretum

William Bayard Cutting Sr. estate,
Westbrook Farm, Great River

Dowling College

William Kissam Vanderbilt Sr. estate,
Idlehour, Oakdale

Environmental Interpretive Center
of Suffolk County

Harold Hathaway Weekes estate,
Wereholme, Islip

The Gatsby Restaurant

Frank D. Creamer estate,
Islip

Gold Coast Museum of Long Island

George McKesson Brown estate,
West Neck Farm, Lloyd Harbor

The Islip Art Museum

Harry Kearsarge Knapp Sr. estate,
Brookwood, East Islip

Meadow Croft

John Ellis Roosevelt estate,
Meadow Croft, Sayville

Joint Industry Board of the
Electrical Industry

Arthur Keeler Bourne Sr. estate,
Lake House, Oakdale

Frederick Gilbert Bourne estate,
Indian Neck Hall, Oakdale

Long Island Center for
Experimental Art

Harry Kearsarge Knapp Sr. estate,
Brookwood, East Islip

Long Island Maritime Museum

Anson Wales Hard Jr. estate,
Meadow Edge, West Sayville

Stony Brook Southampton College

Arthur B. Claflin estate,
Shinnecock Hills

Suffolk County Vanderbilt Museum

William Kissam Vanderbilt Jr. estate,
Eagle's Nest, Centerport

Timber Point Country Club

William Laurence Breese estate,
Timber Point, Great River

West Sayville Golf Course

Anson Wales Hard Jr. estate,
Meadow Edge, West Sayville

NASSAU COUNTY

American Merchant Marine Museum

William Slocum Barstow estate,
Elm Point, Kings Point

Bailey Arboretum

John Clark estate,
Lattingtown

Caumsett State Park

Marshall Field III estate,
Caumsett, Lloyd Harbor

Cedarmere

William Cullen Bryant estate,
Cedarmere, Roslyn Harbor

Clark Botanic Garden

Grenville Clark Sr. estate,
Albertson

DeSeversky Center

Alfred Irene du Pont estate,
White Eagle, Brookville

Glen Cove Mansion and
Conference Center

John Teele Pratt Sr. estate,
Manor House, Glen Cove

Glen Cove School District,
administrative building

Robert Dunbar Pruyn estate,
Glen Cove

Great Neck Village Hall	John C. Baker estate, Great Neck
Great Neck Estates Village Hall	John Jacob Atwater Sr. estate, Great Neck Estates
Great Neck School District, administrative building	Henry Phipps Jr. estate, *Bonnie Blink*, Lake Success
Hofstra University	William S. Hofstra estate, *The Netherlands*, Hempstead
Holocaust Memorial and Educational Center of Nassau County in Welwyn Preserve	Harold Irving Pratt Sr. estate, *Welwyn*, Glen Cove
Long Island University, C. W. Post College	Marjorie Merriweather Post estate, *Hillwood,* Brookville
	John Randolph Robinson estate, Brookville
	John Randolph Robinson estate, (second estate, also unnamed), Brookville
Mill Neck Manor School for the Deaf and Early Childhood Center	Robert L. Dodge estate, *Sefton Manor*, Mill Neck
Museum of Long Island's Gold Coast	George McKesson Brown estate, *West Neck Farm*, Lloyd Harbor
Muttontown Preserve	Benjamin Moore estate, *Chelsea*, Muttontown
	Bronson Winthrop estate, (now called *Nassau Hall),* Muttontown
Nassau County Art Museum	Lloyd Stephens Bryce estate, *Bryce House*, Roslyn Harbor
Oheka Castle Catering	Otto Hermann Kahn estate, *Oheka,* Cold Spring Harbor
Old Westbury Gardens	John Shaffer Phipps estate, *Westbury House*, Old Westbury

Planting Fields Arboretum	William Robertson Coe estate, *Planting Fields*, Upper Brookville
Sagamore Hill	Theodore Roosevelt estate, *Sagamore Hill*, Cove Neck
Saint Ignatius Retreat House	Nicholas Frederic Brady estate, *Inisfada*, North Hills
Sands Point Community Synagogue	Bettie Fleischmann Holmes estate, *The Chimneys*, Sands Point
Sands Point Park and Preserve	Howard Gould estate, *Castlegould,* Sands Point
	Harry Frank Guggenheim estate, *Falaise,* Sands Point
Science Museum of Long Island	Herman Goldman estate, Plandome Manor
Swan Club	Arthur Williams estate, *Brook Corners*, Glen Head
Town of Oyster Bay Golf Course	Victor Morawetz estate, *Three Ponds*, Woodbury
The Unitarian Church	Charles Shipman Payson estate, Manhasset
United States Merchant Marine Academy	Henri Bendel estate, Kings Point
Webb Institute of Naval Architecture	Herbert Lee Pratt Sr. estate, *The Braes,* Glen Cove
Westbury – Syosset Community Park	James Watson Webb Sr. estate, *Woodbury House,* Syosset

Appendix III

TIFFANY WINDOWS IN
SUFFOLK AND NASSAU COUNTIES

Please note that wherever possible the name recorded by Tiffany Studios is the name used here. When a window is not recorded in the surviving Tiffany Studios' records, the name given to a similar window elsewhere in the country has been used to maintain consistency.

Suffolk County

Town of Huntington Tiffany Windows

Trinity Episcopal Church, Northport

Brown Memorial window – *Our Saviour*
  (*documented but unsigned*)

Knight Memorial window – *Christ in Gethsemane*
  (*documented and signed*)

Parrott Memorial window – *Saint John*
  (*documented but unsigned*)

Town of Islip Tiffany Windows and Memorials

William Bayard Cutting Estate Westbrook, Great River

Three-paneled bamboo decorative window in second floor hallway
  (*undocumented and unsigned, possibly Tiffany*)

Two three-paneled decorative windows in front hallway with wreath-decorated
  panels above
  (*undocumented and unsigned, possibly Tiffany*)

353

Two two-paneled decorative windows with two floral/landscape scene insets
each and wreath-decorated panels above in stairwell and annex hallway
(undocumented and unsigned, possibly Tiffany)

Five matching ornamental panels above clear leaded glass on porch
(now, concession area)
(undocumented and unsigned, possibly Tiffany)

Small jewel glass ornamental window (artificially lighted) in dining room to
right of fourteenth-century fireplace
(undocumented and unsigned, possibly Tiffany)

Mosaic fireplace decoration
(undocumented and unsigned)

Emmanuel Episcopal Church, Great River

Hobbs Memorial window – *Christ and Child with Adoring Angels*
(documented and signed)

Floral window with poppies and lilies on north chancel wall
(signed but not specifically documented)

Floral window with poppies on south chancel wall
(unsigned and not specifically documented*)

Sarah Nicoll Memorial window – *Crown of Heaven*
(unsigned and not specifically documented*)

William Nicoll Memorial window – *Jewel Glass Cross*
(unsigned and not specifically documented*)

Five ornamental windows
(unsigned and not specifically documented*)

Dover Memorial window
(signed but not specifically documented*)

*A note in the Tiffany Studios' partial list of completed commissions refers to
ornamental window(s) completed in this church.

Saint Mark's Episcopal Church, Islip

Three chancel (apse) windows – *Saint Mark*
*(gift of Louis Comfort Tiffany to parish in 1895—replacing original 1878
Tiffany window)*
(documented but unsigned)

Redmond Memorial window – *Saint John*
(documented but unsigned)

Peters Memorial window – *Floral Design*
 (documented and signed)

Hyde Memorial window – *Recording Angel*
 (documented but unsigned)

Johnson Memorial window – *Choir of Angels*
 (referred to in Tiffany Studios' records as Carroll Memorial)
 (documented and signed)

Ornamental windows in storage
 (documented and unsigned, possibly Tiffany)

Trefoil Pebble Cluster window over east entrance
 (undocumented and unsigned, possibly Tiffany)

Saint Ann's Episcopal Church, Sayville

Seven chancel (apse) windows – *Christ and Adoring Angels*
 (documented but unsigned)

Round Pebble Cluster window over south entrance
 (undocumented and unsigned, possibly Tiffany)

Prescott Memorial plaque in bronze
 (documented and signed)

Two hemisphere ornamentals in narthex
 (undocumented and unsigned, possibly Tiffany)

Town of Shelter Island Tiffany Windows

Saint Mary's Episcopal Church, Shelter Island

Nicoll Memorial windows
 (documented but unsigned)

Town of Smithtown Tiffany Windows

Saint James Episcopal Church, Saint James

Miller Memorial window – *Good Shepherd*
 (documented and signed)

Miller Memorial plaque in bronze
 (signed but undocumented)

Town of Southampton Tiffany Windows

Church of the Atonement Episcopal Church, Quogue

Benjamin D. K. Craig and Ann Wagstaff Craig Memorial window – *Dove*
(undocumented and unsigned, possibly Tiffany)

Roswell Park Cullen Memorial window – *Jewel Glass Cross* composite
(undocumented and unsigned, possibly Tiffany)

Henrietta Craig Colgate Memorial window – *The Lord my God will lighten
my darkness*
(undocumented and unsigned, possibly Tiffany)

Three Craig Memorial windows – *Angel of Praise and Adoring Angels*
(documented but unsigned)

Edith Beckwith Smith Memorial window – *Seated Angel*
(undocumented but possibly signed, molding obscures signature, possibly Tiffany)

Katharine Van Wyck Memorial window – *Sunset Landscape*
(signed but undocumented)

Mary Livingston Austin Poor Memorial window – *Saint Cecilia*
(signed but undocumented)

Memorial tablet
(documented but not found)

Jewel Glass Chancel Cross
(undocumented and unsigned, possibly Tiffany)

Christ Episcopal Church, Sag Harbor

Belknap Memorial window – *Cross*
(documented but unsigned)

James Herman Aldrich Memorial window – *Jesus' Presentation in the Temple*
and associated 1917 mosaic
(signed but undocumented)

Saint Andrew's Dune Church, Southampton

Mary E. Holbrook Memorial window – *Jewel Glass and Marine Mosaic*
(documented but unsigned)

Ogdon Cryder Memorial window – *Sir Galahad*
(documented and signed)

Louise Holbrook Betts Memorial window – *Landscape*
(signed but undocumented)

Theodore Gaillard Thomas Memorial window – *Christ Blessing the Children*
(documented and signed)

Josephine Churchill Nicoll Memorial window – *Blessed are the pure in heart*
(signed but undocumented)

Margaret H. Schieffelin Memorial window – *Saint Margaret*
(documented but unsigned)

C. Wyllys Betts Memorial window – *Resurrection*
(undocumented and unsigned, possibly Tiffany)

George G. Dewitt Memorial window – *Angel of Resurrection*
(signed but undocumented)

Frederic Henry Betts *Memorial* window – *Landscape*
(documented and signed)

Town of Southold Tiffany Windows

Saint John's Episcopal Church, Fishers Island

Bowers Memorial window – *Our Savior*
(documented but unsigned)

NASSAU COUNTY

Town of Hempstead Tiffany Windows

Saint George's Episcopal Church, Hempstead

Henry Van Rensselaer Kennedy Memorial window
(undocumented but signed "J. A. Holzer, 1917")

Bessie Morgan Belmont Memorial window
(undocumented and unsigned, also possibly by Holzer)

Saint Paul's School, Garden City

Thomas Newcomb Memorial window – *Conversion of Saint Paul on the Road to Damascus*
(documented but unsigned)

United Methodist Church of Hempstead, Hempstead

Thorne Memorial window – *Resurrection*
(documented and signed)

Town of North Hempstead Tiffany Windows

All Saints Episcopal Church, Great Neck

Farnham Memorial window – *Angel with Landscape*
(documented and signed "Edward P. Sperry, 1907")

Hamilton/Messenger Memorial window – *Sermon on the Mount*
(documented but unsigned)

Childs Memorial window – *Angel of Praise*
(documented but unsigned)

Stanton Memorial window – three-paneled ornamental
(documented but unsigned)

Trinity Episcopal Church, Roslyn

Hooper Memorial window
(signed but undocumented)

Five Duer/Duer/Mackay Memorial windows – *The Young Jesus with Children and Adoring Angels*
(undocumented and unsigned, possibly Tiffany)

Other windows credited to Tiffany by church staff can not be confirmed.

Town of Oyster Bay Tiffany Windows

Saint John's Episcopal Church, Cold Spring Harbor

Moore Memorial window – *Angel of Resurrection*
(documented and signed)

John Divine Jones Memorial window – *Good Shepherd*
  (documented but unsigned)

Townsend Jones Memorial window – *Annunciation*
  (documented but unsigned)

Saint Dominic's Roman Catholic Church, Oyster Bay

The back altar of the historic chapel, including the cupola over the crucifix, is undocumented but most probably the work of L. C. Tiffany. Dating of this work and absolute attribution is impossible. The ceiling decoration may be the work of Samuel Coleman during his association with Tiffany in Associated Artists, Inc.

Most of the windows were fabricated by Mayer of Munich.

Saint Margaret's Episcopal Church, Plainview

Lott Memorial window – *Risen Christ and Adoring Angels*
  (originally in Saint Gabriel's Protestant Episcopal Church, Hollis, Queens—presently in storage and unmounted)
  (documented)

QUEENS COUNTY

Far Rockaway

First Presbyterian Church, Far Rockaway

Russell Sage Memorial window – *Landscape*
  (documented but unsigned)

Appendix IV

VILLAGES AND TOWNS

VILLAGE	COUNTY	TOWN
Albertson	Nassau	North Hempstead
Amagansett	Suffolk	East Hampton
Amityville	Suffolk	Babylon
Apaquogue	Suffolk	East Hampton
Aquebogue	Suffolk	Riverhead
Babylon	Suffolk	Babylon
Baldwin	Nassau	Hempstead
Bay Park	Nassau	Hempstead
Bayport	Suffolk	Islip
Bay Shore	Suffolk	Islip
Bayville	Nassau	Oyster Bay
Bellmore	Nassau	Hempstead
Bellport	Suffolk	Brookhaven
Bohemia	Suffolk	Islip
Bridgehampton	Suffolk	Southampton
Brookville	Nassau	Oyster Bay
Calverton	Suffolk	Riverhead
Cedar Beach	Suffolk	Southold
Cedar Point	Suffolk	East Hampton
Center Moriches	Suffolk	Brookhaven
Centerport	Suffolk	Huntington
Cold Spring Harbor	Suffolk	Huntington
Cold Spring Harbor	Nassau	Oyster Bay
Commack	Suffolk	Smithtown
Commack	Suffolk	Huntington
Coram	Suffolk	Brookhaven
Cutchogue	Suffolk	Southold
East Farmingdale	Suffolk	Babylon
East Hampton	Suffolk	East Hampton
East Islip	Suffolk	Islip
East Marion	Suffolk	Southold
East Meadow	Nassau	Hempstead
East Norwich	Nassau	Oyster Bay

VILLAGE   COUNTY   TOWN

VILLAGE	COUNTY	TOWN
East Patchogue	Suffolk	Brookhaven
East Quogue	Suffolk	Southampton
East Rockaway	Nassau	Hempstead
East Setauket	Suffolk	Brookhaven
Eastport	Suffolk	Southampton
Eaton's Neck	Suffolk	Huntington
Elmont	Nassau	Hempstead
Elwood	Suffolk	Huntington
Farmingdale	Nassau	Oyster Bay
Farmingville	Suffolk	Brookhaven
Fire Island	Suffolk	Brookhaven
Fire Island	Suffolk	Islip
Fishers Island	Suffolk	Southold
Flanders	Suffolk	Southampton
Flower Hill	Nassau	North Hempstead
Freeport	Nassau	Hempstead
Garden City	Nassau	Hempstead
Glen Cove	Nassau	Oyster Bay
Great Neck	Nassau	North Hempstead
Great Neck Estates	Nassau	North Hempstead
Great Neck Plaza	Nassau	North Hempstead
Great River	Suffolk	Islip
Greenlawn	Suffolk	Huntington
Greenport	Suffolk	Southold
Greenvale	Nassau	North Hempstead
Halesite	Suffolk	Huntington
Hampton Bays	Suffolk	Southampton
Hauppauge	Suffolk	Smithtown
Head of the Harbor	Suffolk	Smithtown
Hempstead	Nassau	Hempstead
Hewlett	Nassau	Hempstead
Hicksville	Nassau	Oyster Bay
Huntington	Suffolk	Huntington
Huntington Station	Suffolk	Huntington
Inwood	Nassau	Hempstead
Islip	Suffolk	Islip
Jericho	Nassau	Oyster Bay
Kings Park	Suffolk	Smithtown
Kings Point	Nassau	North Hempstead
Lake Grove	Suffolk	Brookhaven
Lake Ronkonkoma	Suffolk	Brookhaven
Lake Success	Nassau	North Hempstead
Lakeland	Suffolk	Islip

VILLAGE	COUNTY	TOWN
Lattingtown	Nassau	Oyster Bay
Laurel Hollow	Nassau	Oyster Bay
Lawrence	Nassau	Hempstead
Lido Beach	Nassau	Hempstead
Levittown	Nassau	Hempstead
Lindenhurst	Suffolk	Babylon
Lloyd Harbor	Suffolk	Huntington
Long Beach	Nassau	Hempstead
Malverne	Nassau	Hempstead
Manhasset	Nassau	North Hempstead
Manorville	Suffolk	Brookhaven
Massapequa	Nassau	Oyster Bay
Mastic Beach	Suffolk	Brookhaven
Matinecock	Nassau	Oyster Bay
Mattituck	Suffolk	Southold
Middle Island	Suffolk	Brookhaven
Mill Neck	Nassau	Oyster Bay
Miller Place	Suffolk	Brookhaven
Montauk	Suffolk	East Hampton
Nissequogue	Suffolk	Smithtown
North Hills	Nassau	North Hempstead
North Sea	Suffolk	Southampton
North Woodmere	Nassau	Hempstead
Northport	Suffolk	Huntington
Northville	Suffolk	Riverhead
Oakdale	Suffolk	Islip
Oceanside	Nassau	Hempstead
Old Bethpage	Nassau	Oyster Bay
Old Brookville	Nassau	Oyster Bay
Old Field	Suffolk	Brookhaven
Old Westbury	Nassau	North Hempstead
Old Westbury	Nassau	Oyster Bay
Orient	Suffolk	Southold
Oyster Bay	Nassau	Oyster Bay
Oyster Bay Cove	Nassau	Oyster Bay
Patchogue	Suffolk	Brookhaven
Peconic	Suffolk	Southold
Pinelawn	Suffolk	Babylon
Plandome Manor	Nassau	North Hempstead
Port Jefferson	Suffolk	Brookhaven
Port Washington	Nassau	North Hempstead
Quogue	Suffolk	Southampton
Remsenburg	Suffolk	Southampton

VILLAGE   COUNTY   TOWN

VILLAGE	COUNTY	TOWN
Ridge	Suffolk	Brookhaven
Riverhead	Suffolk	Riverhead
Riverhead	Suffolk	Southampton
Rockville Centre	Nassau	Hempstead
Roslyn	Nassau	North Hempstead
Roslyn Estates	Nassau	North Hempstead
Roslyn Harbor	Nassau	North Hempstead
Roslyn Heights	Nassau	North Hempstead
Russell Gardens	Nassau	North Hempstead
Saddle Rock	Nassau	North Hempstead
Sagaponack	Suffolk	Southampton
Sag Harbor	Suffolk	Southampton
Saint James	Suffolk	Smithtown
San Remo	Suffolk	Smithtown
Sands Point	Nassau	North Hempstead
Sayville	Suffolk	Islip
Sea Cliff	Nassau	Oyster Bay
Seaford	Nassau	Hempstead
Setauket	Suffolk	Brookhaven
Shelter Island	Suffolk	Shelter Island
Shinnecock Hills	Suffolk	Southampton
Shinnecock Inlet	Suffolk	Southampton
Shirley	Suffolk	Brookhaven
Smithtown	Suffolk	Smithtown
Southampton	Suffolk	Southampton
Southold	Suffolk	Southold
Southport	Suffolk	Southampton
Springs	Suffolk	East Hampton
Stony Brook	Suffolk	Brookhaven
Three-Mile Harbor	Suffolk	East Hampton
Uniondale	Nassau	Hempstead
Upper Brookville	Nassau	Oyster Bay
Upton	Suffolk	Brookhaven
Valley Stream	Nassau	Hempstead
Village of the Branch	Suffolk	Smithtown
Wading River	Suffolk	Riverhead
Wainscott	Suffolk	East Hampton
Wantagh	Nassau	Hempstead
Water Mill	Suffolk	Southampton
West Babylon	Suffolk	Babylon
West Bay Shore	Suffolk	Islip
West Fort Salonga	Suffolk	Huntington
West Huntington	Suffolk	Huntington

VILLAGE	COUNTY	TOWN
West Sayville	Suffolk	Islip
Westbury	Nassau	North Hempstead
Westbury South	Nassau	Hempstead
Westhampton	Suffolk	Southampton
Westhampton Beach	Suffolk	Brookhaven
Westhampton Beach	Suffolk	Southampton
Yaphank	Suffolk	Brookhaven

APPENDIX V

WINERIES

Ackerly Pond Vineyards
1375 Peconic Ln., Peconic
(631) 765-6861

Bedell Cellars
36225 Route 25, Cutchogue
(631) 734-7537

Broadfields Wine Cellars
2885 Peconic Ln., Peconic
(631) 765-6403

Castello di Borghese Vineyards
Route 48, Cutchogue
(631) 734-5111

Channing Daughters Winery
Scuttlehole Rd., Bridgehampton
(631) 537-7224

Charles John Vineyards
3340 Hortons Ln., Southold
(631) 765-9218

Corey Creek Vineyards
45470 Main Rd., Southold
(631) 765-4168

Duck Walk Vineyards
Montauk Hgwy., Southampton
(631) 726-7555

Galluccio Family Wineries
24385 Route 25, Cutchogue
(631) 734-7089

Jamesport Vineyards
1216 Route 25, Jamesport
(631) 722-5256

Laurel Lake Vineyards
3165 Main Rd., Laurel
(631) 298-1420

Lenz Vineyards
Route 25, Peconic
(631) 734-6010

Lieb Family Cellars
35 Cox Neck Rd., Mattituck
(631) 298-1942

Loughlin Vineyards
South Main St., Sayville
(631) 589-0027

Macari Vineyards and Winery
150 Bergen Ave., Mattituck
(631) 298-0100

Pugliese Vineyards
Route 25, Cutchogue
(631) 734-4057

Martha Clara Vineyards
6025 Sound Ave., Riverhead
(631) 298-0075

Raphael
39390 Route 25, Peconic
(631) 765-1100

The Old Field Vineyards
59600 Route 25, Southold
(631) 765-2465

Roanoke Vineyards
3543 Route 48, Riverhead
(631) 727-4161

Osprey's Dominion Vineyards
44075 Route 25, Peconic
(631) 765-6188

Schneider Vineyards
2248 Roanoke Ave., Riverhead
(631) 727-3334

Palmer Vineyards
108 Route 48, Aquebogue
(631) 722-9463

Shinn Estate Vineyards
2000 Oregon Rd., Mattituck
(631) 804-0367

Paumanok Vineyard
1074 Route 25, Aquebogue
(631) 722-8800

Ternhaven Cellars
331 Front St., Greenport
(631) 477-8737

Peconic Bay Winery
31320 Route 25, Cutchogue
(631) 734-7361

Vineyard 48
Route 48, Cutchogue
(631) 734-5200

Pelligrini Vineyards
23005 Route 25, Cutchogue
(631) 734-4111

Waters Crest Winery
22355 Route 48, Cutchogue
(631) 734-5065

Pindar Vineyards
Route 25, Peconic
(631) 734-6200

Wölffer Estate
Montauk Hgwy., Sagaponak
(631) 537-5106

INDEX

Index

Index

Index

Index

Index

391

Index

Index

405